AFTER MODERNITY

AFTER MODERNITY

HUSSERLIAN REFLECTIONS
ON A PHILOSOPHICAL TRADITION

JAMES RICHARD MENSCH

STATE UNIVERSITY OF NEW YORK PRESS

Published by
State University of New York Press, Albany

© 1996 State University of New York

For information, address State University of New York Press,
State University Plaza, Albany, N.Y. 12246

Production by M. R. Mulholland
Marketing by Dana E. Yanulavich

Library of Congress Cataloging-in-Publication Data

Mensch, James R.
  After modernity : Husserlian reflections on a philosophical
tradition / James Richard Mensch.
      p.   cm.
  Includes bibliographical references and index.
  ISBN 0-7914-2985-7 (alk. paper). — ISBN 0-7914-2986-5 (pbk. :
alk. paper)
    1. Time. 2. Self (Philosophy) 3. Methodology. 4. Husserl,
Edmund, 1859-1938—Views on time. 5. Aristotle—Views on time.
6. Thomas, Aquinas, Saint, 1225?-1274—Views on time.
7. Postmodernism. I. Title.
B945.M4853A37 1996
190—dc20   95-33584
                                                                        CIP

10 9 8 7 6 5 4 3 2 1

THIS BOOK IS DEDICATED TO THE MEMORY OF
PROFESSORS EDO GATTO AND REINER SCHÜRMANN

CONTENTS

ACKNOWLEDGMENTS

Some of the chapters in this volume are reworked versions of previously published articles. Acknowledgment is made to the following publishing houses, periodicals, and persons for their kind permission to republish all or part of the following articles: "Aristotle and the Overcoming of the Subject-Object Dichotomy," *American Catholic Philosophical Quarterly* (Autumn 1991). "Between Plato and Descartes—The Mediaeval Transformation in the Ontological Status of the Ideas," *The St. John's Review* (Spring 1984). "Existence and Essence in Thomas and Husserl," *Horizons of Continental Philosophy: Essays on Husserl, Heidegger, and Merleau-Ponty* (Dordrecht: Kluwer Press, 1988). "Husserl and Sartre: A Question of Reason," *Journal of Philosophical Research* 19 (1994). "Phenomenology and Artificial Intelligence: Husserl Learns Chinese," *Husserl Studies* 8 (1991). "Post-Normative Subjectivity," *The Ancients and Moderns,* ed. Reginald Lilly (Bloomington: Indiana University Press, 1996). "Radical Evil and the Ontological Difference Between Being and Beings," *Philosophy and Culture*, vol. 4, ed. V. Cauchy (Montreal: Montmorency, 1988). "The Mind Body Problem, Phenomenological Reflections on an Ancient Solution," *American Catholic Philosophical Quarterly* 68, no. 1 (Winter 1994). "Time and Augustine's Metaphysics," *Energia* (Winter 1984). "Husserl's Concept of the Self," published as "What Is a Self?" *Husserl in the Contemporary Context: Prospects and Projects for Transcendental Phenomenology,* ed. B. Hopkins (Dordrecht: Kluwer Press, 1996). Finally I wish to thank the director of the Husserl Archives in Louvain, Professor Samuel Ijsseling, for permission to quote from the Nachlass.

INTRODUCTION

There are periods in philosophy when a general consensus becomes apparent. As our century draws to a close, we seem to be agreed that modernity has ended. A sign of this is the change in our sense of what it means to be a "self." The self is no longer taken as an autonomous unit, something which in its basic laws and processes is the same for all. In other words, we no longer take it, as Kant did, as an unchanging "ground of the lawfulness" of what we experience. We see the self as dependent on its circumstances, as pluralized by the situations it finds itself in. Rather than being a ground of lawfulness, its rules and processes are derived from its circumstances. Descartes, by contrast, sought in the self the unchanging Archemedian point upon which to found his "system." In this, he initiated the modern project of founding systems on the self, i.e., on its rules and processes. The shift from the modern is, thus, also a shift from the foundational, systematic thinking of modernity. It is a move to a pluralistic view, one which emphasizes the perspectival character of reality. Accordingly, the change is not just one in the understanding of the self, but also in how we comprehend reality. It is a shift in our understanding of being.

What is the nature of these shifts? What is new in them and what is not? What is required to say that we have genuinely left modernity behind? My purpose in this book is to explore these questions. Written separately, the essays forming its chapters can be read apart. They can stand on their own. Yet, when they are read consecutively, they form an ongoing meditation on the philosophical tradition that results in modernity. Historically, this tradition has been set by reflections on the interrelated themes of being, self, and time. It ultimately rests on a specific understanding of these terms. A radical shift in their interpretation marks the end of the modern period. By way of an introduction to the chapters that follow, I will sketch the special character of the relation of these reflections and make explicit the question which grows out of this relationship. My claim is that reflections on the nature of self and being ultimately involve reflections on the nature of time. The response of philosophy to the question of time, of its nature and origin, determines the tradition of modernity. A change in this response is what allows us to pass beyond modernity.

The Interrelation of the Themes

To be conscious is to be a place where things come to presence. This place of conscious presence we call the *self* is the most intimate and yet one of the most mysterious subjects of philosophical reflection. Phenomenologically regarded, i.e., regarded in terms of what we directly experience, the question of the self—of what it is—is the question of such presence. It arises because the self seems to be and yet not be all that fills it. As a place of conscious presence, its content is that of the world that is present to it. Yet, given its vulnerabilities—the fact that it is liable to all sorts of accidents, including death—it distinguishes itself from the world. It is not the world, but rather its presence. This identification of self and presence, which seems to distinguish the self from the being of the world, has, in fact, the opposite effect. It actually links the question of the world's being to that of the self. In fact, the history of the philosophical conceptions of the self—i.e., of the presence (the selfhood) that we are—is also a history of the understanding of being.

The reason for this is that we have no way of apprehending or understanding being except through presence. This can be put in terms of the meaning of *to be*. *Ousia* (being) is related to *parousia* (presence) in the Greek. As Heidegger points out, the "ancient interpretation of the being of beings" is informed by "the determination of the sense of being as παρουσία or οὐσία, which signifies, in ontological-temporal terms, 'presence.'"[1] This understanding of being, he claims, has essentially determined subsequent philosophical reflection. The same understanding can be drawn from the etymology of the word for existence. The English form, *exist*, can be traced back to the Latin, *ex(s)istere* and to the Greek, ἐξίστημι. Both mean to "stand out." This original sense expresses the insight that what exists must distinguish itself from its background. Distinguishing itself, it shows itself, it makes its presence known. If, for example, I walk into a dark room where I have never been before, it is only by bumping into things that I would know that they are there. It is at that point that they stand out, that they "exist" in the original meaning of the word. This existence is their distinguishing presence. Without this capability for presence, I can never ascribe being to them. Given that the self, taken phenomenologically, is the place of presence and that *to be* is *to be present* (or, at least, be capable of presence), the tie between the two follows automatically. Ontological reflections on presence have a natural bearing on the self and vice versa.

They also have a natural bearing on our reflections on time. In fact, time seems to be an essential element in the presence of both self and being. Thus, the word *present* in the expression to be *present* points to a mode of time—that of the present. What is present shares a now with us. When things "stand out," they do so at the moment of our encountering them. Given this, *to be* has a temporal aspect. It indicates presence in the now. For Heidegger, this understanding is the crucial error of the Western philosophical tradition. "Oriented towards the world or nature in the widest sense," it conceives the latter as that which can be present to man.[2] As such, it ignores the being *to which* things are present: human being or *Dasein* in Heidegger's terminology. Referring to Aristotle's account of time, he writes, "time itself is taken as just one being among others"—i.e., one more item which can be present to man. The error here is that, in making time objective, this understanding of being ignores *Dasein*'s role in temporalization. It conceals from him his role in making things present.[3] Is this the case? Is the tradition of modernity determined by a forgetting of the human function of temporalization? Is such a forgetting a concealment of our subjectivity? Or is the reverse the case? To claim this would be to assert that it is precisely modernity's attempt to understand temporalization as a subjective process which is the crucial error. It is this, rather than any forgetting of our role in temporalization, that makes our subjectivity unknowable. Insofar as modernity makes subjectivity foundational, an unknowable subject would lead to its crisis. An unknowable subject cannot be an unambiguous foundation.

Before confronting this issue, I should first note that the understanding of being as presence does not leave out, but rather characterizes, the self. If being qua presence has a temporal dimension, so must the self. As the place of presence, it must also be marked by nowness. In fact, on one level—that of the formal relations of its contents—the self can be described simply as a set of temporal (as opposed to spatial) relations. Thus, reflection shows that spatial dimensions do not directly pertain to the contents of consciousness. One thought is not so many feet (or meters) distant from another. The visual image of an object is not some definite size. I cannot say, for example, that my image of a person is the size of the house I see behind her. The building fills less of my visual field and yet is larger. What gives me a sense of size is not the image but its rate of change as I move toward it. Bringing my hand to my face, I can rapidly fill my visual field. For a distant object, this takes longer. Similarly, I learn to locate myself in space by gauging the rates by which objects seem to turn as I walk by them. This "turning" occurs most strikingly on a train ride. Looking out the window, close objects seem to rush by me, while more distant ones glide by at a more measured pace. Really distant objects hardly seem to move at all. The same thing happens whenever I move. As psychologists assure us, part of learning how to see is learning how to estimate distance in terms of time.

The Question of Time

The fact that spatial dimensions can be reduced to temporal relations implies that when we say that the self is the "place" of presence, we cannot say that this "place" in a spatial sense is ultimately foundational. The self is not a spatial place in which presence appears.[4] Rather, presence, itself, places us—i.e., gives us a definite spatially located "here" through its unfolding. This presence, as we have indicated, is primarily temporal. With this, we come to the question on which these chapters on the history of philosophy turn: What is the status of the temporal relations of contents from which I derive my world as well as my spatial place in it? Is their temporality self-generated or does it come from without?

If we say that time is subjective, i.e., that the self is its origin, we do not, I claim, undo some "error" in the ancient understanding of being. We do not uncover an alternative to modernity, understood as a tradition based on this error. Quite the contrary. With this assumption, we embark on the path that characterizes modernity. When fully developed, modernity links being, presence, and time in a claim about their subjective origin. Taking being as presence, it does interpret presence in a temporal sense. Presence is understood as nowness. But then, it makes a further claim. Assuming that time is subjective, it contends that nowness originates in the self. This position can be extended to include the idealist's assertion that the self is the origin of the being (the temporal presence) of the world. This is because, as the origin of time, the self supplies the successive nows which make the world present and actual.

Needless to say, such a self is both myself and something more than this. Individually regarded, the self is in the world. Spatially and temporally positioned, it appears as one among many selves. Yet, as a ground of the temporal presence or being of the world (and, hence, of the world as a spatial-temporal whole), it is somehow beyond it. It is not part of that which it itself grounds. As a result, the self seems to become depersonalized, even as it undergoes a kind of unlimited inflation. Grounding all that is and distinguished from what it grounds, it is depersonalized in the sense that it loses the personal characteristics that make a self a person among persons, a person in the world. So distinguished, the self is also inflated in the sense that it has no rival or equal. On the level of the ground, it is all that there is. Its uniqueness is such that it cannot recognize another.

A certain order of dependence characterizes this view. It makes being (qua presence) dependent on time, taking the latter as dependent on subjectivity. Such an order—whether or not it is developed into an explicitly idealistic position—is a characteristic feature of the tradition of modernity. It is behind the modern penchant for treating subjectivity as normative, i.e., for drawing prescriptive rules from its processes and performances. If such processes are ultimately those of temporalization and if being's presence is ultimately temporal, then the rules of such processes are prescriptive of the presence of things. The study of the subject, taken as the determining place of presence, should allow one to say *in advance* how things must appear.

The difficulties with this view—difficulties that ultimately bring about the collapse of modernity in the sense thus defined—stem from its depersonalization and inflation of the self. If the self really is the ground of everything, it is distinguished from everything. It cannot have the same characteristics as that which it grounds, since if it did, it would be in their situation, which is that of being grounded or determined by another.[5] This logical necessity drives the self, taken as an ultimate ground, into the region of the unknowable. It turns it from a describable set of temporal relations into something absolutely timeless. As the ground of presence, the self is not "present." Responsible for appearance, it itself cannot appear.[6] The self is thus positioned in what Kant called the *noumenal* as opposed to the phenomenal realm. The questions this raises seem both obvious and unanswerable: If the ground of presence cannot itself be present, how can we characterize it? If presence is equivalent to being, can we even give it an ontological status? As the ground of the categories by which we classify the beings that appear to us, it necessarily escapes their designations. With this, we come to the concealment of subjectivity which characterizes modernity. It is a concealment, *not* by virtue of a forgetting of the subjective function of temporalization. It is, rather, the insistence on this function which makes the subject unknowable. In such a situation, almost any characterization of the subject—so long as it goes beyond the designations of what *it* makes present—is equally plausible. We can position it, as Husserl does, as an "absolutely timeless subject." It can be named *God, the absolute*—Husserl's term. We can call it, as Sartre does, *an impersonal spontaneity*, one which is "a first condition and an absolute source of existence." We can even take it as a presubjective, biologically conceived, "will to power." It can be addressed as the god "Dionysius" when, with Nietzsche, we take it as a primal (preindividual) will to life.

The plurality of the different life forms, each with its own will to life, does not point to this self's pluralization. Neither does the plurality of different phenomenal (appearing) subjects. The ground that makes the world present (and hence existent) for all is the same for all. Except in its crudest versions, this development thus does not face the absurdity of making each subject a creator of "its" private world. As previously indicated, what makes the world present is both the self and not the self. It is the self because it is its acting center; it is not the self, because it is its preindividual "absolute" core.

What causes the problem is the indefinite inflation of the self that is this core. Since the ground is presubjective, while its expression remains subjective, the possibility arises of unlimited subjective claims. Each subject acts out of a ground that, as preindividual, knows no other individual agency. Each, crudely put, acts on the basis of the "god within." Yet, this "god" has no definitely describable characteristics. We may take it as a Christian God with its biblically related absolute claims. We can also understand it as Nietzsche's Dionysius, i.e., as a personification of will to power or will to life.[7] Here, the lack of acknowledgment of others like itself places it outside the moral framework implied by such acknowledgment. It, thus, can lead to the assertion: "Exploitation . . . pertains to the essence of the living thing as a fundamental organic function; it is a consequence of the intrinsic will to power which is precisely the will to life."[8] In either case, the situation it leaves us in, which is one of unlimited claims, is highly unstable. Modernity takes roughly five hundred years to work out the consequences of this instability. Its history is, in general, that of the continuous failure of its appeal to subjectivity as a source of prescriptive norms. Its legacy, as our last chapter indicates, is a plurality of absolute, yet contradictory systems and claims.

After Modernity

The contemporary, "postmodern" response to this plurality is twofold. On the one hand there is the denial of any possibility of a "grand narrative," of an account which would unify this legacy.[9] On the other, the historical basis of modernity's narrative—subjectivity as such—is denied. Yet, for all its apparent newness, this response remains a response conditioned by the modernity that called it forth. Thus, it continues modernity's implicit idealism in its rejection of any extrasubjective determinant of meaning. When it adds to this its denial of the subject, it essentially cuts meanings loose, making them ground-less in that their content is deprived of any nonlinguistic ground.[10] Determined neither by subjective performances nor by objective referents (self-existing, transcendent entities), significance becomes a matter of arbitrary and contingent relations of signs within a linguistic system. With this, it affirms rather than overcomes the arbitrary quality of significance with which modernity ends. Modernity's plurality of contradictory claims becomes one of incompatible language games.[11] The same point can be made for the contemporary denial of the subject. To deny the subject tout court, to say that nothing corresponds to its concept, underlines rather than passes beyond the modern position. This follows because the subject's inconceivability remains a correlate of the modern project of taking it as a ground. It is, as we said, a logical necessity implicit in the distinction between ground and grounded. To this, we may add that the denial of the subject is not necessarily a denial of its function. The function of determining meanings can pass from the subject to a set of linguistic practices. That such practices do not allow of "totalization"—i.e., of the systematization of meanings into a coherent whole—does not avoid the fact that we still remain within the limits of the human (the community of speakers) as a contingent, yet final horizon.[12] To the point that we do, such linguistic practices can be regarded as yet another mask, another aspect, of subjectivity.

The point of these remarks is not to engage in a dialogue with this contemporary response. As with my remarks on Heidegger, my aim is simply to distinguish my own position. Thus, a reader who looks for references to Derrida, Lyotard, Foucault, Lacan, Rorty, or the host of other writers of the "postmodern" movement will come away disappointed from the chapters that follow. The goal of these chapters is not to work out yet another version of postmodernism. On the contrary, from their perspective, to remain at the level of the contemporary response is not to pass beyond modernity, but to remain at the stage of its collapse. To go beyond this is to work out an alternative to the view that makes time subjective. Modernity considers the self as the source of nowness. To overcome this is to make the origin of time external to the self.

The original expression of this alternative is given by Aristotle. According to Heidegger, "Aristotle's treatment of time . . . has essentially determined every subsequent account of time—Bergson's included." He adds, rather surprisingly, "even the Kantian interpretation of time operates within the structures which Aristotle set forth."[13] Given that the modern position, as exemplified by Kant, makes time subjective while Aristotle argues the reverse, this cannot be the case. In terms of my analysis, it is the *forgetting* of the Aristotelian position which characterizes the modern tradition. The implication here is that only its recovery and renewal can move us beyond modernity.

The outline of my understanding of this position can be sketched in a few lines. Its primary proposition is that the continuous up welling of the ever new now does not result from the self, but from *what is present* to the self. Time is dependent, not on the self, but on being. The now is the presence of being. Negatively expressed, when nothing is present to the self, neither is nowness. Furthermore, without the experience of the change of being (of motion), there is no experience of temporal passage. The subjective sense of this passage, which is that of the upwelling of new nows, comes, then, not from the self, but from the changes in its environment. They occasion the change in presence, and this change is the change or passage of time.

The basic point here is that the now we experience is the presence of the entity—in general, the presence of the world of entities. It is our registering it. As the entity shifts its place, it shows a different aspect or side to us. The now registers this change in the change of its content. Thus, the welling up of time *is* this shifting content of the now. It is a shifting content within a remaining now. The now that remains (the now in which we constantly are) continually exhibits new content. In doing so, it seems to shift or stream. Not that it passes away; rather, it remains even though what is present in it—the actual perceptual content displaying the changes—has shifted. Its remaining is a result of the continuity of the world's presence, i.e., of the fact that through all the shifts in its content the world continues to show itself as the same. Thus, the constant presence of our nowness follows from being's constant presence—in general, the constant presence of the world that maintains its identity. Similarly, the continuity of time (the experiential inseparability of its moments) is a result of the continuity of world's presence. By virtue of being's continual presence throughout all the changes in its content, the shifting content of the now does not disperse time into discrete, separate instants. The result is, rather, its seamless flowing as it register's change.

The position I have just sketched has its own order of dependence. It shares with modernity the view of subjectivity as a set of temporal relationships. As a place of presence, the self remains primarily temporal. Its ground, however, is not some inner core of upwelling nowness, but rather the entities the self registers. Thus, the order of dependence reverses modernity's, which had being (as presence) depend on time, which, in turn, depended on the self. Here, the self depends on time, which, itself, depends on being. The upshot is that the self depends on the being of the entities it registers. Thus, the reversal in the order of dependence marks a shift in what counts as a self. In the alternative that characterizes modernity, the self is foundational. On its deepest, most intimate level, it is beyond the vicissitudes of the world. In Descartes's philosophy, it can exist without its body. In Kant's, it is independent of the world of appearances. In Husserl's, it has a timeless "absolute" at its core. As just indicated, my alternative makes the self dependent on what it registers. Open to the shifting presence of being, it is capable in extreme cases of fragmentation. As we shall see, the very temporality which unifies it can shatter it. The splitting of the self's world—the world that gives it its nowness—is also the self's splitting. In cases of extreme childhood abuse, the result can be the clinical state of multiple personality disorder. In its focus on the self's fragility—on the self's dependence on its situation—this alternative presents a sharp contrast to the modern notion of a foundational, impregnable self. In this respect, its conclusions resemble those of the contemporary "postmodern" account. Yet, it differs from the latter, because it arrives at its position by shifting the foundation from the self to being.

An Outline of the Chapters

Modernity, like the alternative we present, cannot claim to be completely new. The continuity of the philosophical tradition is such that its insights can also be traced back to positions occurring in ancient philosophy. The first chapters begin by exploring the roots of modernity before going on to its modern representatives. After "Husserl's Concept of the Self," beginning with the "Remark" that follows, I again turn to the ancient world to find the Aristotelian origins of my view of the self.

This account can be fleshed out by outlining the course of these chapters. To do so will, perhaps, be as helpful in their reading as the sketch just given of their themes. The first chapter sets out the problem whose solution was attempted by one philosopher after another. Ultimately, the attempt to solve it set modernity on its course. I am referring to Plato's problem of participation. In the *Parmenides*, Plato tries to find a common standard of being or presence. Both things and their ideas (εἴδη) are present to us, yet their presence is such that we cannot use the same language to describe them. We cannot say that the *idea* of size is, itself, a certain size nor, to use Frege's example, can we assert that the *idea* of black cloth is, itself, black and made out of cloth. What, then, is the common standard of their presence? How do we relate what changes in time (the individual thing) to what does not (its unchanging idea)? Plato, in drawing his standard of being from the timeless ideas, cannot provide an answer. He cannot because his theory of participation in such ideas is an attempt to think being apart from time. The next essay takes up Augustine's effort to think being in terms of time, i.e., to conceive its presence as temporal presence. Arguing that time itself must be present in order to be, he postulates the presence in the now of both the past and the future. In the "mind," i.e., in the self's memories, direct perceptions and anticipations are "a present of past things, a present of present things and a present of future things." These "presents," he claims, are the reality, the very being, of time. We are thus set on a path that makes time subjective.

Augustine, of course, is not a modern philosopher. His assertion, for example, that "if you did not exist it would be impossible for you to be deceived" gives the essence of Descartes' argument, but is not yet Descartes' "cogito ergo sum."[14] The same holds with regard to the self. Having made time subjective and having assumed that time is unending, the question he faces is that of the subject who is adequate to time's unlimited extension. Given that the subject is the place of time, what place is sufficient to hold all its presents? For Augustine, this place is God's eternity. God is the self who is adequate to time. This conclusion points to the inflation of self that characterizes modernity. Yet, in Augustine's thought, it limits itself to the assertion that man is the image of God. Only when the context of biblically based faith weakens does the inner logic of Augustine's premises lead to the conclusions of modernity. Instead of calling man an "image" of God, the explicit assertion becomes that of a level of identity between man and God—i.e., between the finite and infinite aspects of self.

A great number of the chapters in this book are taken up with Husserl's working out of the details of these conclusions. Beyond its general, phenomenological outlook, it is their presence which gives this book its claim to the title, *Husserlian Reflections*. Husserl's account is central to its project in that he, above all others, fleshes out the claim that time is subjective by giving a detailed account of our experience of the temporal process. The chapters devoted to Husserl examine the notions of presence, existence, and self which arise from his analyses; they also show how he comes to assert a level of identity between the self and "God, the absolute." In the process, they compare him with Aquinas and Sartre, use his ontology to speak about radical evil, and examine the implications of his theory for artificial intelligence.

The reason for this attention is not simply Husserl's metaphysical commitments (commitments which exemplify those of modernity). It is also the excellence of his descriptive, phenomenological accounts. These provide a neutral content which can serve phenomenological reflection quite apart from such commitments. Because of this, I use this content to recover and renew the Aristotelian alternative to the modern tradition. Having considered in a pair of chapters Aristotle's position that time is dependent on being, I use Husserl's account of internal time consciousness to work out the mechanics, the actual processes, of such dependence. The same holds for my account of the self. Husserl's descriptive account of the self as a field of temporal relations keeps its validity whether we assume (as he does) the subjective origin of time or engage in the reversal that positions this origin outside of the self.[15] On one level, everything remains the same except that there is a kind of symbolic change of sign, one that points to the change of the origin. On another level, however, nothing remains the same, in the sense that the self, in its openness to the world, is vulnerable to its assaults on every level of its being. On this level, the self can fall into a state which confirms Nietzsche's hypothesis: "the subject as multiplicity."[16] The penultimate chapter uses Husserl's descriptive insights to explore the self's vulnerabilities. Its susceptibility to fragmentation through trauma is traced to a disturbance of its temporal sense. The splitting of the sense of time through bodily trauma is a splitting of the presence of the world and hence of the self situated by such presence. The final chapter proposes an alternative to the modern tradition in its ways of thinking about the themes of self, time, and being. It concludes by presenting a nonmodern, nonnormative view of that magic place of presence we call a *self*.

1

BETWEEN PLATO AND DESCARTES—
THE MEDIAEVAL TRANSFORMATION IN THE
ONTOLOGICAL STATUS OF THE IDEAS

I

Even the most casual reader of philosophy senses the abyss that separates Descartes from Plato. In Descartes' work, a concern for certainty overshadows and, in fact, transforms the original Platonic conception of philosophy. Such a conception, as exemplified by the figure of Socrates, fundamentally involves a love of wisdom. Wisdom—σοφία—is not the same as certainty. That which I can be certain of does not necessarily make me wise (see *Phaedo,* 98 b ff.)

We can mark out the difference between Plato and Descartes in terms of two contrasting pairs of terms: trust and opinion for Plato, doubt and certainty for Descartes. Plato describes our attitude to the visible realm as one of trust—πίστις (see *Republic,* 511e). Descartes begins his *Meditations* by doubting his perceptions. For Plato, the examination of opinion is a necessary first step in the philosophical ascent to the highest things. He depicts Socrates as enquiring into the opinions of the most various sorts of men. There is in Socrates a certain trust in the existence of "true" or "right" opinions. At times, such opinions can become "hypotheses"; they can become stepping stones leading to "what is free from hypothesis" (*Republic*, 511 b). For Descartes, precisely the opposite attitude is assumed. Because of his lack of such trust, he begins his *Meditations* by withdrawing from society and systematically doubting every opinion he has hitherto accepted on trust. His position is summed up by the statement: "reason already persuades me that I ought no less carefully to withhold my assent from matters which are not entirely certain and indubitable than from those which appear to me manifestly to be false . . ." ("Meditation I," *Philosophical Works of Descartes*, trans. E. Haldand and G. Ross, p. 145).

This lack of assent, of qualified trust, reveals the transformation that philosophy undergoes in Descartes' hands. It changes from a love of wisdom to a love of certainty. Certainty, even if it concerns what is apparently trivial, becomes the philosopher's goal. The certainty Descartes pursues has an absolute, almost mathematical character. His assent will be given only to matters "entirely certain and indubitable." This is a sign that certainty, rather than wisdom, has become the object of his philosophical love. What a philosopher loves and, hence, pursues is generally what he takes as absolute. For Descartes, this absolute is nothing less than certainty itself.

How did this transformation occur? My claim is that it is the result of a transformation in the minds of philosophers of what it means for an idea or εἶδος to be. More precisely put, it is the result of a transformation, occurring in the Middle Ages, in the philosophical notion of the *ontological status* of the idea. Because of this transformation, doubt replaces trust in our perceptions. In the consequent shifting world of doubt, certainty becomes our paramount object. It is both the initial and final goal of our philosophical enquiries.

II

Before I present the historical evidence for this thesis, we must be clear on what is meant by the term *ontological status*. The term signifies "status of being." An entity can be said to have the status of a merely *possible* being. Alternatively, it can be said to have the status of an *actual* existent. Here, we must note that the question of the content of a being—the question of its essence or "whatness"—is a question distinct from that of its ontological status. *Whether* something is, i.e., whether it is actual or merely a possible existent, is not answered by giving a concept delineating *what* the entity is. As Thomas Aquinas puts this, "I can know what a man or a phoenix is and still be ignorant whether it exists in reality" (*De Ente et Essentia*, ch. 4, ed. M. D. Roland-Gosselin, p. 34). Kant expresses the same point by writing, "'Being' is obviously not a real predicate; that is, it is not a concept of something which could be added to the concept of a thing" ("Kitrik" B 636). If it were a real predicate, i.e., part of the concept of a thing, then from knowing the what, I could know the whether—i.e., whether the concept refers to an actual or a merely possible existent. That this is not the case is shown by the fact that there is not the least difference in content between the thought of a possible existent and the conception that arises from its actual presence. As Kant observes, the thought of a hundred possible thalers contains the same number of coins as a hundred actual thalers (see ibid., B 637). Because of this loans can be repaid or, more generally, what we think of as merely possible can be encountered and recognized in reality. If being did make a conceptual difference, if it were something "added to the concept of a thing," then when I was actually repaid, I would reply, "This is *not* what I had in mind when I thought of the possibility of repayment."

This distinction has a technical name. It is called *the distinction between being and essence*. "Essence," as Aquinas says, "is what the definition of a thing signifies" (*De Ente et Essentia*, ch. 2, p. 7). It is *the content of an idea*, the idea, say, of a man or a phoenix as delineated by its definition. Being, as distinct from essence, refers to ontological status. Admitting this distinction between being and essence, we must also admit that what is defined conceptually is not specified according to its mode of being. The question of its ontological status, the question concerning the *actual or merely possible* being of what is defined, is not answered through its definition.

This point applies directly to our thesis about the ideas. It does so because the ideas, considered simply in themselves, are the same as essences. An essence, we said, is the content of an idea or εἶδος. An idea, however, is just its own content and nothing more. It is a *pure* conceptual unit. It is such by virtue of being, in itself, simply the conceptual content that a definition delineates. Given the fact that *idea* and *essence* denote the same thing, what we said about the essence applies to the idea. The latter, too, is necessarily silent on the question of being. Otherwise put, no examination of an idea as it is in itself—i.e., as a pure conceptual unit—can answer the question of actual versus possible being. This silence on the question of being, based as it is on the very nature of the idea, is absolutely general. It, thus, applies to the question of the idea's own ontological status. If we attempt to answer it by considering the conceptual *content that is the idea,* we are always free to answer it in two possible ways. We are free to give the idea the ontological status of a possibility *or* an actuality.

III

The history of philosophy gives ample evidence of this freedom For the moderns, the idea has the ontological status of a possibility. To illustrate this, I shall take three prominent figures: Kant, Whitehead, and Husserl. According to Kant, every conception that the understanding itself grasps is grasped under the aspect of possibility (see "Kritik d. Urtheilskraft," *Kants Werke*, V, 402). For very different reasons, Whitehead concurs: ideas or essences are "eternal objects." But, as he says, "the metaphysical status of an eternal object is that of a possibility for an actuality . . . actualization is a selection among possibilities" (*Science and the Modern World,* p. 144). Husserl, who would not at all be found in Whitehead's camp, agrees on this one point: possibility and essentiality are the same. The reason he gives for this is that the being of an idea is the being of an ideal or pure possibility (see *Logische Untersuchungen,* 5th ed., I, 129, 240, II/1, 115, II/2, 103). Such examples could be multiplied. In modern times, the idea is universally given the status of a possibility: an empirically grounded possibility for the empiricists, an ideal or "pure" possibility for the non-empiricists. In neither case are ideas considered to be actualities.

For Plato, however, this was just what the ideas or εἴδη were when he introduced them into philosophical discourse. He names them οὐσία which is taken from the participle of the verb to be, εἶναι. A corresponding root is found in the word *essence,* in Latin, *essentia.* The root *esse* means "to be." To call something οὐσία or *essentia* was to say that it actually is. It has what is signified by the verb *to be.* The same point can be made by looking at the divided line (see *Republic,* 509 d–511 e). In a proportion involving the ratio between reality and image, the ideas are at the top. They are supremely real. They possess οὐσία in the highest degree.

One of the ways to see why this is so is to look at Parmenides' statement: τὸ γὰρ αὐτὸ νοεῖν ἔστιν τε καὶ εἶναι (*Poem,* Fr. 3). We can translate this as "the same thing exists for thinking and being, and take this to mean: "the same thing can be thought as can be."¹ So understood, we have a statement of logical equivalence: Thinkability implies being and being implies thinkability. Now, whether or not this understanding agrees with Parmenides' original intention, it does yield a notion that for Plato is crucial for the status of the ideas. This is that thinkability and being pertain to the same thing. More precisely expressed, that which makes it possible for a thing to be *also* makes it possible for it to be thinkable. The common ground of these possibilities is self-identity or self-sameness. This self-identity will turn out to be a mysterious quality. For the moment, however, we may define it as the quality of something remaining the same with itself.

That such a quality is at the root of being is affirmed by Plato when he writes that "the very being of to be—αὐτὴ ἡ οὐσία τοῦ εἶναι—is to be "always in the same manner in relation to the same things." As Plato explains, this is to be "unchanging" and, thus, to remain the same with oneself. The ideas "beauty itself, equality itself, and every itself" are called *being*—τὸ ὄν—and this, because they "do not admit of any change whatsoever" (*Phaedo,* 78 d). Plato's position follows from Parmenides' statement and an analysis of what change means. Its fundamental intuition is that change is always change of something. This something is an underlying self-identity. The consequence is that real loss of self-identity is not change, but rather annihilation, pure and simple, of the individual. Now, the presence of self-identity not only makes possible the persistent being in time of the individual, it also makes possible the predication of an idea of this individual. If change negated all self-identity, then nothing in our changing world could have any intelligible name or sense. Let us take an example, a person proceeding from a newborn baby to extreme old age. The presence of some self-identical element in this process allows us to predicate the idea "human" of this individual. When the person dies, this is no longer possible. What answers to the concept "human" is no longer there. The point is that self-identity is required both for being and being thought. What is not self-identical cannot be thought and cannot be.

A number of consequences follow from this reasoning. The first is that the ability to recognize being and the ability to predicate an idea of a thing always occur together. They must, if they are both based on the apprehension of an underlying self-identity. Given that predicating an idea of a thing is the same as the recognition of the thing as intelligible, *being* and *intelligibility* must be understood as coextensive terms. One cannot ascribe the one without ascribing the other; whatever has a share in being must also have a share in intelligibility. Now, participation—μετέχειν—means literally "having a share in." It, thus, follows that participation must be understood as participation in *both* being and intelligibility. We can put this in terms of the Platonic doctrine that a thing is intelligible by virtue of its participating in its idea. The idea itself is the conceptual expression of the self-identity that Plato calls the οὐσία of *to be*. Thus, one can also say that a thing has being by virtue of its participating in its idea—i.e., participating in the self-identity that the idea expresses in terms of an unchanging concept. From this it follows that participation demands a single notion of being, one common to both the thing and its idea. A thing could not possess its being by virtue of its participation in its idea if both thing and idea did not exist by virtue of the same οὐσία of *to be*. This is self-identity or self-sameness. This self-identity is what allows us to take the divided line and see it as a hierarchy of beings with the ideas at the top. Levels of being could not be ordered and ranked if there were not a single standard of being by which to measure them. This, for Plato, is the self-sameness which images, things, mathematical objects and ideas respectively possess to a more and more perfect degree.

IV

How did the transformation between Plato and the moderns occur? How do the ideas, from being understood as pure actualities—i.e., entities capable of being called τὸ ὄν—become, for the moderns, expressions of possibility? From a philosophical standpoint, the answer to this question has already been indicated. Our claim is that self-identity is not a sure criterion of being. In particular, it does not point to the actual as opposed to the merely possible. The reason for this is that, like any other conceptual content, self-identity is part of the essential determination of a thing. As forming part of a thing's essence, it is silent on the question of the status of the being of a thing. Thus, to return to Kant's example, we can say that a possible entity—a hundred possible thalers— possess as much self-identity as an actual identity. Granting this, we must admit that self-identity does not distinguish between the actual and the possible. An argument for the actuality of the ideas, which is based like Plato's on their self-identity, is, thus, bound to fail. Here, indeed, we can find the underlying reason for the ambiguity which, as we shall see, characterizes the use of the term *self-identity*. The concept per se is not ambiguous, its meaning being simply "sameness with self." It becomes ambiguous when we attempt to make it into a criterion of being, something no concept is fitted to do.

For Plato, the attempt to make self-identity a standard of being arises in connection with his doctrine of participation. As we have seen, entities have being to the point that they participate—or have a share—in self-identity. How are we to understand the self-identity that is to be shared in? We cannot understand it as simple *identity with self*. That which shares with another its identity with self would either absorb the other into its own identity or else lose itself in the identity of the other. Thus, if the ideas and things are related by virtue of their sharing in self-identity, either the idea would absorb the thing or vice versa. A similar difficulty arises when we take self-identity as the quality of *being one*. Is the oneness to be referred to the oneness of a thing or to the oneness of the idea?

The *Parmenides* shows Plato's awareness of the difficulty we are pointing to. He has Parmenides ask Socrates if things must participate either in the whole of an idea or in a part of it. Socrates agrees that these are the alternatives. Both, however, seem to be impossible. Participation by parts would make the ideas divisible by parts. It would also make us say that we can predicate "part" of an idea of a thing. Such notions are strictly speaking unintelligible. Ideas, which are not material things, are not materially divisible. But neither are they conceptually divisible. A *simple* idea cannot be conceptually divided. As it has no parts, part of it cannot be predicated of a thing. A *complex* idea, so divided, would become a different idea. Here, the notion of the idea as maintaining its self-identity by virtue of its unity precludes all division. If, however, we say that the *whole* of the idea is participated in, we still cannot maintain the necessary oneness of the idea. If individuals participate in the whole of the idea, then, as Socrates admits, "the whole idea is one and yet, being one, is in each of the many" (*Parmenides* 131 a, in *The Dialogues of Plato*, trans. B Jowett, vol. 2, p. 91). This, however, implies that "one and the same thing will exist as a whole at the same time in many different individuals and therefore will be in a state of separation from itself" (ibid., 131 b). Self-separation seems the opposite of self-identity when we understand this latter as the quality of being one. To be as a whole in many is to be many rather than being one.

As is obvious, at the basis of Parmenides' dialectic is the ambiguity of the meaning of being one. There is being one in the sense that an idea or concept is one; there is also being one in the sense that an individual thing is one. If, with Plato, we understand participation in terms of a single notion of being, one common to both the thing and the idea, then we are faced with the problem of trying to put together these two different ways of being one. This, of course, is the famous problem of the universals: How can the idea or species be present in the individuals, or how can the distinct individuals share in the unity of the species? The endless debate on the question is actually about the notion of being. Both sides agree that the very being of *to be* is being one, but disagree on what this last means. If to be means to be one thing, then the ideas, which have only conceptual unity, are not. They are nothing but "common names" produced by habit, circles of association, historical processes—the list is endless. An illegitimate child who is not owned up puts everybody under the suspicion of parentage. If we reverse this and say that to be means to be a conceptual unity, then the same fate befalls individual things. *What* a thing is, its form or common nature, is what is. In itself, in its own individual unity, the thing is not. Both solutions are obviously one-sided. For just as our senses convince us that there are individual things, so without conceptual unities we would have no specifically human mental life.

The debate points out a problem, but it does not give a solution. When, in the Middle Ages, a solution does arise, it occurs by virtue of a transformation of the ontological status of the idea. The context of this solution is set by Aristotle. More specifically, it is set by his denial that ideas or essences exist in themselves as opposed to being either in the mind or in objects (see *Metaphysics,* 991b, 1–3, 1039a, 24 ff). For his medieval followers, this denial of the self-subsistent idea or essence does not solve the problem of the universals. The denial leaves intact the two notions of being on which the problem revolves. The facts of predication show this. What is predicated is the idea in the mind. Viewed in terms of the activity of predication, the idea has the characteristic of universality. As engaged in the individual object, however, the idea has the characteristic of singularity. Thus, we do not predicate Socrates' "humanity" of Plato. The "humanity" of Socrates is part of his individuality. It is an informing form that makes him into a definite individual—i.e., into what Aristotle calls a *primary substance.* We do, however, predicate the idea of humanity which is present in our mind of both Socrates and Plato. It has the characteristic of universality: the character of one thing being applicable to many. How is this possible? How do we recognize that the humanity of a sensibly perceived singular is the same as the intellect's universal idea of humanity?

This is the question that Avicenna, an eleventh century Persian philosopher, asked himself. His answer is that such recognition is possible only by abstracting the idea or essence from both forms of being one. The unity of a universal and the unity of an individual must both be seen as accidental to the essence considered in itself. Without such an understanding, predication is impossible. Let me quote Avicenna on the essence "animal": "'Animal' is the same thing whether it be sensible or a concept in the mind. In itself, it is neither universal nor singular. If it were in itself universal so that animality were universal from the bare fact of being animality, the consequence would be that no animal would be a singular, but every animal would be a universal. If, however, animal *qua* animal were singular, it would be impossible for there to be more than one singular, namely the very singular to which animality belongs, and it would be impossible for any other singular to be an animal" (*Logica,* III, fol. 12r, col. 1).

Avicenna is here arguing that we cannot explain predication by identifying the essence either with the universality of the concept or the singularity of the thing. Predication requires both the thing and the concept, and they must be brought together through an essence that is recognizably present in each. If this is the case, then Avicenna's conclusion apparently follows. It is that we conceive something "accidental" to animality when beyond its bare content we think of it as singular or universal (see ibid.; see also Avicenna, *Metaphysica*, V, fol. 86 v, cols. 1–2).

Avicenna's position is in some sense a return to Plato, but it is a return that transforms Plato's original conception. Plato has Parmenides ask: "In the first place, I think, Socrates, that you, or anyone else who maintains the existence of absolute essences, will admit that they cannot exist in us?" To this Socrates replies: "No, for then they would not be absolute" (*Parmenides*, 133 c, *The Dialogues*, trans. B. Jowett, vol. 2, p. 94). Now, it seems to be part of the logic of the notions that make up Plato's thought that they are incapable of being completely absorbed in incompatible philosophical systems. They have, in other words, a certain resistance to their being misunderstood. This resistance is evident here. Attempting to follow Aristotle, Avicenna begins with the position that essences are either in the mind or in things. But then he examines predication, and the logic of the notion of an essence compels him to say that essences cannot be identified either with being in the mind or being in things. In themselves, absolutely considered, they are, as Avicenna admits, in neither. Yet the very way in which Avicenna affirms this exhibits the transformation he has wrought in Plato's essence. It is a transformation of the criterion of being which underlies Plato's notion of participation.

The problem with this criterion in Avicenna's eyes is its equation of being and being one. How can we understand oneness with respect to the ideas? How can an idea or essence be—that is, be one—in many individuals, each of which is also called one? Avicenna's answer is to split the category of being by asserting that *to be* does not necessarily mean to be one. Let me restate this. If asked how the idea can be one and yet, being one, *be* in each of the many individuals, Avicenna would reply that it is precisely because unity is *accidental* to the being of an idea that its being in the many does not prejudice the idea's own inherent being. To make the idea one is to make it present either in the mind or in things. It is to make it *either* an idea in the mind which is predicable of many *or* an individual which is a subject of predication but not itself predicable of another. Both forms of being one are accidental to it as it is in itself. In itself, it represents a form of being that is other than predicable notion or physical object. Itself neither, it has the possibility of being either. In other words, from the point of view of mental notion or physical thing, it is just this possibility of being either and nothing more. Its ontological status is simply that of a *possibility*.

The transformation that Avicenna has worked on Plato's original position can be indicated by noting the following. For Plato, participation is based on a single notion of being. As a consequence, participation in an idea is also participation in being. For Avicenna, this is not the case. The essence, insofar as it lacks unity, has not the same being that an individual entity has. Thus, participation in an essence does not mean participation in actuality. How could it if the essence, instead of being supremely actual, represents only a possibility? In fact, for Avicenna, the function of sharing being is taken over by God, the only necessary being. Things cannot become actual by participating in their essence, since essence has, for Avicenna, no inherent status of actuality.

We need a further step to come to the modern notion of an essence or idea. Once again it can be looked upon, at least in a superficial way, as an attempt to return to Plato. This return attempts to restore to essence some notion of unity.

While Avicenna's influence was spreading through the Arab world, the Latin West was independently developing a doctrine of the transcendent properties of being. These are the properties of being irrespective of where it is found. There are a number of these properties, but we need only mention one: unity. The doctrine taught that being and unity are coextensive properties. Where being is present, unity is present. To the point that being is lacking, there is a corresponding lack of unity.[2] When Avicenna entered the West with his assertion that an essence had being but not unity, only two alternatives seemed possible to those who thought being and unity were coextensive. They could accept Avicenna's denial of the unity of an essence, but reject his teaching on the proper being of an essence. Alternately, they could accept his assertion that an essence has a proper being and reject his doctrine that unity does not apply to the essence as such.[3] The first course was followed by Aquinas who writes that essence, considered in itself, abstracts from "any being whatsoever" (*De Ente et Essentia*, cap. 3, p. 26). In other words, lacking unity, it must, in itself, lack being. This is part of what Aquinas means when he writes that essence and being are "really distinct." The famous defense of this distinction is his treatise, *On Being and Essence*.

The second course was taken by Scotus. Scotus agrees with Avicenna that essences have a proper being. He thus argues against Aquinas's attempt to conceive of essence apart from being (see *Opus Oxoniense*, lib. IV, d. 11, q. 3, n. 46, Vives ed.). He also asserts that essences do have a unity—not the unity of a mental idea or physical thing, but something slightly less than this, called *minor unity*.[4] This unity corresponds to Avicenna's being of an essence. Such unity is demanded by the fact that the essence in the individual perceived through sensation and the essence in the mind's universal notion are, in fact, the same essence.

How does Scotus know that they are the same essence? The answer can be drawn from the elements of Scotus's position. The first of these is that essence in itself does not express reality, be this the reality of a mental idea or an extramental thing. It expresses only the possibility of a reality. Its ontological status—i.e., the status of its being—is that of a possibility (see *Op. Ox.*, lib. I, d. 2, q. 1, n. 56). The second is that the examination of this possibility is the examination of the essence's "minor unity." This means, for Scotus, that the terms that make up the definition of an essence must not be contradictory. They must be compatible, that is, capable of forming a unity. The insight here is that, without this capability, the essence defined by these terms cannot be instantiated as a unity either in the mind or in things. It cannot be so instantiated in the mind for, as Scotus observes, contradictories cannot be thought of as single notions (see *Opus Oxoniensen*, lib. I, d. 2, q. 1; *Duns Scotus, Philosophical Writings*, ed. A. Wolter, p. 73). This applies to analytical contradictions such as "p and not-p." It also applies to synthetic contradictions such as the concept of a red tone. In such a case, the notions are so "distant" from each other that neither determines the other. If we leave the notion of figure out of account, color and tonality can only be thought of as separate, unrelated notions. The same criteria of compatibility apply to instantiation in things. To say "this one" in the sensible world implies that there is a subject of predication there. It presupposes that the predicates we express are *unifiable* in this subject. Otherwise, there would not be one but two subjects of predication there.

A further element in Scotus's position is that we never leave the field of being when we talk about an essence. There is a being of an essence; in fact, there is an existence of an essence. Essences themselves are only possibles; but as Lychetus, Scotus's authorized commentator, remarks: "It is simply contradictory for any essence to have its being of a possible and not to have its existence of a being of a possible" (*Opus Oxoniensen*, lib. II, d. 3, q. 1, n. 7). In other words, because essences have being, they also have existence. For Scotus, this means that degrees of existence follow upon degrees of essence (see *Opus Oxoniensen*, lib. II, d. 3, q. 3, n. 1). I can illustrate this by an example, the person of Socrates. We start out with the most general essence we can think of, that of thinghood or substance. We now begin to specify this essence, adding successively the predicates, living, animal, two-legged, rational, capable of laughter, in Athens, engaged in dialectic, snubnosed, and so forth. The essence, as it is further specified, gradually narrows and makes more definite its unity. The possibility corresponding to its unity becomes more defined. The possibility of a rational animal living in Athens is not the possibility of thinghood in general. Now, the ultimate determination is, of course, one of singularity, in this case, the *numerical singularity* of an individual thing. When we reach it, then according to Scotus, we have an existence corresponding to this grade of determination. We have the actual existence of an individual man. This view can be summed up by saying that all individual existents are completely full essences. They are specified down to the here and now of their being. Let me make a comparison. If we say that such essential determinations must take account of every element of a person's life and, in this, also his relations to all other actual existents, we shall be able to see the monads of Leibniz peeping over Scotus's shoulder. Such monads also owe their actual existence to the fullness of their essence (see *Discourse on Metaphysics*, XIII, in *Basic Writings*).

Scotus's proof for the existence of God nicely illustrates this position. The proof involves a redefinition of Anselm's formula for God. In Scotus's version, it runs: "God is that without contradiction than which a greater cannot be conceived without contradiction" (*Duns Scotus, Philosophical Writings*, p. 73). The addition of the words, "without contradiction," points to the fact that Scotus's attention is on the essence of God. Since essences are possibles, to demonstrate an essence is to demonstrate a possibility. Yet, as we said, the basis of essential possibility is minor unity. This is the same as the absence of self-contradiction. Thus, according to Scotus, what one has to first demonstrate is that the essence of God "non contradicit entitati," "does not contradict entityness." This phrase is typical of Scotus. Less literally translated, it means "does not contradict that which every entity must be in order to be." This, for Scotus, is being self-compatible. Every entity must have compatible attributes if it is to be. Thus, the major part of Scotus's argumentation is directed toward showing that God, as Christians conceive him—as causally active, as intelligent, as willing, as infinite and perfect, but especially as the first or highest—is, in fact, a compatible essence. This means, for example, demonstrating that the notion of causality is compatible with that of a first cause. It means demonstrating that the notion of perfection is compatible with the notion of a highest or first degree of perfection (see *Duns Scotus Philosophical Writings*, pp. 39–45, 48–49).

All of these demonstrations, if we grant them, prove that God is possible as an essence. What about the proof that he is an actual existent, that he is a numerical singular? To demonstrate this, we have to establish that he is unique. This is because the grade of actual existence corresponds to that of an essence specified down to the uniqueness and singularity of an actual individual. To manage this step of the proof, Scotus points out that the notion of a first in the order of causality—as well as in the orders of perfection, will, intelligence, and so forth—can involve only the same unique singular. The notion of two firsts, as he argues, is simply contradictory. It is, for example, contradictory to conceive of more than one being which, *as first,* is defined as the necessary and sufficient cause of the world's existence. If there were more than one, neither cause, by itself, would be a sufficient cause. The result of such arguments is the assertion that, if God is possible, he must necessarily be an actual existent. This follows because God's notion specifies in the order of possibility a unique singular. His essence includes his actual existence, for it is an essence which is only possible as that of a unique existent.

There are a number of ways Scotus makes this point. For example, he notes that a first cause is essentially possible only as an actual existent. It is, he argues, contradictory to the notion of a first cause of existence to receive its actual existence from some other cause. Thus, if it is, indeed, *possible* for a first cause to exist, it must actually exist of itself. The *possibility* of its existence, however, has already been demonstrated by Scotus's arguments showing that the essence of a unique first cause is a compatible essence. As a consequence, we must say that a first cause does, indeed, actually exist of itself. It is an actually existent entity (see *Duns Scotus, Philosophical Writings*, p. 46). A similar argument is made about God as the measure of perfection.

Whatever else we might think about this proof, we should keep an essential point in mind. It only works for God. In other words, since nothing else is first, nothing else can be proven to be unique and, therefore, actual by this method. We can express this by saying that God is a deductive singular. From his notion as a *first,* we deduce he can *be* only as an actual singular. All other beings, like our example of Socrates, are singular inductively. They are singular by the inductive addition of conceptual formal note to conceptual formal note, each further conceptual determination working to further specify the essence in question.

What happens when we say that such "notes" or specific differences are infinite in number, that they comprehend the specification of the relations of our finite being to every other finite being? If we believe this, then Leibniz's God is capable of seeing in our essence the necessity of our actual existence. But we, with our limited understanding, are not. In other words, *for us,* every actual existent other than God is, in terms of its conceptual essence, essentially unprovable. The conclusion follows from our adoption of Scotus's metaphysics. The result of this metaphysics is ultimately to collapse being and essence together. In Scotus's words, "It is simply false that being is other than essence" (*Opus Oxoniensen*, lib. IV, d. 11, q. 3, n. 46). Granting this, the proof of a being is also the proof of an essence. Thus, if we say that a finite being has an infinite number of specifying differences in its essence, then a proof of its actual being, as based on the examination of its essence, is a proof necessarily involving this infinity. It requires the demonstration of the compatibility of an infinite number of formal notes. Such a demonstration is impossible for a finite mind. In terms of our limited, human conceptions of individual beings, we never cross the boundary between possibility and actuality. This is because we can never inductively specify an entity down to this one thing, to an actually existing unique singular. We mention this to point out the transformation that Scotus has worked on the original Parmenidean equation between conceivability and actual being, νοεῖν and εἶναι. The equation no longer involves, as it did for Plato, the identification of a *limited* number of underlying, self-identical elements.

V

Let us return to Descartes. In his *Meditations,* Descartes doubts the world and then finds it necessary first to prove God in order to assure himself of the existence, say, of his inkpot. Why begin with God rather than the inkpot? The procedure is in some sense intelligible if we take into account the philosophical world into which Descartes was born. As a number of historians have pointed out, the underlying philosophical influence in this world was that of Scotus.[5] His influence can be seen by comparing Descartes' proof for the existence of God with Scotus' original. The former is actually a truncated version of the latter. Thus, at least historically, the reason that Descartes must begin with God's existence is clear. In the order of demonstration, God's existence comes first because it is, in fact, the only existence that we can, in this tradition, demonstrate.

What about Cartesian doubt? There are, as we maintained at the beginning, two sides to this doubt: doubt of perception and doubt of opinion. Both, we claim, can be traced to the transformation in the ontological status of the idea.

Let us consider, first, the value Descartes places on opinion. As indicated above, the transformation implies that every essential predication we can make about the world grasps its objects only under the aspect of possibility. In other words, the subject of our discourse, insofar as our discourse is concerned, is only a possibility. It is an essence which we can only incompletely specify. For all our talk, in terms of our statements' *essential* content, the object we are talking about may or may not actually be. The implication is that our statements, considered in themselves, express what may be called *mere* opinion. By this, we mean that they have no inherent claim to be "true" or "right." Because of this, their examination is not, as Plato thought, a necessary first step for philosophical enquiry. Since they are, in their essential content, inherently capable of expressing an actual reality, they must, as Descartes believes, be, one and all, doubted.

What about a direct perception of the object? Plato, as we said, associates the realm of the directly perceivable with the attitude of trust. Trust, as opposed to certitude, is all that we can have if we remain on the level of direct (or sensuous) perception. On this level, we cannot confirm a perception except through a further perception, and so we have ultimately to trust our perceptions. Between this trust and the Cartesian doubt of perception, there also lies the change in the status of the idea. The idea, for Plato, is etymologically and philosophically tied to perception. The Platonic term for the idea, εἶδος, is taken from εἴδω, which means "perceive." The philosophical link between the two appears when we take the ideas we garner from our perceptions of the world as the highest expressions of actuality. If we take the ideas as supremely actual, we are inclined to trust rather than to doubt our perceptions; for then we say that our ideas *are* and that their images, the directly perceivable things, also are. The relation here is that of actuality to image as given by the divided line. For Plato, given that the ideas are, the directly perceivable things—which, as images, are dependent on the ideas—must also be.

This philosophical position is, of course, completely undermined once we say that the ideas have the ontological status of possibilities, i.e., that they express the fact that what sensibly instantiates them may or may not be. At this point, they cannot provide a philosophical basis for a belief in the existence of sensible things. Trust, therefore, turns to doubt, and like Descartes we must turn to the benevolence of God to assure us of the world we once took for granted. A sign of the new character of this doubt is the fact that this benevolence itself becomes an object of proof rather than a matter of direct perception. In the absence of any proof to the contrary, it is, for Descartes, possible that God may be an evil, deceiving genius. The direct experience of God's benevolence is grace. That grace could be considered a matter of demonstration is a sure sign that the modern age has been entered.[6]

Was this transition to modernity necessary? Was it necessary for us, with Descartes, to enter an age in which we attempt to demonstrate matters which we formerly took on trust or faith? What about modernity itself? Is *it* necessary? Given that the whole of the history we have recounted turns on the failure to distinguish being and essence, we cannot say this. What we can say is that the question of being, of that which, as Parmenides says, "is and cannot not-be," still remains open.

2

TIME AND AUGUSTINE'S METAPHYSICS

We can say one thing with certainty about time. We all feel that we understand what it is until we are asked to explain it. The goal of this chapter is not so broad. It is to understand Augustine's concept of time. Yet, even with this limitation, I am not going to approach the topic directly. I shall try to flank it by returning to a problem I considered in the first chapter: that of participation. From this, I hope to find an entrance point which shall lead us to the required explanation. I begin, then, with a little fragment of Plato's *Parmenides.* Socrates has just said that the ideas are "paradigms in nature and other things are like them and resemble them." He, then, defines "the participation of things in their ideas as itself nothing more than their having been made like their ideas." Parmenides, the ever-subtle dialectician, seizes on this point. He asks, "If the thing is like the idea, must not the idea be like the thing which has been made like it, at least with regard to the point of resemblance"? Since this statement is almost a tautology, Socrates cannot but assent. Parmenides then draws the dialectical net tighter. "But isn't it necessary," he asks, "for the two things which are alike to participate in one and the same thing?" "Necessarily," says Socrates. Whereupon Parmenides asks, "And that which the two participate in and are alike through such participation, won't this itself be an idea?" (*Parmenides*, 132 d–e, my own translation). Once again Socrates agrees and finds, to his surprise, that he has fallen into an infinite regress.

Let me spell out the difficulty that Parmenides has drawn the young Socrates into. Its first premise is that, when things are alike, we say they are such through their participating in some idea. Thus, chairs are similar by virtue of their participating in the idea of "chairness." We come to this idea through our perceptions of individual chairs. Arising from this basis, the idea cannot be dissimilar from them. Our second premise, then, is that the idea is *like* the individuals participating in it. With this, we return to our first premise. Likeness arises whenever two things participate in the same idea. Thus, "chairness" and individual chairs must be similar by virtue of a new idea common to them both. Yet, this third thing, if similar to the first two, will demand for its similarity a new idea. This last, if similar to the first three, will demand yet another idea, and so on indefinitely.

What is the point that Plato is making here? It concerns, we can say, the being of the idea and the relation of this being to that of a thing. Is the idea of large objects itself a large object? Is the idea of smallness itself small? Is the idea of a piece of black cloth itself black and made out of cloth? As our negative answers to these questions indicate, we cannot predicate of the idea what we predicate of the thing participating in the idea. This distinction of predication points to a distinction in being. The thing is an individual, material entity. It has the predicates appropriate to this state of being. The idea, however, is defined as being one thing present in many. Its being one-in-many rules out any notion that it is a material entity. Thus, as Parmenides notes, one thing can be present in many either as a whole or part by part (*Parmenides*, 131a). A material thing can exist as a whole in many things only by being multiplied. At that point, however, it is many and not one. Similarly, it can exist part by part in many things only by being divided. What would a material part of an idea, for example, the idea of smallness, mean? The silliness of such a notion is apparent when Parmenides invites us to conceive of something getting smaller and smaller as material portions of the idea of the small are progressively added to it. If the idea is not a material thing, then we can say that the predicates appropriate to such things, predicates such as large, small, black, made of cloth and so forth, are not appropriate to it. This conclusion allows us to assert that the idea is *not like* the thing. Insofar as we can affirm this, we avoid the infinite regress of ideas we just described. This, however, leaves us with a worse difficulty. Our knowledge begins with the things about us. How are we to ascend to a knowledge of the ideas when we say that they are *not* like these things? Is it not the case, as Parmenides says, that the ideas "must remain unknown to us"—because in fact, they are not like any of the individual things which we sensibly know (*Parmenides*, 133 b)?

The dilemma presented by the *Parmenides* is not directly soluble. Something else must be added if we are to move away from the sterile dialectic of things being either like or unlike the ideas that they participate in. What we need, in fact, is a medium between the things and the ideas. The medium must possess the qualities of both the things and ideas and must allow the ascent from one to the other.

II

It was Augustine who first suggested that time could be such a medium. In Book XI of the *Confessions*, he writes that "even when we learn from created things, which are subject to change, we are led to the truth which does not change."[1] This truth is the "Word" of God. The Word is eternal and contains in its eternity, as he elsewhere writes, all of what Plato called *ideas*.[2] How is the ascent to the Word and, thus, to the ideas possible? The answer that can be drawn from Augustine is that time itself makes this possible. Time is the medium that links the changing thing to the eternity in which "all is present." The linking point, as we shall see, is the now. Augustine writes, describing time: "Time . . . is never all present at once. The past is always driven on by the future, the future always follows on the heels of the past, and both the past and the future have their beginning and their end in the eternal present. If only men's minds could be seized and held still! They would see how eternity, in which there is neither past nor future, determines both past and future time" (*Confessions*, Book XI, §11, pp. 261–62).

To bring us to the point of holding our minds still, Augustine begins with the following, rather startling fact: The future does not yet exist and the past has ceased to exist. This fact is so simple and so close to us that, like a pair of glasses, it usually escapes our notice. Personal loss and the consequent longing for what is past as well as acute expectation and the tedium of waiting for what will be does, at times, give us a sense of this fact. Out of this sense comes a notion of being. Being means presence, or, to put this in Greek, *ousia* means *parousia*. Now, that which is present is at the present. It shares with us a now. If neither the past nor the future are, if only the present really is, then this last, in its nowness, is the place of being.

What sort of being is this? If being is presence in the now, then the present would seem to be, like the moment that occupies the now, the most fleeting type of being. The present moment is but for a moment and slips into the past, that is, into what is not. As Augustine says: "If, therefore, the present is time only by reason of the fact that it moves on to become the past, how can we say that even the present *is*, when the reason why it *is* is that it is *not to be*? In other words, we cannot rightly say that time *is*, except by reason of its impending state of *not-being*" (*Confessions*, Book XI, §14, p. 264). Augustine's point here is that the moment of the now is constantly present by virtue of being constantly new. Time is a process involving continual change. This means that the moment of the now, regarded as part of this process, *is* only insofar as it changes into what is not—i.e., the past. This annihilation of the moment, does not, however, mean that the process stops. A new moment appears, moving, as it were, from the future to the present. Here we can say two things. The first is that the very being of the present moment demands both the past and the future. The present moment would not be in time, that is, would not *be* at all, if, as Augustine says, it did not "move on to become the past." Similarly, it could not have come to be, if it had not, as part of the future, replaced the present moment. Granting that time is a process of constant change, of moment replacing moment in the ongoing now, none of time's moments can exist as an *independent* being. To give a moment such a being is to think of it apart from what precedes and follows it. But this is to place it outside of time. Since, however, the moment only exists as part of time, this is not to think it at all. The conclusion here is that the moments of time can be conceived and can only exist by virtue of the moments that surround them. They are all dependent members of a whole. We can also say that, like the points on a line, they exist, *not* as discrete (or separate) entities, but as elements of a continuum. The second thing we can say about time is that nowness, with its constant appearing and vanishing of moments, is a pure example of what we mean by becoming. It is, we can say, a pure form of the world of sensible things. This is a world which, to quote Plato, is ever anew "created, always in motion, becoming in place and vanishing again out of place" (*Timaeus*, 52 a, trans. B. Jowett).

How can we say, as we earlier did, that within the thought of the now is the thought of a link between change and eternity—in particular, the eternity of the ideas? To quote Plato again, the being of an idea is "always the same, uncreated and indestructible." It is a being "never receiving anything into itself from without nor itself going out to any other" (ibid.). How can the present now, which continues to exist by receiving the moments of the future and, in the same process, yielding these moments to the past, qualify as a link to the eternal being of the ideas?

That there must be something more inherent in the concept of the now is indicated by the fact that our present conception does not allow us to speak of time as duration; that is, as long or short stretches of time. As Augustine writes, "We speak of a 'long' time and a 'short' time, though only when we mean the past or the future. . . . But how can anything which does not exist be either long or short? For the past is no more and the future is not yet" (*Confessions*, Book XI, §15, p. 264). In other words, if being is presence in the now and if a stretch of time includes by definition more moments than the one that occupies the present, then such a stretch is not yet thinkable.

Here we can state a paradox—a paradox out of which a proper conception of the now can be drawn. As we have stated, the moment of the now is not independent. As a moment of time, it exists only by virtue of the pastness into which it will flow and by virtue of the futurity that will replace it. Since, however, both the past and the future are not, it is, in its own being, dependent on what is not. With this, we can be said to come to the parting of the philosophical ways. Holding fast to the notion of being as presence, we can say, on the one hand, that being as presence depends upon absence; that is, on what is not present. Here, we enter upon the road of Neo-Platonism. We affirm that absence—or what is *beyond* being—is what upholds being. Heidegger, at times, seems to come close to this school of thought.[3] On the other hand, we can embrace Augustine's solution. We can assert that being can be dependent only on being. Thus, for the present, dependent moment to be, both the past and the future on which it depends must *also* be. Being means presence in the now.

This means that both the past and the future must be copresent in the now.

This solution can be understood on two levels. In both of these, time appears—not as an object, not as a thing among the things "outside" of us—but, in Augustine's words, as something "subjective." This does not mean that it is *merely* subjective. On the contrary, we are presented with a notion of a subject that transforms our ordinary understanding of subjectivity.

To see this, we must first give the elements of the solution. When Augustine asserts of the past and the future, "it is only by being present that they are," he means that we have three components of presence: "a present of past things, a present of present things and a present of future things" (*Confessions*, Book XI, §20, p. 269). The first, he says, exists as "memory," the second exists as "direct perception," and the third as "expectation" or anticipation. Since these three exist "only in the mind," it is in the mind, according to Augustine, that time is measured and has its proper being. This means that I measure elapsed time, say, the time of a note that has sounded, by retaining in my memory the moments of its sounding. Similarly, if I hear in succession two sounds, first a short one and then a long one, I must, while hearing the long sound, "retain the sound of the short one in order that I may compare the two for the purpose of measurement" (ibid., §27, p. 276). This retention of moments in the ongoing now gives the now a certain *depth*. We do not apprehend time as an isolated instant. Its apprehension always involves a retained stretch of time that preceded. Augustine makes the same claim with regard to the future. Future moments of time are copresent in the now and are apprehended in the attitude of expectation. Thus, we can, starting from the present moment of the now, view the future as definite stretches of anticipated time.

Augustine illustrates the workings of what he calls the "faculties" of expectation and memory by the example of reciting a Psalm one knows. He writes:

> Before I begin, my faculty of expectation is engaged by the whole of it. But once I have begun, as much of the Psalm as I have removed from the province of expectation and relegated to the past now engages my memory, and the scope of the action which I am performing is divided between the two faculties of memory and expectation, the one looking back to the part which I have already recited, the other looking forward to the part which I have still to recite. But my faculty of attention is present all the while, and through it passes what was the future in the process of becoming the past. As the process continues, the province of memory is extended in proportion as that of expectation is reduced, until the whole of my expectation is absorbed. This happens when I have finished my recitation and it has all passed into the province of memory (*Confessions*, Book XI, §28, p. 278).

Husserl has provided us with a diagram (Figure 1) which we can adapt so as to spatially represent this process.[4] The horizontal line represents successively given time. Reading from left to right, each of the points of the line represent later moments. The *O* point represents the present now. Thus, to its left, *OP* stands for the past, while to its right, *OF* stands for the future. Now, the reason why the line *PF* is drawn dotted is that neither the past nor the future exists except as present. As present, the past and the future are given by *P'O* and *OF'*, respectively. In other words, the vertical line passing through the *O* point of the now gives us in its bottom half, the "province of memory," whose content is the retained past moments. In its top half, it gives us the province of expectation, which consists of the anticipated future moments. The diagonal lines pointing away from the vertical toward the horizontal indicate the temporal references of what we retain or anticipate. Thus, the retained stretch of time *P'A'* has a reference to *PA*, a successively experienced stretch of past time. Similarly, the anticipated stretch, *F'U'*, refers to *FU*, a duration in the future we shall experience. As the arrows indicate, the reference of what we retain is a reference to greater and greater pastness as we descend along the vertical. *P'* is a retention of an earlier moment than *A'*. The same thing holds in a reverse fashion when we ascend the vertical. *F'* is the anticipation of a later moment than that anticipated by *U'*.

To make this diagram represent what happens when we recite a Psalm, we must imagine the diagonal lines as remaining fixed while the vertical line is displaced, parallel to itself, from left to right. Since the intersection of the ver-

FIGURE 1

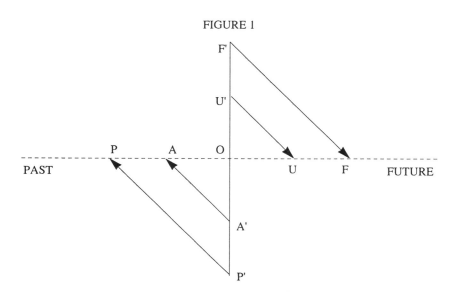

tical and the horizontal lines continues to designate the present now, this motion represents the advance of this now into successively later moments. Let us note that F', U', A', P' are determined as points of intersection between the moving vertical and the fixed diagonal lines. Therefore, as the vertical is displaced to the right, the points of intersection will be seen to move downward. This means that the anticipated duration, represented by $F'U'$, will sink on the vertical, gradually passing through the O point, the point representing the moment of the present. As it does so, the arrows denoting the temporal reference of $F'U'$ will be reversed. When they pointed to future moments to the right of the vertical, they were directed to the right and downward. Pointing to the *same* moments that the moving vertical has placed to the left of the O point, the arrows will point upward and to the left. The reverse of the direction of the temporal reference means that the temporal stretch that was anticipated is now retained. The present of future things, $F'U'$, has now become the present of past things, $P'A'$. We, thus, have achieved a representation of a process in which, as Augustine says, "the province of memory is extended in proportion as that of expectation is reduced." Here we may observe that insofar as the past and future exist only as present, our diagram could have been reduced to the single vertical line with its O point. The movement of the line downward through the O point would, then, represent what is anticipated successively becoming actual and then passing into the retained past.

Augustine's solution, we said, is capable of being interpreted on two different levels. On one level, it can be looked upon as making time merely subjective. So understood, it reduces the reality of time to the memory and expectation of an *individual* subject. That this is *not* Augustine's meaning can be gathered from what he writes immediately following his description of the reciting of the Psalm. He states: "What is true of the whole Psalm is also true of all its parts and of each syllable. It is true of any longer action in which I may be engaged and of which the recitation of the Psalm may only be a small part. It is true of a man's whole life, of which all his actions are parts. It is true of the whole history of mankind, of which each man's life is a part." The claim that Augustine is making is that memory and expectation pass far beyond the faculties of an individual subject. The vertical line which represents the two must, in fact, be drawn as infinite.

This claim should not surprise us once we recall the dependence of the moments of time. The being-in-time of the present moment demands, in its dependence, the being of the past and the future. This implies that we cannot grant time's existence without also granting its indefinite continuance. Indefinite continuance must be assumed since the temporal being of the present moment demands the existence of the moment that replaces it as it slips into pastness. In other words, the present, in its dependence, is never without its anticipated future. This means that the vertical line, which represents on its upper half the series of anticipated moments, must be taken as indefinitely extended. Only by so conceiving it, can we make it represent the inexhaustibility of time. Because, by what we have just said, it follows that time can have no temporal beginning, we must also make the bottom half of the vertical indefinitely long. From that which has no beginning, an indefinite amount of time can be safely assumed to have elapsed.

Let us, for a moment, focus on the conception of time that we have reached. We have asserted that the indefinite continuance of time springs from the fact that every moment, to be in time, requires the being of the moments that surround it. It is easy to see that any finite stretch of time is also in the same condition of dependence. Its first and last moments, as existing in time, demand respectively the being of what precedes and what follows this finite stretch of time. Granting this, the dependence manifested by the moments and the finite extents of time is ultimately on nothing less than the whole of time. If this dependence is to be real, if it is to be anchored in being, then we have to say that the whole of time has an *independent* being. Otherwise put, if we grant the existence of the present moment, the moment at the *O* point of our diagram, then the chain of dependencies that links this with the whole of time demands that this whole be given an independent being. What precisely is this temporally independent being which we are pointing to? Its thought is the thought of its *not* being dependent on another time in order to be. It is, thus, by definition, the thought of the *whole* of time—i.e., time as the abiding totality of its moments. That such a whole (or totality) does not itself move in time, i.e., progress like an individual thing that has a beginning and end, follows from the way we have defined it. There is no "time," i.e., a time outside of the *wholeness* of time, into which it could be said to progress. There is, we may observe, a name for this type of whole. It can be designated as a *unique singular*. Such a singular is defined as that which necessarily exists *simply as one* and not as *one among many* individual singulars, each having the same nature. Given the dependence of the moment on the wholeness of time, we have to say that if time exists— that is, exists as a present, actual moment—then it must also have the being of a unique singular. It must, in other words, have the quality of wholeness that excludes any time beyond itself. There is an here an implicit basis for Augustine's remark that it was not *in time* that God created time. Time as a unique singular must be created all at once. It must, for any moment of it to appear, be entirely present as an inexhaustible whole.

Our representation of this whole is the indefinitely extended vertical line. That this line is drawn vertically signifies the copresence of every instant of time with the present now. Here, of course, we simply follow the necessity that has guided us before. This is that, if being means presence in the now, both the future and the past, in order to be, must be present in the now. The line, then, represents the copresence in the now of every moment of time; it represents the now in which "all is present." This last is Augustine's *definition of eternity*. With this, the now appears with an aspect opposite to that with which we began. Before, the now appeared as a pure example of the notion of becoming. Here, the now appears under the aspect of eternity.

Some philosophers consider eternity an unthinkable concept. Convinced by Kant, they declare that the concept is beyond all experience. This, however, is *not* the case with Augustine's concept of eternity, which signifies the copresence of distinct moments. Fragments of eternity—that is, of such copresence—are experienced by us at every instant of our lives. They are experienced every time we apprehend something in motion. A motion, for example, the falling of a pencil, is a temporally extended event. To apprehend it as such, I must grasp its moments as successive, as occupying distinct temporal positions. The successively grasped moments cannot, however, disappear from my consciousness the instant after their apprehension. To grasp as a whole the falling of a pencil, I must retain such moments in the present, that is, in the present of my act of apprehension. In other words, they must, as distinct moments, be copresent with my ongoing now. Therefore, admitting that such copresence is the characteristic of eternity, it is by virtue of a little fragment of eternity that I grasp my pencil's falling. That the now actually embraces more than this fragment, that, in fact, it must embrace the copresence of the totality of time's moments, follows from what was said earlier: Given the dependence of the moments of time, no part of time can exist separately. In other words, time must exist as a whole or not at all.

We have reached a point where we can begin to understand the assertions of Augustine that we first quoted. He writes that "both the past and the future have their beginning and their end in the eternal present." He also claims that "eternity . . . determines both past and future time." This eternity is the copresence with the now of all the moments of time. It is by virtue of this copresence that the individual moment can exist as present. The moment, as dependent, can only exist—i.e., be present at the *O* point—by virtue of the copresence of the whole of time, the whole upon which it ultimately depends. Now, the relation of the future and the past to the present moment can be looked upon in two ways. We can think of them as standing outside of the present moment. Here, time appears as the horizontal line of our diagram. The *O* point, indicating the present, is both the beginning of the segment representing the future and the end of the segment representing the past. This beginning and end of the future and the past is, however, not just the present regarded as a single moment. Through it is drawn the vertical line that represents the eternal present—i.e., the copresence in the now of all that it depends upon. It is this eternal present which is, thus, always the beginning of the future and the end of the past when the latter are horizontally represented. To see this eternal present as *determining* both past and future time, we have to change our point of view and say that the past and the future do not exist outside the present moment. In Augustine's words, "it is only by being present that they are" (*Confessions*, Book XI, §20, p. 269). If we do this, we are left with what is signified by the vertical line of our diagram. The line signifies eternity. The downward movement of the segments of the line represent the passage from anticipated to retained time. It also signifies eternity's determination of future and past time. The essential point illustrated by this spatial representation is simply this: If, in fact, past and future can *be* only as present, then this determination must be in terms of such presence. The copresence of the past and future moments of time is, however, precisely what Augustine means by eternity.

With these thoughts, we can catch a glimpse of eternity's relation to existence. Let us make a distinction between being and existence. Being, we shall say, is copresence in the now. It is the copresence that is shared by the anticipated future, the actual present, and the retained past. Existence, according to its etymology, means standing out. Accordingly, we shall define it as the outstanding or exemplary condition of being present. It signifies being at the *O* point of the now. With these definitions, eternity can be said to *determine* existence. For its determination of the passage of time is also a determination of the moments of time successively occupying the *O* point or actual present. It is a determination of the welling up of moments that successively take their place at the *O* point of the now. Each of these present moments is also *supported* by eternity. This follows insofar as each is dependent on the whole of time, on the copresence of moments that we have called eternity.

From these reflections, two thoughts can arise. Both have a long history in Western speculative thought about God. The first is that God, through his eternal Word, i.e., through his eternity, both grants existence and supports existence from moment to moment. It is, we can say, through his "grace" that a thing exists and continues to exist. God is, in the eternal copresence of moments, the being which supports the existing thing. For Augustine, as we shall see, such support also involves the presence in the Word of eternal ideas. The second thought is that the notion of time as something subjective leads us, through the notion of eternity, to posit God as the ultimate subject. Put rather simply, only in God can the notions of anticipated and retained time be indefinitely extended. Only in him can they be extended—as they must—to embrace the necessary wholeness of time.

III

I now return to the problem from the *Parmenides*, which I discussed at the beginning. As we recall, the elements of this problem are two necessary, but apparently incompatible demands. On the one hand, the idea must be like the thing. This follows insofar as it is from our perceptions of the thing that we rise to the thought of its idea. On the other hand, if we are to avoid an infinite regress, the idea must *not* be like the thing. In particular, it cannot, as the thing is, be a material, spatial-temporal object. Conversely, a material thing cannot have the being that defines the idea. As we saw, a material entity cannot be one thing and also be present in many.

How, then, can the idea both be like and unlike the thing? An answer informed by Augustine involves, first of all, our defining the idea in terms of the preceding discussion of time. So regarded, the idea is the *shining through of eternity* in each of the present, fleeting moments. It is, in terms of our diagram, the result of the vertical line passing through the ongoing now point. This definition does not make the idea into something material, a spatial-temporal entity. It does, however, allow us to say that the idea is the very *presence* of a thing. In fact, insofar as being and presence continue to be the same for us, the definition allows us to say that the idea is the very *being* of a thing.

This definition may seem somewhat opaque. It is, however, composed of common notions. Thus, when we say that the idea is the very presence or being of a thing, we are affirming that we grasp the thing as there, as present before us, in the very same process by which we grasp its idea. The idea is one thing in many. Thus, our claim is that, through our recognition of identical elements in a multiplicity, we grasp both a thing and its idea.

Where are we to locate this multiplicity? Let us recall our assertion that from the perceptions of a thing we rise to the thought of its idea. It is also from these same perceptions that we apprehend the thing as present, as being there before our eyes. Now, if we take the multiplicity in question to refer to our perceptions of some object, we can begin to see the type of entity required to solve the Parmenidean problem.[5] Let us consider, in abstraction, an individual perception. We say "in abstraction" because, like the moment that contains it, such a perception is never actually discrete or separable from those that preceded and follow it. When we do consider the individual perception, it shows us a remarkable characteristic. It is both like and unlike the thing perceived. It is like it insofar as the content of the perception becomes for us the content of the thing perceived. Thus, the redness I see can, under certain conditions, become for me the redness of an object present to me. We shall mention these conditions later. First, however, let us observe how *unlike* this perception is to its object. The perception, as contained in a moment of time, does not endure. It exists, in the "outstanding" sense of the term *existence*, for only an instant. The object, however, continues to exist and, hence, to endure moment after moment as it affords us continually new perceptions. The object, moreover, is a spatial thing. We can measure it and predicate of it, in relation to ourselves, largeness or smallness. None of this is possible with regard to an individual perception. Suppose I see a tower in the distance. Can I tell from my single perception if the tower is large or small? Can I put a tape measure to my mind and measure my perception as so many inches or feet across? The obvious answer is that I cannot. In fact, only through the temporal ordering and arrangement of my perceptions have I any notion of the size of the tower. I predicate largeness of the tower because, as I approach it, my perception of it takes up more and more of my visual field. Similarly, I take the tower to be a three-dimensional spatial object because, as I walk around it, my perceptions temporally arrange themselves as a series of perspectival views. All of this is, of course, very elementary. It does, however, show us that it is not through a single perception that we arrive at the predicates appropriate to spatial-temporal, material things.

Where, then, are we to locate the multiplicity through which we perceive both the thing and its idea? Taking the multiplicity as referring to our perceptions, the answer becomes apparent. All of our perceptions, along with the moments which contain them, are retained in the ongoing now. Their proper place is in that eternity which is the copresence of the totality of retained and anticipated moments. Now, when we regard what we have called the *shining through of this eternity*, we see the conditions that allow us to grasp an object. We observe, first of all, that although the retained perceptions are distinct in their temporal references, showing themselves as more or less past, this does not mean that we apprehend them one by one. On the contrary, we view them all together. This follows from the nonindependence of the moments that contain them. Such nonindependence means that we cannot think of something as past without also thinking of the moments and contents that follow this in time. What we retain is, therefore, apprehended as a *unified* perceptual experience. It is not apprehended as discrete moments and discrete perceptions. What is the result of this apprehension of retained perceptions "all together"? Such perceptions, when viewed as a whole, are placed in a unity of coincidence. They have a presence that is analogous to that of a series of overlapping transparencies. In this coincidence, contents that are identical—and, to a lesser extent, contents that are similar in quality—reinforce the presence of their qualities. The result of this is the shining through of a one-in-many that allows us to grasp both the thing and its idea.

This can be illustrated by an example. I take my pencil and continually turn it in my hand. As I do so, the contents that I perceptually experience constantly enter into the retention of my memory. The pencil has only a finite number of features and, thus, the contents that I do retain, as I constantly view it from one side and then another, will recur. In the unity of coincidence in which all these contents are placed, the recurrent contents will reinforce one another. They will, as we put it, "shine through." This shining through has, we say, two specific effects. In the first place, it allows me to affirm that my present, momentary perception is not an isolated experience but rather a perception *of* some object. The content of this present perception is re-enforced by the identical, recurring contents that have been previously experienced. It, thus, attains a reference to what I have previously experienced. It becomes a perception of a feature of an enduring object. With this I pass from a judgment of perception, for example, the judgment that I see yellowness, to a judgment of experience. The latter consists in the affirmation that there is something there, enduring before me, *of which* I am presently having perceptions. It is a claim concerning being. The second effect of this shining through is the apprehension, in a primitive form, of the idea of the object. The similar elements that recur and allow me to unify my perceptions as perceptions of definite features of one and the same object *also* allow me to predicate definite qualities of the object. They give me the definite qualities which form the elements of the idea of the object, for example, the yellowness, length, and shape of a pencil.

Several things can be said about this solution. The first is that the idea that arises in this process is both like and unlike the object. Its likeness consists in the fact that its content is identical to that of the object. Its unlikeness consists in the fact that it itself is not a spatial-temporal object. A spatial-temporal object appears perspectivally. It changes its appearance from moment to moment as we view it from different sides. What we retain, however, is fixed in eternity. We cannot take a remembered perceptual experience and examine it like a physical object, turning it around to view it from a side that we have not yet seen. Because of this, the idea which results from the shining through of what we retain is *not* like and can *never* be like the thing in the sense of *itself* being something spatial-temporal. The second point is that the process, which we described as giving us the idea of a *single* object, can be repeated again and again to give us the idea of a *number* of objects. Thus, I can view in succession a number of pencils. The same process of retention, unification, and reinforcement of similar contents will occur. Here, however, the resultant idea will apply not to one but to many pencils.

When we ask how far we can continue this process, two alternative answers appear. We may take our description as purely psychological in the modern sense. It will then be understood as applying only to the individual subject with his limited abilities. Alternately, we may take it as applying to the one subject who is adequate to the necessary wholeness of time. Here, anticipation and retention extend to the totality of moments and possible contents contained in these moments. The shining through that occurs through the coincidence of these contents will then be a shining through of ideas that are truly eternal. In this case, the "place" of the ideas will be in that eternity which Augustine calls the Word of God. We mentioned earlier that God, in the eternal copresence of moments, is the being which supports the existing thing. We may now refine this thought by saying that the ideas that have their place in this copresence support not just the existence but also the definite qualities of the thing.

The philosophical necessity for this second, Augustinian interpretation is contained in the notion of time. Time, as we said, is a unique singular. If it does exist, it must exist as a whole that has no beyond. The same can be said for the idea. Each idea, if it does exist, exists as an all embracing whole. Thus, the idea of man properly embraces *all* men. It is not added to by the multiplication of examples falling under its concept. It is a unique singularity in the same sense as time is: It is one thing and it has no beyond in terms of individuals of a similar type. Granting this, we have to say that, if such an idea is to arise, it must do so through the presence of the wholeness of time. This follows insofar as its notion involves the presence of *all that has been* and *all which will be* an example of its notion. Does such an idea exist? Given the preceding, we can say that it exists as certainly as the wholeness of time exists. If we admit the dependence of the moment, we can also say that it exists as certainly as this present moment does. Both its present existence and the preservation of its being as it slips into the past demand this wholeness—the very wholeness that Augustine takes to be God's eternity.

When Husserl revives this argument some 1600 years later, the same necessities of dependence and independence will apply. His focus as a modern, however, will be on knowing rather than on being. His account of temporality will be advanced to resolve an epistemological, rather than an ontological crisis. In spite of this, the impulse to assume a subject who is something more than an individual person will remain. Such an "absolute" subject seems to be required as long as we assume that time is subjective and is unending.

3

THE TEMPORALITY OF KNOWING

I

The crisis of modernity, which has advanced with this century, is one of confidence. We lack confidence in the efficacy of thought, both scientific and philosophical thought. This lack of confidence extends to consciousness itself. We doubt whether it is revelatory of its object. Even in the supposedly privileged domain of self-consciousness, these doubts occur. Consciousness appears more and more a mystery to itself, something opaque to its penetrating power. Our claim is that one of the roots of this crisis is the modern account of what it means to know. Starting with Galileo, given a further impulse by Locke, and continuing to the present day, there has been an ongoing, yet unsuccessful, attempt to explain knowing in terms of the modern notion of causality.

Two laws give the essence of this notion. The first is that caused facts are dependent on the material makeup of interacting bodies. The second is that what has occurred in the past determines what occurs in the present. Both may be illustrated by the Newtonian law for gravitation. It states that the force presently existing between two bodies is directly proportional to the product of their masses and inversely proportional to the square of the distance between them. Thus, varying the masses, e.g., the material makeup of the bodies, varies the fact of the force. So does varying the distance. In regard to this last, we can see how an event in the past—e.g., an impulse that gave one of the bodies a certain velocity in a certain direction—affects the distances presently obtaining between the bodies. It, thus, affects the *present* force.

What happens when we attempt to interpret the relation of knowing, taken as a subject-object relation, in terms of this schema? As a slight reflection shows, knowing must give up its objective claim. The subject can no longer claim to know the object as it is in itself. According to the schema, the fact of knowing depends upon the material makeup of the subject and object and upon the spatial-temporal relations between them. Thus, keeping the object and the relations constant, if we vary the material makeup of the perceptual and thinking organization of the subject, the caused fact—i.e., the given content of knowledge—will also vary. We cannot say that our knowledge is valid for the object in itself. It is, at least in part, determined by our own material (physiological) organization.

The skeptical consequences implicit in this view can be drawn by noting what the theory of evolution tells us about the variation of this organization. Our material organization has developed from lower forms. Its development has not been determined by the epistemological criterion of the truth or falsity of our knowledge. It has been guided by the criterion of survival. The two do not necessarily coincide. Thus, cognitive mistakes—as the behavior of numerous species indicates—may be necessary in the struggle for survival. The point has also been applied to the forms of cognition—i.e., the basic forms and laws of logic. They have been considered not as valid in themselves, but as peculiar to a particular line of evolutionary development, that of humans. With this, we have a means of relativizing what Aristotle once called the *principle of principles*, the principle required for all further knowledge (*Metaphysics*, 1005b, 15 ff). We can relativize the law of noncontradiction.[1]

The import of this is clear: The scientific-causal account of knowing seems to undermine the very claims of science to state what is objectively true. Sigmund Freud responded to this difficulty in a manner that may be regarded as typical for scientists. He writes, "our mental apparatus . . . is itself a constituent part of the world which we set out to investigate, and it readily admits of such investigation." Granting this, it follows for Freud that "the task of science is fully covered if we limit it to showing how the world must appear to us in consequence of the particular character of our organizations" (*The Future of an Illusion*, trans. W. D. Scott, pp. 91–92). These statements, taken together, are essentially a claim that a study of that which is determinative of appearance can, in fact, be based upon appearance. That which is determinative of appearance is the mental apparatus, as a "consequence" of whose "particular character" the world "must appear" as it does. The appearance which allows us to study this apparatus is that of the world "which we set out to investigate," a world where this same mental apparatus appears as a "constituent part." The fallaciousness of this claim may be shown by returning to the causal explanation of knowing. Expressed in these terms, it is a claim that the mental physiology whose appearing functioning we investigate and causally explain is the same as the physiology *by virtue of* whose causally determinative functioning we make our observations and explanations. Only if this were so could a causal account directed to the appearances of this functioning show us why the world "*must* appear" to us in the way that it does. Now, as is readily apparent, this claim rests on a prior claim. We must assert that our mental apparatus (as determinative of appearances) causes us to correctly ascertain the laws of causality. We, thus, are asserting that we can, from the world's appearance, get the world as it is "in itself"—i.e., get its causal laws and processes as they actually function. Yet, as we have seen, the very notion of causality denies this. When we interpret knowing in terms of causality, we can never get the object as it is in itself. As

laws of knowing a content distinct from that of the natural causal laws. The question is whether such temporality can be maintained. Is cognitive apprehension necessarily structured by a temporality that is teleological, a temporality in which the not-yet plays a determining role? Our position is that a reading of Husserl's texts on internal time-consciousness suggests that this must be the case. Within them, we can find an answer to the crisis with which we began this chapter.

First, however, we must begin with some elementary considerations. Husserl represents the basic structure of time in terms of a simple time diagram (Figure 2). The horizontal line of the diagram, *AE*, represents successive time. Reading from left to right, each of the points of the line represents a later

FIGURE 2

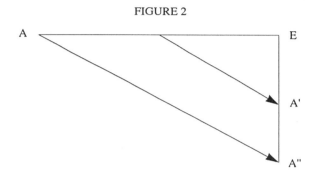

moment.[2] The diagonal lines represent the "sinking down into pastness" of each of the successively given moments. The moments, having been experienced as present, are experienced as "just past," and then as just "just past," and so forth. This experience is one of time's expiration, of time's passing away—which requires, of course, an experiential sense of time's moments as *having* passed away. Husserl draws the diagonal lines parallel to one another. This parallelism designates the equitability of the sense of expiration. Contents are apprehended as sinking into pastness at the same rate. This signifies that their original order of succession is not temporally scrambled while they are grasped as expiring. In other words, the order of points given by the intersections of the diagonal lines with a vertical line is also the order of the successively given now points. The length of the vertical line represents the quantity of pastness. All but one of the points of the vertical line of our diagram are simply endpoints of the diagonal lines. Thus, as you descend the vertical, you come upon point moments that have more and more expired—i.e., sunk deeper and deeper into pastness. Its initial, topmost point is the present, actually given now.

For Husserl, the vertical line also represents enduring time: time apprehended as duration. To see how this is so, let us examine a problem for which the diagram is supposed to represent a solution. Suppose I see a bird flying through the garden. How have I been able to "see" this? What is required, with regard to my sense of time, to grasp this flying or, for that matter, any motion at all? To grasp the flight as temporally extended, I must grasp its moments as successive—i.e., as occupying distinct temporal positions. But the successively grasped moments cannot disappear from consciousness the instant after their apprehension. To grasp the flight as a whole, I must retain them in the present— the present of the ongoing act of apprehension. Thus, what is required is both the temporal distinctness of the moments and their simultaneous presence in the ongoing now of the act of apprehension. The vertical line represents the fulfillment of both demands. Its points signify temporally distinct, successive moments insofar as to each is attached a successively greater sense of expiration. The points, however, are all given along with the now (the topmost point of the vertical line). They, thus, represent a *retention* in the ongoing now of the moments that were successively apprehended. This retention, which preserves the successive (or temporally distinct) quality of moments, is termed by Husserl *primary* or short-term *memory*.

Let us take a closer look at this solution. The diagonal lines represent, as we said, the sense of expiration, of sinking down into pastness. Now, this sense is that of greater and greater removal of a moment with its impressional content from the ever new, actual now. This sense of constant removal, of removal proceeding at a uniform rate, is that which first gives us a sense of the content-laden moment as occupying a definite position in the past. The moment, according to Husserl, is sensed as sinking into pastness at just such a rate as to fix it in a definitely given order of past (or expired) moments (See *Zur Phänomenologie des inneren Zeitbewusstseins* [hereafter cited as *Ph. d. in. Zb.*], §31, ed. R. Boehm, Hua X, 64). In other words, with every new now, the moment is experienced as being a moment later. Diagramatically represented, with each new now, the retained moment moves down a point on the vertical line in Figure 3.

FIGURE 3

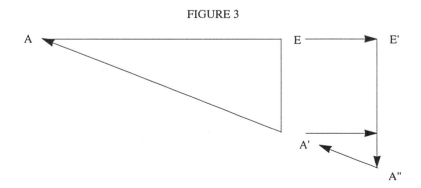

The downward movement thus corresponds to the movement of the vertical line to the right as it advances to the next now point in the horizontal line of successive now points. The downward movement of expiration is, accordingly, precisely what is required to keep the retained moment having the same diagonal (or "retentional") reference to the same point in the past. One can also put this by saying that our sense of constant expiration constitutes for us the givenness of a content at a definite point of time. Applied to a multitude of contents, all expiring at the same rate but distinct in the degree of their expiration, this sense allows us to apprehend, in the now, successively given time.

What precisely is this sense of expiration? Husserl describes it as a "steady continuum of retentions such that each later point is a retention of an earlier" (*Ph. d. in. Zb.*, §11, p. 29). In other words, we have an impression of a content in the now. This impression is retained in the following moment. In the next, this immediate retention is itself retained. We, thus, have "a continuous chain of retentions of retentions" of the original content (*Ideen zu einer reinen Phaenomenologie, Erstes Buch* [hereafter cited as *Ideen I*], §81, ed. W. Biemel, Hua II, 199). Each retention retains all the retentions that preceded it and, thus, retains the original content to which they are all serially related. Each, however, also modifies this content. It adds a sense of greater expiration or "pastness" to it. Otherwise put: the sense of the pastness of a content that a retention contains becomes, in a retention of this retention, a sense of *past* pastness, i.e., a sense of greater pastness or further expiration. If we ask what, strictly speaking, is the sense of pastness, we have to say that it is a relational sense. It is a sense of the amount of the serially ordered relations—i.e., retentions of retentions—that intervene between the present moment and that of an original impression of a sense content.

According to the above, the sense of expiration is a sense of a serially ordered, constant process. The nature of this process can best be seen by considering in somewhat greater detail what cognition requires of our sense of time. Apart from Augustine, the first serious consideration of these requirements is Kant's in his *Critique of Pure Reason* (hereafter cited as "Kritik d. r. V."). Two of them have already been mentioned by us. We can, however, profitably review them by following Kant's formulations. The first involves the fact that the apprehension of a temporally extended object involves a "multiplicity" of temporally distinct impressions. Such an apprehension, as Kant writes, would be impossible "if the mind did not distinguish time in the succession of impressions following one another" ("Kritik d. r. V.," A 99, *Kants gesammete Schriften*, IV, 77). The impressions must be given distinct temporal positions. They must, we can say, be inserted into definite, unchanging positions in objective, successively given time. The second condition is that of reproduction. As Kant says, "if I were to lose from my thought the preceding impressions . . . and not reproduce them when I advance to those which follow, a complete presentation would never arise . . ." (ibid., A 102, IV, 79). The requirement, then, is that of making copresent the impressions which I must distinguish according to successive temporal positions. For Husserl, the retentional process satisfies both requirements by retaining (or reproducing), at each temporal position, the content which was retained in the previous position. Thus, at every moment of my apprehension, the past is brought up to the present. In the series of such moments, the past is serially retained. Yet, these copresent retentions continue to be temporally distinguished. This follows when we grant that the sense of their distinction—of greater or less pastness—is a relational one: a sense of a retention being related to its original impression *through* the intervening retentions of retentions.

This admission allows us to meet a third requirement for cognition. Retention can fulfill its function of bringing the past up to the present only if we are capable of recognizing that the retained content is the same as the content originally given in the past. In Kant's words, "Without the consciousness that what we think is, in fact, the same as what we thought a moment before, all reproduction in the series of presentations would be useless" (ibid., A 103, IV, 79). In other words, without this consciousness, the reproduced would appear as something *new*. Rententions would not be temporally distinguished from the impressions which we are presently experiencing. Now, the consciousness that a retention is not a new presentation is a consciousness that what it retains—i.e., its content—is something past. This consciousness is guaranteed if we grant that a retention presents what it retains through a series of retentions and grant as well that a consciousness of this series is, in fact, that of the pastness of the retained.

The precise nature of this consciousness of pastness can be elicited by contrasting the independence of a new presentation with the dependence of a retention. The former does not exhibit a dependence on what is not presently given, the latter does. Husserl writes that a retention, in itself, "is a momentary consciousness of an expired phase and also a basis for the retentional consciousness of the next phase"—i.e., a basis for a retention of *this* retention (*Ph. d. in. Zb.*, Beilage IX, p. 118). This means that a retention cannot be given unless what it retains is first given, the latter being the retention that serves as *its* basis. The same holds for each of the members of the retentional chain. Together, they form a chain of dependencies. The chain is anchored in its first member, which is here understood as an originally given presentation.

How does the attachment of this chain to the presentation exhibit the latter's pastness? The answer takes us to the origin of time's intentionality. We are aware of a retention's dependence by virtue of its functioning as a sign; that is, by its pointing beyond itself. The dependence of its being in the now upon what is *not* now is exhibited by its reference. It refers beyond itself, in its present givenness, to that upon which it is immediately and, then, mediately dependent. Reference to something else is, however, the primitive form of intentionality. We, thus, have two possible descriptions of the retentional chain, the first being the inner of which the second is the outer manifestation. Because the members of the chain are all dependent, the chain can be described as a "continuity of constant changes . . . inseparable into phases and points of the continuity that could exist for themselves" (*Ph. d. in. Zb.*, §10, p. 27). Since dependence, or incapability of existing for oneself, shows itself in intentionality, the chain can also be described as possessing a "diagonal intentionality" (*Langsintentionalität*), one proceeding back from the present retention to the independently given "primary datum" (ibid., §39, p. 81).

The phenomenological distinction between a new presentation and a retention should now be apparent. The former presents its content immediately without any further temporal reference. As for the latter, it presents what it retains through a serially structured intentionality. In other words, it presents it through a continuous chain of retentions of retentions, each of which is understood as retaining all the previous members of the chain. Now, because each of the members, by virtue of its dependence, is intentionally "of" the previous members of the chain, none of them, as a retention, can claim an independence or newness. Thus, each member presents itself as a nonnew or *past* moment. With this, we can see how each adds the modification of pastness to what it retains. To grasp an originally given content through a series of retentions, each of which presents itself as a past moment, is to grasp it through a stretch of past time. Temporally speaking, the content's appearance is also the appearance of the pastness through which it is given. This follows since we cannot retain this content without *also retaining* the pastness which is presented by each of the retentions of the content. Thus, the content is presented as an impression which is at a temporal remove from our present act of retention—i.e., our retention of *all* the retentions which are dependent on the content's original givenness. We can also say that the increase of this chain of retentions involves the increase in our sense of the pastness of the impressional content since each additional member of the chain adds the modification of not-newness or further pastness to it.

The crucial point in this analysis is that of the serially structured dependence of the members of the retentional chain. Each retention, *in its now*, is dependent on a retention which, relative to it, is *not now*. This dependence of the now of each retention on the relative not-nows of what precedes it must be assumed if we are to explain how the resulting diagonal intentionality involves a sense of pastness, i.e., a sense of the givenness that is no longer now. Otherwise put: dependence on the not-now manifests itself in an intentionality that presents this not-now. This intentionality proceeds along the retentional chain, whose members are dependent, each upon the next, until it ultimately results in a presentation of the impressional content *in its pastness*. We must, a fortiori, also assume this dependence to explain our apprehension of successively given time. Such time corresponds to the increasing sense of the *pastness* of a content as from moment to moment we successively move from *retention to retention* of this content. The simultaneous apprehension of a multitude of successively given moments, all expiring at the same rate, arises from our retentional chains being linked to a multitude of contents. The different lengths of these chains give us our sense of the different degrees of pastness pertaining to such moments.

There is a further necessity for the possibility of cognition. Beyond the recognition that the retained impressions are the same as the originally given ones, we must, according to Kant, have the recognition that the retained "form a whole." The multiplicity of contents that we retain in the now must be viewed as united "into a presentation" ("Kritik d. r. V.," A 103, IV, 79). Thus, turning a die in our hands, the impressions we have of its different faces, corners and edges must be united into the presentation of the die itself. This requires, we can say, the same inseparable unity in the vertical direction as we uncovered in the diagonal. As we have seen, each moment of the diagonally represented retentional chain is "of" a previous moment in this chain because it cannot exist or be conceived without the latter. To repeat Husserl's remarks: "We know with regard to the phenomenon of expiration that it is a continuity of constant changes, that it forms an inseparable unity, inseparable into temporal stretches that could exist for themselves and inseparable into phases and into points of the continuity that could exist for themselves." Now, the diagonal lines of retentions end, at every moment, in a vertical line, one that represents the presence of the retained at that moment. With this, we can say that the same inseparability exists in the vertical direction. No single retention of the vertical line can be grasped in isolation from the later members of this line. This follows because the present retention's reference to a past moment occurs serially through all the moments separating it from this past instant. Its reference, thus, demands the moments that *followed* this past instant. These moments, however, are *themselves retained* on the vertical. Accordingly each moment of the vertical line, by virtue of the fact that it has sunk down and is grasped as such, implies these later moments of time. Its having sunk down is, we can say, a consequence of the presence on the vertical of those retained moments which separate it from the topmost, now point of the vertical. The result is that each of the presently retained moments points beyond itself—or has a vertical reference—to retentions of later moments. The "retention" of what has been implies, in Husserl's language, the "protention" or reference to what occurs later. As before, the root of this protentional reference—or, in Husserl's words, "vertical intentionality" (*Querintentionalität*)—is simply dependence.

Husserl writes, "Enduring is the form of something that endures, the form of an enduring being, of something *identical* in the temporal succession that functions as its enduring" (*Ph. d. in. Zb.*, Beilage VI, Hua X, 113, italics added). Kant makes the same point when he calls the synthesis which allows us to intuit an enduring object, one of "recognition in a concept" ("Kritik d. r. V.," A 103, IV, 79). A concept is a one in many. Thus, we must be able to recognize identical characteristics within the multitude of our distinct impressions in order to say that our impressions are *of* something identical, i.e., are impressions of an appearing object with definite qualities. The same point holds when we abstractly consider our awareness of duration per se. The moments are recognized as moments of a duration when they exhibit an identical character. Since we are considering time as abstracted from all content, the characteristic in question can only be the quality of the moments as empty containers of possible contents. How does the recognition of this characteristic actually occur? According to Husserl, the temporal process exhibits a twofold structure of dependence. Dependence in the diagonal direction results in moments being retained with definite temporal referents. In the vertical direction, it results in the retained moments being united with one another in the ongoing present. The retained moments, thus, have a twofold reference. Each is distinct insofar as it retentionally refers to a distinct moment in the past. Each, however, is unified with a portion of the retentions along the vertical insofar as the pastness of what it retains implies later moments that are themselves retained. We, thus, have a situation where we are required to think the retentions along the vertical as temporally distinct in their reference to past impressions and, yet, as forming a continuous whole—i.e., as incapable of "existing for themselves." The former thought gives us the multiplicity necessary for "recognition in a concept." As for the latter, it points to the required element of unity. To grasp the retained as a whole is to grasp them in their coincidence. It is also to grasp them such that their similar qualities reenforce one another. As we noted in the preceding chapter, this present coincidence and consequent reenforcement of an element of quality is the appearing of one in many.

When, for example, we take an object and, in turning it, continually view its features, the object is experienced as the same—as one in many—by virtue of the coincidence and reenforcement of the recurring contents of our experience. Each of the contents is retained in the ongoing present. This means that each is placed in a "unity of coincidence" with the other retained contents. This coincidence does not affect their temporal references; each content remains in its reference something experienced in a given point in successive time. The coincidence, however, does generate the reenforcement of qualities that are the same. Like a series of overlapping transparencies, the coincidence of moments results in the reenforced appearance of what is the same and, to a lesser degree, of what is similar (See *Ph. d. in. Zb.*, §18, Hua X, 44–45). The analogy with the transparencies should not mislead us. The contents, by virtue of their distinct temporal referents never lose their character of multiplicity.

They become contents *of* the object by virtue of the unification of their qualitative elements. With respect to the hypothetical experience of empty or pure duration, this point of identification is simply the quality of the temporally distinct moments being, one and all, *containers* of some possible content.

IV

This analysis of the temporality of cognition has for us an important result. It is that cognition requires the dependence of the moment. Dependence along the retentional chain gives us the "diagonal intentionality" of each retained moment. Each is intentionally "of" an originally given past impression. Dependence in the vertical direction gives us a corresponding "vertical intentionality." Here, the retained content is intentionally "of" the enduring object that appears through the coincident union of impressions. Thus, without the moment manifesting its dependence, we would not have the consciousness of either succession or duration.

What does the quality of a moment's dependence, its quality, as Husserl expresses it, of being "nothing for itself," imply about the nature of the temporal process? If we admit that the moment is nothing for itself, then we also admit Husserl's "a priori law" according to which "there pertains to every time an earlier and a later time" (*Ph. d. in. Zb.*, §2, Hua X, 10). The moment is linked retentionally to an earlier moment and protentionally to a later moment. Since these relations express dependencies and these dependencies are serial in character, we may speak here of both the immediate and the mediate dependence of the moment. The moment is immediately dependent upon those that surround it. The latter are also dependent on their surrounding moments, so the moment is also mediately dependent on these. In other words, every moment is linked to every other through a serial chain of dependencies. Its ultimate dependence is on nothing less than the whole of time expressed as the totality of its retentionally and protentionally related moments.

When applied to experiences, the preceding gives us Husserl's claim that temporality "designates not just something universally pertaining to every experience, but a *form necessarily* binding experiences with experiences" (*Ideen I*, §81, Hua II, 198). An experience, in having its time, is necessarily and formally bound to other experiences. It is such by virtue of its time—at the limit, its moment—being *dependent* upon the times that surround it. Two conclusions can be drawn from this. The first is that the independence of a content-laden moment—i.e., a moment of experience—is a formal impossibility (see ibid., §83, p. 202). The second is that every experience, by virtue of its duration, necessarily "takes its place in an unending continuum of durations—a filled continuum. It necessarily has an all-sided, infinite, filled horizon of time." The individual experience, in having its finite duration, can begin and end, "but the stream of experiences can neither begin nor end" (ibid., §81, p. 198).

The Kantian tone of Husserl's remarks is unmistakable. They imply that, although time *in its moments* is transitory, time itself, considered *in its wholeness*, is not transitory. In Kant's words, "time . . . is unchanging and abiding." This means that "time does not flow away (*verläuft sich nicht*)," for, if we regard it as a whole, then there is no "time"—i.e., a time outside of the wholeness of time—into which it could flow ("Kritik d. r. V.," B 183, III, 137). For Husserl, this quality of time as a whole is also the quality of the stream of experiences. The latter, as structured by the form of time in its wholeness, "can neither begin nor end"—that is, progress into another time.

A whole that does not permit of a "beyond" is termed a *unique singular.* Such a singular exists *simply as one* and not as *one among many* singulars, each having the same nature. Why is it that we must regard time as unique? Why can we not think of it only in terms of finite durations, as finite times *among* finite times? The answer comes from the condition we uncovered for the possibility of our apprehending successive and enduring time. The condition is the dependence of the moment and, indeed, the dependence of any finite stretch of time through the dependence of its first and last moments. As we have said, this is a mediate dependence on the whole of time. If a moment or any finite stretch of time must be conceived as "nothing for itself" and, as a consequence, ultimately dependent on the whole of time, then the thought of their existence implies the thought of the latter's existence; that is, the existence of the abiding totality of moments. Here, we can say that the dependence of the moment ultimately demands the *independence* of time in its wholeness. Independence means not being dependent on another time in order to be. The thought of the moment in its dependence, thus, necessarily leads to the thought of time in its unique singularity. It leads to its thought as an abiding totality of its moments, a totality that excludes another time and, thus, has no "beyond" in terms of its dependence.

V

If the relation of dependence is one of grounded to ground, the preceding asserts that the abiding wholeness of time—time as an "all-sided" horizon—is the ground of each moment's being. Yet as our foregoing analyses indicate, the moment, in its dependence, exists as part of an atemporal process which results in the presence of abiding time. The retention of moments in the ongoing now yields the presence of time as *that which abides* while its moments, retentionally fixed in their temporal positions, are regarded as *passing away.* Thus, the abiding totality of moments is not just the ground, but also the goal of every moment in its coming to be. Every moment, as nothing for itself, exists only as part of the ongoing temporal process. Yet, the objective of this temporal process—that which it is determined to accomplish—is nothing less than the progressive realization of the *same* abiding of time which grounds each of its moments in its dependence.

This thought can be considered as leading Husserl to write in a manuscript of 1933:

> In my former doctrine of internal time-consciousness, I treated the intentionality that is hereby exhibited simply as intentionality: directed to the future as protention and modifying itself, but still preserving its unity as retention. . . . May we not or, rather, must we not presuppose a universal, driving intentionality (*Treibintentionalität*), one which unifies every original present into a lasting temporalization and which, concretely, propels (*forttreibt*) it from present to present in such a way that every temporal content is the content of a fulfilled drive and is intended before the goal? Must we not presuppose that this drive propels it in such a way that in each primordial present there are transcending impulses (*transzendierende Triebe*) of a higher level that reach out into every other present, binding them like monads together, in the course of which they all are implicit in one another—implicit intentionally?

Husserl concludes this reflection with the assertion, "This would lead to the conception of a "universal teleology," one based on a "universal intentionality" (Ms. E III 5, reprinted in *Zur Phänomenologie der Intersubjektivität Dritter Teil* [hereafter cited as *Ph. d. Inters*. III], ed. Iso Kern, Hua XV, 594–95).

What, precisely, is this "universal, driving intentionality"? Husserl claims that it is productive of the temporal process and that, as such, it leads to the notion of a universal teleology. Let us analyze the first part of this claim to see how the second—the teleological conception—arises from it. According to Husserl, this universal intentionality does not just unify already given moments into a "lasting temporalization"—that is, unify them into given duration—it also propels this duration from "present to present." In this, it is productive of the ever new present or the ever new now that adds to the quantity of accomplished duration. The precise sense of this productive intentionality is given by Husserl when he writes that this enduring and the now are to be regarded as contents of "a fulfilled drive" and adds that as such they are "intended before the goal." What we have here is an intentionality that produces what it intends. The contents whose presence would fulfill its intended reference are intended before they exist, and this intending is, in fact, a bringing into existence of these same contents. The result is, then, a driving intentionality directed towards temporalization, one that has as its "goal" moments (and a consequent increase of duration) which do not yet exist. It is an intentionality that fulfills itself by bringing into existence and retaining in existence new moments. As Husserl also expresses this, we have here to do with an intentionality that arises before the given existence of its referent. "This intentionality," Husserl writes, ". . . possesses in its primordiality its goal as its own; it is, thus, at its core a primary mode of intention, one which simply arises and fulfills itself" (*Ph. d. Inters.*, p. 594). It is, in other words, an intentionality that is responsible both for its intention and its fulfillment.[3]

The teleological character of this process becomes apparent once we translate Husserl's description into the terms of the dependence of the moment. We, then, assert that, like the intentionalities of retention and protention—the "diagonal" and "vertical" intentionalities discussed above—this universal, driving intentionality is also an expression of dependence. It is an intentionality which takes its character from the mediate dependence of every actual moment on the abiding wholeness of time. Every moment is immediately dependent on the moments that surround it. This means that, as "nothing for itself," its actuality requires the actuality of the latter. Its being in the now demands their being in the now. Thus, with regard to the future or not yet existent moment, we can say that the very *being* of the present moment is one with an intentional drive, a drive that propels it to appropriate the future moment and bring it to present existence. In other words, a drive exists in each "original present," one that, by virtue of its dependence, "propels it from present to present." Each present that is brought into existence is a fulfillment of this drive, even though it did not yet exist when it stood as the drive's goal. The same dependence and consequent intentional drive also exist with regard to the past moment. This moment, which no longer exists, is appropriated by the present in the form of a retention. The dependence of the moment, understood as the origin of a process, thus, gives us both the progression of time and the retention of its expired moments. It results in an increasing duration that is propelled from present to present. As for the ultimate goal of this process, this cannot be anything less than the whole of time. This follows from the fact that time, in the abiding totality of its moments, is the ultimate object of each moment's dependence. Now, the actual existence of the moment does not *immediately* demand the actual, present existence of this whole. The moment is immediately dependent only on the presence of the moments that surround it. It is, we can say, the serial nature of this dependence—one where the actuality of one moment demands immediately only the actuality of the next—which results in time's serial (or successive) actualization.

The teleological nature of the temporal process should now be apparent. The abiding wholeness of time is not something that, in any finite time, could be made actual. It is, with respect to any finite period of time a not-yet—i.e., something to be actualized. Each present, actual moment is, however, ultimately dependent on this whole. It is this serial dependence which gives rise to the driving intentionality that results in the ongoing temporal process.[4] We, thus, have a pure example of a teleological system in which what is to be actualized—time as an enduring whole—determines the being of what is actual and, in so doing, *brings about its own progressive actualization.* Otherwise expressed: the very same enduring which is the *goal* of the temporal process is also, by virtue of its being the *ground* of the moment's dependence, that which directs the process itself. It determines its own progressive actualization through mediately determining the dependence (and the driving intentionality) of each actual moment. A ground, which is also a goal, is a determining factor that stands to the determined in the relation of a not-yet. It is, thus, by definition, a *telos* or final cause of a teleological process.

VI

The conclusion we can draw from this can be briefly expressed in a series of implications. The temporality necessary for cognition implies the dependence of the moment which, itself, implies the teleological character of the temporal process. Thus, if cognition is to be possible, its temporality must be teleologically conceived. The goal of our knowing—what we intend to grasp—must be determinative. This means, for example, that perception must be taken as an intentional process, one where the sense intended guides the process of interpreting what we sense and retain. The exact description of this must be the subject of a separate essay. Our concern is to note how Husserl breaks the circle of reasoning we initially described. The circle arises when we interpret the laws of knowing as natural causal laws, having first asserted that our knowledge of natural causal laws is determined by the laws governing our knowing. To break it, we must distinguish the laws of knowing from those of natural causality. The required distinction follows because cognition, by virtue of its temporal basis, is teleologically structured. Given this, the laws of cognition cannot be interpreted as laws of natural (material-efficient) causality. They have a different temporality, that of formal-final causality.

There is a certain moral implication in the distinction just drawn. Teleological temporality pertains not just to knowing but also to human freedom. It is implicit in our actions of choosing and pursuing goals. To be determined by a goal as something to be actualized by ourselves is very different from being determined by past, perhaps forgotten events. The latter determination, as Freud and others have pointed out, is the paradigm of the lack of human freedom. As for the former, it opens up to us both the possibility of error—in the ancient sense of missing the mark or goal—as well as the possibility of recognizing our errors and correcting them. Such recognition can be described in terms of comparing what we had in mind with where we presently are. The possibility of this is the same as that of taking self-responsibility. With regard to our self-knowledge—i.e., our being transparent to ourselves—this implies that what we ought to do is as revealing as what we actually do.

For Husserl, this self-knowledge and corresponding self-responsiblity implies something more than ourselves. It involves a depth dimension that includes not just other subjects, but also an absolute subject whom he takes to be God. To see this, we must show how his account of time functions in his description of our recognition of other subjects. It is to this task that we now turn.

4

INTERSUBJECTIVITY AND THE CONSTITUTION OF TIME

As is well known, Husserl remained dissatisfied with the *Cartesian Meditations*. The German edition of this work never appeared in his lifetime. It was constantly delayed by Husserl's attempts to refine and revise its solution to the problem of intersubjectivity. The *Nachlass*, the collection of his unpublished manuscripts, bears witness to the immense efforts he expended on this problem in the last years of his life. In these late manuscripts, Husserl attempts to find a phenomenological solution to the problem of knowing other minds through an analysis of time. The focus of his efforts is to show that the experience of other subjects and the experience of time have one and the same foundation. This may be put in terms of a claim present throughout the late manuscripts. It is that an analysis of the experience of time reveals the direct, phenomenological evidence for affirming that others are, indeed, subjects like myself, subjects perceiving as I do and constituting together a common objective world. In this chapter, I shall first delineate the nature of the problem and then give some of the arguments of the *Nachlass*'s solution.

I

For phenomenology, the problem of intersubjectivity—that of establishing that others are, indeed, subjects perceiving and thinking like oneself—is, first of all, a problem of methodology. To be more precise, it is a problem connected with its own method of procedure: the method of the phenomenological reduction. As its name implies, this is a method of *reducing* to *phenomena*. A thesis of judgment—for example, the thesis that I am perceiving a spatial-temporal object—is to be reduced to the phenomena and connections of phenomena that form its evidential basis. In this case the evidence is the presence of perceptual contents that are perspectivally arranged—i.e., those contents that show first one side and then another of the object. The method by which this is accomplished is essentially that of suspension or epoché. I suspend the thesis of my judgment, my belief in its validity, to free myself to regard with unprejudiced eyes the phenomena that lead me to this belief.[1] Here, we may note the logical requirement for this suspension: one cannot include the validity of a thesis as a part of the evidence brought forward for this validity. If one did, one would assume what one was trying to evidentially validate. The phenomenological suspension of belief—or epoché—is, we can say, exercised to avoid this *petitio principii*.[2]

For Husserl, this method of reduction runs into difficulties when we raise the question of objective knowledge. Such knowledge involves, in its very notion, intersubjectivity. It asserts more than a merely private, subjective validity. Objective knowledge claims to have a universal validity; that is, one involving not just myself but all other subjects as well. What is the evidence for the judgments that make this claim? Can such evidence be uncovered by the phenomenological reduction? If validity is to be judged by direct perceptual evidence of the phenomena, then objective validity, as validity *both* for myself and others, seems to include a range of phenomenal evidence that is not directly available to me. This unavailability is simply a function of the fact that I cannot see through another's eyes. I cannot directly intuit the phenomena that form the basis of another's assertions. Husserl puts this objection to the phenomenological method in the following terms: "without wishing to admit it, it falls into a transcendental solipsism, and the whole step leading to another subjectivity and to genuine objectivity [of knowledge] is possible for it only through an unconfessed metaphysics . . ." (*Cartesianische Meditationen* [hereafter cited as *CM*], ed. S. Strasser, Hua I, 174). This solipsism springs from my ability to verify through direct perception only those statements that are true for me—i.e., those which have a merely private, subjective validity. To claim more than this, I must apparently make what Husserl terms a *metaphysical* assertion. This is a statement that cannot be phenomenologically grounded—i.e., reduced to the immediately experienced phenomena which could directly justify it. Insofar as objective knowledge involves others, the objection Husserl is raising is that the very existence of others as *perceiving subjects* must, for phenomenology, remain a metaphysical assumption. The phenomenological reduction, beginning as it does with the suspension of belief, demands, when it examines objective knowledge, a suspension of the belief in the claims to objectivity of such knowledge. This necessarily involves a suspension of belief in the existence of others as having the same perceptual evidence for an assertion as I myself have. The objection, then, is that there is no way to re-establish this belief in terms of direct perceptual evidence. Such evidence would demand the perception of the other, not as an embodied subject standing over and against me, but rather as an actively functioning subject, as the active center of his consciousness and world.[3]

It is easy to see why the solution proposed by the *Cartesian Meditations* does not satisfy the objection Husserl raises. Stripped to its essentials, the solution concerns what Husserl calls the process of *analogizing appresentation*. As the term *analogy* indicates, this is a process whereby consciousness spontaneously acts to set up a proportion. Three of the terms are directly presented; the fourth is not directly given, but rather inferred or, as Husserl says, "a-presented." The proportion is this: my bodily behavior is to my perceptual experience of the world as the other's bodily behavior is to his perceptual experience. Given this analogy, similarity of behavior in well-defined circumstances indicates similarity of perceptual experience. In other words, given that the other acts as I would in the perceptual presence of a given situation, I can assume that his perceptual experience is similar to mine. I can, in Husserl's words, "associatively transfer" the sense to him of being a subject "like myself" (*CM*, Hua I, 144, 148 f).

The problem with this solution does not concern its description of our recognition of others but rather a principle presupposed by this description. In terms of the project of phenomenologically grounding our assertions, the solution commits the *petitio principii* described above. Thus, to genuinely establish that the other is a subject like myself, I cannot assume this in advance. This means that I cannot assume, as a matter of principle, that another's perceptual experiences are similar to mine. This, however, is precisely what I must assume in determining whether behavior is to count as similar or "harmonious" with my own. Such harmonious behavior is, as indicated, behavior that I would have in the perceptual presence of a given situation. A subject who had a different perceptual experience of the given situation and who acted accordingly would *not* have a behavior similar to mine. For Husserl, this means that he would *not* be recognizable as subject by me (*CM*, Hua I, 144). The crucial point here is that the behavior recognized as harmonious with mine—and, thus, as indicating the other as a subject—is behavior in accord with my perceptual experience of a given situation. Thus, the assumed commonality of this perceptual experience serves me as a criterion for what I take to be harmonious behavior. Here, the *petitio principii* of Husserl's argument is revealed in its circularity. Its criterion for similarity of perceptual experience is harmonious behavior; its criterion for harmonious behavior is the assumed similarity of perceptual experience.

II

The collapse of this argument returns us to the original requirement for the phenomenological verification of the other. The demand is for an experience of the other as a functioning center of *his own* experiencing. As Husserl expresses it, it is a demand for an experience in which "there is no distance" between my own subjectivity and that of the other. Only if we meet this demand can we avoid the suspicion that our perceptual experiences—rather than revealing the other—conceal his essential difference from ourselves. For Husserl, perceptual experience, including the senses of the world it affords us, is a constitutive process. The suspicion, then, is that our constitution of the senses according to which we act or "behave" in the world is such as to conceal another person who is genuinely other—i.e., who constitutes differently—than ourselves.

This thought led Husserl in the final years of his life to a radical investigation of the notion of constitution. In this, he focused on the most primitive level of constitution, the constitution of our sense of time. Its fundamental claim is that at the basis of this sense is a layer of phenomena that satisfies our demand, one that allays the suspicion we just raised.

Constitution is a notion implicit in the reduction. It is, in fact, the reverse of the reduction. The reduction, as we said, is a method of reducing a thesis to the phenomena whose connections form its evidential basis. If, in fact, these founding phenomena owe their own appearing to the connections occurring between even lower level phenomena, the reduction can be exercised on the former—i.e., on the thesis of their own immediate or "original" givenness—to uncover the latter, more primitive, founding layer. Once we accept with Husserl that constitution is this process of founding, two points immediately follow. The first is that one layer of evidence founds (or constitutes) the next through the ordering of the connections existing between its phenomena.[4] The second, which is implicit in the first, is that the individual phenomena on the founding level are distinct from those they found through their connections. An example of this distinction would be between a perspectivally appearing spatial-temporal object and the individual appearances of its perspectival views. The individual appearance, as Husserl says, "does not show itself perspectivally" in the way that the object does (*Ideen I*, ed. W. Biemel, Hua II, 97).

These points apply directly to Husserl's position that our experience of time does involve founding or constitution. Husserl writes, "The phenomena which constitute time are, in principle, evidentially different objectivities than those that are constituted in time" (*Zur Phänomenologie des inneren Zeitbewusstseins,* ed. R. Boehm, Hua X, 74–75). They cannot be the same, because, if they were, we would not have two layers of phenomena, one founding and one founded. We would have only one layer. This means that if we say with Husserl that the constituted (or founded) layer of temporal phenomena display such characteristics as persistence, succession or simultaneity, then we cannot say that the constituting (or founding) phenomena individually have these qualities. With this, we are led to Husserl's assertion that "we can no longer speak of a time of the ultimately constituting consciousness" (ibid., p. 78). As composed of the data that found the experience of time, such consciousness must itself be made of phenomena whose experience does *not* involve time. Given Husserl's equation between being in time and being experienced as an individual object, we cannot even state that the data composing this consciousness are experienced as individual objects. What we have to say, according to Husserl, is that "subjective time constitutes itself in an absolutely timeless consciousness which is not an object" (ibid., p. 112).

A first picture of such a consciousness can be given by recalling what Husserl considers to be the essential condition for the experience of time. This is the process of retention. Let us say that I experience a temporal event; for example, the falling of a pencil. To grasp it as such, the successive impressions I have of its falling cannot disappear from my consciousness the instant after their apprehension. To grasp the falling as a temporally extended event, I must *retain* these impressions in the present—i.e., in the constant nowness of my ongoing act of apprehension.

The description of this condition is common to Husserl and a number of empirical psychologists. Where Husserl differs from them is in his viewing it through the perspective of the reduction. According to the reduction, we cannot assume that time is something immediately given since the reduction's focus is, in fact, on uncovering the conditions of this givenness. In the most original sense, what is immediately given is our nowness with ourselves, the nowness of our own ongoing act of apprehension. What is constituted out of this nowness is time in its successive ordering of past, present, and future moments. Thus, it is not the case that time is first successively given and then its apprehension occurs through the retention of its moments in the now. The reverse is the case for Husserl. In other words, the retentions are themselves to be regarded as constitutive of successively ordered temporal positions. The details of this process of constitution cannot engage us here. They were, in part, the subject of our previous chapter. For our present purposes, we need only recall that the sense of increasing pastness of an impressional moment is a sense constituted by a process of constant retentional modification of this moment. This modification adds the interpretation of pastness to it. Iteratively applied to the same impressional content, the result is not just a series of retentions of retentions of this content. In Husserl's words, it is a series of *"interpretations* which in their flowing connectedness *constitute the temporal unity of the immanent content in its sinking back into pastness"* (*Ph. d. in Zb.*, ed. Boehm, Hua X, 92). As Husserl elsewhere expresses this, "it is precisely through this [process of retentional modification] that it is constituted as the same, as an individual point in the fixed form of the primal now and the just past, etc. . . ." (Ms. C 2 I, p. 13a). The content's insertion into time is the result of the retentional process. In fact, viewed from the perspective of the primal nowness uncovered by the reduction, temporalization is simply "a constant letting loose (*Aus-sich-ent-lassen*) of retentions . . ." (Ms. A V 5, p. 5).[5]

For Husserl in the 1930s, this analysis was seen as establishing a number of points with regard to the nature of the "timeless consciousness which is not an object." The first concerns our sense of the now of the subject as an ongoing or flowing now. This sense is actually that of the relation of the subject's constant now to the positions in successively ordered time that it constitutes. To be constantly now for Husserl is to be "timeless"; it is not to be *in* time in the sense of being a moment fixed in successively ordered time. It is, rather, to constantly transcend the positions of such time as they slip successively into pastness. The sense of this continual transcendence *is* the sense of our nowness as flowing. At its basis is the necessary distinction between levels of constitution we earlier mentioned. The now as constituting is distinct from what it constitutes. As such, it constantly distinguishes itself, constantly transcends and, hence, constantly yields the sense of its flowing with regard to the constituted, fixed temporal positions.

The second point is that this flowing is what first makes possible the subject-object relation. *Object* in German is *Gegenstand.* It is that which *stands against* the subject. This "againstness" indicates a certain nonidentity, a certain distance, between the subject and its object. In transcending temporal positions, the now of my actively constituting subject constantly opens up a *temporal distance* between itself and the constituted positions (see Ms. C 7 I, p. 21a). In this, it also opens up the original distance between itself and its objects which are positioned in definite stretches of successive time. All objectification involves such positioning in successive time. This follows because all objectification is, in this analysis, a constitutive process. As we said, the connections of the data on one level found or constitute the appearance of the object on the next. This means that such data must be experienced with a certain ordering and, hence, must be *successively* experienced in time for the constituted object to appear. The simplest example of what we are pointing to is a physical object that shows itself first from one side and then from another. The condition of the possibility of this ordering of perspectives is the departure of each of the momentary perspectives into pastness. We can thus say that, although we constantly share a now with the object as we continue to view it, the now of this object, as a *constituted* now, constantly departs from us. It slips away from the now of the subject as the latter, in remaining constantly now, transcends fixed, temporal positions.

The third point is that the subject, as actively functioning, i.e., as actively constituting, remains nonobjective. To be objective, it would have to allow itself to be fixed in time. There would have to open up that original, temporal distance which first permits the subject-object relation. The subject, as actively constituting, is, however, the present subject. It is, thus, constantly transcending those fixed temporal positions whose departure into pastness forms the original, temporal distance. What this means is that we can never grasp ourselves, through reflection, as actively functioning. In Husserl's words, "I am always ahead of myself" (Ms. C 16 VI, p. 78b). The subject that stands against me as the object of my self-reflection is one that is fixed in time. It is not the subject that is presently reflecting, but rather one that *has* reflected. As remaining now, the active subject is already ahead of it in time, the temporal distance between them, being, in fact, what allows the latter to appear as an object.

III

The tie between this analysis and the problem of intersubjectivity can be introduced by a conclusion Husserl draws from it. He writes: "The structural analysis of the original present (the lasting streaming present) leads us to the structure of the ego and the underlying levels of egoless streaming which constantly found it . . ." From thence, "it leads back to the radically pre-egological" (*Zur Phänomenologie der Intersubjektivität, Dritter Teil*, ed. I. Kern, Hua XV, 509). The reference here is, on the one hand, to the individual ego, enduring through time with its own individual, temporally extended history. On the other hand, it is to the constant now that founds this by constituting temporal positions. "The ego," Husserl writes, "is itself constituted as temporal unity. It is, as a lasting and remaining ego, an already acquired (and, in constant acquisition, continually acquired) ontical unity" (ibid., p. 348). The basis of this acquisition is the production of its moments of pastness, moments whose retention forms its temporal history and, with this, its own constitution as enduring through this history. Its ultimate basis is the being-now that is productive of such moments. In Husserl's words, "This *present* is absolute actuality, is actuality in the strictest sense as originally active or productive. As such, it ontifies itself into the temporal modes and, as originally temporalizing, it has temporal being as its ontical acquisition" (ibid.).

The reason that this "present" is something radically "pre-egological" is clear. It follows from the necessary distinction between layers of constitution. Thus, given that the individual ego is a temporal or ontical unity, the present that constitutes it cannot be such. This necessity can be put in two different, yet complementary ways. The first is that all the distinctions in space and time by which we characterize an individual unity are distinctions occurring on the constituted level. This means that, when we come to the originally constituting present, we are not on a layer of phenomenal evidence that would allow us to assert distinct individuality. The constant now, considered in itself, has no distinct position in time; still less has it such a position in a spatial-temporal sense. It is, in fact, "worldless" in a spatial-temporal sense.[6] The second way to express this is to note that the individual ego is *such* by having a world, more precisely, by having intentional relations to its surrounding world. It is an ego as a subject for this world, a world that stands against it as an object for its perceptions, questions, actions, and so forth.[7] None of this is applicable to the original present considered in itself. In itself, it remains constantly now, constantly self-present. In itself, it has no temporal distance which would allow of objectification, allow of there being a world standing against it. Our very inability to objectify ourselves in our nowness, to make ourselves, as actively functioning, objects of our self-reflection is, for Husserl, the phenomenal evidence of this fact. What we can say about this original present is that it is, in its constitution of definite temporal positions, what first allows of a definite temporal distance and, hence, yields the appearance of the ego as a subject.

For Husserl, it is precisely this nonobjective, original present which is at the basis of his claims in the C manuscripts that other egos are "implicit within me" (see, e.g., Mss. C III 3, p. 44a; C 17 I, *Zur Phän. der Inters.*, Hua XV, 332; C I, ibid., Hua XV, 668). It is what allows him to speak of "My 'coincidence' with others in the original level of constitution, my coincidence, so to speak, before there is constituted a world for myself and others ... " (Ms. C 17 V, p. 84a). The coincidence is one of the nowness of our being. This is the nowness which exists before all constituted differences, being what first constitutes the ego's individual, ontical unity. It is the nowness of ourselves as actively functioning *centers* or, in Husserl's term, "*poles*" of our lives. The very nontemporality and, hence, nonenduring of ourselves as poles is, we said, what makes it impossible for us to reflectively grasp ourselves as objects—i.e., to make the thesis of our present being in the now as an individual "this" standing against ourselves. Husserl expresses the notion of the resulting coincidence in the following words: "There is, indeed, a community [of self and others]. . . . Everything that is temporalized, everything temporalized by the streaming modes of appearance in the immanent temporal stream and then, again, by the 'external' (spatial-temporal) appearances has a unity of appearances, a temporal unity, a duration. But the ego as a pole does not endure. Therefore, my ego and the other's ego also do not have any extensive distance in the community of their being together. But also my life, my temporalization, has no distance from that of the other" (Ms. C 16, VII, *Zur Phän. der Inters.*, Hua XV, 577).

The conclusion Husserl draws from this is that, in my direct, preobjective experience of my nowness, I satisfy the demand phenomenology sets for a verifying experience of the other. In this experience, I view the other, not as an embodied subject, not as a constituted unity, but rather as a functioning center of constitution. The conclusion, then, is that I possess an experience of the other in which, by virtue of the coincidence of our nows, there is no "distance" between ourselves as poles or functioning centers. Husserl expresses this in the following way: "The original source point of time constitution is, for each individual, the experience of his present in its original mode and also the capacity of each to experience others . . . i.e., the capacity, within his own living present, to experience others in an original manner and with this, indeed, to experience the original coincidence between his own and the other's being" (Ms.C 17 I, *Zur Phän der Inters.*, Hua XV, 334). This assertion is, for Husserl, not the result of some "unconfessed metaphysics." It is rather the result of following the phenomenological reduction to its end, that is, to the now that stands as the source of all constitution.

Two further points must be mentioned to complete our sketch of this solution to the problem of intersubjectivity. The first is that all the egos, in their coincidence in the now, form what Husserl terms a *primal ego*. This ego, which is, in fact, radically "pre-egological," exists as a unique singular—i.e., exists, not as one among many but simply as one. As Husserl puts this: "In an absolute sense, *this ego is the only ego*. It is not meaningfully multipliable, more precisely expressed, it excludes this as senseless" (Ms. B IV 5, p. 26). The reason for this exclusion is that this "pre-egological" ego, in its existing on the level of the constant now, exists on a level before any of the constituted distinctions (and, hence, multiplications) of being. It is, we can say, the original unity of all egos before their constituted objectification as enduring temporal entities. Given that this ego is uniquely one and given that it is, as Husserl here adds, "itself nothing other than a continual, original, streaming constitution . . . ," we have the answer to the objection we raised in considering the argument of the *Cartesian Meditations*. This was that our constitution of the senses of the world, senses that determine the appropriateness of our behavior, is such as to conceal the subjectivity of another individual who is genuinely other—i.e., who constitutes and, hence, behaves completely other than ourselves. If the source of the "original, streaming constitution" is, indeed, uniquely singular, this differently constituting subject cannot exist. As originally constituting, we all are functioning from the nowness of our beings. As such we all are in an original coincidence with each other, a coincidence within the uniquely singular now. This very coincidence is, in fact, the ultimate meaning of Husserl's notion of an "intersubjective community."

The final point returns us to the reflections with which we concluded our chapter on Augustine. The unique singularity of the nowness of the primal ego is all embracing. Preobjectively, it embraces the whole of time. Because of this, Husserl does not shrink from referring to the "absolute subject" or "primal ego" as God. He writes, for example, "we humans as knowers are, indeed, egos into which the absolute ego has split himself . . ."(Ms. F I 22, p. 22). The latter ego is nothing other than the divine being. In Husserl's words, "God, who in himself is a constant and unchanging absolute being, reveals himself in eternal necessity in the form of a pure ego. He expresses himself in an infinite ladder of self-reflections in which he . . . finally comes to the purest self-consciousness. In this process of development, he splits himself, as it were, into a plurality of finite human subjects . . ." (ibid., p. 39).[8] That the self-consciousness of God demands his pluralization into a number of finite, temporal egos should not surprise us. It follows from the position that all consciousness, including self-consciousness, demands a temporal distance between the knower and the known. Such a distance is required for consciousness to be intentional. Thus, not even God, considered as the constant now of the intersubjective community, can grasp himself as presently active. To be self-conscious he requires his temporal objectifications—these objectifications being our individual selves.

To explore this matter further, we have to engage in "metaphysics," phenomenologically conceived. Having performed the reduction, we must raise the question of being. What is the nature of being which permits us to affirm both our individual existence and our ultimate coincidence with "God, the absolute." As the next chapter shows, the results afford a striking parallel between Husserl and one of the greatest of the classical metaphysicians, Thomas Aquinas.

5

EXISTENCE AND ESSENCE
IN THOMAS AND HUSSERL

In a series of conversations recorded towards the end of his life, Husserl is quoted as saying, "Yes, I do honor Thomas . . ." and "certainly I admit Thomas was a very great, a colossal phenomenon."[1] With this, however, is the assertion that one "must go beyond Thomas."[2] What is this going beyond Thomas? The purpose of this chapter is to explore this in terms of the distinction between existence and essence we considered in our first chapter when we inquired into the ontological status of the ideas. Our claim is that, on this point at least, Husserl is in agreement with Thomas Aquinas. The demand that we go "beyond" him does not concern this distinction. It rather amounts to an implicit call to bring Thomas's epistemology—in particular, his view of consciousness—up to the level achieved by his metaphysical insights.

I

For Thomas Aquinas, the distinction between existence and essence begins with the observation that I can know *what* something is without knowing *whether* it is. As we earlier cited him, "I can know what a man or phoenix is and yet not know whether it exists in reality. It is, thus, clear that existence (*esse*) is other than essence or whatness."[3] If they were the same, then from knowing the what, I could know the whether, i.e., existence would be included among "those things which are the components of the essence."[4] The fact that existence is not so included makes it inconceivable. This does not mean that we cannot speak about existence or categorize it in various ways. It does, however, mean that existence is not originally known through conceptualization. It cannot be because it is not one of the concepts which I can abstract from an entity so as to formulate its definition.[5]

A consequence of this distinction is the contingency of the entity. My concepts correspond to the entity's inherent forms. The inconceivability of existence is, correspondingly, existence's distinction from such forms. Not that we can speak of forms apart from existence. Apart from its existence—i.e., from the act of existing or the actuality whereby it has real or cognitional existence—a form is obviously a nothing. Yet, the fact that existence is never absent from it does not mean that the form exists through itself. For Thomas, if the form is to have its "to be," it must have an "external existing cause," one that is not itself a form (see *Quaestiones disputatae de Anima*, a. 6, ad 9m). Granting this, the "informing" forms—the forms that make an entity be what it is—do not give it an inherent claim to exist.[6] The entity does exist and yet, in Thomas's words, existence can be regarded as "accidental" to what it is. It comes to it "from another."

An example Thomas uses will make his position clear. Fire will heat water; and water, for a time, will preserve this heat. With air, however, the action of the sun's illumination never results in the air's *remaining illuminated* after this action has ceased. Aquinas explains this difference by observing that water is such that it can receive the form of heat. This form can, for a time, be inherent in its matter as a formal set of relations determining its what. These relations—one thinks here of the modern notion of the relations of mass and motion determining the kinetic energy of a system—are the same as those found in the water's source of heat. This source, in other words, causes heat by imparting to water a form that it itself embodies. This explanation of water's reception of heat does not hold for the the illumination of air. Air, according to Aquinas, "is not at all of such a nature as to receive light in the same way as it is in the sun, namely, to receive the form of the sun which is the principle of light. Therefore, since the light has no root in the air, the light at once ceases with the action of the sun."[7] He follows this with the assertion that the same point holds with regard to the existence of creatures. Existence is not a form; therefore, it cannot, like heat in water, become rooted in an entity. It cannot be considered something which an entity can preserve by virtue of having assumed a certain set of formal relationships. To say that an entity is existentially contingent is, thus, to assert that existence is not "what" it is. It is other than the forms that determine the entity's inherent qualities. This means that an entity's continued existence, like the continued illumination of the air, is dependent on the action of an external agent. In Thomas' words, "everything whose existence (*esse*) is other than its nature has its existence from another."[8] It is contingent on a giving that is external to it. This is a giving of existence which, for the entity, never becomes a self-giving, i.e., something provided through its inherent forms.

To complete this brief survey, we must observe that existence, for Thomas, is never to be considered as one thing and essence another. A thing exists through their composition. As Etienne Gilson puts this, the distinction between existence and essence is "real," not because they are separate, thinglike realities, but because "their composition alone is what makes up a thing."[9] The composition is of elements which are *prior* to the thing. It is a composition of the grounds or causes of the thing's being a finite reality. The reality's essence is the thing's formal cause. Conceived as a set of formal relationships, the essence can become *inherent* in it. As such, it makes the thing be what it is in its own nature. It helps make it finite—i.e., a being which is capable of definite description. An entity cannot be definitely described without those forms which make it a "this" rather than a "that."[10] Existence, for Thomas, is what makes the "this" which we can know "stand out" or "exist." As that which makes all agents be, it is the ultimate *efficient cause*.[11] Existence can be thought of as the action of all acts, an action that is there, present in each agent's acting. Each particular action is its expression, its manifestation in some formal character which makes it be this action rather than that one. In this context, to say that an agent is contingent is to say that it is not self-caused. It is contingent because the underlying action of its existing, taken as the *ground* of its particular acts, is not itself *grounded* by such acts. The same point holds for the totality of finite existences. They are contingent insofar as they are the result rather than the cause of existence per se.

Such existence is capable of being characterized in a number of ways. The first we may call its essential anonymity. By this we do not mean that we cannot name individual existents or that most languages have not a name for existence. Anonymity points rather to the fact that, as Kant put it, "existence is not a real predicate"—not "a concept of something which can be added to the concept of a thing" (*Kritik d. r. Vernunft*, B 626). Anonymity signifies existence's not being a formal character of reality. In other words, existence is nameless insofar as its designation is not one of the names or "predicates" taken from the forms that make up the essence of a thing. We can also observe that existence is not per se characterized by the relations of space and time. Such relations are added to it when it manifests itself as the existence of a spatial-temporal thing. They are inherent in the latter by virtue of its materiality, its being definitely describable as a body. Its presence as the existence *of* such a body is, in other words, one with its transcendence of such presence insofar as it is not, per se, the relations which make existence bodily existence. What it is, in itself, is the nonformal cause of such relations. It is the "pure act" that makes them, along with what they relate, present and actual. Thus, it is not the successive moments of time in terms of which a finite body can be said to exist at a certain time. It is, rather, what makes such moments be. Existence is their successive presence, their act of "standing out," which makes them successively actual. For Thomas, existence in its purity can also be characterized as God. Here, God appears as the actuality, the pure act, through which things are actual. In his purity, he constantly transcends the things that he actualizes. Because he is *esse tantum*,[12] he is not a combination of existence and form that could be finitely described.[13] He is not the conjunction of this with matter which would make such a description include being located in a specific point of space and time.[14] His purity from such additions makes him the nonfinite ground of the world.[15] He is a cause which constantly escapes being described in terms of the things he causes to be.[16]

II

When we turn to Husserl, the same characterizations of existence appear. Their locus, however, is determined by his epistemological interests. More precisely, their locus is the knowing subject. Husserl asserts: "The effort of my phenomenology has always proceeded from the subjective back to the existent."[17] It is at the very heart of the subjective that he finds the existence which makes everything be. He calls such existence "the prebeing which supports all being, including even the being of the acts and the being of the ego, indeed, even the being of pretime and the being of the stream of consciousness [understood] as a being."[18] The term *prebeing* means that this ultimate factor is not a being—not an individual, finite entity. Thus, to reach it is to reach something "radically pre-egological"—i.e., something prior to the ego considered as a finite entity.[19] It is to reach that which "supports" it as a being by causing its existence.[20]

The phenomenological method for reaching this ultimate factor is termed the *reduction*. As our last chapter made clear, the reduction is a move from the constituted to the constituting. Its principle is that one layer of phenomena constitutes or founds the next through the connections that order them in time. Thus, the connections that give us a spatial-temporal object are those that order its appearances into perspectival series. These are the series which, in a graduated progression, exhibit first one side, then another of the object. When we suspend these connections, bracketing the thesis that arises from them, we are performing the reduction. We are moving from the appearing spatial-temporal object to the appearances that form its constitutive basis.

In the 1930s, Husserl applies this suspension or bracketing to the subject. His question is, What allows a subject to be a subject? What is the ultimate phenomenon at the basis of its functioning? He writes in this regard: "I must not terminate the reduction with the bracketing of the world, including my spatial-temporal, real human being in the world." I must exercise it "on myself as a transcendental ego and as a transcendental accomplishing, in short, as a transcendental life."[21] Now, if I do suspend all the connections which successively order appearances in time, I bracket as well time itself in its successive character. It is no longer regarded as something objectively spread out before me—something *in which* appearances are ordered according to the distinctions of past, present, and future. Such temporal distinctions, which Husserl shows as constituted through connected chains of "retentions" and "protentions,"[22] are themselves bracketed. Understood as the suspension of *all* possible connections, "the performance of the phenomenological epoché" thus appears as "a radical 'limitation' to the living present and a determination to speak only about this . . ."[23] As Husserl elsewhere puts this: "The regressive inquiry which begins with the epoché . . . leads to the '*nunc stans*', the stationary 'present.' Insofar as it indicates a modality of time, the word 'present' is strictly speaking unsuitable."[24] According to Husserl, the present that is a "modality of time" is a present that will slip into pastness. The momentary present is not "stationary," but rather fleeting. It is, objectively regarded, part of the flowing order of successive time. It approaches the present from the future, passes through it, and departs into pastness. The present that remains present is not "in time" in the sense of being carried along with its streaming moments.[25] It is rather the present of my constant self-presence, a present which is "now and only now."[26]

Two points can be made about the result of this reduction. The first concerns the reduction's effort to grasp what is originally present. A spatial-temporal object is not *per se* originally present. The origin of its presence is, in the first instance, the appearances which have been ordered perspectivally. Original presence is, then, the reverse of constituted presence. It is the presence of the *constituting or founding phenomena*. Granting this, the claim that ultimately the reduction reaches what is "now and only now" is a claim about original presence. What is radically present is neither the anticipated future nor the remembered past. It is simply the present in its nowness. Insofar as that which is originally given is, phenomenologically, the *constitutive ground* of that which is not, a second claim appears: this "primal present" can be conceived as an ultimate origin. Thus, *before* the reduction, the stationary present appears as *that through which* objectively extended time flows. *After* the reduction, after we limit ourselves to immediate or primal nowness, this passing through the present appears as a "welling up" within it. Passing through, in other words, is exhibited as the *successive production* in this present of what comes to be regarded as the fleeting moments of successive time. With this, we have Husserl's assertion that this "present is 'absolute actuality' in the proper sense as that which is primally productive."[27] It is, in other words, actuality in the sense of being in act, the act being the welling-up that is productive of the distinct moments of time. Switching to the term *absolute*, which he uses to designate an ultimate ground, Husserl writes: "The absolute itself is this universal, primordial present. Within it 'lie' all time and world in every sense. Itself streaming, [it is] actuality in the strict, worldly sense of 'being present'."[28] "Both time and world are temporalized in the absolute which is the stationary-streaming now."[29] Thus, the present, in "temporalizing"—i.e., in producing the moments of time—is that which makes things actual in the worldly sense of being present in time. It is called a *stationary-streaming now* insofar as the successive moments of time stream or well up from its stationary presence.

The second point which follows from this reduction is a consequence of its being performed on the subject. The nowness that makes things present is nowness at the heart of the subjective. It is, in fact, what makes a subject be a subject. It is the basis of its being a functioning subject. To function or to act is not to have functioned; it is to be *presently* functioning. My present actions become, through their temporalization, past actions. "But I," Husserl remarks, "[who am] the identical subject of my acts, am 'now and only now.' I am *still* the accomplisher of my actions in my being as an accomplisher."[30] The insight, here, is that what becomes past becomes objectively fixed. One cannot change the past, which means that pastness is not the place of newness and, hence, is not the place of the the action that results in the new. Only nowness is this place insofar as it is the locus of the arising of the new moments of time that contain the new acts. For Husserl, the original action is simply the welling-up of the new moments of time from the stationary present. This action is called the *primal form* of the ego who exists, *qua* accomplisher, in and through this present.[31] From this we have the notion of the ego's action: "this acting," Husserl writes, "is a letting loose from itself. It is a primal welling up, a creative allowing to depart from itself of that which itself streams, namely the acts."[32] In other words, the departure of the moments of time from the stationary present allows the departure of the acts and, hence, the possibility of new action. A corollary of this is that this departure is the origin of transcendence. The original transcendence is that of *pastness vis-à-vis presence*. It is the arising of the "temporal distance" between the two as each moment departs from the present to make way for the next. Insofar as I exist in the stationary now, "I exist," Husserl writes, "in the streaming creation of transcendence, in the creation of self-transcendence, of my being as self-pastness . . ."[33] Thus, the departure of my acts into pastness makes them my *past* acts. It makes them part of my already constituted temporal environment that stands "over and against" my existence in the stationary present.

There is, for Husserl, a dual result of this creation of transcendence. First we have objectivity understood as the quality of "standing against" a subject. The opening up of temporal distances creates the successive time in which such standing against can first appear. The principle, here, is that an object stands against a subject in its otherness from the subject's present, momentary apprehension. The object is *more* than what the subject presently perceives. It transcends the latter insofar as it exhibits itself, not as a perception, but as the unity of a series of perceptions—i.e., as the one thing which each perception is said to be a perception of.[34] So understood, the object's transcendence requires the multiplicity of time. It requires it as the locus of the multiplicity of perceptions. It, thus, presupposes temporalization as the process by which one perception of the object gives way to the next. The second result is the reverse of this. As Husserl expresses it, "the ego which is over against everything else is anonymous. It is not over against itself."[35] For it to have an objective name or sense, it would have to undergo the process of objectification. It would have to be seen as departing, moment by moment, into pastness. Yet the ego which is constantly over against everything else is the functioning ego. It is the ego which is "now and only now." As such, it lacks the self-transcendence that would allow it to be "over against itself." Strictly speaking, the conclusion here is simply that "functioning is constantly anonymous."[36] My ego, insofar as it *has* functioned, is objective. It can stand against me in the objective regard of what I have been—i.e., what I have done or failed to do.[37] Anonymity, then, is descriptive of nowness per se, the nowness that, as the "giving" that is prior to all givenness in time, is prior to all the names that apply to the given.[38]

III

The relation of this nowness to essence follows from Husserl's account of the latter. As in Thomas' philosophy, essence, first of all, is the whatness of a thing. It is what is inherent in its concept. For Husserl, however, this whatness undergoes a "transcendental reinterpretation." It is taken as expressing the "essential connections" of experience that must be present if a thing with a particular essence is to appear.[39] It is, in other words, a rule for ordering our experiences in time which is required if a particular, synthetically constituted "what" is to to be experienced. Thus, if I am to experience a spatial-temporal object, my experiences must be connected to form a perspectivally ordered series. The essence of a spatial-temporal object, qua spatial-temporal, is the rule for the perspectival unfolding of its contents in time.[40] Now, if we say that such an object exists, it is, in Husserl's words, "because it passes from present to present."[41] An existent or entity (*Seiendes*) signifies "persisting presence."[42] An entity exists insofar as it is now and continues to be now. As should be obvious, nowness in itself is, for Husserl, existence per se. It is the "primally productive," inherently "anonymous" cause of a thing's being present and actual. Granting this, a concrete being is both existence and essence. Existence (or continual nowness) is required if it is to pass from present to present. Its essence is required as an ordering of contents involving this passage. What existence does is make the essence into a rule that obtains for an actually occuring temporal passage. It becomes an actually obtaining "what"—i.e., a rule for successively ordering contents which is embodied in an actually given, "persisting presence."

That both existence and essence are required for an entity to be does not mean that they are the same. Existence, by its very anonymity, is *other* than the nameable essence and, hence, is other than the finite entity that possesses a definite essence. This can be put in terms of the persisting presence of a spatial-temporal thing. This entity persists through the departure of its contents in time. The *fact* of this departure results in its objectivity. The *order* of the departure yields its essence, its being this rather than that type of objectivity. This

departure, however, is a *departure from* that stationary or nondeparting nowness which is the very *act of existence*, the very "to be" of the thing. Thus, the
thing is objectively present with a definite essence in its constant separation—
in its dynamically flowing otherness—from its existence. Another way of
expressing this is to say that a thing exists only through a process which constantly surpasses its given being. This process is that of temporalization. Temporalization surpasses the given by constantly giving; that is, by constantly
adding to the given yet another now. This next now is required for a thing's
continual presence, yet it is not inherent in it. The persisting thing is present
only through its departure into pastness. But this ongoing departure requires the
continual production of additional moments which, as they become successively past, increase the pastness of those that preceded them. As we said, the
next now or moment is not inherent in the thing's given unity. The latter consists of *already given* contents and temporal positions, which means that the
addition of moments *surpasses what is already given* in an objective sense.
With this, we can say that temporalization is a giving that both surpasses the
objective givenness of the thing and, in so doing, brings the latter about.

The contingency of a thing follows as a matter of course from the preceding. What is given is always given as contingent insofar as it relies on an
addition to itself for its continuing givenness. Thus, the source of its "to be,"
understood as the welling-up of time in the stationary streaming now, is *not
inherent* in the thing's objective givenness. Its contingency is its dependence in
its "to be" on an *external cause*. This contingency is present in the whole of
nature considered in its objective character and essential knowability. As
Husserl writes in 1935: "But isn't it apparent that the being (the actual existence—*'die wirkliche Existenz'*) of nature is an open pretension."[43] The pretension involves the fact "that time and world are temporalized in the absolute
which is the stationary streaming now."[44] It involves the fact that "the absolute"—conceived as a pure act—"is nothing but absolute temporalization."[45]
The pretension is that this temporalization will continue. Nothing in the objectively given world can assure us of its continuance. This follows from the fact
that what is at issue is not its givenness, but rather giving—that is, the constant
addition to such givenness.[46]

Because the essence of a thing pertains to the ordering of its contents in
already constituted time, it pertains to the objective realm—i.e., to the realm of
what is already given. As such, its consideration does not remove this "pretension." An appeal to the essential structures of givenness cannot establish that the
addition to givenness will continue—that the given will continue to be present and actual. As Husserl writes of the the laws springing from the essences
of things: "These laws . . . cannot pronounce with regard to an actuality—i.e.,
whether or not there exists an actuality which corresponds to them. Essential
laws possess a meaning for the real if something real (an individual being)

can be given which falls under the essences, the ideas."[47] In other words, "such laws . . . only specify facts with regard to possibility."[48] The same point is expressed in terms of the transcendental logic which delineates the formal relations between essences once the latter have undergone their "transcendental reinterpretation": "Transcendental logic, which as transcendental is led back to consciousness, contains the grounds for a possible nature, but none for an actual nature."[49] The basis for these assertions is that, when we consider an entity's essence, we bracket the giving by which the entity persists. As such, in considering its essence, we abstract from the consideration of its existence.[50] Thus, an essence, regarded in itself, is no longer a rule for a presently obtaining temporal passage. It has only a hypothetical character. It asserts, *if* an entity of a certain type is to be given, *then* a certain ordering of contents in time is required. The giving of the moments of time is not a result of this rule; it cannot be derived from it. On the contrary, it is what the rule itself presupposes for its actual obtaining. Thus, when Husserl writes, "the phenomenological *a priori* consists simply in the essences of the types of consciousness and in the *a priori* possibilities and necessities based on these essences," the "necessities" referred to are only hypothetical. They specify only the "possibilities" of entities' being given.[51] The *fulfillment* of such possibilities requires "the absolute which is the stationary-streaming now." It requires, in other words, the act of existence (or "primal temporalization") which fulfills the essence by progressively making it be in time as the essence of a persisting entity.[52]

IV

How far can this absolute be identified with God? Our context for this question is Husserl's statement: "Philosophy as an idea [is understood] as a correlate of the idea of God. [It is understood] as an absolute science, namely as a science of the absolute being, as the science of the pure idea of divinity (*Gottheit*) and as the science of the absolutely existing being." Its question is "whether and how far the absolute being as the existing God . . . can come into existence and be known."[53] Pursued phenomenologically, this inquiry involves a suspension of everything which would prejudge its result. Thus, it involves the withholding of judgment on the assertions of the Bible and on the "proofs, methods and positions" employed by confessional theology. It is in this sense that Husserl, while claiming that phenomenology "ultimately leads to God, the absolute,"[54] also is reported as asserting, "I am attempting . . . to reach God without God."[55] The "without God" refers to the practice of the phenomenological epoché on the received tradition of theology.

Understood as the absolute now, the God he does reach is both timeless—i.e., constantly present—and the cause of everything's being in time. As the nowness in and through which I function, God, as we saw in the last chapter, is both *my* ego pole and a "super-worldly, super-human pole."[56] He is the former because my being as "pole" is my being as a "center" of my constituted environment; but this is my being in the nonconstituted now.[57] His identification with the "super-temporal, super-human pole," follows from the fact that constituting nowness is prior to all divisions into "mine" and "thine." In Husserl's words, "When in self-meditation, I return to my living present . . . , it is not, for me, my living present as opposed to that of other human beings; and it is not mine as the present of an existent real human being with a body and soul."[58] As the ground of the ego's being an ego, this nowness is, in fact, "radically pre-egological." Since it is before the ego, its action, Husserl claims, "is a temporalizing-temporal primal occuring (*Urgeschehen*) which does not occur from egological sources (*aus Quellen des Ich*); it therefore occurs without the participation of the ego."[59] The "ego" of this passage is the ego as a pole or center. Husserl's point is that, prior to its being as a center, the ego must have a *centering*, already constituted temporal environment.[60] Thus, the welling-up of time that creates this environment is not something that results from the central ego. It is rather what grounds the central ego.[61] In other words, nowness per se (nowness considered apart from the time it constitutes) is prior to all such centering and, hence, is prior to all individual egological being. Thus, it is not *my* nowness any more than it is another's. It is the nowness by virtue of which every subject has its environment and functions within it. As such, it is the common, "preindividual" ground of the "letting loose" of those acts by which subjects' have their real temporal world.[62] When, with Husserl, we take God as such nowness, we can say that he is *immanent* in subjects as the nowness in and through which they function; but we can also say that he is *transcendent* to them, not in the sense of being objectively transcendent, but rather in the sense of being *before* their individual givenness.

With this, we have the answer to the question we posed at the end of the last chapter. It is Husserl's account of existence and essence which allows him to affirm both the individuality and coincidence of subjects. Their coincidence with "God, the absolute" occurs by virtue of the nowness that is existence per se. Their individual existence arises through the ordering of the contents filling the moments let loose by this nowness. It is a function of their essence as it is individualized in a given stream of experiences. As with Aquinas, the ultimate priority is given to existence per se.

The nature of this priority of "God, the absolute" can, perhaps, be best understood in terms of his necessity. Husserl writes: "The absolute has his ground in himself; and in his nongrounded being (*grundlosen Sein*), he has his necessity as the single, absolute 'substance'."[63] The key to understanding this statement is Husserl's assertion that "what is ultimately constituting is not itself constituted."[64] Thus, considered as ultimately constituting, the absolute is without a prior constitutive ground and can be called "ground-less" (*grundlos*).

It can, in other words, be described as a *self-caused* substance, i.e., one having "his ground in himself." A further feature of the absolute's necessity is given when Husserl continues these remarks: "His necessity is not an essential necessity which permits the contingent. All essential necessities are moments of his fact (*Factums*), modes of his functioning in relation to himself—his modes of understanding or being able to understand himself." The functioning referred to here is that of primal temporalization. The latter results in temporal transcendence and, with this, in "objectivity" understood as the quality of standing over and against a subject. Insofar as they are objective, all essential necessities are "moments" of the absolute's "fact"—i.e., are dependent on the fact of his functioning. When Husserl asserts that they are also "modes" (*Weisen*) of the absolute's self-understanding, we must take this in an objective sense. He cannot grasp himself as actually objective without being so, without objectifying himself in time through his functioning.[65] Whether or not such modes are the *only* ways in which he can understand himself is not at issue in this passage. Its point is the priority of the absolute's functioning to all essential necessities.[66] This priority follows from what we have said. Essential necessities are only hypothetical. The essences upon which they are based only specify possibilities.

For actual existence, we require the "fact" of the absolute's functioning. It is this which turns a possible ordering of contents in time into an actual ordering. The "absolute temporalization" of such functioning is, thus, prior to all essential necessities as that which allows them, whatever their particular character, to be actually obtaining necessities. It is in this sense that Husserl speaks of "the absolute" as "lying at the basis of all possibilities, all relativities, all limitations, giving them their sense and being."[67] The necessity of the absolute is not that of a specific possibility or specific set of objectively given entities, but rather that of the presence that makes them be—this, no matter *what* they are. What we confront here is not a necessity based on essences, but rather one based on existence. In Husserl's words, we confront the necessity of "actuality, itself streaming, in the strict worldly sense of being present."

Unlike the essential necessity "which permits the contingent"—i.e., leaves open contingency in areas not specified by its general rules—this existential necessity is all embracing. To express this tautologically, everything that is is. The necessity of its being is prior to the obtaining of any further necessities. Considered as the necessity of nowness per se, nowness in its otherness from objectively given entities and their essential structures, it is an absolute necessity. We may express this in terms of the anonymity of such nowness. For Husserl, we can conceive of something being different by varying in imagination its objective features—i.e., its given ' what." Yet, the absence of objective content in nowness *per se* means that we cannot conceive of it as other than it is through this process of "free variation." Can we conceive of it as simply not being? We can, after all, imagine the nonexistence, the permanent absence from nowness, of an entity which *once* was present. Against this supposition is the assertion that such nowness is "not a modality of time." Its nontemporal character is its being constantly present—i.e., its being a "nunc stans." Thus, as stationary, it cannot change. Its existential necessity is its inability to depart from the constant nowness that it is. Therefore, given that it is, that is, given that anything is present and actual, it must always be.

Is this an advance, a "going beyond" Thomas? Husserl believes that it is. He is reported as saying: "In spite of everything, I once believed—today, it is more than belief, today it is the knowledge—that precisely my phenomenology, and only this, is the philosophy which the *church* can use—this, because it goes together with Thomism and extends Thomistic philosophy."[68] The claim of an advance arises from the conviction that its positions are phenomenologically grounded. This signifies, for Husserl, that they spring from an epistemology whose radicalness corresponds to the depths of its metaphysical insights. The question of a theological advance is, of course, another matter. Husserl's concern is with a "philosophical" as opposed to a "confessional theology." The former is "a nonconfessional way to God" and, as such, probably cannot satisfy any church's confession of faith.[69] The same point holds with regard to ethics. Although they are not reducible to any particular faith's ethical code, the metaphysical assertions we have just considered do have definite ethical implications. As the next chapter makes clear, his "philosophical theology" has a practical and moral side.

6

RADICAL EVIL AND THE ONTOLOGICAL DIFFERENCE BETWEEN BEING AND BEINGS

Ludwig Landgrabe makes the point that Husserlian phenomenology sees itself as reestablishing metaphysics. The traditional metaphysical question concerns the being of beings, the being by virtue of which we can say that something is. For phenomenology, this question becomes one of the *origin* of beings. In Landgrabe's words, "According to this [the last period of Husserl's work], the sense of the phenomenological method must be understood as the question concerning the origin of each thing which is given to us as a being."[1] The answer to this question is pursued through a phenomenological analysis of the *giving* of being. It is an analysis which takes up the question of human being and human consciousness as things which are "already in the world," possessing their "objective time," and asks how these are given.[2] The result of this radical inquiry into the origin or ground of every individual being is an awareness of the distinction between being and individual beings. The being of the ground, the being that is ultimately giving, cannot be interpreted in terms of the individual beings—including human beings—which it grounds. As Landgrabe expresses this insight, "Being itself, however, is not a being but rather that which allows us, at any given time, to say of the beings, the 'things,' it exists' and 'it is such and such.'"[3]

We have already met this distinction in terms of our discussion of the Husserlian analogue of Thomas' distinction between existence and essence. There we considered being in terms of temporalization. In this chapter, we propose to consider it in terms of the content actually filling up the moments of time. When we do, the distinction between being and beings has a practical and a moral side. In particular, the distinction between finite, human being and being itself becomes exemplified by a phenomenon which has especially characterized our age to its detriment. I am referring to the appearance of radical evil as witnessed by our century's destruction of cultures—the cultures, for example, of Turkish Armenians, Eastern European Jews, and Moslem Bosnians. One may even include here the possibility of wholesale destruction, through nuclear war, of much larger areas of culture.

Husserl's method for reaching the being at the origin of all individual beings is that of the phenomenological reduction. As we have seen, the reduction's practice consists in suspending in thought all those connections of experience through which we are given individual beings. Husserl's two favorite terms, *constitution* and *reduction*, actually signify the reverse of each other. *Constitution* means the connecting or ordering of experiences *through which* there is present to us the synthetic (or connected) unity that we call an individual being. Reduction, on the contrary, means the abstracting in thought of such connections. Actually, two reductions are possible. There is the reduction that abstracts from the connections which give us the temporal presence of the object. In it, we suspend the ordering of retentions and protentions responsible for this presence. Its ultimate residue is the "living present." Functioning to make things present, it is the "Absolute" that Husserl defines as "Absolute temporalization." Another reduction is also possible. Just as we can abstract time from content and consider it apart from the content which fills it, so we can consider content apart from time. In this reduction, we abstract from the connections which yield the object's specific content, its content as this rather than that entity. To take the standard example, through the connecting of experiences into a perspectival series, there is present to us a perspectivally appearing, spatial-temporal object. The latter, we can say, is given to us through that sequential arrangement of experiences that presents first one side and then another of the object. Now, when we systematically abstract the connections through which objects are given, we ultimately arrive at what Husserl calls "the domain of experiences *qua* absolute essentialities."[4] These are those elemental experiences through whose connections all else arises and which themselves do not exist through any further connections. Husserl calls this domain "the totality of absolute being in a definite sense"—the sense, that is, of being the nonconstituted origin of all individual, constituted being.[5] In the late manuscripts, it is often simply termed the *absolute*. This is the same "absolute" that is the origin of time. The two reductions simply uncover different aspects of it. The reduction of the *Ideen* considers it under the aspect that makes it the origin of content. Taken in terms of the elements forming its domain, it has none of the features of a constituted, individual being. It is, to use an analogy, simply an alphabet of experiences. Our written alphabet does not per se spell words, it spells them through the sequential ordering of its letters. With such ordering, the whole of written literature becomes possible. Similarly, this absolute's domain does not, itself, have the characteristics of any given, individual being. It yields the latter through its own ordering, i.e., though the insertion *into the before and after of time* of its elemental, "essential" experiences. To complete this analogy, we note that just as the alphabet underlies the possibilities of our literary culture, so in a general sense this alphabet of experiences is that which makes possible all our experiences of individual beings. In Husserl's words, "there is no actor here. There is just the absolute . . . which lies at the basis of all possibilities, giving them [through its connections] their sense and their being."[6]

We can move into the human realm by mentioning the role this aspect of the absolute plays in making possible intersubjective relations. Such relations require an acknowledgment of both the identity and difference of subjects. According to Husserl, I acknowledge another person as different than myself insofar as I take him as "there"—i.e., as experiencing the world from a different location from that occupied my myself in my "here." Our identity is acknowledged when I assert that his "there" could have been my "here" and that were I to take up his standpoint in space and time, I would experience the same world that he does.[7] What is the condition of the possibility of these acknowledgments? Phenomenologically speaking, my unique "here" is the result of the perspectival ordering of my experiences. The latter are ordered so as to point to myself (in my "here") as the unique "center" or "O-point" of my spatial-temporal surrounding world. The same must be said of the Other in *his* "here," if he, like myself, is to be regarded as an *ego* or, what for Husserl are equivalent terms, as a *center* or *focus* of experiences.[8] This points to a double role of this absolute in making possible intersubjective recognition. The latter requires that the elements of our experience—the alphabet—be the same. It also requires that inherent in the possibilities generated by this alphabet are those of the perspectival arrangements of its elements into various surrounding worlds, each with its own unique O-point or "here." My assumption that were I able to simultaneously occupy with the Other his "here," I would experience the same surrounding world he presently does, rests, therefore, not on my actually being able to do this. It rests, rather, on my view of the absolute as *common* ground of myself and the Other, one which underlies *both* our possibilities as unique, experiencing egos. Another way of putting this is to say that my acknowledgment of the Other presupposes an implicit phenomenological reduction. Beyond the reduction which reveals the commonalty of our pre-egological nowness, there is also a move to the possibilities inherent in the "domain of experiences qua absolute essentialities."

Aside from its part in recognition, Husserl's absolute—his being of beings—has another role in intersubjective relations. Husserl asserts that "human being is teleological being and being as an ought to be."[9] This claim finds its ultimate justification in his analysis of our experience of time. This experience, which structures all that we do and accomplish, is, as we saw, inherently teleological. If it is, then, in Husserl's words, "this teleology prevails in each and every egological act and project."[10] This claim is extended when Husserl comes to see even the arising of new egos as a function of the constitution of time. Granting that such pre-egological constitution is *itself teleolog-*

ical, we have, in Husserl's words, "The new awakening of egos . . . as a teleology included within the universal teleology . . ."[11] With this, teleology
becomes understood as the "form of all forms." This means that "teleology
can be exhibited as that which determines, concretely and individually, all
being in its totality, as that which ultimately makes it possible and, by virtue of
this, actual."[12]

    As we quoted Husserl, it is "the absolute which lies at the basis of all pos-
sibilities . . ." This is what gives such possibilities "their sense and being" as
actual entities. Taken together with the remarks on teleology, we thus have
the claim that the absolute's action of grounding individuals is to be understood
as a *teleological* action. Broadly speaking, such action may be described as a
process where *what is to be actualized*—the telos or goal of the activity—
determines what is presently actual and, in so doing, *brings about its own progressive actualization*. To take a common example, we may note that a student's goal of passing an examination, if sincerely held, determines his present
actuality, which is one of studying for this examination; and, in so doing, it
brings about its own fulfillment. Having studied, the student actually passes the
examination. Teleology, in other words, is a process where the not-yet—the
goal which exists only as a possibility that may be realized—determines the
present and does so to bring about its own eventual realization in time.

    If, as Husserl claims, the absolute's action is teleological, the same pat-
tern can be applied to its process of grounding or constituting beings. To do so,
we must see the *possibilities* suggested by its position as an alphabet *as goals to
be realized*. The infinity of experiential being such an alphabet is capable of,
thus, becomes understood as a teleological goal that informs all the actual connections or ordering occurring among the elemental experiences forming the
"letters" of this alphabet. In terms of our analogy, we can say that the "writing"
of the existent world occurs through the insertion in the *before and after of time*
of such elements. The connection of experiences, through which the synthetic
unity of individual being is given, is the connection of such experiences *in
time*. Now, what makes the process of connecting experiences—i.e., of the
"writing" of the world—necessarily teleological is the aforementioned doctrine that the temporal process, the process of the constitution of time, is itself
inherently teleological. As we cited Husserl in Chapter 3, it is a process in
which time is propelled "from present to present in such a way that every content is the content of a fulfilled drive and is intended before the goal," i.e.,
before the next temporal content, which is intended as a goal, actually (or
"presently") *exists*.[13] If time is teleological, then all connecting or ordering in
time must be teleological. If the absolute grounds being through such connecting, then such grounding must be understood teleologically. Thus, in terms of
our first remarks which defined Husserl's being of beings as the origin which
"gives" all individual beings, we have to say that the absolute is this origin by

being, itself, the goal that all constitution of being is striving to realize.

This "striving" takes on a recognizable form once we turn to human being. According to Husserl, such being is, in an exemplary manner, the "self-expression" or "self-objectification" of the absolute in the world.[14] This signifies that human subjects, once they arise, become the locus in and through which the absolute's self-constitution takes place. The teleological process of such self-constitution becomes manifest as a teleology "immanent" within "the transcendental totality of subjects." It manifests itself, in other words, "as a universal form of their individual being, as the form of all the forms in which this totality exists."[15] Such subjects, then, exhibit their own teleological grounding by virtue of the teleological character of the constitution occurring within them. Constituted by the teleological process of time, they themselves experience time teleologically. They intend the future before it actually exists, which means that the future is a matter of concern to them. It becomes a matter of practical valuation, of goals to be realized, of possibilities to be brought about or avoided. With regard to the possibilities of their own being, the general "will to live," which they share with all animate existence, becomes a teleologically directed "will to true being."[16] This "true being" is, we can say, a "fullness" of being. Such fullness is not to be taken as a completion in a static sense. It is, rather, to be understood in terms of an indefinitely extended horizon involving anticipation and fulfillment. So understood, every human accomplishment is taken as a *fulfilling* of the notion of being human and as an *anticipation* of further possibilities of being human. According to such a conception, we can, e.g., say that the accomplishment of human speech opens up a whole range of further possibilities—civil society, commerce, etc.—to the possibility of being actualized. Each of these, when actualized (or fulfilled) in some particular way, points, in anticipation, to further possibilities. In such a situation, "fullness" represents a teleological ideal. It is a goal toward which this horizonally structured process of anticipation of the future and fulfillment tends. Husserl writes in this regard, "the totality of monadic [or human] being exists in horizonality, and infinity pertains to this, infinite potentiality." The claim implicit in the word, *infinity*, is that the ultimate goal of the intersubjective community is nothing less than the synthetic (collective) actualization of the harmonious possibilities inherent in the absolute. The absolute itself is the goal which this constituting-accomplishing community continually strives to realize.

Let me turn to the theme of radical evil. Evil may be considered as radical when it strikes at the root of things—when, as a consequence, there is no remedy for its effects. In other words, the destructive work of this evil is such that it cannot be "made good" again. What cannot be made good again is a possibility foreclosed to us. Applied to human being, its effect is, thus, the permanent closing off of the possibilities of being human. Such evil may take the form of the destruction of the historical records of a society; it may proceed beyond this and involve the loss of the society's native language. Its ultimate expression is the wholesale destruction of the members of the society—such an action being intended to eliminate the possibilities of behavior and thinking these members manifest. As the experience of our century demonstrates, this radical, exemplary evil exists in a continuum with the more common, everyday forms of intolerance. Intolerance of an ethnic group precedes their destruction. Intolerance contains the germ of radical evil insofar as it expresses the attitude that other persons who think and act in a certain way are not to be accounted as genuinely human. Adopting this attitude, not just my relation to these other persons but also my tie to the ground of these relations is *partially severed*. Such other persons are *not recognized* as human subjects "like myself," which also signifies that I do not recognize the absolute as implicitly containing both my human possibilities and those of the group I cannot tolerate. This can be put in terms of the absolute considered as the teleological goal of human fullness. Intolerance, both in its minor and radical forms, is an attempt to bracket the striving toward this goal. It directs itself against already realized human possibilities or against possibilities present as anticipations springing from these. It, thus, typically takes the form of attempting to *narrow* or, at least, *hold static* the meaning of being human. In the former case, it attempts an actual *regress* from the ideal of human fullness. In the latter, its attempt is to eliminate the teleological action of this ideal as a goal toward which to advance. Once again, we can speak of our tie with the absolute as being partially severed. Coincident with our nonrecognition of the human possibilities manifested by others is our nonrecognition of the absolute. The absolute's *presence*, in the form of a concrete teleological goal, *becomes withdrawn*.

This connection between recognizing others and the presence of the absolute can also be expressed in terms of human finitude. My finitude is shown by the fact that I can only actualize one possibility of my being—i.e., engage in a specific course of action—by neglecting other possibilities. Because of this, my finitude implies a plurality when it is viewed in a teleological framework which points to the harmonious actualization of *all* possibilities. Given human finitude, it is only through a plurality of individual subjects that possibilities can be *collectively*—and not just successively—actualized. The conclusion, here, is that my recognition of others and their possibilities is tied to my recognition of the absolute as a teleological ground. Seen in terms of this ground, my finitude situates me in a self-acknowledged being with other persons. Yet, this collective being of subjects *is itself something finite*. This is shown by the fact that it can, through its collective actions, permanently close off its own possibilities, for example, those of Eastern European Jewry. Thus, like the individual, it is finite in the sense that it can, through its actions, eliminate possibilities for itself; though, unlike the individual, this cannot be made up by an appeal to a greater collectivity—i.e., others. This follows because it, itself, is this very collectivity.

As we said, this permanent foreclosure of possibilities is the phenomenon of radical evil. Radical evil—or the potentiality for such—thus shows itself as the mark of the collective finitude of humanity. It is also, we can say, the phenomenological sign that human *beings* do not equal *being itself.* The ontological distinction between the two is shown by the fact that the possibilities represented by the absolute—Husserl's being of beings—can be permanently lost to humanity. If this ontological distinction did not obtain, humanity could find within itself the potentialities to make good again all those losses which have made its history so calamitous. That it cannot signifies that it is not its ground, that it can *partially* or even, in an ultimate catastrophe, be *totally* cut off from the latter. These possibilities are, in fact, themselves inherent in the absolute conceived as the totality of possibilities. It, itself, grounds radical evil by including even the possibility of foreclosing possibilities.

Radical evil is, thus, a permanent human possibility. Indeed, the attempt to completely foreclose it as possibility would involve the very foreclosing of possibilities that it, itself, is. It would be rather like attempting to overcome evil by engaging in it in its radical sense. The fruitlessness of this attempt can be seen in the fact that the very possibility of such evil is also that of our finitude. It is inherent in the ontological distinction and, thus, in the transcendence of being itself (of our ground and our goal) from ourselves. That such being is teleologically conceived signifies, we can say, that "value" remains "value." It can never be reified and considered a permanent possession like some human, physical feature. It always remains transcendent as a goal directing our life. Husserl's *Krisis* reflects on the fact that this direction can be lost. His remark, "the dream is over," broadly refers to the dream of inevitable human progress. Because the absolute both draws humanity toward itself *and* includes humanity's possibility of turning away and *losing* its way—this dream is rightly over. In its stead, we have the awakening of self-responsibility. An "awake" humanity, in Husserl's view, knows that evil and intolerance can never be permanently overcome but only continually and responsibly combated.

7

PHENOMENOLOGY AND
ARTIFICIAL INTELLIGENCE:
HUSSERL LEARNS CHINESE

It is time to put the insights of the previous chapters to work on a current problem. We can do so by considering John Searle's ingenious argument against the possibility of artificial intelligence. For over a decade, it has held a prominent place in contemporary discussions of philosophy and cognitive science. This is not just because of its striking central example and the apparent simplicity of its argument. As its appearance in *Scientific American* testifies, it is also due to its importance to the wider scientific community. If Searle is right, artificial intelligence in the strict sense, the sense that would claim that mind can be instantiated through a formal program of symbol manipulation, is basically wrong. No set of formal conditions can provide us with the characteristic feature of mind, which is the intentionality of its mental contents. Formally regarded, such intentionality is an irreducible primitive. It cannot be analyzed into nonintentional (purely syntactic, symbolic) components. This chapter will argue that this objection is based on a misunderstanding. Intentionality is not simply something given which is incapable of further analysis. It only appears so when we mistakenly abstract it from time. When we regard its temporal structure, it shows itself as a rule-governed, synthetic process, one capable of being instantiated both by machines and men.

Searle's Double Thesis

Searle's position is actually twofold. The first part is that the semantics which characterize mental contents are irreducible to syntax. By *semantics* he means the ability that thoughts and perceptions have, through their mental contents, "to be about objects and states of affairs in the world."[1] This aboutness is their intentionality, their being thoughts or perceptions *of* something. This first part is buttressed by a second. For Searle, consciousness with its mental states is a biological product. As such, computers can simulate it, but they cannot reduplicate it. Thus, the computer simulation of the digestive system does not itself digest anything. Similarly, the simulation of the oxidation of fuels in an automobile engine does not itself power an auto. Given that consciousness is also a physically caused effect, Searle concludes, "the computational model of metal processes is no more real than the computational model of any other natural phenomenon."[2]

In defense of his first thesis, Searle has contrived an ingenious example. He invites us to consider him as a computer, specifically a Chinese-speaking one. Although he does not know Chinese, he does have a rule book "in English for matching Chinese symbols with other Chinese symbols."[3] Identifying them entirely by their shape, he finds the cards with the matches to the symbols he receives and passes them on to his interlocutor who hands back "more small bunches of symbols." According to Searle, "the rule book is the 'computer program.' The people who wrote it are the 'programmers.'" And he is the "computer." Unbeknown to himself, he is actually carrying on a conversation in Chinese, successfully passing the Turing test for artificial intelligence. His overt verbal behavior indicates that he knows Chinese, that he is in fact an intelligent Chinese speaker. That he is, on the contrary, totally ignorant of this language does not mean he fails the test, but rather that the test itself fails.[4] His example, then, is meant to show the general failure of all tests based on such behavior to identify intelligence.[5] Because he fails to understand Chinese "solely on the basis of running a computer program," Searle claims that "any other digital computer [also fails] solely on that basis."[6] The basis is the process of formal symbol manipulation. Given that computer programs are formal (or "syntactic") systems and admitting that they fail to understand Chinese in the sense of grasping the semantics or intrinsic meanings of the symbols they manipulate, the first part of Searle's position follows. Syntactic or purely formal relations are incapable of resulting in semantics. This means that "programs" which operate on the level of such relations "are neither constitutive of nor sufficient for minds" which do understand the intrinsic meanings (or "about-ness") of the symbols they manipulate.[7]

If such an understanding is not based on any rule-governed procedure, how does it come about? Searle's answer returns us to the second part of his position, which is that consciousness, as a biological product, is a caused fact. In his words, "Mental states are as real as any other biological phenomena. They are both caused by and realized in the brain."[8] The same holds for the intentionality of such states. "Intrinsic intentionality," he asserts, "is a biolog-ical phenomenon, caused by brain processes and realized in the structure of the brain."[9] Given that mental processes are causally determined—in Searle's words, that "the brain operates causally both at the level of the neurons and at the level of the mental states"—such processes can only be simulated by a computer.[10] To actually duplicate them, the formal elements which compose the computer program would have to have equivalent causal powers. But their only power is to move the program forward to the next manipulation of purely formal symbols.[11]

Applicability and Validity

This conception of consciousness as a caused fact ignores an important distinction. Turing seems to have had it in mind when he advocated "drawing a fairly sharp line between the physical and the intellectual capacities of a man." There was, he remarked, "little point in trying to make a 'thinking machine' more human by dressing it up in . . . artificial flesh." The latter was irrelevant to its intelligence.[12] Similarly, we should not "penalize the machine for its inability to shine in beauty contests" since, while success in such contests is biased toward the human, it is not clear that intelligence is.[13] If we grant this, then the question facing us is not, can we make machines *human*, but only, can we make them think. In drawing this distinction, we are separating thinking from any species specific function. We are also, at least implicitly, distinguishing the laws of thought from those governing their application in a specific circumstance. The laws of arithmetic, for example, can be instantiated both in men and machines. Both can "do" sums. Very different causal laws, however, are involved in the process. Sticking just with machines, a favorite pastime of systems experts is to dream up nonelectronic computers. Perfectly good logical gates can, for example, be constructed by channeling the impacts of billiard balls.[14] Here, the laws governing the applicability of the program to the machine are those of classical mechanics. In standard, silicon chip machines, they are those of electronics. Given that the laws governing the instantiation (or application) are different, but the laws actually instantiated (e.g., those of arithmetic) are the same, the two sets of laws cannot be identical.

Husserl puts this point in terms of the distinction between the validity and the applicability of the logical laws. For the law of contradiction to be applicable to our mental processes, we must be subjectively capable of maintaining constancy among our concepts. This condition for the applicability of the law is not the same as its validity. The latter depends only on certain relations obtaining once meanings are, in fact, held stable. If we fail to make this distinction, then, as Husserl notes in the *Logische Untersuchungen*, we would have to call the law of contradiction *invalid* whenever we did not fulfill the condition of keeping constant the meanings of the expressions we use (*Logische Untersuchungen*, Hua XVIII, 106f; J. N. Findlay's trans. [*Logical Investigations*, New York, 1970], p. 127). Similarly, we would have to see the development of the conditions for the applicability of logic to our mental life—i.e., the development of the psychological ability to hold concepts constant—as the development of the *validity* of the logical laws.[15] The skepticism implicit in this brand of psychologism is readily apparent. It makes logical validity a contingent fact, a matter of the obtaining of a specific set of causal conditions. The same skepticism is also implicit in making thinking into a species specific act—e.g., something which is inseparable from the particular conditions in which it occurs in human beings. At this point thought becomes, as one of Searle's followers asserts, "a natural kind" of entity. Rather than being a function, it becomes so identified with its material conditions that we have to say that it is "matter of a certain sort."[16] The difficulty with this kind of reductionism is that it leaves us almost defenseless against the assertion that "logic alters with the development of the brain" (*Logische Untersuchungen*, Hua XVIII, 152; Findlay's trans. p. 162). If intelligence is a type of matter and if we fail to distinguish its material from its formal conditions, then a material change is also a transformation in what counts as intelligence. Here, the skepticism regarding artificial intelligence turns into one about intelligence itself. As such, it ends by undermining all claims to knowledge.

Intentionality and Meaning

Searle's first thesis can be simply stated: Syntax is not sufficient for semantics. We cannot generate semantics out of nonsemantic elements.[17] Behind this simplicity, however, lies a mystery. *Semantics* signifies both meaning and intentionality. It thus embraces the phenomenon of *x* meaning *y*, as when we ask about the meaning of a word, an event, or even (at times) an object. It also includes the phenomenon of *x*, as a mental state, being *about y*. Here it is the ability of thoughts, perceptions, etc. through their mental contents "to be about objects and states of affairs in the world." The mystery is: how does it embrace both? How does intentionality involve meaning and meaning involve intentionality? Is there some common root to the two phenomena?

Husserl asked himself such questions throughout his career. His answer to them begins with his refusal to follow Frege in separating the sense from the reference of an assertion. An assertion, according to Husserl, refers through its meaning. Conversely, in language, in the sphere of signs that function by virtue of an inherent sense, reference to an object must involve sense.[18] The same inseparability also occurs in the realm of the meanings (or senses) that we find embodied in our perceptual experiences. Such senses (*noematic Sinne* in Husserl's later terminology) involve a reference to the objects whose senses they claim to be. Conceptually, we can distinguish between "the object as (*sowie*) it is intended and the object, simply, which is intended," the former being the sense, the latter being the reference of our particular presentation (*Logische Untersuchungen*, Hua XIX/1, 414; Findlay's trans., p. 578). But in an actual perception, we always grasp the intended object with a particular sense. Indeed, if we cannot make sense of our perceptual experiences, if we cannot make them "fit together" so as to say that they are perceptions of some definite object, then their referent is also lost to us. In a successful perceptual experience, there is, then, a simultaneity of the theses of *Sinn* and *Sein* (of sense and being). We grasp the object as being there at the same time as we grasp it as having a determinable sense. Intentionality (or reference to the object) thus always appears as an inherent feature of this sense.

These facts have led some commentators to draw a parallel between Husserl and Searle. McIntyre, for example, asserts that "Husserl says of noematic *Sinne* essentially what Searle says of mental states themselves: they have 'intrinsic', as opposed to 'derived', intentionality."[19] This means that they "are conceived by Husserl as intentional, not because of any relations they bear to anything *else* (e.g., not because they are 'interpreted' by someone or caused in some particular way) but simply because they are a sort of entity whose very nature is to *be* representational."[20] In other words, just as a mental state is conceived by Searle as having an intentional character by virtue of its very (material) being, a similar thesis is here asserted about meanings. Intentionality is considered to be one of their "primitive features" and as such "cannot be reduced to causal roles, computations, or to anything else."[21] Granting this, Husserl would also agree with Searle on a further point: the impossibility of artificial intelligence in the strict sense. In McIntyre's words, Husserl's position would be that "artificial intelligence is 'artificial' precisely because it is only formal and so devoid of what is truly 'mental.'"[22] What is truly mental is a mental state's intentional character. It has this character "by virtue of its relation to a noematic *Sinn*."[23] Since, however, intentionality is "an intrinsic and irreducible" feature of such *Sinne*, it cannot be generated by the purely formal means employed by artificial intelligence.

McIntyre's position bases itself on two unexplained mysteries: the relations of mental states to meanings (*Sinne*) and of meanings to intentionality. Both are assumed as simply given, as somehow irreducible. If, however, we take such states as the immanent contents or experiences of consciousness, it is precisely their relation to meaning that explains meaning's intentional character.

To see this, we must first note that for Husserl intentionality and meaning are related by having a common (constitutive) origin. As we indicated, both the reference and sense of the perceptually embodied meaning are the result of the fact that our individual perceptual experiences fit, or are "harmonious," with one another. If they do fit, then we say that the appearing object bears an intelligible sense. We also assert that we are not experiencing a hallucination—as well we might if a series of perspectival views did not fit together. We say, rather, that we are experiencing the object as something existent. Now, as Husserl observes, we continue to regard it as existent as long as we grasp it as one and the same thing showing itself in different aspects or perspectives. This very same process of grasping a one in many, however, also results in a grasp of the object's sense (its *noematic Sinn*).[24] For Husserl, then, the object is not just apprehended as something real, a "real unity." Its constitutive basis also makes us grasp it as a unity of sense. Indeed, as he constantly stresses, all "real unities" are "unities of sense" (*Ideen I*, ed. R. Schuhmann, Hua III/1, 120).

The notion of sense at work here is that of being a one in many. To grasp Husserl's position, it is essential to observe that he understands not just kinds or species as unities in multiplicity. The same universality, he claims, is also to be found in the senses attributed to individuals (*Logische Untersuchungen*, Hua XIX/2, 564; Findlay's trans., p. 692). The only difference is in what constitutes the "many." For a kind, it is the individual objects falling under its notion; for an individual existent, the multiplicity of its sense is composed of the perceptual experiences through which we grasp it (ibid., 565, Findlay's trans., pp. 693–94). When such experiences reveal an identical content, we grasp both the object *and* its "fulfilling sense" (*Logische Untersuchungen*, Hua XIX/1, 56; Findlay's trans., p. 291). In such a context, it is almost a tautology to say that the sense bears an inherent reference to the object and, hence, has some sort of "intrinsic intentionality." For Husserl, the presence of the object is the presence of its perceptually embodied sense. As he writes of the way the object is "in" consciousness, "This in-consciousness is a completely unique being-in. It is not a being-in as a real, inherent component; it is rather a being-in as something intentional . . . it is a being-in as the object's *objective sense*" (*Cartesianische Meditationen*, Hua I, 80).[25]

Once we accept this equivalence between the intentional presence of an object and that of its sense, the locus of intentionality falls where it should. The intentional relation is not primarily between an object and its sense, the object being conceived of as a thing "in itself" independent of and distinct from its sense. (The positing of such an "in itself" would be a "metaphysical" thesis shut off by the reduction). The relation is, rather, between consciousness with its immanent experiences or "mental states" and this presence of a sense. By virtue of its temporal structure, consciousness, as we saw in our third chapter, retains the multiplicity of its past impressions. Thus, within it are the multiplicities of those perceptual experiences which provide the material for (and hence correspond to) the unities of sense that it grasps. As embracing the relation between consciousness and its object—in Husserl's phrase, as designating the fact that consciousness is "consciousness of" some object—the intentional relation is between such experiences and their object. It is, in other words, the relation between multiplicity and unity that results in sense. This means that to constitute this relation is to constitute the intentionality of consciousness. As we shall see, such intentionality is coconstituted in the same process which results in the presence of the object with its perceptually embodied sense. By virtue of this process, the individual experience becomes an experience *of* the object, the experiential content being a concrete example (or instantiation) of the content of the object's noematic *Sinn*. The experience, in other words, is considered to be *of* the object insofar as it is taken as an instance of what the object in its content can continually exhibit as it shows itself. Its being "of" the object is, then, its being part of the indefinite multiplicity that is correlated to the object's being as a "unity of sense."

Perception as Interpretation

How, then, does an experience become part of this multiplicity? In the *Logical Investigations*, Husserl's answer begins with the fact that "perception is interpretation." He writes in explanation: "It belongs to perception that something appears within it, but *interpretation* makes up what we term appearance—be it correct or not, anticipatory or overdrawn. The *house* appears to me through no other way but that I interpret in a certain fashion actually experienced contents of sensation. . . . They are termed 'appearances' or, better, appearing contents precisely for the reason that they are contents of perceptive interpretation" (*Logische Untersuchungen*, Hua XIX/2, 762). The doctrine, here, is that nonintentional elements—say, particular "contents of sensation"—become intentional through our taking them as appearances of some object. To take them as such is to place them in a framework of identity in multiplicity. We do so when we continually take them in the same sense. As Husserl writes in describing how "we suppose ourselves to perceptually grasp one and the same object through the change of experiential contents," "different perceptual contents are given, but they are interpreted, apperceived 'in the same sense,' . . . the interpretation (*Auffassung*) according to this 'sense' is a character of experience which first constitutes 'the being of the object for me'" (*Logische Untersuchungen*, Hua XIX/1, 397; Findlay's trans., 566). What we have, then, is a threefold structure. On the objective side, we have the object as an appearing sense. On the subjective side, the side of what is "truly immanent" in consciousness, we have the "contents of perception." On the same side, we also have the "perceptual acts in the sense of interpretative intentions" (ibid.). The acts make the contents intentional by transforming them from senseless sense data to "representing contents"—contents which point unambiguously to the corresponding features of the object (*Logische Untersuchungen*, Hua XIX/2, 609; Findlay's trans., p. 730). They do this through assuming that the experiential contents have a single referent, i.e., fit together to form the recurring pattern of perceptions through which an object exhibits its specific sense.[25]

Later on we shall have to review more closely the mechanisms by which this is accomplished. For the present, however, a number of points can be made. The first is that the intentional relation is not a causal relation, since it is a relation to a sense rather than to a physical reality (*Logische Untersuchungen*, Hua XIX/1, 384–86; Findlay's trans., pp. 557–58). Furthermore, the existence of the relation does not guarantee the real existence of its object. This follows because it is based upon an interpretation, and the interpretation may be wrong. If further perceptual evidence fails to confirm our particular interpretation, then the interpretation will be abandoned along with the reference to the object it embodies.

Our third point concerns the fact that the theses of sense and being can become separated. This occurs each time we verbally report what we have seen. So detached, the thesis of sense continues to carry with it a reference to the thesis of being—i.e, the being there of the object we report having seen. But the hearer of the report can directly confirm it only when experiencing the intuitions which can be subsumed under the sense's range. As a one in many, the sense embodies the thought of a possible existence which stands as a correlate of a range of possible perceptions. In this way, it does have an intentionality (a "representational character" in McIntyre's phrase) to the object. The intentionality, however, is not "primitive" in the sense of being unanalyzable. At its basis are the perceptions which could fill up the sense's range. These perceptions, when actually present, embody the intentional relation in the Husserlian sense of relating consciousness to its object. This object is not something outside of the sense. It is the perceptually embodied sense; it is, in other words, the unity which is the correlate of the perceptions a given consciousness has retained and synthesized. This implies that the sense which becomes separate from perception in a verbal report (the nonperceptually embodied sense) has only an indirect intentionality. It refers the object through the perceptions (the "mental states" as defined above) which form the multiplicity of its range.

Implicit in the preceding is a position directly opposed to Searle's. Given that interpretation is essential for the setting up of the one in many relation that embodies intentionality, without interpretation there is no intentionality. In other words, if we admit with Husserl that through interpretation senseless sense data become "representing contents," then we also agree that interpretation is the constructing of semantic or intentional structures out of nonintentional elements. There is, we may note, an immediate, nontheoretic evidence for this position. It occurs whenever interpretation fails or, in cases of fatigue or stress, is temporarily wanting. For example, the person suffering from certain forms of dissociation perceives and yet those perceptions have no referent. He cannot put them together to get a world of objects, a world that is somehow "out there" beyond the immediate presence of the sensations which crowd in on him. Only when the interpretation does succeed does the world regain its depth. Our perceptions again become *of* something beyond them. Objects then appear which exhibit the sense we make of the experiential flow of perceptual multiplicities. If this is at all accurate, then Husserl's position follows: Intentionality is not a fact but rather an analyzable performance (*Leistung*). As such, we can uncover its nonintentional components.[27]

Perception and Passive Synthesis

After the *Investigations*, Husserl expresses the same points in terms of synthesis. He writes in the *Cartesian Meditations*: "The object of consciousness, in its self-identity throughout the flowing of experience, does not enter into this flowing from outside. It lies included within it as a sense; it is this [sense] as a result of the intentional performance (*Leistung*) of the synthesis of consciousness" (*Cartesianische Meditationen*, Hua I, 80). Without this performance, there is no intentional object and hence no intentionality. Synthesis, in other words, is prior to intentionality. Thus, the individual elements of an intentional experience do not themselves generally have "the basic character of intentionality, that is, the characteristic of being 'consciousness of something'" (*Ideen I*, Hua III/1, 74). They gain this only when they are part of a successful synthesis, one which can establish an ongoing objective sense.

On one level, synthesis can be described as simply a matter of putting together or connecting our perceptions. To describe the objective sense as a result of this process thus implies that it can be established by the proper ordering or connecting of our perceptions. If, for example, our perceptions can be connected to form a perspectival series, a series showing first one side and than another of an object, then the result should be the sense of a spatial temporal object. Now, generally speaking, we do not consciously connect our experiences in time. They are simply given to us in a certain order that we recognize immediately. Synthesis, unlike interpretation, tends to denote something involuntary, something that can go on without any active participation of the subject. In fact, the move to describe intentionality in terms of synthesis occurs as Husserl begins to work out his doctrine of the "passive constitution" of the intentional relationship. In this, both its poles, both the subject and its object, come to be seen as the results of the connections of experience. The same holds with regard to the subject's interpretive act. It, too, is seen as founded on a given ordering of experience. The ordering of experience which results in the intentional relation is, thus, seen as *prior to*, and hence as occurring *without the active participation* of the subject.[28]

What does determine it are rules. According to Husserl, "*any object whatever* (including any immanent object) *points to a rule bound structure* (*Regelstruktur*)" (*Cartesianische Meditationen*, Hua I, 90). Correlated to the notion of an experiencing subject and its possible experiences, there is "a strict rule of possible syntheses" which would provide the subject with a coherent surrounding world (ibid., p. 24). Thus, the rule of perspectival ordering provides

us with a spatial-temporal world. The dissolution of this ordering is the dissolution of this world. It is also the dissolution of the ego, or subject, because it,
too, is established through such ordering.[29] If we grant this, then we can see why
Husserl has been called a *father of cognitive science*.[30] For Husserl, not just
intentionality but also the intending subject, can be constructed from nonintentional elements. Taking such elements as Husserl's absolute, both can be
seen as the results of following rules for ordering (or processing) the data of
experience. This implies that nothing prevents such rules from being imple-
mented by a machine.

Synthesis and Intelligence

To really see Husserl as a father of cognitive science, we must specify
more precisely what we mean by *synthesis*. We have to ask, what are the general features of its rule governed operations that are directly transferable to
machines? Yet, before we consider this question, a word of caution is in order.
As C. A. Fields observes, "It is not at all clear that intelligence (the ability to
solve antecedently specified problems of certain types) is or even has anything
to do with intentionality."[31] Machines with traditionally written programs can
perform a large number of functions from game playing to medical counseling.
These machines have not been programed to be intentional, yet such functions
have traditionally been considered to be "intelligent." To reverse this, a large
number of animals, obviously incapable of such functions, seem to possess
the ability to be directed toward an external object. They possess intentionality,
but not intelligence. The same point can be put slightly differently by suggesting that when we say that a machine does not "understand" or acts without
understanding (as in Searle's Chinese room test), what we are really claiming is
that *it is not a subject*. By a "subject" is meant simply something that has a
world; *has* it rather than *is* it, since the "aboutness" of the intentional relation
implies a certain nonidentity. If other animals can also be subjects, we grant
that to be a subject does not mean that one has to have intelligence in the above
defined sense.

Two reflections follow from this. The first is that the rules which make
machines intentional need not as such make them intelligent. One can well
imagine a machine that processes data according to the rules of intentional
synthesis, and so sees as we do, and yet fails the Turing test. This is not to say
that there are not advantages to making machines intentional. To realize them,
however, we should first make them intentional and then work on making
them intelligent. The same insight allows us to counter Dreyfus's position. He
attacks the concept of artificial intelligence by focusing on the "infinite task" it
implies.[32] Admitting that intentionality is a rule-governed procedure, such rules,
according to Dreyfus, become unimaginably complex once we realize with

Husserl that "intelligent behavior also presupposes a background of cultural practices and institutions."[33] Even though this may be the case, it does not follow that such knowledge is essential for intentionality per se. If it were, we would have to exclude most of the animal world from it. Once again, what we should do is first attempt to make machines intentional and then work on making them culturally adept.

Intentionality and Transcendence

What then are the features of intentional synthesis? What characterizes it quite apart from the skills of problem solving intelligence or cultural adaptation? To begin with the most obvious, its action, as we have stressed throughout these chapters, is temporal. Its underlying level is the temporal ordering of experience. The basic feature of such ordering appears whenever we regard a spatial-temporal object. As we turn it, one appearance gives way to the next. A new side shows itself, while the experience of the previous side sinks into pastness. The perceiving subject, however, remains constantly now. It remains a kind of marker point against which the departure into the past is measured. The basic feature, then, is the distinction between the nowness of the subject and the flowing into pastness of what it perceives. In Husserl's words, what we confront "in the primordial sphere" is a continuous process where "worldly perception (*Wahrnehmung von Weltlichkeiten*) and the world separate themselves."[34] There is a twofold necessity for such separation. Given that all action occurs in the present, if the subject is to continue to act (to continue, for example, to perceive), he must remain present. If, however, the object is to show more than one side to the subject, the appearances it shows to him must depart into pastness. Thus, on the one hand, if the subject were to remain fixed in the fleeting moment when he perceived a particular appearance, he could not apprehend any others. On the other hand, if the particular appearance remained constantly now with the subject, it could not give way to any others. What is required, then, is the separation occasioned by the departure into pastness.

Such departure brings about transcendence. In Husserl's words, "the not now transcends the now; in particular, it transcends the [present] consciousness of the not now . . . what is transcended is always consciousness."[35] With this, the original nonidentity required for intentionality opens up: consciousness, in remaining now, is transcended by what departs into pastness. Such departure opens up an original distance between subject and object. The object, which is grasped as enduring, is more than my present, momentary experience of it. As enduring, it is grasped as including both my present and my past experience of it. Thus, to the transcendence of the now by the not now, there is added a second transcendence: that between my present consciousness and its object. The content I presently experience becomes "of" what is beyond this momentary experience. It becomes, in its departure, the content of an object that endures.

The Pastness of an Experience

The second feature of synthesis is that it involves an ontological distinction. There is a distinction in being between the individual experiences and the object that appears through their synthesis (*Ideen I*, Hua III/1, 86). This distinction shows itself in a corresponding distinction in the types of allowable predication. Thus, we cannot predicate of the object what we predicate of the experience. The object shows itself perspectivally. It manifests the sense of a spatial-temporal entity, one subject at the very least to the laws of kinematics. The experience, however, does not show itself first from one side and then another (ibid.). It cannot, accordingly, be regarded as some sort of physical reality or be considered as subject to the corresponding laws. Admitting this, we cannot say with Searle that "mental states are as real as any other biological phenomena." Rather than being an inseparable part of a physical process, they have a status which allows them to be considered as information for processing.

Behind this distinction between the experience and the spatial-temporal object are very different temporal modes. If we are not to be confronted with a chaos of sensations, each individual experience, once obtained, must remain unchanged. Yet each must, as we noted, also give way to the next. It must sink back into pastness. The requirement, then, is that its content be retained unchanged and yet possess a changing temporal tag, a marker showing its increasing distance from the present. The object, by contrast, has the temporal mode of persisting through change. Appearing through a succession of different sensuous contents, it must continue to show itself as *that of which* such contents are contents.

Kant, as we have seen, was the first to systematically consider these conditions for synthesis. Let us take a moment to review them. When Kant defines the "synthesis of apprehension" as the act by which we run through a multiplicity of perceptions and hold them together, he notes that the first requirement is simply that of grasping the multiplicity as a multiplicity. This requires that the mind "distinguish time in the succession of impressions following one another."[36] Each impression must, in other words, be distinguished through its distinct time. Once distinguished, the impressions must be preserved. If they are to be grasped together, then they cannot vanish from consciousness the moment after their apprehension. In Kant's words, "if I were to lose from my thought the preceding impressions . . . and not reproduce them when I advance to those which follow, a complete presentation [of an enduring object] would never arise . . ."[37] Thus, not only must the impressions be temporally tagged (and so distinguished), they must also be "reproduced"—i.e., brought up, moment by moment, to the present. The result is their retention with their temporal tag. As Kant implies, this tag must itself be preserved, for otherwise what is reproduced would be indistinguishable from "a new presentation." What we require, then, is "the consciousness that what we think is, in fact, the same as what we thought a moment before."[38]

The consciousness that the retained impression is *not something new* is the consciousness that it is something past. Each time the impression is reproduced, it must therefore be brought up to the present as something not new. Husserl, as we saw, expresses this condition in terms of a chain of "retentions of retentions." An impression is retained, and then this retention is itself retained, and so on serially: the result being a "constant continuum of retentions such that each later point is a retention of an earlier" (*Zur Phänomenologie des inneren Zeitbewusstseins*, Hua X, 29). Each retention thus retains the previous retention. Each also tags what it retains as not-new, i.e., as old or past. Since the retention that is retained is itself not-new, what we have in its retention is a modification which adds a further degree of pastness to its content.[39]

When we satisfy these conditions, we have the special type of being which characterizes the momentary experience. This is a being which does not show itself perspectivally. Rather than offering us anything new, the experience departs unchanged into increasing degrees of pastness. Such departure is, as we said, the occasion of the original transcendence which marks the intentional relation. Now the conditions for such departure, those of reproduction or retention, may seem quite complex in their verbal expression. Mathematically, however, their algorithm is simplicity itself. It can be expressed in a series of parentheses, each further set representing a retention of a latter set. Thus, in the series, i, (i), ((i)) . . . , each later member can be taken as a retention of the earlier. What allows us to do so is the operational value we give to the parenthesis. This demands that we proceed through the parenthesis, going from the outer to the inner, for all processing operations having to do with "i," the original impression or datum supplied by a traducer. In this way we duplicate the fact that in intentional synthesis the access to expired impressions is *through* the retentions of retentions which preserve them.[40]

The Persistence of the Object

In distinction to the momentary experience, the object has a being which endures through change. Persisting, it exhibits itself as the same in a number of different appearances. This exhibition is, for Kant, the result of a "synthesis of recognition in a concept."[41] A concept is a one in many. Thus, to relate to an object, our representations "must necessarily agree with one another, that is, must possess that unity which constitutes the concept of an object."[42] For Husserl, this means that the recognition of the object requires the grasp of the elements of this agreement. The object is intentionally present as a sense, as a one in many. The grasp of its content thus depends on the recognition of identical elements within the multitude of our distinct impressions.

Such recognition happens more or less automatically. It is the effect of the retentional process which preserves our expired experiences. Since the experiences are not themselves real, spatial temporal objects, their retention does not result in a heap of disparate elements. The effect is rather a "unity of coincidence." This coincidence does not affect their temporal references; each experience remains, in the reference attached to its retention, something encountered at a given point of time. The coincidence does, however, generate the reinforcement of the qualities that are the same. Like a series of overlapping transparencies, the coincidence of what we retain brings about the reinforced appearance of what is the same. As Husserl writes, this occasions "a certain relatedness (*Aufeinanderbezogenheit*) which . . . prior to all 'comparison' and 'thinking' stands as a presupposition for the intuitions of likeness and difference" (*Zur Phänomenologie des inneren Zeitbewusstseins*, Hua X, 44). In the C manuscripts, the same point is expressed in terms of "a continuous merging (*Verschmelzung*)" of like contents occasioned by the retentional process. By virtue of it, the merged qualities "stand out." They reinforce each other and, hence, distinguish themselves from the heterogeneous qualities whose union does not result in their merging.[43]

With this process, we have a certain overlay of simultaneity on succession. The merged experiences retain their successive temporal referents, yet each, in its content, becomes one with others with the same content. The result, then, is the object which presents itself as simultaneously possessing all of the features we successively experience. It is also a further expression of the transcendence that characterizes the intentional relation. An experience becomes an experience *of* a particular object by virtue of the merging of its content. It does not, however, become this object insofar as it keeps its distinct temporal tag. The tag, then, preserves the "manyness" of the the object's appearing. Distinct temporal tags give us the multiplicity in which the object appears as one and the same thing. As for the intentional relation, it is just this many to one relation. The continuous merging which grounds it thus explains the inherent relation between intentionality and meaning. The merging makes our experiences (or "mental states") relate to the object; it also allows the object to present itself as a sense. Thus, by virtue of it, the intentional relation necessarily embodies both "of-ness" and meaning.

Pattern Recognition

The point of this review of the phenomenological account of temporal synthesis is to apply its insights to machine intelligence. To do so is to talk about pattern recognition. Three major difficulties confront a machine when it attempts to grasp a pattern. The first is that of attention focusing. How do you get a machine to attend to a particular item and yet be open to something new? If we divide the visual field into an attended and nonattended part, the latter is precluded from influencing the attended set of data except at some mechanically set level. How, then, do we introduce flexibility into attention?[44] Once we do attend to a part of the visual field, we face the difficulty of discriminating the object from its background. As Pylyshyn notes, if we just use "contrast gradients, light or dark regions, etc.," then "the lines defined in this manner do not correspond to figure boundaries." If we turn to the figure boundaries in actual perception and attempt to capture them through such gradients, such boundaries "more often than not do not produce lines . . ."[45] Sentient animals have, of course, already learned to see. They have a large store of residual knowledge which helps them pick out objects against their backgrounds. One could certainly add such knowledge to a machine in the form of stored patterns and elements of shapes, but the difficulty of using it effectively would still remain. Blind searches and process by elimination are too cumbersome. What we need, in Pylyshyn's words, are systems "designed to facilitate the use of all available knowledge in working towards their goal—including knowledge gained from the analysis of interim failures."[46] The point is to produce systems which "zero in" on their goals.

The main insight that phenomenology can bring to these problems is the thought that pattern recognition cannot be static if it results from synthesis. To say that the "synthesis of recognition" is temporal means that it grasps the features of the object, not in themselves but rather *through their recurrence*. We can put this in terms of the doctrine we began with: Husserl's position that perception is interpretation. Such interpretation always implies anticipation. When, for example, I interpret the shadows I perceive in the bushes as a cat, I anticipate that further perceptions will confirm this interpretation. This means that, rather than attempting at once to distinguish a figure through contrast gradients in my present perception, I move to get a better look. If it is a cat, then a certain pattern of perceptions will unfold itself over time. The recurrent elements of this perception will, I anticipate, become for me the features of the object.

The commonsense interpretation of this is that I always take my perceptions as determined by some object "out there." Because of this, my perceiving is marked by a special, teleological relationship. In this, the whole that I am attempting to grasp—i.e., the whole which, in anticipation, stands as the *telos* or goal of my perceiving—determines the interpretation I place upon my individual perceptions. This shadow is seen as part of the cat's ear. Another is his eye, and so forth. If my interpretations are correct, then the data should form part of an emerging pattern that exhibits these features.

For a machine to imitate this behavior, it must, first of all, process its data according to a series of expanding temporal wholes. The brain scans its data for processing every few seconds, but there is no need to repeat the human interval. We can, for example, choose a single second interval for the machine. The first scan for an emerging pattern would then cover the one second whole of $w1$, the second would cover the whole, $w2(w1)$, for an evaluation of the data of the past two seconds, and the third would examine the three seconds of data accumulated in the whole, $w3(w2(w1))$. The fact, as indicated by the parentheses, that these are wholes within wholes points to the temporal tagging (or "retention") of the data of each sweep. This is required if the machine is to grasp a pattern which involves the recurrence of data in the fixed relations of before and after which characterize the perspectival series.

The strategy, then, for distinguishing an object from its background is to turn this into a temporal process, one which imitates our activity of moving to get a better look. We can duplicate this by making the machine attentive not just to contrast gradients but to their relative rates of change. The same general strategy can be applied to the problem of attention, i.e., of making it flexible. The key here is to note that interpretation is not just anticipation, it is also discrimination. As the machine scans its data, any emergent patterns could be given a reënforcement index number. As the patterns repeat, the numbers would be increased. At any given time, they could be read out as the strength of the machine's objectifying interpretations of what it is seeing. They could also be seen as a discriminatory factor. According to its strength, the machine could be instructed to discriminate against (or set aside) a certain amount of the inharmonious data it is receiving—i.e., the data that does not fit into the patterns it has thus far found. This is, in fact, what we do when we perceive. Generally, we process only the information we anticipate we will receive. Within certain limits, the rest is not attended to. To build this flexible focus into the machine, we could have each whole in which an emergent pattern has established itself throw an anticipatory shadow which would be equal to its length. Thus, the whole, $w3(w2(w1))$, which repeated the same pattern, would establish a discriminating tendency equal to its length. During this time, the data that did not fit in would, according to the strength of the factor, be stored but not processed.

With our limited capacities, we would suffer breakdown if we had to process everything we received. The same holds for any reasonably finite machine. Giving it the ability to discriminate or focus its attention avoids this. It also, however, makes it capable of mistakes. We are often mistaken in our perceptual interpretations. What we took to be a cat dissolves into a collection of shadows when we get a better look. Our capacity for mistakes is, we can say, a function of the teleological temporality of our perceptions. This, as we said, is a temporality in which the *future* (what we anticipate) determines our *present* interpretation of what we have experienced.[47] Because our anticipations can turn out to be ill founded, the interpretations based on them may turn out to be wrong. We are mistaken, but, on the other hand, we are also capable of realizing and rectifying our mistakes. This happens when our discrimination factor starts making us set aside more and more of what we receive as the latter increasingly fails to fit into an anticipated pattern. At a certain point, we snap back and start increasing the amount of data we attend to and process—this, until a new pattern is established.

To give the machine the same flexibility of focus, its discriminatory factor must vary according as the sequence, w1, w2(w1), w3(w2(w1)) . . . , confirms or fails to confirm a pattern. Thus, when a pattern stops being re-enforced through repetition, the discrimination factor should progressively decrease and the machine's acceptance of new data for processing should increase until a new pattern (a new interpretation) is established. With this, we have an answer to the difficulty of getting the machine to attend and yet be open to the new. When a changing context disrupts the patterns it has established, it automatically opens up. Similarly, when a pattern begins to emerge, it "zeros in" on it.

Husserl describes our grasp of an object as "polythetic," that is, as built up from a number of syntheses. Individual syntheses give us the individual features of an object while an overarching synthesis yields the object as the unity of its particular features (*Ideen I*, Hua III/1, 303–4). Insofar as we do attend to a number of objects and grasp their unity through some relation, an even higher level of synthetic activity is possible. Such activities go on in parallel. We simultaneously grasp the different features of an object and, at the same time, attempt to unify them. The insight here may be expressed in contemporary language by saying that the brain is a massively parallel processor. To reduplicate this in a machine it is probably necessary, as Churchland suggests, to give it the architecture of a neural network.[48] In this, different levels of the nodes of the network would correspond to different levels of synthesis, with each individual node performing a particular synthetic function.[48]

Whatever the ultimate architecture, the move from one level to the next would have to involve the retention of the results of the earlier. The temporality of the process would have to be respected, which means that the results must be processed according to the order of their temporal tags. Only then could the basic structure of intentionality be respected. This structure is synthetic; synthesis, as the grasping of unity in multiplicity, is an inherently temporal process. If this is correct, then there is no theoretic difficulty in generating intentional or semantic elements out of the nonintentional. What is required for machines to have the intelligence which implies intentionality is practical work. We have to make them process their information according to the temporality determinative of synthesis. The work consists in expressing the processes of synthesis in the appropriate algorithms.

As the next chapter will show, the result of this synthesis is not just the presence of the object. The temporal departure which occasions the latter also brings about the presence of the self which grasps the object. Both self and object are the outcome of the same law-based synthetic process that results in the intentional relation. As our comparison of Husserl and Sartre makes clear, the question of reason, of its nature and extent, is for Husserl the question of this synthetic process.

8

HUSSERL AND SARTRE: A QUESTION OF REASON

Sartre's first major philosophical work, *The Transcendence of the Ego*, attacks what he assumes to be a major Husserlian theme: the pure ego understood as a synthesizer of the stream of consciousness. Sartre takes his own philosophy as beginning with the demand that such an ego fall to the reduction. Husserl's defenders almost invariably oppose this demand. They argue that the pure ego, because of the functions it fulfills, cannot be reduced. Without an ego, we are left with a "paralyzing" spontaneity. We lose any ground for our "unity and identity" with the result that "our experience and consciousness are rendered irrational."[1] For such defenders, "the dead end of the reduction" must be "the ego," the latter being the irreducible guarantor of the rationality of experience.[2] The debate, thus, seems to be over a question of fact: whether there actually is a pure ego. Yet, for a reader of the last works of Husserl, in particular, the unpublished manuscripts, there is no disagreement between the two philosophers on this point. Spurred on by his studies of passive synthesis and temporal constitution, Husserl, as we have seen, accepts the need to exercise the reduction on the ego. Passing through the ego, he explores the layers of "pre-egological" functioning, a functioning which is constitutively responsible for the ego. The resultant doctrine of the constitution of the ego, which Husserl shares with Sartre, is the occasion for another similarity. Both philosophers agree on the impossibility of grasping oneself qua functioning in any thetic (or objective) manner.

In spite of these agreements, there is a fundamental difference. For Sartre, the result of these positions is that reason cannot be grounded by an appeal to the ego. We cannot say that the world is rational because of the rationality of the ego's syntheses. Along with the ego, this supposed guarantee falls to the reduction. As a result, Sartre, in a long and difficult analysis, attempts to find the source of rationality in the interplay between our freedom and the resistance the world offers to its expression. As we shall see, the rationality that arises is shot through with contingency. Contingent on the circumstances of its practical employment, reason also runs the constant risk of being denied by the freedom which first makes it possible. For Husserl, by contrast, the reduction of the ego does not call reason into question. This is because reason has a pre-egological source. It arises from the rationality of the "passive syntheses" which first make the ego possible. Husserl's final position, then, is that "the world must . . . constitute rational persons within itself. Reason must already exist and must be able to bring itself to a logical [rational] self-disclosure in rational subjects."[3]

This chapter will explore the reasons for this difference. It will show that the opposition between Sartre and Husserl is not, as Sartre believed, over the scope of the reduction, that is, over whether or not it can be exercised on the ego to reveal the pre-egological. It is, rather, over the nature of the pre-egological, over what Sartre calls the *impersonal spontaneity* of consciousness. The disagreement concerns how it functions as a ground of reason. Is such grounding, as Sartre believed, to be found in this spontaneity as it manifests itself in our practical freedom? Is it, rather, as Husserl thought, to be found in the automatic processes of temporal synthesis? As we shall see, this opposition will also appear as a difference regarding intentionality: Is it, along with the ego, to be regarded as a constituted product? In other words, is intentionality, as Husserl believes, to be seen as a result of the processes of temporal synthesis or is it, rather, as Sartre thought, a presupposition for them? Ultimately, the issue concerns what precisely is the "openness" of consciousness.

The first part of this chapter will focus primarily on Sartre. The goal of its analyses will be to set the framework for and then analyze what he means by *reason*. In the sections that follow on Husserl, I will be constantly drawing comparisons between the two philosophers, my goal being to draw the balance between their views on reason.

The Reduction

In *The Transcendence of the Ego*, Sartre begins his attack on Husserl by noting the points of their agreement. He writes: "we readily acknowledge the existence of a constituting consciousness. We find admirable all of Husserl's descriptions in which he shows transcendental consciousness constituting the world by imprisoning itself in empirical consciousness" (*TE*, p. 36).[4] With Husserl, he agrees that this consciousness is "not a set of logical conditions. It is a fact which is absolute. . . . It is a real consciousness [something actually at work, constituting the world], accessible to each of us as soon as the 'reduction' is performed" (*TE*, p. 35). For Sartre, their disagreement comes with regard to the ego's relation to this consciousness. Is the ego that "which in fact unites the representations [the individual experiences of consciousness] to each other?" Or, "is the I that we encounter in our consciousness made possible by the synthetic unity of our representations . . . ?" (*TE*, p. 34). In other words, is it a cause or a result of the syntheses of constituting consciousness? Sartre's answer is unambiguous: "consciousness . . . makes possible the unity and the personality of my I" (*TE*, p. 36). It does this by constituting the ego. As he writes, "the ego is the spontaneous, transcendent unification of our states and our actions" (*TE*, p. 76). This means that "consciousnesses [*Erlebnisse*] are first; through these are constituted states; and then, through the latter, the ego is constituted" (*TE*, p. 81).

The particular modality of such constitution is reflection. Spontaneously, I reflect on my states, e.g., my states of joy, hatred, kindliness, etc. Grasping them together, I assert that I give rise to them. I posit myself as their origin. This positing, according to Sartre, is my ongoing constitution of myself as an ego. As just indicated, this constitution has its layers: "consciousnesses are first," then "states," and then, "the ego." This means that first I reflectively posit my states as the origin of particular consciousnesses, then, through a second reflective act, I posit myself as the origin of the states. To use Sartre's example, my feelings of repugnance, of disgust, when I see Peter are grasped, when I reflect on them, as emanating from a state, that of my hatred of Peter. The occasion of the reflection can be as simple as the question, "Why were you so unpleasant to Peter?"—to which I reply "Because I detest him" (*TE*, p. 67). Here, the state, "hatred, appears through the consciousness of disgust as that from which the latter emanates" (ibid., p. 68). The same process, in a second reflective act, attaches the states to *me*. In Sartre's words, "the unifying act of reflection fastens each new state, in a very special way, to the concrete totality, *me* . . . reflection intends a relation which traverses time backwards and which gives the *me* as the source of the state" (ibid., p. 77). Thus, I am reflectively posited as a source of the state, a source which existed *before* the state was given. This does not mean that I actually exist as such. As Sartre notes, were I to "plunder" the ego of its states and qualities, I would not uncover it pure and simple (as it in "in itself" apart from its effects). Quite the contrary, "at the end of this plundering, nothing would remain; the ego would have vanished" (ibid., p. 78).

The best way to see why this must be so is to recall the relation of constitution to the reduction. Constitution is the action of connecting phenomena and the positing belief in the unity that appears through such connections. It is, we can say, the mostly spontaneous action of founding. The reduction is the self-conscious reversal of this action. When we suspend a positing belief to examine the evidence for it, we engage in the reduction. As we do so, we move from the constituted to the constituting—i.e., from the founded to the founding phenomena. What we do is attempt to look at the evidence of the phenomena through whose connections the founded appears. If these founding phenomena owe their own appearing to the connections occurring between even lower level phenomena, the reduction can be exercised again. We can employ it on such lower level phenomena. We can suspend our belief in their own independent or "original" givenness to uncover the evidence provided by an even more primitive founding layer. Thus, to say that the ego is founded on its "states and actions" is to assert that its appearing presence is that of a unity appearing through their connected multiplicity. Similarly, to assert that each of these states and actions is, in turn, constituted from individual experiences (momentary "consciousnesses" in Sartre's terminology) is to make the same claim in their regard. If the claim is justified, we can engage in the suspension called the *epoché*. We can "suspend" or "restrain" our belief in the unconstituted ("absolute") givenness of the unity in question and turn our attention to the phenomena *through which* it appears. Granting this, the implication for the ego is obvious. Once we admit that it is constituted unity, we also admit, as Sartre says, that it is not "absolute," i.e., irreducibly given. It is not, then, in reality, the "source" of its states. The relation is rather reversed. The states are the source for the ego's givenness insofar as they provide the material for its constitution. This is why, plundered of them, it "vanishes." It is also why, as Sartre says, the ego "falls like other [constituted] existences at the stroke of the ἐποχή" (*TE*, p. 104; see also pp. 36, 78). If it is a constituted unity, then exercising the epoché, we can show its founding layers; i.e., the states, actions, and experiences without which it cannot be given.[5]

For Sartre, this assertion does not just hold for the "psychic and psychophysical me," the "me" that is given in the natural attitude. It also holds for the "pure ego" Husserl claims to uncover in the reduction. This means that the ego that synthesizes, the "transcendental" constituting ego, must also be considered as subject to the reduction. This, Sartre feels, is his point of departure from Husserl. Yet, as we have seen, Husserl also came to feel the necessity for exercising the reduction on the pure ego. He writes, for example, "I must not terminate the reduction in my bracketing of the world and, with this, my spatial-temporal, real human being in the world." I must exercise it "on myself as a transcendental ego and as a transcendental accomplishing, in short, as a transcendental life."[6] As with Sartre, the basis for this demand is the view that the ego (along with its "life") is a constituted unity. In other words, once Husserl admits that "the individual egological life is passively constituted in immanent time," the way is open for him to perform the reduction so as to examine its constituting, "pre-egological" elements.[7]

The Question of the Pre-Egological

For both philosophers, the descent into the pre-egological is a descent into an "absolutely impersonal consciousness" (*TE*, p. 37). For both, this is an absolute, unconditioned origin. Husserl describes it as "the prebeing that bears all being, including even the being of the acts and the being of the ego, indeed, the being of the pretime and the being of the streaming of consciousness [understood] as a being."[8] Sartre writes that "absolute consciousness, when it is purified of the *I*, no longer has anything of the *subject*. It is no longer a collection of representations. It is quite simply a first condition and an absolute source of existence" (*TE*, p. 106).

Their disagreements begin with the consequences of this descent. For Husserl, as we shall see, it is a descent into the origin of rationality. For Sartre, this cannot be the case—this, at least, if we accept what he assumes to be Husserl's view of the ego. In Sartre's interpretation, Husserl takes the Kantian notion of the ego or subject and turns it into an actually functioning reality. So transformed, it is no longer "a set of logical conditions" for the rationality of the world. It is not a "hypostatization of validity" by which we imagine the conditions for the obtaining of synthetic a priori judgments. Rather, the Husserlian ego becomes a presently functioning reality, one whose syntheses give the world its a priori rationality (*TE*, p. 35). If we accept this interpretation, then, from the Husserlian perspective, the suspension of the ego is the suspension of rationality *tout court*. This follows because to say that the "source" of rationality is egological and that it falls to the epoché is to distinguish this source from the pre-egological. It is to distinguish the source from what appears *after* the ego's reduction. It is, thus, to assert that the latter is *not* rational. As we said, the reduction is the move from the constituted to the constituting. It is, in this sense, a move to the source or origin of the constituted. Given that the reduction can be exercised on the ego, taken as a source of rationality, its status as such can be relativized. Both it and the rationality it grounds are not ultimate. What is ultimate is a nonrational, that is, purely spontaneous, source.

Does this mean, as one critic writes, that "through the radicalization of the phenomenological reduction Sartre did not only reduce the ego to consciousness but he also reduced the artificial rationalistic structure of the world and the ego into nothingness"?[9] Do we face here a "radicalization of absurdity"?[10] From a Sartrian point of view, this does not follow. What does follow is that he can no longer avail himself of what he takes to be the Husserlian guarantee of rationality. He cannot assume an ego synthesizing according to pregiven rational rules. What about the consciousness which remains once we suspend the ego? Can we find the guarantee in consciousness considered as an impersonal spontaneity? For Sartre, its very spontaneity stands in the way of its fulfilling this function. If by *spontaneity* we mean an absence of prior determination, then, by definition, the total spontaneity of consciousness seems to exclude any necessary rational determination. In other words, its spontaneity seems the opposite of any notion of rules determining its syntheses, a determination which would translate itself into a pregiven rational order of experience. For Sartre, then, a lack of determination in the syntheses of "absolute consciousness" is implicit in its notion as "a first condition and absolute cause or source of existence" (*TE*, p. 106). As first, nothing can determine absolute consciousness, but such lack of determination is precisely its pure spontaneity. As first, it is, therefore, "an impersonal spontaneity," one which "determines its existence at each instant, without our being able to conceive anything *before* it" (*ibid.*, p. 98). As Sartre was later to write, "consciousness, such as we have defined it, is never anything before existing, . . . there is no law of consciousness, but rather a consciousness of law . . ."[11] Such laws, in other words, exist, not as a source, but only as an object of the ultimate consciousness.

It is easy to see why, for readers of *The Transcendence of the Ego*, such statements lead to what may be called the *irrationalism* of existentialism. The work seems at times close to adopting an idealistic position. Not only does consciousness seem to be an ultimate origin of the *me*, it also seems to be the source of the world in which the *me* finds itself. Sartre writes, "The World has not created the *me*; the *me* has not created the World. These are two objects for absolute, impersonal consciousness; it is by virtue of this consciousness that they are connected" (*TE*, pp. 105–6). The suspicion that to be an object of this consciousness is to be creatively constituted by it is reinforced by Sartre's adding that "purified of the *I*," consciousness "is no longer a collection of representations. It is quite simply a first condition and an absolute source of existence" (*ibid.*, p. 106). Here we seem to assert the existence of the experiences of consciousness *prior* to their being representations—i.e., presentations, within a given subject, of some given object. We are, thus, reminded of William James's "world of pure experiences." For James, experiences, through their connections, are what first give rise to the subject-object dichotomy, a dichotomy which then allows us to take these experiences as subjective representations of already existing objects.[12] In such a view, consciousness becomes a first condition of existence through the connections that allow the positing of existent objects. Now, were this Sartre's position, two conclusions would follow. First, he would have to be seen as embracing a constitutive idealism. At its basis would be an absolute consciousness conceived not just as *a* "source of existence," but also as its necessary and *sufficient* "first condition." Second, the spontaneity of this condition would mean that the existence thus generated would have no basis for its rationality. The stable ordering of our experience that allows us to anticipate, to draw inferences, and generally to make use of reason in dealing with the world would be without foundation. It would be simply a fact, one, however, that would seem to be a miracle given the spontaneity at the basis of our experience. For a reader of this early work of Sartre, the question of the pre-egological is, then: "How can we understand it without forcing it into the inappropriate mode of a constitutive idealism?"

The Extension of the Pre-Egological

The "Introduction" to *Being and Nothingness* stands as a kind permanent defense against the interpretation of our last section. It answers its question by, in the first instance, continuing the attack on Husserl. Having, in the earlier work, freed himself from what he considers Husserl's erroneous concept of the ego, Sartre now distances himself from what he takes to be Husserl's constitutive idealism. Husserl, he writes, "defines consciousness precisely as a transcendence. . . . This is his essential discovery. But from the moment that he makes of the *noema* an *unreal*, a correlate *of* the *noesis*, a noema whose *esse* is *percipi*, he is totally unfaithful to his principle" (*BN*, p. 23).[13] The accusation here is that Husserl is engaged in a kind of Berkeleyan idealism, one that asserts that the *being* of the noema (or object of consciousness) is its *being perceived*. As is obvious, this view makes the noema something "unreal." It has its being, not in itself, but only as a correlate of a noesis or act of consciousness. The consciousness that grasps it does not ontologically transcend its own acts. It is not really consciousness *of* an object that transcends its being. Yet, this for Sartre is what it means to say that consciousness is intentional. Husserl, thus, misunderstands the "essential character" of intentionality when "he makes of the *noema* an *unreal*" (ibid.). In fact, he misunderstands the being of consciousness. For Sartre, "To say that consciousness is consciousness of something means that for consciousness there is no being outside of that precise obligation to be a revealing intuition of something—i.e., of a transcendent being" (ibid.). Intentionality means, in other words, "that transcendence is the constitutive structure of consciousness; that consciousness is born *supported* by a being which is not itself" (ibid.). If we grant this, then we also grant that consciousness in its very being implies a "nonconscious" being. It cannot exist without the latter. As such, it "is powerless to constitute the objective" in any Husserlian sense (*BN*, p. 24).

Whether or not this attack on Husserl is justified is beyond the scope of this chapter to judge. The issue of Husserl's idealism, of its precise nature and limits, is one of the thorniest in Husserl studies.[14] Our own purposes are satisfied by noting its effect on the notion of the pre-egological. For Sartre, the "ontological proof" we just sketched out for the existence of nonconscious or transcendent being implies that the pre-egological cannot be conceived in idealistic terms. It must, in other words, include what consciousness cannot constitute, i.e., the being which is not consciousness. Thus, the impersonal spontaneity of the absolute consciousness must be thought of in its relation to this "nonconscious" being. It must be conceived in terms of its openness to it.

In point of fact, two new categories appear. Absolute consciousness is now seen as the "For-itself," while the being which transcends it, the being which it cannot constitute, occupies the category of the "In-itself." The *For* of the *For-itself* expresses the inner distance (or nonidentity) required by the intentional relationship. To say that consciousness is consciousness *of* something is not to say that it *is* that thing. Intentionality, insofar as it implies transcendence, is an "openness to," rather than identity. This holds even when we speak of self-awareness, i.e., of the fact that consciousness is always conscious of itself, that even before any explicitly reflexive act, it is always present to itself. In Sartre's words, "*presence to* always implies duality. . . . If being is present to itself, it is because it is *not* wholly itself. Presence is an immediate deterioration of coincidence, for it supposes separation" (*BN*, second italics added, p. 124). Given that consciousness, to be consciousness, must be self-aware, such separation must also characterize it. The intentionality which defines the being of consciousness can thus be viewed as implying a self-separation (a "nothingness") at the heart of this being. To quote Sartre again, "The being of consciousness qua consciousness is to exist *at a distance from itself* as presence to itself, and this empty distance which being carries in its being is Nothingness. Thus, in order for a *self* to exist, it is necessary that the unity of this being include its own nothingness as the nihilation of identity" (*BN*, p. 125). With this, we have the new category of the For-itself. As Sartre paradoxically expresses it, "The For-itself is the being which determines itself to exist inasmuch as it cannot coincide with itself" (ibid., pp. 125–26). It is, as it were, being in its continual self-separation, being in its continuous deterioration of identity.

As for being-in-itself, it is simply the polar opposite of this. The In-itself has no gaps. Nothingness is entirely excluded from it. We cannot say that it is active or passive because such concepts involve the differentiation of agent and patient and, with this, the implicit assertion that one is *not* the other. It lacks even the differentiation that would allow us to speak of it as a self-affirmation. The "undifferentiation of the In-itself is beyond [this]." Faced with the Parmenidean quality of its sheer identity, the only thing we can say about it is that "being is itself" (*BN*, pp. 27–28).

Nothingness and Freedom

What breaks up this identity is the For-itself. In an analysis which mirrors elements from both James and Heidegger, Sartre employs the themes of nothingness, freedom, and finitude to describe how we differentiate the In-itself into an articulated whole. We have just seen how nothingness is required for intentionality and presence to self, i.e., for the two features which give consciousness the ontological character of a For-itself. The same nothingness is next positioned as the ground of freedom. The possibility of freedom, he asserts, is that of withdrawal, of detachment. He writes, "For man to put a particular existent out of circuit is to put himself out of circuit in relation to the existent. In this case he is not subject to it; he is out of reach; it cannot act on him, for he has retired *beyond a nothingness*. Descartes, following the Stoics, has given a name to this possibility, which human reality has, to secrete a nothingness which isolates it—it is *freedom*" (*BN*, p. 60) We "secrete" this nothingness every time we reflect upon ourselves, every time we "step back" from ourselves and grasp our relation to some existent. The fact that intentionality is not identity signifies that the reflecting consciousness is not the consciousness reflected upon. This nonidentity is the possibility of our withdrawal, of our detaching or *freeing* ourselves from the self we reflexively grasp. Because of this, it is a withdrawal from the conditions determining the latter. This detachment is a possibility implicitly present in our prereflexive self-awareness. As such, it is a possibility grounded in our very being as a For-itself, i.e., as a mode of being which is a continuous decomposition of the identity of the In-itself. For Sartre, then, "Human reality can detach itself from the world—in questioning, in systematic doubt, in sceptical doubt, in the epoché, etc.—only if, by nature, it has the possibility of self detachment" (*BN*, p. 60). The possibility of this detachment is the same as that of its freedom, which is the same as that of its self-presence or consciousness. Given this, it follows that "what we call freedom is impossible to distinguish from the *being* of 'human reality.' . . . there is no difference between the being of man and his *being-free*" (ibid.).

Sartre asserts that through freedom "nothingness comes into the world" (ibid.). Freedom is the channel between the nothingness within the For-itself and the nothingness which distinguishes the world of the In-itself into an articulated whole. It does this, not directly, but through a whole series of conducts (questioning, imagining, seeking causes, etc.) which it grounds. As Sartre describes the first conduct: "Every question presupposes a being who questions and a being which is questioned. . . . I expect a reply from the being questioned. . . . The reply will be a 'yes' or a 'no.'" This means that to pose a question, I must grasp the world in terms of "two equally objective and contradictory possibilities" (*BN*, p. 35). This, in turn, requires that the world free itself from presenting itself in just one way. It must allow an alternative, one that *negates* the way it is now presenting itself. Suppose, for example, I ask the mechanic if my car is ready. Questioning, I envisage two possibilities: one, a world in which my car is ready, where I pay the mechanic and drive away to continue my business (I return to work, go shopping, etc.), the other, a world where I continue to wait. Not only the world is different, I am different. Questioning, I face the possibility of the "not," of the negation of one of the alternatives by the other. As Sartre describes this: "negation is a refusal of existence. By means of it a being (or a way of being) is posited, then thrown back to nothingness" (*BN*, p. 43). As is obvious, to question, I must imagine. I must step out of my given world—the world, e.g., in which I wait for the mechanic—and conceive of an alternative. To imagine, I must detach myself, but to do this, I must be free. My freedom thus expresses itself in an action (that of imagining) whose result embodies the very separation which is at its core. The result of the action of imagination is the *image*. As expressing its origin, "the image must enclose in its very structure a nihilating thesis." Actually, Sartre adds, "it carries within it a double negation;

first, it is the nihilation of the world (since the world is not offering the imagined object as an actual object of perception), secondly, the nihilation of the object of the image (it is posited as not actual) . . ." (*BN*, p. 62). The same sort of negations are implicit when we ask why something is one way rather than another. To be able to raise this question, we must believe that things have a cause, that "nothing is without its reason" as Leibniz expresses it. But to be able to entertain such a thought, we must be able to imagine alternatives. Thus, to ask why something is this way is to implicitly assume that it could be otherwise. Indeed, it is the assumption that it is not necessary, but rather could be otherwise, which first raises the question of a cause, of the circumstances upon which its present being is dependent. The assumption, however, is dependent on a double negation: first, the negation involved in imagining the alternatives (which as imagined are taken as not real); second, the negation involved in ranging the being of the thing questioned among such alternatives. Here we take its existence as non-necessary, i.e., as simply one more imagined possibility which may, given a change in circumstances, *not* obtain. As before, the ground of this process is our freedom, it is the very self-detachment (the "nothingness") by virtue of which we are.[15] Expressing itself through the various forms of conduct it makes possible, this nihilating detachment introduces the negativities of "distance, . . . absence, change, otherness, repulsion, regret, distraction, etc." into the In-itself (*BN*, p. 55). It thus introduces the distinctions (the assertions that one thing is *not* another) which makes possible the breakup of the sheer self-identity of the In-itself.

Finitude and Embodiment

To complete this sketch of the articulation of being, we must bring in the theme of human finitude. Such finitude is actually implicit in the account of freedom. A nonfinite being cannot detach itself, cannot separate itself from a given position. By definition, its infinity implies its *occupation of all positions*, the actualization of all possibilities, all the alternatives, that confront the For-itself. An infinite For-itself thus collapses into an In-itself. It becomes an immobile identity in the sense of having no place to move. For freedom to arise, then, the For-itself must be confronted with alternatives, alternatives that present it with real choices, with possibilities which it may or *may not* realize. For this, however, finitude is required. In Sartre's words, "my finitude is the condition of my freedom, for there is no freedom without choice" (*BN*, p. 432). This demand for finitude is actually a demand for embodiment. My body is the concrete expression of my finitude. Limited as I am in my bodily being to one place at one time, whenever I engage in one action, I forgo its alternatives. I cannot travel north and south at the same time. I cannot stay at home and go out to meet Peter. The same cause prevents me from simultaneously engaging in any number of life courses. In each case, my "body is precisely the necessity that *there be a choice*, that I do not exist *all at once*" (ibid.).

Sartre thus presents us with a line of implication that begins with consciousness and ends in embodiment. The self-presence of consciousness implies the self-separation, which implies the freedom, which implies the noninfinity—i.e, the finitude—which implies the embodiment of consciousness. Given this, embodiment is not something that happens to consciousness, under the pattern, say, of a soul being thrust at birth into a body. It is rather part of its notion. In Sartre's words, "the body conditions consciousness as pure consciousness of the world, it renders consciousness possible in its very freedom" (ibid.). This means, as Sartre rather strikingly puts it, the body is "our original relation to the world—that is, our very upsurge in the midst of being" (*BN*, p. 428). It is such because it is through the body that consciousness engages in the original conduct that differentiates the world. At the basis of its questioning, doubting, or imagining alternatives to the world is the conduct of its finite, embodied freedom.

Before we describe the rationality that results from this, two further implications in this chain must be noted. The first is contingency. My body, as the concrete embodiment of my finitude, is by definition contingent. To take the simplest example, its being in space is its being in a system of possible positions. Its finitude is expressed in the fact that only one of these can be occupied at a single time. The body's contingency finds expression in the one occupied, i.e., in the sense of its being just *one* possible position, in the sense, in other words, of its being a position in an *available* space. The same sort of analysis can be carried on with regard to all the features that make up our embodiment. The very positionality, taken in a broad sense, of such embodiment implies contingency. Sartre expresses this with his typical flair: "Birth, the past, contingency, the necessity of a point of view, the factual condition for all possible action of the world—such is the *body*, such it is *for me*. . . . From this point of view we must recognize both that it is altogether contingent and absurd that I am a cripple, the son of a civil servant or of a laborer, irritable and lazy, and that it is nevertheless *necessary* that I be *that* or else something else, French or German or English, etc. . . ." (*BN*, pp. 431–32). The necessity springs from my finitude. Because I cannot be all, I must be one; and the one that I am, since it does not embrace all, is contingent. It is something that could have fallen out otherwise. The second implication that follows from our embodiment is that of having a point of view. As we just cited Sartre, "the necessity of a point of view . . . is the body . . ." We can, in fact, "define the body as a contingent point of view on the world" (*BN*, p. 433). Such a body, of course, embodies consciousness. As implying the body with its contingent situatedness, consciousness itself must be understood as contingently situated. We cannot, then, think of it as a set of pure experiences that is somehow prior to subjects and objects.

More particularly, we cannot think of it as a sort of prepersonal pan psyche which, as prior to subjects, is the same for each of them. Individualized by the circumstances which compose its embodiment, the nothingness it engenders is itself individual. As Hazel Barnes, Sartre's translator, puts this, "consciousnesses are particular since they appear at a definite time and place, thus nihilating being from a particular point of view."[16] The world they reveal in articulating the In-itself is thus, itself, contingent. Its contingency follows from the contingency of its conditions. It follows from the body, understood as the whole set of contingent conditions which individualize consciousness. Sartre thus can write, "My birth . . . my race . . . my nationality . . . my physiological structure . . . my character . . . my past, as everything I have experienced . . . all this . . . is *my body* as the necessary condition of the existence of the world and as a *contingent realization of this condition*" (*BN*, p. 432, second italics added).

Sartrean Reason: The Project

With this, we come to the point of the preceding analyses; namely, to pose the question of reason. What is the character of reason in this world that Sartre has so carefully constructed? An initial view shows it as manifesting a blend of necessity and contingency. Necessity enters in as a feature of the transcendent character of being. If being transcends me, so does its appearing. As Sartre writes in this regard, "The reality of that cup is that it is there and is not me. We shall interpret this by saying that the series of its appearances is bound by a principle which does not depend on my whim" (*BN*, p. 5). This principle is the meaning—the Husserlian "noematic sense"—of the object. It is what appears *through* the series of appearances. From a phenomenological perspective, the object manifests its transcendence in the indeterminate number of its possible appearances. In other words, it transcends our actual, finite experience of it through its ability to continuously offer yet further experience. Turning the cup, I can indefinitely continue to view it first from one side, and then another. To claim that the cup, as transcendent, does not depend upon my whim is thus to claim that the indefinite series it affords me is ordered by a principle equally independent. I transcend my actual (finite) experience and grasp the cup itself when I grasp the transcendent principle ordering this series. In Sartre's words, "If the phenomenon is to reveal itself as transcendent, it is necessary that the subject himself transcend the appearance toward the total series of which it is a member. He must seize Red through his impression of red. By Red is meant the principle of the series . . . the object shows itself as the structure of the [individual] appearance which is at the same time the principle of the series" (*BN*, p. 6). This structure of the individual appearance is the *principle uniting it* to the other appearances in the series; it is the sense of the unitary object which they manifest. Sartre also calls it the *essence* of the object: "The essence is not *in* the object; it is the meaning of the object, the principle of the series of appearances which disclose it." (*BN*, p. 8). Now, to say that such an essence does not depend on our whim is to say that perception has a rational structure. The ongoing series which make up our perceptual experience are ordered by principles, principles that manifest themselves in the structure of the appearances, what Husserl would call the "rules" governing the pattern of their appearing. With such rules, we thus seem to have an inherent logic of experience, one that provides the basis for our use of reason.

This, of course, is not the whole story. As indicated by our last section, the actual employment of reason by an embodied self is shot through with contingency. Over against the few pages devoted to the notion of the principle of the series, dozens are spent describing the radical contingency of my embodiment. As we cited Sartre, the body is my "contingent point of view on the world." It is my "upsurge in the midst of being" that, however "contingent and absurd," sets the starting point for the use of reason. How can these two themes of necessity and contingency be combined?

For Sartre, the point of their combination is the *project*, the practical activity that seeks to attain some contingent goal. The logic of experience does not present itself to me as an abstract necessity. It is rather revealed to me by my practical projects. In other words, objects, with their necessary essences, reveal themselves to me as means for the accomplishment of my contingently given goals. Thus, in hanging a picture, a nail appears as that-which-is-to-be-hammered-into-the wall. Similarly, the hammer is that-which-is-to-be-struck-against-the-nail. All of these projects come from me. They are the ways in which I try to shape the world according to my purposes. Strictly speaking, these purposes or goals are not something real when they are conceived. Temporally, they express the "not yet," i.e., a future possibility which I have determined to realize. Such possibilities, Sartre emphasizes, are *my* possibilities. In my action of hanging a picture, I realize the possibility of *myself* having this picture on the wall. Similarly, in making an appointment—say, calling Peter, arranging times and places, marking them in the calendar, traveling to the location, and so on—I realize the possibility of *myself* being there with Peter. When I do, a whole host of instruments—telephone, calendar, map, car, and clock—achieve their sense as materials that are necessary for my purpose. Given that our primary way of being in the world is practical, the same point holds for it in general. The world with its essences reveals itself through our projects. The world, in other words, appears as the correlate of the possibilities we realize; it appears as the correlate of *our* possibilities. In Sartre's formulation, "the world as the correlate of the possibilities which I *am* appears from the moment of my upsurge as the enormous skeletal outline of all my possible actions. Perception is naturally surpassed towards action; better yet, it can be revealed only in and through projects of action " (*BN*, p. 425). The project, in other words, determines ("reveals") the perceptual quality of the world.

Sartre's position is, here, strikingly similar to that of William James's pragmatic approach to reason. For James, the cardinal fact is: "My thinking is first and last and always for the sake of my doing, and I can only do one thing at a time."[17] What I actually do determines my thinking about what a particular object is. The paper, for example, appears to me not as "combustible, rectangular, and the like." It is rather "what you write upon." But it is this only because I employ it this way for my particular purpose.[18] As James expresses the general point, "The essence of a thing is that one of its properties which is so *important for my interests* that in comparison with it I may neglect the rest."[19] The essence, in other words, is its instrumental character; it is its function as a *means* for the accomplishment of my projects. The same holds for all the particular properties of the object. They appear only as correlates of the projects that reveal them. In fact, only in terms of such projects does the world appear at all; that is, as articulated into objects with given properties. Per se, "every reality has an infinity of aspects or properties."[20] It is simply undifferentiated—what Sartre would call an element of the "In-itself"—before my purposes inform it. Once they do, however, the properties of interest to me, i.e., which can serve as the means or instruments for my purpose, immediately stand out.

The same sort of pragmatism lies behind Sartre's assertion that properties are the "correlates of the non-thetic projects which we are, but are revealed only as structures of the world: potentialities, absences, instrumentalities" (*BN*, p. 425). Engaging in my projects, things show their potential to help me reach my goals; they are either present or absent as means (instrumentalities) for my purposes. As is obvious, what we are describing is the concrete process by which we articulate being in itself—in James's terms, differentiate the "infinity of aspects or properties" of the realities about us. The process is the opposite of the creative idealism Sartre attributes to Husserl. As Sartre sums up his position, "Thus, the world appears to me as objectively articulated; it never refers to a creative subjectivity but to an infinity of instrumental complexes" (*BN*, p. 425). Such instrumental complexes—a hammer for the nails, nails for the board, the board for the shelf to be erected—are not the creative constitutive product of some disengaged "pure" subjectivity. They are rather the result of our "being-in-the-midst-of-the-world." In Sartre's terms, I am in the midst of the world "because I have caused the world to-be-there . . ." I have caused it to-be-there "because I have caused instruments in general to-be-there by the projection of myself towards my possibilities" (*BN*, p. 429).

Hodological Space

The world that results from this "practical and active" determination has a certain ordered character. Just as an overall project involves a number of subsidiary projects, each of which may, in turn, require further projects for its realization, so we find a corresponding hierarchy of means. Thus, to get to the store, I must drive; to get to the car, I must descend the stairs. To drive, I require a car, but to use it, I must take my keys. I must also be careful to fill the car with gas so that it will not run out. This, however, requires cash and a stop at the filling station. If I am out of cash, I must first stop at the bank and use my teller card. This use, however, first requires that I have applied for one. As is obvious, were I so minded, this description could continue until I have exhausted the instrumental complexes by which I make my way (sketch out my paths) in my world. The order of these complexes is, in fact, "the practical organization of existents into a *world*." Within it, "each instrument refers to other instruments, to those which are its *keys* and to those for which it is the *key*" (*BN*, p. 424). The "paths" connecting these determine the "hodological space" (from the Greek *hodos* for path) that characterizes this world. Thus, just as the "place" of an object is here "not defined by pure spatial coordinates, but in relation to axes of practical reference," so such axes give me my space. In Sartre's words, "The space which is originally revealed to me is hodological space; it is furrowed with paths and highways; it is instrumental and is the *location* of tools" (ibid.).

The center of this network is, of course, myself: "while each instrument refers to another instrument and this to another, all end up by indicating an instrument which stands as the *key* for all" (*BN*, p. 425). I am, in my bodily being, their necessary "center of reference," the place where all these paths meet (ibid.). Thus, "the nail refers to the hammer and the hammer refers to the hand and the arm which utilizes it" (ibid., p. 426). Yet the hand and the arm are not just another instrument. I don't just use them. I am them. Thus, in writing, "I use my hand in order to hold the pen. I am not in relation to my hand in the same utilizing attitude as I am in relation to the pen; I *am* my hand" (ibid.). Am I, then, an instrument or am I not? There is here a certain paradox. The Jamesian pragmatics we have adopted implies that a thing can appear as only a means or instrument. Being in the world, in the sense of being present, is to be such. Hence, on the one hand, as Sartre writes, "the structure of the world implies that we can insert ourselves into the field of instrumentality only by being ourselves an instrument" (*BN*, p. 426). On the other, however, I cannot be myself an instrument if I am to be the key to them all, concretely, if I am to determine what is to count as an instrument. Here I have to say that the "instrumental complex can be revealed only by the determination of a cardinal meaning of this complex," that of myself in my bodily being. Such being is not the means, the instrument, for the accomplishing of some project. My bodily being is, insofar as it is what I am, the project itself. I am, in my possibilities, the goal of every action. Given this, my bodily being can be revealed only by its revelations, i.e., by the hodological space created by its projects. In Sartre's words, "We do not use this instrument, for we *are* it. It is given to us in no other way than by the instrumental order of the world, by the hodological space, by the univocal or reciprocal relations of machines, but it cannot be *given* to my action" (*BN*, p. 427). What can be given, in the sense being revealed by my action, are the means, the instruments it employs. My bodily being, however, is not the means but rather the action (the project) itself. It therefore appears, not as an object in the space it defines, but rather as its condition. It is both a central point of reference and an absence, a hole in its fabric. As Sartre also puts this, "The body is *lived* and not *known*" insofar as it is "*given concretely* as the very arrangement of things" (ibid.). This paradox of the body insofar as it is an instrument and yet not one, both inserted into and yet absent from the world is, we may note, the paradox of consciousness itself. Functioning, the body lives but does not objectively know itself. Functioning, it is objectively absent to itself. The same holds, as we shall see, for consciousness itself. The set of implications from self-presence to freedom to embodied finitude by which Sartre has expanded his notion of consciousness does not alter this paradox. It has simply occasioned its statement in terms of its bodily being.

With the description of the space set up by our projects, we have reached our goal of characterizing Sartrean reason. This is because the structure of this space is that of reason. Reason, here, is primarily practical and active. "My thinking," as we cited James, "is first and last and always for the sake of my doing . . ." Admitting this, the structures set up by such doing—the paths of hodological space—give us the structures of thinking or reason. They are, as it were, its concrete embodiment. Accordingly, we can define rational conduct as the behavior that recognizes these "paths and highways" and proceeds *through* them. When I try to proceed crosswise—for example, by attempting to get money from the machine without my teller card—I do not just act irrationally. I also encounter a "coefficient of adversity." This resistance points out that what is articulated by this space is the transcendence of being-in-itself. Not that I encounter such transcendence directly. It is always mediated by particular instruments. In Sartre's words, "instrumentality is primary: it is in relation to the original instrumental complex that things reveal their resistance and their adversity. The bolt is revealed as too big to be screwed into the nut, the pedestal too fragile to support the weight which I want to hold up, the stone too heavy to be lifted up to the top of the wall, etc." (*BN*, p. 428). Recognizing this, I recognize the necessity, the transcendence of the In-itself. Although it is only articulated through my projects, it is nonetheless real. I act irrationally when I do not take account of it, when I ignore or deny the instrumentalities that organize it. Reason, by contrast, is their acknowledgment. As Barnes describes Sartre's position: "Reason . . . always takes this organized world into consideration, for by definition knowledge is the one real bridge between the For-itself and the In-itself." Reason, in other words, "is consciousness' perception of those organizations and relations which the brute universe is capable of sustaining."[21]

The Contingency of Pragmatic Reason

Does this mean that "Sartre's philosophy," as Barnes asserts, "is a philosophy of reason"?[22] Have we actually overcome the irrationality which in the *Transcendence of the Ego* seemed to appear as a consequence of the sheer spontaneity of the Absolute? To answer this, we must first take note of the infectious quality—the virulence, as it were—of the contingency which I am as "a point of view on the world." My projects are determined by the circumstances of my birth, my race, my nationality, my physiological structure, my character, my past, etc. All these, as we cited Sartre, are my body. Yet, all are contingent. Given that my body, the instrumental "key" to all other instruments, is contingent, contingency attaches to all the particulars of the hodological space that these instruments organize. We thus have a chain of contingency stretching from my bodily being to my projects to what these project reveal; that is, entities as the means (the instruments) for their accomplishment.

The same point can be made with regard to the essence taken as the principle of a perceptual series. The grasp of this principle depends, by definition, on what we perceive. But this is a function of the use we make of the object. Very different perceptual experiences are given by paper if we burn it or write on it. One usage hides another. The burnt paper can no longer be written upon. Yet as obvious, my finitude demands that only one use at a time is possible for me. This point may be put in terms of James's assertion that "every reality has an infinity of aspects or properties." As we cited him, its essence is just that property which is "important for my interests." The essence, thus, depends upon my interest. But this interest conceals as it reveals the reality because it is always finite. As James writes, in "classing it under one aspect or another, I am always unjust, always partial, always exclusive. My excuse is necessity—the necessity which my finite and practical nature lays upon me." The necessity, in other words, is that while "my thinking is . . . for the sake of my doing, I can only do one thing at a time."[23] If we accept this, then the essences we do discover in the world become relativized. They become correlates to our projects or "interests." Admitting this, we must also accept, as James asserts, "there is no one quality genuinely, absolutely, and exclusively essential to anything."[24] Sartre's adoption of his pragmatic account of reason must have a similar effect. It cannot but undermine his original assertion of an objective essence, i.e., of an objective "principle of the series," independent of "my whim." Such a perceptual series does depend upon me since only because of my interest would I ever run through it. The contingency of the series is, then, the contingency of its principle. It is its being contingent on my projects.

It, thus, seems that the sheer spontaneity of the earlier work has not disappeared but only changed its place. More precisely, what has changed is not the spontaneity but the notion of the "absolute consciousness" which manifests it. This now includes embodiment and finitude. As a result, its spontaneity appears under the guise of the contingency, the "absurdity" (the irrationality) of the facts of birth, physical state, race, etc. Borrowing a term from Heidegger, we seem to be simply thrown into the world which manifests these facts. Our "thrownness" (*Geworfenheit*) appears in the contingency of our embodiment, in our being "there" in one situation rather than another. It appears as well in the instrumental complexes which we happen to inherit. The inherited hodological spaces, say, of Paris and a remote Andean village, are as much features of our thrownness as the facts of our birth, race, or physical condition. Both Paris and the village exhibit a rationality, a set of paths connecting their respective sets of instruments. That this rationality is contingent, i.e., takes its origin from contingently given circumstances, does not lessen its necessity for those who live within it. It does however localize it. In so doing, it points out that the world exhibits only the rationality that men and women put into it. Insofar as the contingency of a specific, by and large inherited situation determines this "reason," we can say that the beginning, the choice of projects, is irrational, though the end, the particular hodological space, is not.

This, of course, presupposes that the projects we engage in have some coherent unified structure. Whether they do depends, we can say, on our ultimate project, the project into which all others are more or less integrated. For Sartre, this project is that of achieving selfhood. I achieve it both by projecting myself towards my possibilities and by determining my essence through actions realizing such possibilities. This project of selfhood is inherent in his definition of man. Man, for Sartre, is the being who is what he is not, and who is not what he is (*BN*, p. 112). Separated from myself by the inner distance which allows me to be a self, I am *not* what I am. This "not" is, indeed, what makes me a For-itself rather than an In-itself. Given this, I can "be" only as what I am not, i.e., as a goal which I am not yet. Otherwise put, I can be only as projected toward those goals or possibilities which I actualize through my projects. Now, if my ultimate project is irrational, that is, if it involves some fundamental contradiction, its irrationality must affect all the projects and, hence, the instrumentalities and the paths of the hodological space it orders. They must, in some sense, share its contradiction.

To see what this might be, we need only ask what it would mean to achieve selfhood—i.e., determine our essence by realizing our possibilities. A fully determined self with a fully specified essence would, it seems, manifest the determinate features of an In-itself. It would appear as fixed in its given qualities. Were it to achieve its end, it would thus collapse as a For-itself. It would lose the inner distance which first allowed it to have the project of selfhood. The contradiction, then, is between it and its goal. The For-itself seeks to be an In-itself and yet remain a self. It seeks to fix itself without giving up the inner distance which is its freedom. That the For-itself can never succeed in being an In-itself has an important implication: The Sartrean subject that engages in world-constitution is not and can never be a unity. This, however, means that its divided being as a For-itself continually threatens the unity of its action and hence the unity of the rational, hodological space such action constructs. As a For-itself, it can always distance itself from the self which has engaged in such construction. It can abandon its projects or turn them in a different direction. Granting this, we have to say that the rationality that arises as it marks out the paths of its space, the rationality of the particular hierarchy of instruments required for its projects, does not just have a contingent beginning, a starting point marked out by the contingencies of birth, race, nationality, and so forth. It is continually contingent. The rationality of our world always faces the risk of the divided selves which constructed it, turning and radically transforming it. The result, then, is the contingency of all its self-proclaimed necessities. Such contingency is rooted in the freedom of the selves which construct it. But this is their inability to be determined or fixed. The contingency is, thus, just another appearance of the absolute in its spontaneity. If Sartre's philosophy is a "philosophy of reason," it is one of a reason continually undermined by the freedom inherent in its pragmatic basis.

The Ego as a Form

The basis for "reason" in the Husserlian sense lies beyond all such pragmatics, beyond all the actions and choices of the practically engaged self. Its origin is, in fact, the process that makes the self possible. To see this, we must first note the nature of his concept of a self or ego.

Reading Husserl's texts, we are confronted by a remarkable, if deceptive similarity. Both Husserl and Sartre agree on the relativity of the ego. Sartre's consciousness is individualized by the particular circumstances it finds itself in. The ego it constitutes is, thus, relative to them. For Husserl, the ego appears in its full concreteness only insofar as it is a correlate of a given world. In his words, "The ego is only possible as a subject of an 'environment,' only possible as a subject who has facing it things, objects, especially temporal objects, realities in the widest sense . . ."[25] This means that, for Husserl as for Sartre, the ego's identity is tied to that of its world. As Husserl expresses this, "The assertion that I remain who I am as the same transcendental ego—as the same personal ego—is equivalent to the assertion that my world remains a world."[26] Both the ego and the world are, thus, relative to each other. For Husserl, however, both are dependent on a deeper structure. The dependence of the ego is not, for him, a Sartrean dependence on the In-itself as it is articulated into the hodological space of an inherited, contingently given world. It is, rather, a dependence on the stream of consciousness taken as ultimately constituting.

The ego, Husserl asserts, is a numerical (individual) singular by virtue of its relation to this stream.[27] It is, in fact, "constituted as a unity with reference to this stream unity."[28] The same unitary stream is, in fact, seen as grounding both the ego and its world.

Before we discuss the ego's grounding, we must, of course, clarify how Husserl understands it. What is the "pure" or "transcendental ego" for him? One of its best descriptions comes from the first volume of the *Ideas*, where it is proposed. The ego, he asserts, is not the changing acts (the *cogitata*) of consciousness. It is, rather, something self-identical, something which, in its self-identity, must be distinguished from the real, changing contents of consciousness. In his words, "The ego seems to be constantly, necessarily there . . . its 'glance' goes 'through' every actual cogito to the objectivity. This ray of the glance (*Blickstrahl*) is something that changes with each cogito, shooting forth anew with the new cogito, disappearing with it. The ego, however, is something identical. Every cogito, at least in principle, can change, can come and go. . . . But, as opposed to this, the pure ego seems to be *something necessary* in principle. As something absolutely identical in all actual and possible change of experiences, it cannot *in any sense* be taken as a real component or moment of the experiences."[29] There is an important implication here. If the ego is actually distinct from the experiences, it is distinct as well from their content. But this means it has no "material content" of its own. "It is," Husserl says, "quite empty of such."[30] This emptiness does not mean that it is nothing. Lacking "a material, specific essence," it is rather simply "an empty form which is only 'individualized' through the stream: this, in the sense of its uniqueness."[31] The ego, in other words, is a structure or form of experience, one individualized—made unique—by the particular contents of a particular experiential stream. Given this, we can see how Husserl can assert what seems on the surface to be two opposing doctrines. We can see how he can maintain, as he does in the *Cartesian Meditations*, (1) that the "transcendental ego [is] inseparable from the processes making up its life" (that it "is what it is solely in relation to intentional objectivities" and is, in fact, "only concrete" in relation to them), all the while affirming (2) the identity and purity of this ego.[32] The purity in question is a purity *from* the changing contents of experience. It is the purity of a self-identical form. As James Edie puts this, what we confront here is "an impersonal, necessary, universal, eidetic structure," one which, however, "is lived in and through each unique consciousness, each ego-life."[33] What particularizes this structure is the actual contents making up a particular ego-life.

Given this, we still have to ask what the nature of this structure is. Husserl's answer to this is relatively straightforward. Having asserted that "the ego is the 'subject' of consciousness," he goes on to explain: "subject, here, is only another word for the *centering* which all life possesses as an egological life, i.e., as a living in order to experience something, to be conscious of it."[34] The best way to describe this "centering" is to note that each self is at the center of its surrounding world. Spatially, each is always at the "here," at the zero point of the coordinate axes of its space. It is from it that distances radiate out. It is about it that the perspectival series unfold, their relative rates of unfolding giving it the sense of the near and the far. Thus, as I walk through a park, trees close by match my progress by receding at the same speed, objects at a middle range glide by at a more stately pace, and objects marking the distant horizon scarcely seem to move. Each in fact, has its rate of showing its different aspects; and each rate is coordinated to the self taken as a spatial center. The same holds, mutatis mutandis, for the self as a temporal center. For such a self, it is always now. It always occupies the point of passage between the anticipated future and the receding, but still retained, past.

With this, we may observe that the original distance that marks the subject-object dichotomy is not, for Husserl, a transcendence based on Sartrean nothingness. What generates it is simply the departure into pastness of moments (and contents) that once were now. While I remain now, they depart into pastness. The result, as we saw in our last chapter, is that "in [temporal] streaming a self-transcending is originally accomplished; namely, a past is constituted . . ."[35] This past transcends me in my "stationary nowness," i.e, in my being as a *temporal center* of consciousness. As we cited Husserl, "The not now transcends the now, in particular, the consciousness of the not-now. Thus, the continuity of intentional modifications [which yield the sense of pastness] is a constant continuity in which one originally apprehends transcendence. What is transcended is always consciousness." This implies that, as my own appearances depart into pastness, this transcendence becomes *self*-transcendence. My presence to myself is, Husserl would agree with Sartre, a function of the distance between the seer and the seen. But this, he would add, is a result of *my remaining now* as a "central ego," even while the experiences which just now particularized me depart into pastness. As Husserl adds here, turning to grasp them, I apprehend myself "not as the self I am, but as the self I was."[36]

This positioning of the ego as a structure of experience, although giving it an identity with respect to the changing contents of experience, should not be understood as making it independent of them. The ego for Husserl is not some Platonic ideal. It is not a form that could exist apart from what it informs. Rather, as he says, "the transcendental ego is a relative ego, an egological structure facing what is pregiven to the ego."[37] Its relativity, then, is to what is "pregiven" to it. As the sense of "pregiven" implies, a relativity to particular contents must *first* be given for it to exist as their form. Admitting that it is the "centering" arrangement of such contents or experiences, we have its contingency. As Husserl expresses this, "One can also say: a complete dissolution of a world in a 'tumult' [of experiences] is equivalent to a dissolution of the ego . . ."[38] This cannot be otherwise, given the ego's dependence on them, i.e., on their manifesting the centering structure which it is. Thus, a dissolution of the perspectival ordering of experiences would not just deprive me of the sense of the spatial world; the jumbling of perspectives in which different sides of objects showed themselves randomly would also necessarily deprive me of my sense of *myself* as a spatial center. I could no longer grasp myself as the zero point from which distances were marked. The same holds with regard to the disordering which leaves me "perplexed in my inner temporality." Such temporality is a function of my retaining my impressions in the temporal order in which they occurred. If the order of before and after is scrambled, then, as Husserl writes, "I would not have the spatial-temporal field of a human life. Spatial-temporality, [spatial-temporal] persisting being would have been nullified (*wäre zunichte geworden*). It would not have been nullified in a worldly sense"—i.e., the sense whereby an entity within an existing world is considered to be destroyed. "Rather, being itself, the being of the world per se (*das Welt-sein überhaupt*) would have been nullified. It would have ceased ever to have been through the loss of its validity, its validity for me as an ego who would remain perplexed in my inner temporality."[39] Such a world would never "have been" for me because I would have lost the sense of anything "having been," i.e., of pastness as an ordered continuum stretching away from me. Its loss, of course, is also that of myself as a temporal center.

Passive Genesis

That the ego can suffer such dissolution shows that it is not an origin. It is not an informing form in the sense of being an *agent* responsible for the ordering of experiences. Cogiven with this order, both the ego and its world must rest on something prior. The same holds for the rationality, the "logic of experience," which is implicit in this structuring. Given that its origin is not some egological agent, the suspension of the ego is not that of this origin. We can thus say that, with the reduction of the Husserlian ego, we do pass beyond its correlate world with its corresponding rational structures. Both the ego and its world suffer a kind of "dissolution" once we suspend the ordered connections—e.g., the patterns of perspectival unfolding—which make the centering of experience possible. Yet the suspension of the Husserlian ego is not, as Sartre's interpretation of it would imply, a passing beyond the rational basis for the world. This is because the ego, as a form or structure, is not an agent and hence *not* this basis.

This point can be put in terms of Husserl's distinction between active and passive synthesis. The ego, as we cited Husserl, is "only possible as a subject of an 'environment'." It must have "facing it things, objects." The latter, however, are *passively* given; they are not the result of its *active* syntheses. "In *active syn-*

theses," Husserl writes in the *Cartesian Meditations*, "the ego functions as productively constitutive . . ." The examples he gives are those of collecting, counting, dividing, predicating, and inferring. In each act, I produce new objects for myself on the basis of already given objects.[40] Passive synthesis is what originally provides me with the objects I start with. In Husserl's words, "anything built by activity necessarily presupposes, at the lowest level, a passivity that gives something beforehand. Pursuing this, we encounter constitution through passive genesis. The ready-made object that, so to speak, steps forward complete as an existent, as a mere thing . . . is given, with the originality of the 'it itself,' in the synthesis of a passive experience."[41] The conclusion, then, is, "Thanks to this passive synthesis, . . . the ego always has an environment of objects."[42] This, however, is the very environment that makes it possible. Similar assertions are made with regard to the stream of experiences, understood as the "life" that makes the ego possible. The life, whose ordered ("rational") connections establish the ego as a center of experience, is passively given. As he defines this term, "'Passive' signifies here without the action of the ego . . . the stream does not exist by virtue of the action (*Tun*) of the ego, as if the ego aimed at actualizing the stream, as if the stream were actualized by an action. The stream is not something done, not a 'deed' in the widest sense. Rather, every action is itself 'contained' in the universal stream of life which is, thus, called the 'life' of the ego . . ."[43] For Husserl, then, the "life" of the ego is not the result of its action. Rather, as he says, "the individual, egological life is passively constituted in immanent time."[44] Here we may note that one of Husserl's earliest formulations of this position occur in his interpretation of Kant. He writes: "What is called constitution, this is what Kant obviously had in mind under the rubric, 'connection as an operation of the understanding,' synthesis. This is the genesis in which the ego and, correlatively, the surrounding world (*Umwelt*) of the ego are constituted. It is passive genesis—not the [active] categorial action which produces categorial formations . . ."[45] Whether or not this is an accurate interpretation of Kant, Husserl's own position is clear. There is a passive constitution whose processes account for the presence of both the ego and its surrounding world—both the subject and object of traditional philosophy.[46] Insofar as this presence is also that of the rational structures (the logic of experience) without which neither would be possible, rationality, here, has an origin quite different from what Sartre supposed. Its source is not the activity of the practically engaged self which is Sartre's embodied consciousness. Its source is, rather, a prior "passive genesis."

Intentionality and Rationality

Insofar as this genesis results in the presence of both subjects and objects, it results as well in the intentional relationship between the two. What this means is that, for Husserl, intentionality is not prior to the syntheses of consciousness. It is not, as Sartre would have it, the result of a nothingness taken as an ontological structure of the For-itself. It is rather an "accomplishment" of the syntheses that give the world its rational structure. Now, the original syntheses which occasion intentionality are temporal. Intentionality first arises as the "original distance" opened up by departure into pastness. As we have seen, this departure is from the nowness which I constantly occupy as a temporal center. It is a result of "the continuity of intentional modifications" of what departs. The reference here is to the "retentional modifications" of experience. By virtue of these, an experience, when it is first retained, is interpreted as a just-past experience. The retention of this retention adds a further modification. It is now interpreted as a just just-past experience. The interpretation, in other words, adds a further degree of pastness. The result, then, of the ongoing series of retentions of retentions of some originally given experience is a corresponding series of interpretations, interpretations which, when synthesized, give us the sense of departure into pastness. As we cited Husserl, the result is a chain of "interpretations which in their flowing connectedness constitute the temporal unity of the immanent content in its sinking back into pastness."[47] Sinking back, it transcends me; and in this transcendence we have the origin of the intentional relationship.

To go beyond this to an actual intentional relation, we have to examine a specific perceptual series occasioned by the departure of some object's appearances into pastness. Here, Husserl's position can best be recalled by considering the perception of a die. Turning it in our hands, we view first one then another of its faces. Yet, as Husserl writes, "all these continually changing appearances are *of* one and the same die."[48] They all show the basic character of intentionality which is a linking of each of our experiences to *that of which* they are experiences. The intentional character of consciousness, i.e., its quality of being *of* some object, is, for Husserl, a feature of the experiences which form the object's appearances. Each is *of* an object insofar as it points beyond itself to that which transcends its momentary givenness. In Sartre's terms, each is only an "aspect of the object" (*BN*, p. 6). As such it points beyond itself to the object's "transphenomenal" being, to the being which transcends the series of its appearances. Now, for Sartre, this intentional character of the appearance is a function of two ontological categories: the Nothingness of consciousness and the In-itselfness of this being. It is a function of the openness of the former to the latter. Husserl, by contrast, sees it as a result of a "unity of synthesis."[49] It arises through the positing belief in the unity which appears when we grasp the common, recurring elements of our ongoing experience.

The mechanics of this process need not concern us as they have been covered in earlier chapters. For our purposes, only three points need be noted. The first is that the experience points beyond itself in its momentary character by virtue of the identification of its contents with those of other similar experiences—experiences exhibiting the same recurring sensuous contents. Identified through its content with the latter, it becomes associated with what it is beyond its fleeting here and now. It becomes an experience *of* something that endures through a given stretch of time. Our second point is that the object which appears through this synthesis is a one-in-many, a unity which shows itself in a multitude of appearances. Its presence as such a one-in-many is that of a *sense*. As Husserl describes the way in which an intentional object is said to be immanent in consciousness, "This in-consciousness is a completely unique being-in. It is not a being-in as a real, inherent component. . . . it is a being-in as [the object's] immanent *objective sense*. The object of consciousness, in its self-identity throughout the flowing of experience, does not enter into this flowing from outside. It lies included within it as a sense; it is this [sense] as an intentional accomplishment (*Leistung*) of the synthesis of consciousness."[50] The accomplishment is, broadly speaking, that of passive synthesis. It involves both an act of identification, whereby the recurring contents of our perceptions are passively "merged," and the positing belief in the unity that results from this. Our descriptions of this simple act of positing have, in fact, taken many pages.[51] A complete account would detail the rational structures and rules of positing which must be followed if the act is to succeed. It is by virtue of such structures that Husserl calls the positing act an *act of reason*, i.e., a "rationally motivated" act.[52] For the same reason, he asserts that "an all-sided . . . solution of the problems of constitution"—i.e., problems which would involve the positing of being—"would obviously be equivalent to a complete phenomenology of reason in all its formal and material formations . . ."[53] With this, we have our third point, which is that intentionality and rationality are always cogiven for Husserl. The rules of the syntheses which establish the presence of intentional objects have as their objective correlate, reason "in all its formal and material formations."[54]

For Sartre, on the contrary, intentionality does not imply rationality. With the reduction, we can pass beyond the ego and, hence, beyond the syntheses that gave rise to it. Yet intentionality remains. Rather than being based on syntheses with their implied rationality, intentionality is an irreducible feature of the "absolute consciousness" that remains as a residuum. Its basis is the nothingness, the openness, that makes this consciousness a For-itself. For Sartre, as we have seen, the very being of consciousness is its intentionality. It is its being open to (and, hence, its being a consciousness *of*) what is not itself. As Sartre puts this in *The Transcendence of the Ego*, consciousness is not a being with given qualities, a definite essence. Rather it is a "*non-substantial absolute*" (*TE*, p. 42). Its qualities are those of the object it is currently grasping. Indeed, "consciousness is aware of itself *insofar as it is consciousness of a transcendent object*" (*TE*, p. 40). At this point it has a content to be grasped.

Conscious of itself, it is "simply consciousness of being consciousness of that object" (ibid.). If we attempt to grasp it apart from its relation to what is not itself, we are left with nothing at all. In Sartre's words, as a "transcendental field, . . . it is a *nothing*, since all [things] . . . are outside it. . . . But this nothing is *all* since it is *consciousness* of these objects" (*TE*, p. 93). The same points are repeated in *Being and Nothingness*. Once again consciousness is called a "*non-substantial* absolute." Again the assertion is made that "it is total emptiness (since the entire world is outside it)" (*BN*, p. 17). The important point here is that this irreducible intentionality is prior to the synthetic act and hence prior to the rationality implicit in the structures of this act.

Sartre's attack on Husserl's notion of *hyle*, taken as the "pure flux of experience and the matter of synthesis," is instructive in this regard. For Husserl, this *hyle* or "sensible data presents itself as material (*Stoff*) for intentional shapings or sense bestowals at various levels."[55] It is the material which can, for example, be cast in the form of perspectival unfolding to yield the series of appearances of some particular object. For Sartre, such material is impossible. He writes: "The hyle in fact could not be consciousness, for it would disappear in translucency and could not offer that resisting basis of impressions which must be surpassed toward the object. But if it does not belong to consciousness, where does it derive its being and opacity?" (*BN*, p. 20). His point is that consciousness, as a sheer emptiness, cannot have such material within it. Its emptiness is its openness, its translucency to what is not itself. Thus, either the hyle would disappear in this translucency or else it would obscure it. A similar set of Sartre's objections apply to Husserl's "intentional form" or "morphe." The constitutive rules (and hence "rationality") implied by such cannot be inherent in consciousness. If they were, they would only serve to "darken" or "obscure" the translucence, the openness of consciousness. Giving consciousness specific features, such rules would limit its receptivity. They would make it a thing, a definite being rather than a receptivity to every possible being or thing.[56] In Sartre's view, then, rationality in the Husserlian sense stands fundamentally opposed to intentionality. With its rules and *conditions* for the possibility of objects' being present, it serves not to enlighten, but to "darken" consciousness. It does so by obscuring its *unconditioned* transparency to objects.

This, of course, does not mean that there is no rationality in the Sartrean universe. It only implies that this rationality cannot be thought of as grounded in the structures of passive synthesis. Its origin, from a Husserlian perspective, must be the *active* syntheses of consciousness. It has to be something we freely construct. This means that its ultimate ground is the freedom of the practically engaged self. From the Sartrean perspective, we essentially say the same thing when we assert that its ultimate origin is the nothingness which makes the self completely open. Given that this is also its freedom to turn from (or reject) what it has constructed, this rationality has, as we noted, an essentially contingent character. Such contingency is the price the Sartrean self pays for its openness.

Anonymity

This is the place to note another striking, if fundamentally misleading, similarity between Sartre and Husserl. If consciousness, in an objective sense, "is a nothing," it cannot be grasped. Objectively speaking, it is anonymous, since any attempt to grasp it as an object—as a being with some definite, nameable qualities—must misfire. Thus, as Sartre writes, "the consciousness which says *I Think* [i.e., the consciousness which appears through reflection as the subject of thought] is precisely not the consciousness which thinks" (*TE*, p. 45). What we grasp in attempting to make consciousness an object of reflection is not the consciousness which thinks, but rather "the *I* [which is the object] of the reflected consciousness" (ibid.). The consciousness which actually thinks is not, then, the consciousness which stands as an object of its thought. It always splits itself off from the latter; it always escapes its "thetic" or objectifying grasp. Husserl makes a similar point about the ego when he writes, "The actively functioning 'I do,' 'I discover,' is constantly anonymous." When I turn my attention to the latter, "it is brought up by a new functioning ego," an ego which is not, itself, attended to.[57] Thus, "functioning subjectivity is constantly presupposed" whenever there is attending to objects. Yet "this functioning is constantly anonymous . . ."[58]

For Sartre, we may note, the insistence that one can objectively grasp this functioning subjectivity is part of what he calls *bad faith*. Bad faith involves assuming two contradictory positions. Unwilling to take responsibility for my situation, I can assume I am an In-itself with given properties, a thing like other things. Unwilling, however, to be reduced to such, I can also insist that I am not as I appear, that I am something more, something different. Thus, in Sartre's example, the young coquette lets her escort take her hand. Unwilling to assume the implications of this action, "she *does not notice* that she is leaving it." She lets it rest "inert between the warm hands of her companion—neither consenting nor resisting—a thing." Thus, on one side of the contradiction, she engages "in the divorce of the body from the soul." She is actually not the body that appears. On the other side, however, "she is profoundly aware of the desire which she inspires." It is this that gives the situation its "charm." Enjoying the fact that it is directed to her, she must identify herself with her body, this even though "the desire cruel and naked would humiliate and horrify her" (*BN*, p. 97). The result is that her actual conduct is a continual sliding from one thesis to the other. She exists in the flickering of the assertion of herself as a For-itself and an In-itself.

Husserl, of course, does not use such language. Our essential anonymity does not prevent him from affirming that we do have a character—what he calls an "ego of habitualities." For Husserl, we can authentically function in and through such a constituted ego.[59] This fact points to a basic difference between the two philosophers. Even though both philosophers base their assertions of the anonymity of functioning on the fact that such functioning is ultimately pre-egological, they are in sharp disagreement over the character of the latter. For Sartre, bad faith is possible because the pre-egological is an unstable assemblage of the In-itself and For-itself. It is an assemblage where "nothingness haunts the face of being," one where we encounter "the unity of being and non-being" as our own "being-in-order-to-not-be" (*BN*, pp. 84–85). For Husserl, by contrast, the pre-egological has the unity of a single, synthetic process. Beginning with "primal temporalization," the process results in the egological centering of experience and ends in the constitution of the ego of habitualities, i.e., the "personal ego" with personal characteristics. Now, the fact that this process is a unity does not exclude the anonymity of the functioning that drives it. Anonymity is, in fact, inherent in the temporalization at its origin. More precisely, it is a result of the "continuity of retentional modifications" which constitute temporal departure and, hence, self-transcendence. Such self-transcendence signifies that my apprehending ego remains now while the appearances which are required for its synthesis of apprehension depart into pastness. Grasping myself through these appearances, I apprehend myself "not as the [functioning] self I am, but as the self I was." In fact, I can never intentionally grasp myself as now, i.e., as functioning, given that the intentional relation is based on synthesis with its corresponding requirement of contents-there-to-be-synthesized. Synthesis requires the temporal unfolding of contents, an unfolding which allows them to be sequentially given (as opposed to being given in an instantaneous "all at once"). It, thus, requires temporal departure. Grasping myself through what departs, I must remain anonymous in the sense that I can never grasp what I presently am.

Absolute Consciousness

As we have seen, both philosophers presuppose the reduction. Both speak of the self-objectification of consciousness which results in the constitution of the ego. For both, the reduction and constitution imply each other, the one being the reverse of the other. Only for Husserl, however, is rationality the tie between the two. Engaging in the reduction, one undoes the rational, positing act that is constitution. The motion of the reduction is, thus, a suspension of reason and a descent into irrationality, but only in the sense of uncovering its founding layers. Indeed, from the Husserlian perspective, without rationality, there is nothing to reduce, since rationality, from the phenomenological perspective, is the layered structure of thesis and evidence, of assertion and grounds, by which we constitute our world. For Sartre, of course, the reduction is also a descent into irrationality. It is a descent as well to the pre-egological "absolute." Its action, however, is not an uncovering of the founding layers of rationality. Rationality for him is not inherent in being, but is rather what we create through our practical activity. What is revealed by the reduction is, in fact, the groundless quality of this activity. The reduction reveals the nothingness which gives reason its contingent character.

More exactly regarded, the end of the reduction for Sartre presents an ambiguous face. The absolute it leaves us with is both a nothingness and a pure spontaneity. Regarding it, we regard a "tireless creation of existence of which we are not the creators" (*TE*, p. 99). A phenomenological description of its spontaneity "renders impossible any distinction between action and passion, or any conception of an autonomy of the will" (ibid., p. 101). This is because it is prior to such distinctions. In Sartre's words, "At this level man has the impression of ceaselessly escaping from himself, of overflowing himself, of being surprised by riches which are always unexpected. . . . Indeed, the *me* can do nothing to this spontaneity, for *will is an object which constitutes itself for and by this spontaneity*" (ibid., p. 99). The question that here arises is how this creative source can also be a nothingness. How can the absolute of consciousness be a "total emptiness" and also be this "overflowing"? The answer is to be found in the absolute's intentionality. Precisely because it is a "total emptiness," it manifests the openness of intentionality. The absolute quality of its openness signifies that things appear within it without its imposing any preconditions. This means that what it is "of," what appears within it, is absolutely everything. The spontaneity of consciousness is, then, its nothingness understood as its total openness, its total lack of prior conditions for appearance. Because of this, anything and everything can appear within it. Here, of course, the word *within*, as implying something other than appearance (a container or a frame that might *place a condition* on appearing), is misleading. For Sartre, "consciousness is pure appearance." It is an "identity of appearance and existence." Indeed it is "because of this identity . . . that it can be considered as the absolute" (*BN*, p. 17). It is "absolute" as appearance and nothing else. In other words, it is absolute as the unconditioned and, hence, spontaneous appearing of the world.

Sartre's position here sounds like Hume's when the latter describes the mind as a "theater, where several perceptions successively make their appearance; pass, re-pass, glide away, and mingle in an infinite variety of postures and situations." This is especially the case when Hume adds: "The comparison of the theater must not mislead us, They are the successive perceptions only, that constitute the mind" (*Treatise*, Book 1, sec. vi, p. 253). Sartre's position, however, is not a Humean idealism, one where much of what counts as the external world is devalued as a "fiction." For Sartre, there is a world in itself. The pre-egological, as we noted, includes the In-itself. Consciousness can, in fact, be regarded as a kind of form in the pre-egological, a structure (that of the For-itself) arising from the nothingness that "haunts" it. As the For-itself, it is the pre-egological coming to self-presence by virtue of this nothingness. It is an ontological form, one manifested by the continuous processes which we are.

For Husserl, the reduction can also be described as uncovering a form. This form, however, is one manifested in each stage of the reduction, each descent from one layer to the next. It is that of synthesis. The universality of this form is what makes Husserl equate positing and rationality. It is what makes reason the tie between the reduction and its opposite motion, constitution. Now, given that synthesis is a temporal process, one involving both time and content, two reductions, as we said in our chapter on radical evil, are possible. Each fastens on a different side of the synthetic process. We can reach the aspect of absolute that is "the domain of experiences qua *absolute* essentialities" where we consider our experiences independent of their temporal ordering. We can also uncover the aspect which is the origin of such ordering. It is in regard to the latter that Husserl writes, "The absolute is nothing other than absolute temporalization."[60] Performing the reduction on my sense of temporal passage, I ultimately encounter a "primal temporalization."[61] This temporalization is prior to me. As Husserl writes, "temporalization possesses its 'layers' . . . the 'layers' beneath the ego (*unterichliche 'Schichte'*) and the egological 'layers'."[62] On the ultimate level there is "the primal being, the inherently self-temporalizing absolute . . . then [there is] the primal being as [an] ego . . ."[63] This second is the result of the first, i.e., of its activity as primal temporalization. To cite Husserl again, "even [the absolute's] interpretation as the absolute which I directly encounter as my stationary streaming primordiality is a temporalization, a temporalization of this into something primally existing."[64] What we have is, thus, a temporal process which "times itself" into a being—into an ego understood as something "primally existing."

Our earlier chapters gave some of the details of the analyses by which Husserl attempts to justify this claim. Here, we need only recall two items. The first is that the temporal process can time itself "into something primally existing" by virtue of the fact that it is inherently synthetic. Incapable of existing by themselves, time's moments exhibit the kinds of interdependence which yield the retention and merging of already expired content filled moments.[65] The result of this is not just the constitution of pastness—this through the interpretations such retentions bear. It is also the constitution of the ego as the above-described temporal centering of experience—i.e., as a now point through which the future passes in its becoming past. Now, when Husserl performs the reduction on this structure, he suspends the positing of both the past and the future. Directed to the subject, "the performance of the phenomenological epoché" is, he writes, "a radical limitation to the living present"—i.e., to the nowness through which the future passes to become the past.[66] So regarded, the present no longer appears as a point of passage. When we view it without the past and the future, it appears as the stationary place (the "*nunc stans*") where the moments of time well up.[67] This exhibition of *passing through* as *welling up* points to the absolute as the ultimate source of time. It also points to the ego itself as an acting center. What is revealed here, Husserl asserts, is "the primal phenomenon of my 'I act' ('*Ich tue*'), in which I am a stationary and remaining ego and, indeed, am the actor of the '*nunc stans*.' I act now and only now, and I 'continuously' act."[68] As Husserl also describes it, the ego's "acting is a letting loose from itself. It is a primal welling up, a creative allowing to depart from itself of that which, itself, streams, namely, the acts."[69] With this we have our second point, which is that the ego's action is its own and yet is also an action of the primal temporalization. The latter provides the welling up of moments whose retention gives us our sense of pastness. It thus provides the basis for that escape into transcendence (into pastness) which is the presupposition for new action by the ego. On a constituted level, its action appears as egological because the departure into pastness appears to be from the nowness in which we function. Yet on the nonconstituted level, the action is that of the absolute itself, the absolute in its constant creation of ever new moments.

Given the dependence of such moments, they will conjoin to produce an ego understood as a temporal midpoint or center of experience. Such a midpoint will be the nowness in which we always find ourselves. In Husserl's words, the result will be ourselves as a "remaining primal now" within the stream of time. A good description of the constitution of this stationary or "fixed form" which is the ego is contained in the following passage: "A lasting and remaining primal now is constituted in this streaming. It is constituted as a fixed form for a content which streams through it and as the source point for all constituted modifications. In union with [the constitution of] the fixed form of the primally welling primal now, there is constituted a two-sided continuity of forms that are just as fixed. Thus, in *toto*, a fixed continuum of form is constituted in which the primal now is a primal welling middle point for two continua [understood] as branches of the modes of [temporal] modifications: the continuum of what is just past and that of futurities."[70] Despite its somewhat labored prose, this passage has a clear doctrine: The egological now is constituted as a "fixed form," *through which* time appears to flow and *in which* its moments appear to well up as present and actual. This constitution occurs "in union with" a second constitution—that of the continua of the past and the future. With the latter, we have the constitution of the temporal environment which allows the source of time to *appear* as a "middle point" within this environment. In other words, we have the constitution of this source as an acting ego. Given that the same constitution, when material content is added, results in the elaboration of this tem-

poral environment into an actual surrounding world, it also produces the rationality which, as a feature of the latter, is always cogiven with the ego. Rationality, we can say, is simply the drawing out of the consequences of the temporal aspect of Husserl's absolute.

Drawing the Balance

Summing up, we can say that, like Sartre's For-itself, Husserl's ego is
also a form embedded in the pre-egological. As we have seen, it is a temporal
form, one individualized by a specific content. In this, it is like Sartre's consciousness which becomes individualized by the "body," this being understood as a general category for the factors of birth, race, physical condition, past
experience—in short, of all the features that give us our contingent situation. A
further point of similarity involves the fact that the absolute acts through the
individual. Because of this, Husserl can affirm that temporalization is a function
of a pre-egological absolute and yet can also assert: "I am. It is from me that
time is constituted."[71] What is really affirmed here is the *Uebersein* of the individual ego. As Husserl defines this, "The 'surpassing being' (*Uebersein*) of an
ego is nothing more than a continuous, primordially streaming constituting. It
is a constituting of various levels of existents (or 'worlds') . . ."[72] Within the
individual ego, this is particularized in the constitution of *its* world. The same
general notion is present in Sartre's calling the individual consciousness an
"*individuated* and *impersonal* spontaneity" (*TE*, p. 98). Particularized by its
environment, consciousness, for Sartre, still remains impersonal insofar as its
origin is not some ego, but rather the spontaneity of his pre-egological absolute.
Such similarities have prompted some critics to assert that the difference between the two philosophers is merely verbal. Both simply call the form
of consciousness by different names.[73] This is not our position. What makes
these similarities deceptive can best be illustrated in these philosophers' understanding of the openness of consciousness. For Husserl, this openness is the
openness of time. It is a consequence of the fact that time's moments may be
regarded as capable of containing every possible content. Because they are
simply empty containers, i.e., place holders devoid of any qualitative content,
such moments have an unconditional openness. Thus, for Husserl, what Sartre
calls the *translucent quality of consciousness*, i.e., its openness or intentionality, is actually a feature of its being as a temporal structure. So, for that matter,
is its spontaneity understood as Sartre's "tireless creation of existence." The origin of this is the welling up of the absolute out of which comes the ever new
existence of the now.[74] If this contentless character of time were a sheer nothingness, then one could argue that all the disagreements between them were
merely verbal. The function of the Sartrean Nothingness could then be understood in terms of the Husserlian absolute of temporalization. So regarded, both

might be understood as making the same assertions about the anonymity of functioning consciousness and hence about the inner distance required by self presence. Their basis would be time understood as a sheer nothingness. This, however, is not the case. Thus, when Sartre comes to speak about temporality, he gives a completely different account from Husserl's. It is an account essentially informed by a Jamesian pragmatism.[75] More important, for Husserl, the contentless character of time does not make it a nothingness. By virtue of the interdependence of its moments, it has an inherent structure. As our third chapter pointed out, this structure manifests itself in the diagonal and vertical intentionalities which begin the synthetic process. It further appears in the rationality (the rules and forms) that characterize objective synthesis. Noematically, it manifests itself in the results of this synthesis, i.e., in the rationality of the resultant objects and intentional relations.

So regarded, the difference between the two philosophers is actually a question of reason. Is reason based on the passive synthesis that first gives us a world or does it find its origin in the kind of Jamesian pragmatics we discussed above? For Husserl, reason is what opens us up to the world. Given that the original openness is that of time, the rationality embodied in egological synthesis is simply this openness' appearance, its self-objectification on the human level. It is, in other words, a result of the original openness achieving egological focus through the processes of temporal synthesis. For Sartre, on the contrary, the original openness of consciousness keeps its character. Appearing on the human level as freedom, it maintains its power to call everything into question—and this includes all our carefully constructed rational (hodological) spaces.

Who is closer to the mark? Many of the images Sartre uses remind us that he wrote *Being and Nothingness* during the Second World War. The breakup of Communism presents us on a smaller scale with similar scenes of destruction. Again and again we see freedom turning on the space reason has constructed, the space of hospitals, schools, apartment complexes, factories, etc., and subjecting it to an actual (practical) negation. The hodological space that makes a given, human world has in our century constantly been subject to human destruction. Husserl, of course, was not ignorant of this fact. He, however, saw this as a crisis of reason, a crisis brought about, not by freedom, but by reason's *self*-alienation. In his last work, *The Crisis*, he argued that this alienation could only be resolved by overcoming reason's self-forgetting. This is a forgetting of its phenomenological roots. What he proposed, in essence, was a rational solution to the crisis of reason. Was he naive? Husserl would probably reply that reason alone can give the context in which an answer to *its* question could be justified. He would probably also add that the question of evidence is a question of reason. In so doing, he would be taking rationality as the structure of thesis and evidence which, as constitution, results in our world. Our forgetting this structure is, from his perspective, our self-forgetting. It is our self-alienation, our "bad faith" with regard to what we are and what the world and the "absolute" are. As we mentioned in an earlier chapter, the ultimate danger of such self-forgetfulness is that of radical evil. The forgetfulness that loses sight of our finitude—i.e., of the level of our *non*identity with our absolute ground—leaves us open to permanent loss. In our identity with this ground, we can uses the resources it offers to separate ourselves from it. Concretely, we can use reason for destructive, irrational purposes. Such use is the ultimate "bad faith" from the Husserlian standpoint. Sartre would probably reply its very possibility depends on a nothingness such as he describes. The question of reason, however, remains: Does Sartre's nothingness allow of an adequate response to this question? Can it ground Sartre's own elaborately reasoned response in anything like the necessity it so obviously claims for itself?

If it cannot, we must look elsewhere for an account of reason, one which escapes the problem of self-referential inconsistency. For Husserl, this difficulty is avoided by identifying reason with the synthetic process. The account reason provides of itself is grounded as a level of this process (one involving the synthesis of higher level, categorial formations). "Reason," taken generally, is a many layered structure, its levels being those of constitution or synthesis. As we shall now see, the same multiplicity of layers characterizes the Husserlian answer to the question of the self.

9

HUSSERL'S CONCEPT OF THE SELF

The question of "what is a self" is probably the most puzzling and persistent in philosophy. It announces itself with the oracle at Delphi's injunction: "Know thyself." Such an injunction, of course, presupposes that there is something there to be known, that the self can stand there as an object of knowledge, that the knower can know himself. Knowing himself, he can know himself as knower. This means that he can grasp the very performance which is himself as knower, is himself as this grasping of himself. As even these slight reflections show, the task of fulfilling the oracle's injunction involves a certain mystery. Either the self is empty or it involves everything. The circle of my apprehending myself apprehending myself is, in its self-reference, devoid of content. Content seems to arise once I admit that, knowing myself, I do not know *an object*. I know that by which objects are known. Here I assert that the self is that in and through which objects are present. Its modes of presence are their modes of coming to presence. As such, it hides itself behind them. Presenting itself as their place, it itself seems placeless. Its content is given by its objects and *their* modes of appearing. This implies that to know the self, I would have to know what could fill it, what objects I could possibly know. For this, however, I would have to know the knowable world itself. Is the self then a world? It does not seem so. Embodied, it is subject to various accidents, including injury, decay, and death. Psychologically, it also has its vulnerabilities, its habits, its peculiarities. An entity among entities, a being *within* the world, how can it claim to be *a* world?

Much of philosophy has been driven by an attempt to come to terms with this mystery. In fact, if Western philosophy has a persistent goal or telos, one which gives it its identity as a historical process, this may very well be provided by the oracle's injunction.[1] Certainly, the whole of Husserl's philosophy can be understood as an attempt to fulfill it, i.e., to actually know what a self or ego is. In Husserl's understanding, phenomenology is a "systematic egological science," one which engages in an "explication of my ego as a subject for every possible cognition, and this with regard to every sense of entities . . ."[2] This means, as Ricoeur writes, "to do phenomenology of the ego is to do phenomenology itself."[3] Doing phenomenology, I explicate what is a self. In doing this, according to Husserl, I accomplish the telos of philosophy. I satisfy the goal that has animated it from the beginning. In the view of the *Krisis*, philosophy is our self-explication. Phenomenology's claim to historical importance is that of presenting the most systematic, most all inclusive answer to the question: "What is a self?"[4] Given this, it is not surprising that we have touched on this issue before. The purpose of this present chapter is to gather up our previous insights and examine it directly. How does Husserl, in confronting the mystery of the subject, come to see philosophy as its self explication? More precisely: what is the notion of self (of "ego," to use his preferred term) which allows him to do this?

How Many Egos Are There?

The texts of Husserl prevent any simple answer to this question. His descriptions of the self present the commentator with an embarrassment of riches. He has multiple concepts of the ego. From these, each commentator draws his list.[5] Ricoeur,[6] for example, has four of them: 1) The ego that stands as the pole of the acts that radiate out from it. 2) The ego that expresses the identity of the reflecting and the reflected upon self. This ego, Husserl writes in *Ideen II*, is "an identity in immanent time." It is the identity which allows me to say "I am and was the same."[7] Next we have 3) the ego as "a nonperspectival unity." This ego "does not appear, does not present itself merely from a side" as a thing does. It is, in fact "incapable of and in no need of constitution through manifolds" of perspectives.[8] It is, Ricoeur says, "an absolute ipseity," a "point like I." Ricoeur ends his list with 4) the ego taken as the substrate of its habits. These habits pertain to the subject as an actor. They are persisting styles of behavior, of positing, doubting, inquiring, etc., which give acting its coherence. Husserl calls their result the "personal ego." Seebohm[9] adds two further concepts of the self to this list: 5) The eidos ego, which is "the sum total of the eidetic structures which can be discovered in phenomenological experience" once we practice the reduction; and 6) "the ego in its concreteness." This is the "monad." It is the whole assemblage of ego-cogito-cogitatum concretely considered according to some given stream of experience. It includes, then, not just the stream, but everything which pertains to it: both the ego, with its given habits and dispositions, and the totality of objects which the streaming experiences are experiences of. If we regard the ego as constitutively responsible for these objects, a further concept of the ego appears. This is 7) the ego taken "as the subjectivity which constitutes both sense and being,"[10] the subjectivity which constitutes the "actuality" of objects.[11] Regarding it, I can say with Husserl, "the world derives its whole sense and existential status from me as the transcendental ego." Such an ego, Alfred Schutz claims, is "creative."[12] Schutz, we may note, adds yet another concept of an ego, that of

8) the primal, pre-individual ego. He asks: "But is it conceivable and meaningful to speak of a plurality of transcendental egos? Is not the concept of the transcendental ego conceivable only in the singular? . . . is it . . . a *singulare tantum*?[13] Husserl, in a manuscript, confirms this intuition. On a certain level, the ultimately constituting ego is in fact unique; it cannot be "meaningfully multiplied."[14]

The list we have been compiling can, in fact, be considerably extended. Among further candidates for ego concepts are the ego as the anonymous, "I function," the ego as the lasting now (the *nunc stans*) in which I function, the real ego, the empirical ego, even the ego as an "all-temporal, ideal, irreal" object, the ego, in other words, that has the being of an idea.[15] To this, we must also add at least a reference to those commentators who attempt to read Husserl as presenting an essentially egoless philosophy. The ego, according to such readers, is no different from any other constituted reality. Rather than being an active center of constitution, it is a result of the syntheses of a non-personal, ego-less consciousness. Advocates of this view include Aron Gurvitch and James Edie.[16] Sartre, as we saw, began his career by advancing this view.[17]

Each of these ego concepts can find some ground in the works of Husserl. Although some overlap, others seem so widely disparate that the temptation arises to choose among them. Sartre, in his early work, opts for the constituted empirical ego, replacing the transcendental constituting ego with the "impersonal spontaneity" of an "absolute consciousness."[18] Marbach dismisses the ego as a pole, asserting that "it does not deserve the title of ego." He prefers the "ego as principle of the unity of consciousness." Only the latter, with its ability to remember and identify itself is, he claims, a human self.[19]

The position I want to advance is quite different from this. Rather than making a list, denying the ego tout court, or choosing among the ego candidates, I want to assert that all the options mentioned have some claim to validity. It is not just that they all can find support in the writings of Husserl (which they can). It is that his theory actually finds room for this plurality. The plurality is a consequence of the fact that *there are as many concepts of the ego as there are of time.* Their plurality can, in fact, be regarded as a transcendental "clue" to the process underlying them, that of temporal constitution. For Husserl, this process originates in the anonymity of pre-egological functioning, exfoliates in the streaming life of a particular consciousness, and ends in the world of constituted, objective sense. Viewed in terms of its result, the temporal process can be seen as that of the ego's self-objectification, its coming to objective presence in time. The different ego concepts correspond to the different stages of this process. In fact, given that the process's origin is pre-egological, even the denial of the ego finds its place here. If we ask, then, what is a self, we have to point to this process itself. Our reference, in other words, is to "the ego in its concreteness," the whole assemblage of ego-cogito-cogitatum, not as a static formula, but rather as set in motion by a pre-egological functioning. The motion is that of temporalization; and the ego first appears as its persistent form.

The Formal Aspect of the Ego

Husserl develops his notion of the ego between the poles of two opposing influences. The first stems from William James—specifically from his doctrine that "the states of consciousness are all that psychology needs . . ."[20] This means the unity of consciousness is their unity. As for knowing or thinking, there is no substantial knower. Rather, "the [individual] thoughts themselves are the thinkers."[21] Husserl in the *Logical Investigations* adopts essentially the same position. He writes, "The phenomenologically reduced ego is therefore nothing peculiar, floating above many experiences: it is simply identical with their own interconnected unity." Its unity is the unity of its experiences or states of consciousness. It is founded on their "contents and the laws they obey."[22] The opposing influence comes from the Neo-Kantian, Paul Natorp. Contrary to James, Natorp stresses the irreducibility of the ego to its contents. "The ego," he writes, is the "subjective center of relation for all contents in my consciousness. . . . It cannot itself be a content, and resembles nothing that could be a content of consciousness." The reason for this is that to be a content is to stand over against an ego. It is to be an object—a *Gegen-stand*—for an ego. Contrariwise, "To be an ego is not to be an object, but to be something opposed to all objects."[23] Such an ego is necessarily anonymous. It cannot be named or grasped in any objective manner. In the *Logical Investigations*, Husserl quotes Natorp only to dismiss him. Phenomenology cannot deal with a nonappearing ego. It is, thus, "quite unable to find this ego, this primitive, necessary center of relations." However, in a footnote to the second edition of the *Investigations*, he admits rather sheepishly: "I have since managed to find it."[24]

What exactly has he found? Seebohm cautions us that Husserl's use of traditional philosophical expressions is often influenced by "rhetorical reasons." To determine their meaning, one must examine "the descriptive analysis of the topic" in question.[25] This applies in particular to the ego. Husserl's terminology is often Neo-Kantian, yet the descriptive analysis points to something quite different. A good example of this occurs in the passage of *Ideen I* which we cited in our last chapter: "The ego . . . is something identical. Every cogito, at least in principle, can change, can come and go. . . . But, as opposed to this, the pure ego seems to be *something necessary* in principle. As something absolutely identical in all actual and possible change of experiences, it cannot *in any sense* be taken as a real component or moment of the experiences."[26] On the surface, the doctrine here seems perfectly Neo-Kantian. The ego, Husserl is asserting, is not the changing acts (the *cogitata*) of consciousness. It is rather something self-identical, something which, in its self-identity, must be distinguished from the real, changing contents of consciousness. This implies that it has no "material content" of its own. "It is," Husserl writes in 1921, "quite empty of such."[27] Yet, this emptiness does not point to the ego as a hidden or noumenal agent. It does not position the self as a Kantian uncombined combiner (or synthesizer) of its stream of experiences. Rather, as we saw in our last chapter, the ego becomes a *form or structure* for such experiences. In Husserl's words, lacking "a material, specific essence," the ego is "an empty form which is only 'individualized' through the stream: this, in the sense of its uniqueness."[28] What individualizes this structure is the actual contents making up a particular ego-life. As for the structure itself, it is that of the centering which makes the subject a subject. Thus, for Husserl, "'subject' here is only another word for the *centering* which all life possesses as an egological life, i.e., as a living in order to experience something, to be conscious of it."[29] The experienced world is always centered; experiencing it, we are always at this center. Our "here" serves as the O point from which we mark off distances. As such it, locates us in the world. The same holds for our "now" which centers us between the retained past and the anticipated future.[30]

Two forms of transcendence appear in this analysis: the spatial one of physical distances and the temporal one which marks the temporal remove from my nowness. For Husserl, "The transcendence of the spatial world is a second level transcendence."[31] "The first, primally welling transcendent is the stream of consciousness and its immanent time."[32] This is the stream whose temporal sequencing of contents results in the relative rates of perspectival unfolding of objects—objects, for example, which surround me as I move through my room. The rates at which objects appear to turn give me my sense of the "near" and the "far" and, hence, my sense of self as a spatial center. Such a sense, with its transcendence, thus, depends on the temporal sequencing of the contents as they depart. But this departure into pastness is what creates the first transcendence. What is originally transcendent is, then, the past over against my nowness. As we cited Husserl: "In [temporal] streaming a self-transcending is originally accomplished; namely a past is constituted . . ." This past transcends me in my "stationary nowness," i.e., in my being as a *temporal center* of consciousness. In other words: "The not now transcends the now, in particular, the consciousness of the not-now. Thus, the continuity of intentional modifications [which yield the sense of pastness] is a constant continuity in which transcendence is originally apprehended (*bewusst wird*). What is transcended is always consciousness." This implies that as my own appearances depart into pastness, this transcendence becomes a *self*-transcendence.[33]

Two conclusions follow from this doctrine. The first is what Husserl calls the ego's *anonymity*. Here Husserl repeats the assertions of Natorp that every objective name or sense we could apply to the ego misses the mark since "to be an ego is not to be an object, but to be something opposed to all objects."[33] The descriptive analysis, however, is anything but Neo-Kantian. Anonymity here is the result of *my remaining now* as a "central ego," even while the experiences which just now particularized me depart into pastness. Grasping myself through their objective synthesis, I apprehend myself "not as the self I am but as the self I was."[35] Every object I grasp is, in other words, already transcendent by virtue of the pastness of the retained contents *through which* it is grasped. As transcendent, it is other than what I am in my central nowness.

The second conclusion that follows from the priority of temporal over spatial transcendence concerns the constitution of the self. Such constitution begins with the institution of temporal transcendence. It is, in the first instance, the constitution of a temporal center as a *point from which* such transcendence is measured. One can also think of it as the specification of the anonymity of this center by (1) the constitution of the temporal environment which makes it a center and by (2) the filling of this environment with the contents which particularize it. As we saw in the last chapter, the temporal environment is formed by the streaming continua of the departing past and the advancing future. Their constitution is the constitution of a "remaining primal now" situated between them. It is, in other words, the constitution of myself as the stationary or "fixed form" of this now.[36] Stationary within this streaming, my now appears as a fixed point of passage—i.e., as that *through which* time appears to flow and *in which* its moments appear to well up as actually present. Its being stationary is its being situated between the continua of the past and the future. Their constitution is, thus, the constitution of the temporal environment which allows the source of time to *appear* as a "middle point" within this environment.

We say *appear* because, although Husserl asserts: "I am. It is from me that time is constituted,"[37] the constitution of time, he also makes clear, is ultimately pre-egological.[38] The best way to put this is in terms of our discussions of the reduction. Exercised on the temporal structure which is the ego, the reduction directs itself to the syntheses of retentions and protentions which yield the positing of the past and future. Suspending this positing, it suspends the temporal environment, the "continua," that give the ego its necessary centering. In Husserl's words, "the performance of the phenomenological epoché" results in a "radical limitation to the living present"—i.e., to the nowness through which the future passes to become the past.[39] So regarded, the present no longer appears as a point of passage. When we view it without the past and the future, it appears as the stationary place, the ("nunc stans"), where the moments of time well up.[40] This exhibition of *passing through* as *welling-up* points, on the one hand, to the pre-egological source of time. It points, on the other, to the ego itself as an acting center. What is revealed here, Husserl asserts, is "the primal phenomenon of my 'I act' (*'Ich tue'*) in which I am a stationary and remaining ego and, indeed, am the actor of the 'nunc stans.' I act now and only now, and I 'continuously' act."[41] As Husserl also describes it, the ego's "acting is a letting loose from itself. It is a primal welling up, a creative allowing to depart from itself of that which, itself, streams, namely, the acts."[42] The point of this is that the ego's action is both its own and that of the primal temporalization. The latter provides the welling up of moments whose retention and protention yields the temporal structure of the now that remains between the past and future even as the latter, in their moments, stream. It thus yields the ego as a "fixed form" for such streaming. On a constituted level, my action therefore seems to originate from this fixed form, i.e., from the now that remains now in the stream of experiences. Yet on the nonconstituted level, the action is that of primal temporalization. It is a function of what Husserl calls the *nonego* in its constant creation of ever new moments.[43] Action, here, has a dual character: its ground is pre-egological; its result is egological. The result, in other words, makes us view the ground *as if* it were an egological source. Viewed in itself, the ground appears as a *singulare tantum*, a unique singularity which is prior to all contrast between unity and plurality. Viewed in terms of its results, however, it can appear simply as a "this one," a one among many possible selves.[44] Commentators have felt forced to choose between one or the other in trying to establish just what an ego is. My position, however, is that no such choice is necessary. What we actually confront is the process that leads from one to the other.

Husserl's Transcendental Aesthetic

An important element in this process is provided by the notion of a "transcendental aesthetic." The term refers to our sensibility, in particular, to the passive syntheses that first give us our objects.[45] Husserl criticizes Kant's aesthetic with its "system of transcendental syntheses" because he sees it as excessively focused on the constitution of spatially transcendent objects. How just this criticism is, indeed, how indebted Husserl's own account is to Kant's, are issues which cannot be answered here.[46] What is certain is that, for Husserl, the prior constitution is that of the "inner world," i.e., of the "purely immanent objectivity" with its temporal transcendence. He calls this constitution "prior" not just because, as he asserts, "the spatial world constitutes itself" by virtue of this prior constitution,[47] but also because the ego itself achieves through these prior syntheses its own lasting character. As he puts this in the second volume of the *Ideas*, the syntheses allow the ego to "find itself as identical in its course"—to find itself as the same ego with the same characteristics.[48] To understand this last assertion, we must note with Husserl that the "numerically singular" central ego "belongs to 'its' stream of experience." The stream is what particularizes it, gives it its character. This means that, just as the stream "is constituted as a unity in unending immanent time," so "the singular pure ego is constituted as a unity in relation to this unity of the stream."[49] Thus, "it could not be constituted as a lasting and remaining ego if a lasting and remaining stream of experience were not constituted . . ."[50] To make this concrete, we need only note that for the stream to have some persistence, what transpires within it—e.g., a perception—cannot vanish the moment after its occurring. It must be retained so that it can be returned to again and again. In Husserl's words, we must have the possibility of "the reproduction of the earlier perception and of its perceptual theme."[51] This means that the content-filled moments of the perception as well as the synthesis that originally bound them together must be retained. To form an identical unit located within departing time, they must be preserved with a distinct temporal referent. If we fulfill these conditions then, as Husserl says, "that which is posited by an act of the cogito, the theme, is . . . something lasting." It becomes one of the "possessions" of the ego.[52] It is there for us even when we do not regard it, do not reproduce it by actively remembering it.

We have already discussed the temporal syntheses by which experiences are retained and fixed in their temporal positions.[53] Here, we need only note that their consequence is a kind of inertia of position takings. Once laid down, a position remains. In Husserl's words, "Each 'opinion' is an endowment (*Stiftung*) which remains a possession of the subject as long as motivations do not arise which require the position-taking to be 'varied' . . ."[54] This is a result of the constitution of a past act as past, as part of the past which *remains the same*. Not that "I" do this. The temporal syntheses which accomplish this are passive. What they accomplish is the basis for my finding myself (if I really am consistent) as the same position taking self. The ego, then, "finds itself as identical in its course" of position takings if, as it performs some act, it recalls having performed the same act in the past.

This argument can be extended to all the features which make up what Husserl calls a *personal ego*—e.g., to our judgments, beliefs, attitudes, etc. Insofar as what I have done remains, the same "inertia" occurs. An interesting point here is that the reproduction of the remembered is also a reproduction of the doxic attitude that accompanied it. Given that nothing has intervened, the latter must reoccur. If it did not, memory would not really reproduce what had gone before. This means that in reproducing an earlier conviction, "I participate in the belief." "The participation," Husserl asserts, "is not a separate step." It is part of the "homogeneous unity of the memory."[55] The result, then, is that not just my experiences, but also my beliefs become part of my "lasting possessions." The important point to remember in all this is that this result is occasioned by the very same processes—those of temporal syntheses—which yielded the central or polar ego. Given this, we cannot, as Marbach advised, choose between the ego as a pole and the ego that can remember and identify itself. Both aspects of the self, in Husserl's view, are co-constituted in the laying down of temporal objectivities.

The transcendental aesthetic includes more, of course, than just the laying down of self-identical temporal unities. In Husserl's words, it involves "the regularities grouped under the title of 'association' which pertain to everything present in the stream of experiences."[56] As such, it includes the Gestalt qualities of fusion, contrasts, and pairing. *Fusion* designates the merging of what we retain. This is "a continuous merging according to similarities."[57] By virtue of it, the merged qualities "stand out." They reenforce each other and, hence, distinguish themselves from the heterogeneous qualities whose union does not result in their merging.[58] This merging gives us the object's "noematic nucleus"—i.e., the connected, relatively stable features which allow us to recognize the object in its appearances. Insofar as the merged qualities pertain to its content, the "contrast" arises between it and the heterogeneous qualities of its background. "Pairing" signifies the linking of similarities. By virtue of it, a present perception recalls a past one with a similar content. Together they may recall a third. The ultimate result here can be a whole horizon of acts, all with similar contents. Once again the phenomenon of merging can occur, though this time its focus can be on acts, rather than on objects and their contents. The result can be the prominence of the relatively stable features which characterize me as a personal ego. In Husserl's words, the consequence of these "regularities" is my "pregivenness" as a personal ego, i.e., my givenness before I reflect on my behavior.[59]

To complete this picture, one further feature must be added. As a personal ego, I am not a solitary self, but rather a person among persons. This means that my objects are not just present for me but for others as well. The same holds for my acts. A layer of their sense structures is intersubjective. As Alfred Schutz points out, this layer cannot be considered as constituted from lower level, private senses—senses drawn from the "sphere of my ownness." If we are ever to solve the intersubjectivity problematic, they must be taken a primordially given.[60] Now, there is nothing in the concept of the ego we have just presented which prevents us from doing this. Regarding the ego, we actually regard a process, one which proceeds from unique to numerical singularity. Temporally speaking, the origin of this process is *neither private nor intersubjective. It is rather prior* to all such distinctions. This means that the actual contents, the senses actually given through the "regularities" making up the transcendental aesthetic, are the source of these distinctions. They determine what counts as just "my own" and what counts as intersubjective. Thus, in spite of certain indications to the contrary in the *Cartesian Meditations*, there is nothing to prevents us from assuming the primordiality or irreducibility of intersubjective sense structures. Learning to see, to feel, to touch—in short, learning how to engage in the syntheses which pertain to our senses—may very well involve the

other as a teacher. It may be that parents help a child to "make sense" of his earliest experiences. If this is the case, then the meanings these learned syntheses
generate are primordially intersubjective. This is what most child psychologists
assert. The egological form of temporal synthesis would not contradict them. As
the "empty form" of the ego, it is simply neutral.[61]

What, then, is a Self?

Summing up, we can say that there are two types of phenomenological
responses to the question: "What is a self?" One of them is static. Here, we
point to the form of egological self-objectification. As a form of constitution, it
is ultimately a temporal form: that of the egological "centering" of experience.
The second answer is dynamic. In it, we point to the continual passage from one
stage to another of this self-objectification. Regarding the anonymity of its
origin, we can give a Neo-Kantian answer to the question of the self. We can
oppose the ego, as a pole or center of this process, to all its constituted results.
A Jamesian answer, one which fastens on the streaming itself, is also possible.
Egological inquiry is here a matter of uncovering the structures of the "transcendental aesthetic," i.e., of the "regularities" which pertain to the streaming. Finally, we can answer the question in terms of this process's ultimate
result: the person among persons, the fully concrete member of the intersubjective world.

Husserl's answer to the question embraces all these features. It is an
answer which explains how, in asserting our essential unknowability, we can
stand outside our worldly givenness, how, in other words, as a feature of our
objective anonymity, we can deny our intersubjective persona. It is also an
answer which explains how we can take the opposite stance and affirm this persona. It, thus, allows us to say that we are both our habits, our personal and
social roles, and our ability to step out of them.[62] We are both determined and
free. Husserl's theory of the ego is nothing less than the attempt to grasp the self
in all its possibilities. The fact that such possibilities are ultimately those of temporal synthesis returns us to the claim that to do phenomenology of the ego is to
do phenomenology itself. The claim takes phenomenology as the study of
those subjective performances (or syntheses) by which the world comes to
presence. What makes phenomenology and egology equivalent is the fact that
the appearing of the world is, correlatively, the appearing of the ego. As a center, the ego is defined by the world as that to which the world appears. Husserl's
insight is that the concreteness or individuality of the one is also that of the
other. This cannot be otherwise given that he sees the same processes of synthesis as underlying both of them.

10

REMARK

With this chapter on the self, we come to a natural conclusion of a line of thought we have followed since the beginning. The original problem we confronted was that of the incompatibility of two different types of being. In our first chapter we asked, how are we to mediate between things and ideas, i.e., between individual and unique singularity? The problem of participation was actually that of categorizing being such that both types of entities could share in being—i.e., achieve a compatible ontological status. The second chapter proposed positioning time as the required mediator. Time in its wholeness seemed to embrace the unique singularity of the unchanging ideas, while its constant passage mirrored the flux of individual being. This solution seems inevitable and it has, in different forms, been embraced by a number of thinkers. As initially proposed, however, it comes with a fateful addition. In its Augustinian form, it makes time subjective. The subject becomes the place where time can have its extension, i.e., be present in both its past and future. This addition, which seems so natural, has a surprising implication once we take account of the unending quality of time. Given that every moment, to be *in* time, must be surrounded by others, there is no first or last moment of time. With this, the question arises as to the subject that could be adequate to time, the subject in which time could have its unending extension. For Augustine, such thoughts point to an absolute subject—to God. The same necessities drive the Husserlian reworking of Augustine's insights. Making time subjective, he, too, is led to an ultimate subject. Containing all time, it is not itself in time. In Husserl's words, "We can no longer speak of a time of the ultimately constituting consciousness" (*Zur Phänomenologie des inneren Zeitbewusstseins*, Hua X, 78). Given that the distinction between the constituting and the constituted is that between ground and grounded, the implication is that "subjective time constitutes itself in an absolutely timeless subject who is not an object" (ibid., p. 112). This timeless, preobjective origin of time also comes to be called *God* or the *Absolute*. As our chapter on radical evil indicates, we can distinguish this Absolute from our own subjectivity. Such a distinction, however, does not prevent us from calling it a layer of our subjectivity. As primally temporalizing, we are identical to the Absolute. It is our most primordial core.

The conclusion, then, is that, for both Augustine and Husserl, the logic of the philosophical path they have chosen leads to God as the ground of the self's being in time.

The danger of this conclusion is one of an infinite inflation of what we call a *self*. Involving, as it does, a totality of layers which includes God, there seems to be no natural limit to its action. The notion, thus, seems to lead to a radical idealism, one which would see everything as a subjective product. This point can be put in terms of Augustine's equation of being and temporal presence, an equation Husserl also shares. If the two are the same, then the constitution of time is also that of being. Thus, if time is subjective—has its reality through subjective constitution—what prevents us from making the same assertion about being? If the being of entities is their temporal presence, it too must be a subjective product. In terms of the present chapter, the implication is that subjectivity in its self-constitution, i.e., in its movement from the pre-egological to the egological, is also constitutive of the world. We, thus, seem to be forced to affirm with Husserl: "Every conceivable sense, every conceivable being, whether the latter be called immanent or transcendent, falls within the realm of transcendental subjectivity as that which constitutes sense and being" (*Cartesian Meditations*, Hua I, 118). What prevents Augustine from embracing this conclusion is the biblical doctrine of creation. The inflation of subjectivity in his thinking remains within the framework of seeing man as an image of God. It is with the decline in belief in creation that the way opens to this radical conclusion. In point of fact, the specter of idealism, from Kant onward, seems to haunt the Augustinian legacy. Such idealism, we should stress, is not one that makes the world a "merely subjective product." It does not engage in the absurdity of making each individual subject a creator of his world. It is rather a consequence of the inflation of the subject. The creative element of the subject is that pre-egological core which is its point of identity both with God and all other subjects.

Given the mutual implication of its notions, we cannot avoid this idealism by working within this tradition. To break out of it, we must abandon its fundamental principles. In particular, we must break the link between the constitution of time and that of being. Rather than making being depend on time, we have to make time depend on being. In other words, instead making time (and, hence, being) be a subjective product, we must reverse the order of this dependence and make temporality the result of being. Accepting that our own subjective being is a field of temporal relationships—in particular those relationships which make up subjective synthesis—this solution makes our selves dependent on being. In the tradition that includes Augustine and Husserl, the order of dependence is that of being depending on time depending on subjectivity. The order that would break out of this is, then, that of subjectivity depending on temporality which would depend on being.

To find the origin of this way of thinking, we must turn to the great rival of the Platonic-Augustinian tradition we have been tracing. Our next chapter will, therefore, examine Aristotle's thoughts on temporality and being. As with our initial encounter with Plato, we shall use Descartes' position as point of contrast for drawing out the insights of an Ancient position

11

ARISTOTLE AND THE OVERCOMING OF THE SUBJECT-OBJECT DICHOTOMY

The idealistic standpoint solves the problem of knowledge—of its possibility and extent—by making the object a product of the subject. It accounts for knowledge by detailing the subjective performances—broadly speaking those of synthesis—which yield the presence of an object. The resulting entity is by definition compatible with such performances. Its categories can always be traced back to the subjective performances which underlie them. In such a situation, we never doubt the possibility of grasping the object. Doubts on this score arise from within a different tradition, one which recognizes the independence of subjects and objects. In modern times, this tradition finds its origin with Descartes. The framework it has left us with has been one in which we picture the subject as something "here," the object as another thing "there," and their relations as describable according to the laws of causality. In this chapter, I am going to relate some very obvious ways in which this framework does not work and then turn to the basis of this failure. This is the notion of the Cartesian grid as somehow prior to and determinative of being. I shall then show how Aristotle, in relativizing both space and time, systematically undermines the possibility of such a grid and, thus, cuts off from the start the Cartesian problematic of the subject-object relation. It will do this by undercutting the supposed independence of subjects and objects, though in a way quite opposed to the idealist alternative. Rather than making objects dependent on subjects, it will affirm the reverse dependence.

The Nature of the Problem

From the Cartesian perspective, the question of the subject-object relation essentially one of transcendence. It concerns our ability to transcend our "here" and to reach the object that appears to be "there," at a physical remove. Can we really reach it so as to get it *as it is in itself*? This reaching of the object depends, of course, on its reaching us. Can it, through its influence on its environment reach our sensory organs? Given that it physically remains there, we seem to be driven to talk of its image reaching us. We begin to wonder whether it can reassemble itself from our multiple perceptions and produce in our brains a replica or image of itself. The question then becomes how we could know whether the image so produced is "like" the original. Do we have to again transverse the distance between ourselves and the object to compare image and object? If we do, then how can we tell whether this second attempt at transcendence with *its* resulting image is successful? Its verification seems to require a third effort, which requires a fourth for its confirmation, and so on indefinitely.[1]

The problem deepens when we try to scientifically explain what we mean by the object and its replica or image within us. Is the image the electric currents coursing through our synapses? Is it also the chemical processes that accompany them? Perhaps it is the pattern of the changing molecular arrangements that occur during the perceptual process. Once we pursue this line of thought, we face the question of the sense in which the physical replica or image could be made "like" the original. The original is itself a collection of mathematically describable space-filling processes, some of which set up parallel processes by impinging on our own sensory organs. The two sets of processes (the original and its subjective replica) are linked through the law of causality. This states that caused events are determined by the material make up of the interacting bodies and the spatial-temporal relations existing between them. A change in any one of these changes the event. If the event is the production of the replica of the object, then the law makes this relative to (among other factors) the particular material structure of the perceiving organism. Different organisms—say, a cat, a parrot, and a man—have different structures and, hence, different replicas of the original within their heads.

Here, the ideal of grasping the object *as it is in itself* collapses once we make causality the bridge between the object and ourselves. As long as perception requires an embodied perceiver, the object that is grasped will be relative to the structure of this embodiment. As post-Darwinian thinkers were to realize, the fact that this structure is the result of an evolutionary line of development, one whose purpose was survival rather than epistemological correctness, also places limits on our understanding of the world.[2] According to this view, each species (man included) will grasp the world in the way which allows it a particular advantage in its struggle for survival. The result is that there are as many appearing worlds as there are ecological niches. As for the world "in itself" which supposedly contains all of these, this can be posited, not as an empirical (observed) reality, but only as a kind of logical necessity. Even this becomes questionable once we say that logic itself is a biologically grounded process, for this implies that "even logic alters with the structure of the brain" (*Logische Untersuchungen* [Tübingen], I, 147, n. 1).

The ontological premise of the preceding description is that of the Cartesian grid with its associated time line. With it, we can identify each object with a mathematical set of coordinates giving its position and time. As such, it opens the way to the mathematical description of nature. Crucial to this account is the assertion that nothing can exist without being in space and time; these, however, can continue even while the things within them come and go. If we accept this, then space and time become grounding conditions of the objects within them. The mathematical account of something according to its spatial-temporal relations becomes not just a description but also an explanation of its very being. It claims to explain why it is as it is. If we accept this, then we have to say that in describing perception, we must take account of two separate realities, those of the image and the original. Both take up space and have their positions in time, and hence both have an equal claim to reality. At this point, if we claim that we predicate an idea in our minds (e.g., of redness), of some external reality, we are actually claiming to predicate one distinct reality of another.

The Relativization of Space and Time

From an Aristotelian perspective, this claim is absurd. Predication is an activity which attributes what cannot exist by itself to what can. The crucial distinction is between a subject of predication (the reality or entity itself) and the attributes that form our description of the reality. To call such attributes "realities in a primary sense" (the sense of being able to exist independently) is simply to commit a category mistake. It is to confuse an attribute such as the place, time, position, quantity or quality of a reality with the reality itself (*Categories*, 1b 25–2a 15). The reality can, by changing, take on different attributes. It thus can continue to be while its former attributes lose their existence as its descriptions.

With this, we already have the basis for Aristotle's relativization of both space and time. Rather than being primary realities, they are regarded as nonindependent attributes of them. It is not the case that entities exist by virtue of being placed in a spatial-temporal environment. Rather, entities are what first make possible this environment. They themselves spatialize and temporalize it. Thus, a place without a body, an empty space or "void," is impossible (*Physics*, 213b 31–33). Considered in itself, it is a kind of "nonbeing or privation." One can no more positively characterize it than one can find "differences in nothing" (215a 11).[3] A place with a body does exist, but it only exists as an attribute of a body.

Aristotle, in trying to determine what sort of an attribute it is, notes that place can in no sense be considered as a cause of an entity. It answers to none of the four causes or reasons why a thing behaves as it does. It is not a body's matter; it is not its form (or intelligible structure); neither is it the goal of its development nor any particular agent causing it to move (*Physics*, 208a 21–25).

Not being a cause, it is, in fact, dependent upon the body. As we said, place without body (empty space) cannot exist. It cannot, because the body itself is what first spatializes—causes us to apply spatial categories. The body does this through its motion. In Aristotle's words, "we must keep in mind that, but for local motion, there would be no place as a subject matter of investigation" (*Physics*, 211a 13). This can be illustrated in terms of Aristotle's definition of place as "the first unmoved boundary of what surrounds [the entity]" (*Physics*, 212a 20). Place answers to the question, "where?" My answer to the question of where I am depends upon my motion. If I am seated writing at my desk, I am in my chair. If I get up and walk about my office, its walls are now my first unmoved boundary. If I now pace the hallway, perhaps visiting other offices on the floor, the appropriate answer to the question "where" is "on the fifth floor." If I take the elevator and visit other floors, my "where" is the building itself. Similarly, during the day, I am at the university; during the week, I am in this university town; during the month, I am in Nova Scotia, and so on. The point of this is that the entity itself determines through its motion its first unmoving boundary and, hence, what constitutes the limits of its environment.[66]

For Aristotle, natural entities move on their own. To have a nature is to have an inherent "beginning" or source "of movement or rest" (*Physics*, 192b 12). Given this, the ultimate cause of spatialization is nature itself. "Nature" in Greek has the sense of growing, developing, and unfolding so as to manifest an entity; the acorn, for example, grows and develops to manifest the goal of this process: the fully formed tree.[67] This last, as determining the pattern and direction of growth, sets the parameters of the environment. Both as an origin and as an accomplished goal of this process, the fully formed tree is the entity itself. The process is its manifestation. As occurring in and through this process, spatialization can be defined as a dimension of the entity's self-revelation, its self-manifestation through time.

Time itself is also part of this self-manifestation. Like place, it cannot be considered apart from the moving body. In itself, it is nothing at all. In Aristotle's words, a stretch of it "consists in non-beings" because it "comprises the past, which no longer is, and the future, which is not yet" (*Physics*, 218a 2). If we ask why neither the past nor the future are, we come to the basis of this assertion. Neither the past nor the future are in the strict sense present. They are elapsed or anticipated temporal presence. To become past is to depart from this presence, while to be future is *not yet* to be present. The premise, then, is that being is correlated to temporal presence. If we are to affirm an entity's actual existence, it must be capable of sharing a now with us. In this now, it must manifest itself, i.e., appear and show itself as it is.[6] If an entity can be on its own, that is, be a reality in the primary sense, then it can manifest itself by itself. It has a "nature" in the above defined sense. Contrariwise, things "not formed by nature"—things which depend on something else to presently appear, such as human artifacts—"are not primary beings" (*Metaphysics,* VIII, 3, 1043b 23).

Admitting that being must be capable of temporal presence, two different paths seem open to us. Either we can assert that being is an ultimate ground or we can ask after the ground of being in the sense of seeking the ground of this presence. As we have seen, the modern period (particularly in the tradition sketched out in our chapters) has pursued the second alternative. It takes time as the ground of being insofar as it sees time as that which makes being temporally present—this, through its flow from now to successive now. This alternative is not limited to the idealistic tradition. It is also implicit in the logic of the Cartesian grid. If to be requires being locatable on the grid, then time along with place is a grounding condition of being. The Aristotelian alternative reverses this, asserting that the presence of time requires the presence of being. In this view, it is not the case that temporality grounds being, but rather that being (in its capacity for presence, i.e., for manifesting itself) grounds time. The entity itself is at the origin of the timing or temporalization of its environment. The modern view, by contrast, takes the flow from now to successive now as the movement from presence to presence and equates temporal presence and being. Time, in making something now, makes it present and, by this definition, makes it be.

The two positions can be distinguished by the different senses they give to the word *presence.* For the modern view, which ultimately stems from Augustine, time can ground being only if being is reduced to presence and only if the sense of the latter is limited to temporal presence, i.e., to nowness. For such a position, the being of an entity is its nowness. For Aristotle, as we shall see, being is understood as the functioning (ἐνέργεια) which results in the entity's presence to its environment. The presence of an entity is the *totality* of its effects, one of which is the present, i.e., temporal presence taken as nowness. Since such presence is only one effect of being, one which Aristotle speculates, requires the presence of soul to occur, it cannot logically be equated with being (see *Physics,* 223a 15–17). To make them equivalent is to embrace the modern position which, in equating nowness, presence, and being, allows us to say that time, in making an entity now, makes this entity be.

For time to do this, it must be composed of nows. In the modern view it is. For Aristotle, however, "the present is not a part of time (τὸ δὲ νῦν ου μέρος)"; for "a part is a measure of the whole, whereas the present is not such a measure." As he also puts this: "time does not seem to be composed of 'nows' (συγκεῖσθαι ἐκ τῶν νῦν)" (*Physics,* 218a 7–8). The necessity for this is more than the logical one that no number of atomic (partless) nows can be summed to produce a whole. It follows from the fact that the presence that grounds time cannot be a part of time. If it were a part of time, then it would, itself, require the same ground or reason for its being that time does. Thus, to function as a ground, this presence—which concretely is the presence of the entity to us—must be *prior* to time. In other words, it is because being (in its presence to a soul) grounds time, that "the present is not part of time."[7]

As in the case of place, such grounding occurs through motion. It is not being's presence pure and simple which occasions time but rather the change of presence. The temporal result of an unchanging presence is an unchanging present. But, as Aristotle observes, "there would be no time" if there were "only a single, self-identical present" (*Physics*, 218b 28). In other words, "when we have no sense of change, . . . we have no sense of the passing of time" (218b 24). The entity, then, grounds time through the change of its presence. This does not mean that this presence manifests a sheer otherness. It combines both identity and difference. The identity comes from the identity of the entity whose presence it is. The difference stems from the differences created by the entity's movement. As Aristotle writes: "The moving body . . . is the same . . . , but the moving body differs in the account which may be given of it." In particular, it differs by being in different places "and the present (τὸ νῦν) corresponds to it as time corresponds to the movement" (*Physics*, 219b 20–23). The assertion, here, is that the present or now which "is not a part of time," but rather its ground, is the presence of the body. It "corresponds" to the body by virtue of being part of the body's continuous self-manifestation. The continuity of time depends upon this continuity, this lack of any gaps in the body's presence.[8] Similarly, time corresponds to the body's movement insofar as it manifests the body's shifting relation to its environment. Thus, "it is by reference to the moving body that we recognize what comes before and after in the movement" (*Physics*, 219b 24). We say, "before, the body was here, afterward it was there." If, on reflection, we distinguish the before from the after, then the present appears as a division between the two: it is the presence of the body after it left one place and before it went to another. With motion comes the shift of the before and the after and, with this, the appearance of the flowing present or now. This shifting center of the temporal environment is simply a dimension (an attribute, an aspect) of the presence of the body as the shifting center of its environment. Subjectively, then, time appears with the phenomenological characteristics which Husserl first described. It appears as a kind of stationary streaming. We experience it as a flow, that is, as a constant succession of the "before and after." Yet we also have to say that the present in which we experience this streaming is itself stationary and remaining. It is always now for us. The continuity of this now is the continuity of the presence of being. We experience it as long as we are aware of being or, what is the same, as long as an entity's presence is manifested to us.

The Ontology of Knowing: Actuality

Aristotle asserts that "before it thinks," that is, before it grasps and apprehends an object, "mind has no actual existence" (*De Anima*, III, iv, 429a 24). It is, in other words, "potentially identical with the objects of its thought, but is actually nothing until it thinks" (ibid., 429b 31). This implies that apart from an entity's presence, mind ceases. Separated from the presence of being, mind (νοῦς), which is the perceiving (νόειν) of being, collapses. When it is perceiving, mind (or rather the knowledge which forms its content) is identical with its object (ibid., 430a 20). The removal of the object is the removal of its content. It leaves it in a state where it has "no actual existence."[9]

Such statements point out the ontological ambiguity of the subject object relation. They undermine from the start any attempt to define subjects and objects in terms of independent positions on the Cartesian grid. Thus, the subject seems to be only in the presence of the object. More precisely, in mind's identity with the being of its object, its "actual existence" is just the presence which is the manifestation of the object to it. When Aristotle says that before it thinks, mind has no "actual existence," he is literally asserting that it has no existence "in the at workness (ἐνεργείᾳ) of beings (τῶν ὄντων)." The *object* is actual, is "at work," in its self-manifestation, yet such self-manifestation is also the *subject's* actual being. When the object is a moving body, then such subjective being involves temporality. It manifests the character of persisting presence—an ongoing nowness—within a shifting environment of the before and after.[10] To attempt to attribute this presence to either pole of the subject object relation is to miss the essential ambiguity of the relation. It is an ambiguity which from the start undercuts the fruitless dialectic of original and replica with which we began.

At the heart of this ambiguity is the fact that "being . . . may be only actual or potential or both actual and potential" (*Physics*, 200b 26–27). The process from the potential to the actual is motion, something which, because it embraces both the actual and the potential, is and yet, as Aristotle says, "is hard to grasp" (201b 33). As he explains it, "since any kind of being may be distinguished as either potential or completely realized, the perfecting (ἐντελέχεια) of what is potential as potential, that is "being in movement" (201a 11). Motion, then, is the perfecting of the entity through the functioning of its potential. Such functioning is the actual operation of the powers that lie dormant in an entity. Thus, dormant in an acorn is the power to grow and to develop so as to ultimately manifest its being as a full grown tree. The motion that is the operation of this power is growth. It is also, we can say, its ongoing result. It is the tree itself in its ongoing presence (or self-manifestation) as a living, growing entity. To take another example, we can say that dormant in the student is the power to learn. The functioning of this power is the perfecting of the student in the sense that it makes him actually become what he is capable of being: in learning, he becomes an actual student.[11]

The student, however, requires a teacher to learn. If we ask where this teacher is, the ambiguity implicit in this description of motion becomes apparent. Considered in terms of his functioning, i.e., his activity of "perfecting" the student, the teacher *is* in the student. The student's perfecting is also the teacher's perfecting as a teacher. Thus, generally speaking, as Aristotle puts it: the "movement is in the movable," this because "the movement is the perfecting (ἐντελέχεια) of the movable by some mover, and the functioning (ἐνέργεια) of this agent is not different [from the perfecting of the movable]" (*Physics*, 202a 13–15). As identified with the perfecting of the movable, the agent's functioning is in the movable. Since this functioning is, in fact, the agent's own perfecting—that is, its own operation of its powers—its identification with the perfecting of the movable means that in this relation of mover and movable there is just one perfecting. In Aristotle's words, "movement must be the perfecting (ἐντελέχειαν) of both; since a thing is an agent or mover because it has the power of moving, and is actually moving when that power is functioning [or, is 'at work']. Hence, there is a single functioning (ἐνέργεια) of both alike" (*Physics*, 202a 16–20). This means that the teacher cannot function as a teacher without the student functioning as a student. They must "work" together. Their "being at work," their actuality, is in this instance one.

To appreciate the strength of this claim, we must note again that for Aristotle the being of entities is this functioning or being at work. An entity has an actual existence (and hence a capacity for temporal presence) through the operation (or functioning) of its powers (*Metaphysics*, 1045a 24, 1045b 19–20). In such a context, to ask where an entity actually is *is* to ask where this functioning is. In the case of the teacher, the answer is clear. The functioning is "teaching," and the place of this is where it is presently at work. It is "in the one taught" (*Physics*, 202b 7–8). Thus, the teacher must actually function in the learner if the latter is to actualize his potentiality to learn. His teaching is "there" in the learner since this is where his being as a teacher is "at work." It is there as the operation or functioning of his power to make the learner learn. Given that the functioning of teaching requires that of learning, what we have are not two different functionings but rather aspects of a single functioning, one which requires both teacher and learner if the potentiality inherent in their relationship is to be realized in the learner. To attempt to represent this on the Cartesian grid, we would thus have to collapse the two spatial temporal positions of the teacher and learner to represent the single actuality that is their combined functioning.[12]

The Ontology of Knowing: Potentiality

Given that being is functioning, on the most basic level, the functioning that results in the being's self manifestation, does this mean that in teaching I really am "there" where my students are, actually present in their learning?

What happens to me when I cease teaching? Does my being as a teacher vanish entirely? The same questions can be asked about the perceptible object. For Aristotle, "the functioning of the sensible object" *is* "in the sensing subject" (*De Anima*, III, 2, 426a 10). It is where the perception of the object is actually operative. In fact, it is "one and the same" with the functioning of such perception (ibid., 425b 27).[13] Does this mean that its being *is* its presence in some subject? What happens when it is not perceived? Does its being as a sensible object cease entirely? Does it cease being even something that *can* be perceived?

To avoid this last assumption, Aristotle makes a distinction in the "to be" of the perceived and its perception. He asserts: "The functioning of the sensible object and that of sensation is one and the same, but not their 'to be'" (ibid.). The same claim is made about the teacher and the student. The identity of their functioning does not exclude a difference in their "to be" (see *Physics*, 202b 10). Thus, you can "be" a teacher after class ends in the sense that you *can* teach again. You have the capability to re-engage in the functioning which identifies you with the learner. Similarly, we can say that although the functioning of the perceived and its perception simultaneously arise and cease, "it is not necessary to assert this of their potentialities" (*De Anima*, 426a 20). The sensible object still "is" apart from its being sensed insofar as it *can be* sensed.

This distinction between functioning and the capacity to function is an *ontological* distinction, one which manifests the ambiguity of an entity's "to be." Given that being is the functioning that manifests itself in presence, this is an ambiguity in the ways in which entities can be present. Thus, behind the question of how an entity can "be" without being perceived is the question of how it can "be" capable of being perceived. What, in other words, is the ontological status of potentiality? Behind this is the still more fundamental question: How do we understand potentiality as a mode of presence? How, in other words, are we to understand it as a manifestation of the functioning of being?

Even when it is not perceived, a sensible object, we say, is there available for perception. Its potentiality signifies its being there, its *being available* for perception. In appealing to it, we do not assert that being equals perception, but only perceivablity or capability to be perceived. Being is what *can* be brought into presence. What is potential can become present. Its potential for presence is its ability to take part in a process involving its self-manifestation. The Aristotelian name for this process is *nature*. *Nature*, as we said, designates that activity whereby something emerges, grows, and develops so as to show itself as it is, i.e., so as to be present in its completed reality (ἐντελέχεια). Thus, as involving presence—more specifically, as a type of being toward being completely present—potential being exists in a context structured by nature.

Nature brings things to presence in a quite definite way. Its temporality is *not* that of the past determining the present, which determines the future. In this unidimensional view of temporal determinism, the state of the world at one moment is viewed as being its necessary and sufficient cause for its state at the next, as in Figure 4. Nature, viewed in an Aristotelian manner, may be symbolically regarded by taking this line and bending it in a circle, as in Figure 5. Here, the future determines the past in its determination of the present. As

FIGURE 4

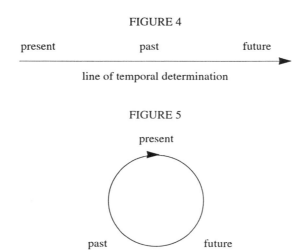

present   past   future

line of temporal determination

FIGURE 5

present

past   future

determinative, the future stands as a goal, as a "final cause" of the natural process. The goal makes the past into a resource, into a "material" as it were, for the process of its own realization. The goal thus determines the past in the latter's determination of the present by structuring it as a potential for some particular realization.

What we are pointing to can be illustrated in a number of ways—all of which are slightly misleading. Suppose, for example, that a woman decided to become a marathon runner. Her being as an actual runner is not a present reality. Neither is it past. It "exists" as a *future* whose determining presence is that of a goal. How long she has to train is determined by the resources she brings to the goal—i.e., how long she has trained in the immediate *past*. Thus, as the circle indicates, determination by the future is not absolute but occurs through the past. The determining presence of the past is that of the materials or resources it presents us to accomplish the goal. Of course, the goal is what allows us to see such materials as materials for some purpose. The goal is what turns the past into a potential to be actualized by our ongoing, *present* activity. To take another example, it is the goal of building which first makes timber into building material. Similarly, the potential of stone to be a statue as opposed to a shelter demands the entertaining of a corresponding goal. What makes these examples somewhat misleading is that they are all from "art" (τέχνη). They are taken from that type of activity where, according to Aristotle, man "imitates" nature. This imitation is an imposition of goals whereby he makes nature participate in his future. Quite apart from man, natural entities have their own goals. Different plants, for example, turn earth, sunlight, water as well as a host of other factors into materials for their own particular ends.

What is common to all such processes is the teleology we encountered in Husserl's description of time. For Husserl, such teleology is implicit in the temporal process per se. It is a function of the nonindependence of time's moments. For Aristotle, however, it is a function of being. It results because, in natural processes, the complete reality that stands at the end is not just the goal but also the cause of its own realization. Thus, as causally determinative, the goal gives us the movement of nature which time mirrors in its passage from the future through the past to the present. What situates potentiality as a category of reality is just such "natural" movement.[14]

To speak of determination by the goal, we must, of course, accept our earlier assertion that it is not time that makes being "be" but rather the reverse. Being is the ground of time, this through the presence which is the result of its functioning. The presence which directs the teleological flow of time—the flow from the future through the past to the present—is the presence of the goal. This point can be put in terms of Aristotle's doctrine that actuality is prior to potentiality. This priority of actuality is, ontologically, the priority of the completed reality (ἐντελέχεια), or the *being at the end* of the process, which the process itself is directed to realize. It is also the priority of functioning (ἐνεργέια) over the capacity to function (δύναμις). What can fully function is the completed reality. Taken as a goal or end of a process, its functioning is that of the process' final cause. As Aristotle expresses this relationship: "everything that comes to be moves towards its source (ἐπ᾽ ἀρχὴν), that is, towards its goal (τέλος); for its wherefore [final cause] is its source. Its coming into being is directed by the end which is the actuality (ἐνέργεια), and it is thanks to the end that potentiality (δύναμις) is possessed" (*Meta.* IX, viii, 1050a 8–10).

A number of points are made in this passage. Together they give us the answer to our question: What is potentiality as a mode of presence? The first point is that it is the end, the completed reality, which directs coming into being. It is, thus, responsible for the motion of nature, the temporal reflection of such action being time grasped as a teleological flow.[15] Without this end or, more precisely, without its functioning (ἐνέργεια) as a final cause, there would be no natural coming into being and, hence, there would be *no potentiality* as a category of reality. Thus, what is potential can "be" without being presently actualized, but not without that which directs its coming into being. The same point can be expressed slightly differently by noting that the causality is exercised by being. It is, in fact, an effect of its functioning. Given that being is what appears at the end of a natural process, we cannot talk of causality in the sense of the past being a necessary and sufficient condition for the present, which serves, in turn, as a similar condition for the future. The presence which could function as such a condition must be that which has achieved completed being (ἐντελέχεια); but in natural, developmental processes, such being is at the end.[16] It is thus "thanks to the end that potentiality is possessed." In other words, the end acts as a final cause determining coming into being; and as such, it makes potentiality possible.

Let us relate this to our point that entities, rather than being a result of their spatial temporal determinations, are what first determine space and time. Both space and time, we said, result from motion. Their ultimate basis is found in those "natural" entities which have within them a beginning or source of the motion whereby they manifest themselves. This source is the completed reality which stands at the end of this process and determines it as a final cause. Understood as an aspect of the entity's self-manifestation, space can be seen as a system (or "place") of those places an entity occupies as it unfolds itself under the direction of this cause. Similarly, time can be taken as a parallel aspect. It is the temporal dimension of this unfolding as it manifests itself to us. It is our registering the changes in the entity's presence. The determination of this motion by the completed reality at the end of this process is, then, the determination of the space and time through which such manifestation occurs. Rather than being independent realities, space and time exist "for the sake of" such manifestation. They are, as it were, its material or medium. We essentially say the same thing when we say that they exist "thanks to the end." They are aspects of the potentiality which the end, in determining coming into being, makes possible. As teleologically determined, they are potentiality as a mode of presence.

There are two complimentary ways of expressing this. We can note that insofar as space and time depend on motion, they are determined by the end that acts as the final cause of such motion. To reverse this, we can say that the final cause makes possible both potentiality and the motion that is the actualization of this potentiality. As a consequence it also grounds the space and time which are the measures of this motion. This implies that space and time are grounded by entities only insofar as they are capable of motion, i.e., possess a potentiality which is not completely actualized. The complete actualization of a potentiality exhausts the capability for motion and hence for being determined by space or time. As Eva Brann remarks with regard to the latter, "When a moving thing has come to the state of being-at-its-own-end or fulfillment it straightaway cuts out of the continuum of time and becomes, with respect to its being, timeless" ("Against Time," p. 74). The same can be said of the entity's location within the system of places which forms its "first unmoving boundary." To the point that it is, with respect to its being, truly incapable of motion, it is also incapable of place. Thus, when the goal is realized, the potentiality, the movement and the spatial temporal determinants all vanish. What remains is a being present (a completed reality) which in directing the process has remained unmoved and which now simply shows itself as its accomplished goal.[17]

This, of course, holds only for the case of complete actualization. What is completely actual, for Aristotle, is the nonmaterial or formal aspect of the reality. As long as a material substrate remains, a certain potentiality, if only for locomotion, also exists. With this, however, we continue to have the potentiality for spatial temporal determination. Thus, the fully formed entity continues, at least with respect to its material substrate, to have a "here"—i.e., a position or membership in a set of places that are possible for this substrate. Similarly, even if it is not *in* time according to its being or form, its material substrate still makes it be *while* time lasts.[18] If however, the end of the process is without a material substrate, if, as in perception, it involves the reception of the form "without the matter," then all such spatial-temporal determinations vanish (*De Anima*, 424a 18–20).

The Overcoming of the Dichotomy

We can conclude by applying these insights to the difficulty we began with. We asked how we could transcend our "here" so as to reach the object that appears "there" at a physical remove. If the object reached *us* through processes resulting in its image, we asked how we could know whether image and original ever matched. Following Aristotle, we have to say that these questions are the result of a couple of category mistakes. The first mistake takes space and time as essential rather than accidental determinants of being. The second compounds this error by confusing potential with actual being. If Aristotle is right in asserting that the sensible object is actually one with its sensation, there is no original out there with which we could compare our sensation. In Gertrude Stein's phrase, there is no "there there," since the *actuality* (the functioning) of the perceived is its *manifestation through our perception*. Qua sensible object, this manifestation is its completed reality. It is, in other words, the final cause of the process resulting in its perception. As such, it is what directed the process from the start.

What about the sensible object when it is not being perceived? As we cited Aristotle, even though the sensible object and its perception have a single actualization, "we need not assert this of them according to their potentialities." We can, in other words, speak of the potentially sensible. Does this make the latter a standard we can apply to judge the validity of our perceiving? Can the potentially sensible object with its different "to be" count as an original against which we can judge the "replica" in our heads? Such an interpretation reverses their true relation. We can speak of potentiality only in terms of actuality. The "to be" of the former is that of serving as material for the latter. Thus, the potentially sensible object is such only as offering the material basis for an actual perception. The latter, rather than being a dependent replica in our head, stands as a final cause directing the process. It is what, in the first instance, makes possible the sensible object's potentiality. Given this, there is no replica and original to compare. To attempt to do so would be rather like attempting to evaluate a finished statue by comparing it with the material it came from. In fact, admitting that the original is the perceptual presence, we have to say that "the perception of proper objects is always true" (*De Anima*, 428b 19).[19] We can err when we attribute something to objects we do not perceive, but we cannot err (in the sense of failing some correspondence test) when we do perceive them. We cannot because, as we said, there is no "there there"—no object actually possessing the sensible qualities we perceive other than the one that manifests itself in us.

Given that this process involves the presence of a form "without matter," the notion of the perceptual object being "in us" has to be qualified. Strictly speaking the presence of the object has no place. The potentially sensible object, to the point that its actualization can be said to involve motion,[20] can be characterized by spatial temporal predicates. It can come to be in us at a certain time. Once the process stops, however, such predicates no longer apply. The object's content can contain a *reference* to a place and a time, but the *content itself* will not be spatially or temporally determinate. This is why it can be handed on: why an event occurring in a specific place at a particular time can be grasped, spoken of, and passed on in the coin of an unchanged meaning. This, of course, underlies the very possibility of teaching insofar as it consists of handing on a received body of knowledge.

All of this affects our answer to the question of where the teacher is. In Aristotle's doctrine, the "self" of the teacher experiences a kind of expansion of its boundaries. This inflation, however, is quite different from that implied by the Augustinian-Husserlian tradition. For Aristotle, there are as many answers to the question of the place of the self as their are senses of being, i.e., of functioning. As a teacher, I am wherever my functioning has effect. Writing at the blackboard, pushing the chalk along, I am at the place of this physical functioning. Speaking and setting up the movements of perception and understanding, I am also present in my students' learning. Here, my place, taken as the first unmoving boundary of my functioning, is the classroom. In general, I am, in my being, wherever my presence (as grounded by my functioning) extends. Other beings may also be in the same "place." Indeed, my own actual being or functioning may be an essential part of their functioning. Since the senses of my being include the "to be" of potentiality, the same assertions can be made with regard to my serving as the material for another's actualization. Finally, insofar as my teaching is successful, i.e., results in the actuality of genuine perception (νοῦς), my presence escapes both time and place. It becomes simply part of the cogitational actuality of unchanging contents.

If all this looks like an ambiguous situation where beings interpenetrate beings and assist in establishing one another in their functioning, it cannot be helped. It may just be the way that reality is. To limit being to a definite position on a Cartesian grid obscures the multiple senses of its being. From the Aristotelian perspective, it also makes unintelligible our own being which, in the actuality of cognition, includes the grasp of being.[21]

12

THE MIND BODY PROBLEM, PHENOMENOLOGICAL REFLECTIONS ON AN ANCIENT SOLUTION

The relation of the soul—and, as part of this, the mind—to the body is an ancient problem. Plato and Aristotle consider it. So does Descartes, the founder of modernity. With the latter, however, the shape of their relation receives a peculiar cast, one which ultimately makes their interaction unintelligible. This lack of intelligibility affects the very notion of a person (or self) as composed of mind and body. In this chapter, I first show how this unintelligibility arises from Descartes' method of doubt. I then continue the reflections of the previous chapter on the Aristotelian tradition to present its solution to the problem of the mind's (or soul's) relation to the body. The use of this tradition does not mean that the insights of Husserl are left behind. To the point that these insights are phenomenologically grounded, they display the kind of neutrality that allows their use to fill some of the descriptive lacunae in the ancient account. I use them to give my own response to the question of what a person (or self) is. This involves reflecting on subjectivity as "flesh." Flesh is proposed as a category which, standing between soul and body, grounds the possibility of their relation and, hence, that of the unity of a self.

Descartes and the Modern Problematic

As is well known, the soul or self in Descartes' *Meditations* suffers a dramatic reduction. It becomes the *I* of the "I think." Normally, when I say "I," I refer to my psychological and physical presence. I include my social relations, my psychological characteristics, and certainly my physical body. For Descartes, however, the "I" is only what I can be absolutely certain of. It is the residuum left by his method of doubt. This method invites us to consider "an evil genius, as clever and deceitful as he is powerful," who has bent all his efforts at deceiving us.[1] Descartes asks, "how do I know that I am not deceived every time I add two and three or count the sides of a square or perform an even simpler operation . . .?"[2] His reply, in the first instance, is to admit the doubtfulness of every object of thought, every conclusion of the judgment. The only thing he cannot doubt is the existence of the "I" or self that is being deceived. This, however, is a reduced "I." It is not the self with a social position. It is not even the self having a "face, hands, arms and this entire mechanism of bodily members." It is, rather, the self that doubts whether any of this pertains to it, the self which assumes that "I . . . have no senses: body, shape, extension, movement, and place are all figments of my imagination."[3] Reduced, then, to what Descartes can be certain of, the self becomes "only a thing that thinks." Its "essence," he asserts, "consists in this alone."[4] Thinking, here, is a generic term. It includes such things as doubting, understanding, affirming, denying, willing, imagining, and sensing.[5] What it does not include are the objective correlates to these actions. Thus, for Descartes, all the objects the self can attend to can be doubted; what cannot be doubted is simply the attending itself. In other words, the self that remains is actually not an object, but rather that which directs itself to objects.

If my essence consists solely in such attending—"thinking" in the broad sense in which Descartes defines it—I must, he argues, be completely nonextended. Given that bodily extension is one of the things I can doubt, it follows "that I am truly distinct from my [extended] body." Indeed, reduced to what I can be certain of, it seems that "I can exist without [this body]."[6] The distinction between mind and body here is deceptively simple. Bodies are divisible and, hence, extended; the self or mind, by contrast, is a thoroughgoing unity. Thus, as Descartes argues, "it is one and same mind that wills, senses, and understands . . . [whereas] no corporeal or extended thing can be thought of by me that I did not easily in thought divide into parts."[7] Since I cannot say I am a different mind when I will or understand or sense, as I often perform these activities simultaneously, I cannot be divided and, hence, cannot be taken as something extended. In fact, as later philosophers were to point out, insofar as I persist as I pass from one form of mental activity to another, I cannot be identified with any of them. Not only am I nonextended, I am also not my sensing or my willing or my understanding, but only a sort of unity of attending underlying these and all other conscious states.

With this we come to the classic mind-body problem: how can this nonextended subject interact with the body. Relaxing his method of doubt, Descartes concludes that the clearest and most distinct aspect of bodies is their extension. Certainty, in the first instance, extends to this alone. This holds even with regard to my own bodily being. "I have," he writes, "a distinct idea of a body—insofar as it is merely an extended thing, and not a thing that thinks . . ." I also "have a clear and distinct idea of myself—insofar as I am a thing that thinks and not an extended thing."[8] Given this, the two are "distinct." But with this distinction comes the question of how to mediate between them. In *The Passions of the Soul*, Descartes proposes that the soul communicates to "the machine of the body" by means of a "little gland," the pineal. Moving it, it moves the body.[9] Yet, given that between the extended and the nonextended there can be no point of physical contact, this obviously will not do. If we reduce mind and body to what we can be certain of, it is possible to arrive at extension as that which distinguishes bodies from minds. But the price we pay is the apparent lack of any mediating category. Mind and body seem mutually exclusive.

The Mind as a Theater

The notion that the mind is nonextended does not originate with Descartes. Earlier thinkers also hold this view. There is, however, an important terminological shift. They prefer to speak of the mind as "immaterial." Its lack of extension is a function of its not possessing matter. The nature of this shift can be seen in terms of a different set of epistemological motivations. Descartes was motivated by the search for a being he can know with absolute certainty— an *ens certissimum*. The requirement of certainty makes him abstract from the mind all that he can doubt. The motivations of the earlier thinkers focused, not on an indubitable item of knowledge, but rather on the nature of the knowing process itself. For the process to be possible, the mind, they argued, must be immaterial.

Their argument can be put in terms of the view that sees reality as informed matter. According to this, a particular thing is such by virtue of its matter having assumed a particular shape. Its organizing itself as this sort of thing, rather than that, is what makes it "stand out" from its background—*ex-(s)istere* in the Latin, ἐξίστημι in the Greek. Standing out or "existing" by virtue of its formal organization, it can appear as a "this"—a particular entity. Now, if knowing is to be taken as the process by which the forms of the world "inform" the mind, an obvious limitation to this view must be made. They cannot inform or shape the mind in the way that they shape a material reality. If they did, then as Aquinas says, "the forms of the things known would make the intellect to be actually of the same nature as that which is known."[10] In knowing fire, for example, the mind would become fire. It would undergo the same sort of material organization as that which the form of fire imposes on a burning object. If this is not to be the case, then the form must be received immaterially. For this to be possible, the mind itself must be immaterial. Aquinas introduces a host of other arguments to the same effect.[11] One by one, they point out the difficulties of having a mind involved in the particularities of matter know different objects. In each case, he argues that mind cannot be a particular thing, a "this," and yet be open to other types of objects.

The insight behind these arguments comes from Aristotle. If, in fact, the mind is to be *open* to all objects, "it can," he argues, "have no characteristic except its capacity to receive" (φύσιν μηδεμίαν ἀλλ᾽ ἢ ταύτῃ ὅτι δυνατόν).[12] If it were "mixed with the body . . . it would become somehow qualitative . . . or even have an organ."[13] It would, in other words, display the definite qualities which bodies must have as particular organizations of matter. Far from being a pure openness, it would itself be some particular thing, its qualities standing in the way of its receiving each thing as it is. This point can be put in terms of the consequences of assuming that mind, like the senses of sight and hearing, has a definite organ. According to Aristotle, each of these senses exists as a "ratio," a formula involving its material components. An excess of the sensible object—a blinding light or a deafening sound—disturbs the ratio and, hence, impedes the sense's capacity to function.[14] Now, if the mind were like this, it would not just be the case that it would be disturbed by an excess of its own object—i.e., after thinking what is excessively intelligible it would be unable to grasp what is less intelligible. It would also be limited by its ratio to one type of object rather than another. Each sense receives "according to its ratio" (κατὰ τὸν λόγον).[15] To give the mind a material organ would thus be to limit its receptivity to those things which are conformable to its material makeup. Rather than being a pure receptivity, it would be open only to those things which fit its particular ratio. Changing the ratio, that is, changing its material makeup, would thus change the very nature of its understanding. With this we face the ancient parallel to the modern attempt to explain knowing in terms of material causal processes. The skeptical consequences implicit here may be considered by reflecting on the words of the nineteenth century psychologist G. Ferrero. As we cited him in our last chapter, "Even logic alters with the structure of the brain."[16] An Aristotelian would say that if the brain is the mind's material organ, then changing its structure changes our receptivity to the logical forms.

The alternative to this is to view the mind as a sheer openness. Capable of receiving the form of every possible object, it is in itself just this capability. It is not itself a form, but rather "a place of the forms" (τόπον εἰδῶν).[17] Any matter would make it a "this"—a particular existent, a particular piece of shaped matter. But as Aristotle asserts, "before it thinks," that is, before it grasps its object, "mind is actually none of the existents" (οὐθέν ἐστιν ἐνεργείᾳ τῶν ὄντων πρὶν νοεῖν).[18] This means that it has no inherent content, all such content being derived from the existents it does think. As a "place of forms," it is, to use Hume's analogy, rather like a theater.[19] The sense organ is where the sensible object can appear as sensible, the actuality of the sensible object qua sensible being, as Aristotle says, in the sense organ.[20] Just so the mind is place, the "theater" in Hume's terms, where the intelligible forms can appear. The motivation for asserting its immateriality is, then, to secure its position as such a "place." The goal is not to secure it as an item of knowledge (a particular "most certain being" in Descartes' phrase); it is to position it as an unlimited openness to every possible being.

One Way Touch

How then does this openness that is immaterial interact with the body? As Aquinas notes, it cannot be by "contact properly so called. For there is contact only between bodies" which touch by coming "together at their extremities."[21] An immaterial substance, however, has no extremity. It also cannot interact by virtue of the mind's being somehow "mixed" with the body. Things mixed are "altered in [their] relation to one another."[22] But this presupposes some "matter in common," which is just what is lacking here. Having listed the difficulties, Aquinas proposes his solution. He writes, "There is, however, a certain kind of contact whereby an intellectual substance [a soul] can be united to a body. . . . if attention is given to activity and passivity, it will be found that certain things touch others and are not themselves touched."[23] This, he asserts, is the soul's relation to the body. The relation is that of one-way touch. It is distinguished from two way or mutual contact insofar as "by this contact the indivisible can touch the divisible." The contact is not between the extremities. Rather, "the whole thing" is "touched" by the indivisible agent. It "is touched according as it is acted upon," that is, "inasmuch as the thing is in potentiality" to such action, the potentiality involving the whole of the thing. With this comes another distinguishing characteristic. The relation of agent to patient is not an extrinsic relation, but rather an intrinsic one. In Aquinas' words, "the contact . . . extends to the innermost things, it makes the touching substance to be within the thing touched and to penetrate it without hindrance."[24] The two are actually "one with respect to acting and being acted upon."[25]

An example he gives makes clear the type of phenomena he has in mind. We are often, he notes, affected by things we are not in physical contact with. It is "in this sense that we say that a person in sorrow touches us."[26] If we have a sympathetic disposition, we can be touched to the quick by his plight. The potentiality of our disposition allows it to "penetrate" us "without hindrance." It allows us to be *inwardly* moved. The motion, we can say, is through our mind or soul. But it is through it as an *openness* to the world, in particular, to the sorrowing person's plight. By virtue of this openness, we can be moved or touched by someone even if that person remains unaware of us. He moves us and yet remains, himself, unmoved.

Once again, the basic insight is Aristotle's. There are, he says, two types of movers: "one kind of mover can only impart motion by being itself moved, another kind can do so through remaining itself unmoved."[27] The distinction, he explains, is actually one of touch. Moved movers touch and are touched. Unmoved movers act through one-way touch. In Aristotle's words: "if anything imparts motion without itself being moved, it may touch the moved and yet itself be touched by nothing—for we say sometimes that the man who grieves us 'touches' us, but not that we 'touch' him."[28] When he touches us, he does not grieve. We are the ones who grieve. The grieving is an action of our soul; it penetrates our entire bodily being. Yet the basis is our openness to the man who grieves us. As unmoved, he is the first or prime mover of this sequence. He moves us, not physically, but as an object of our thought. As Aristotle states the general position: "The object of desire (τὸ ὀρεκτὸν) and the object of thought (τὸ νοητὸν) move without being moved."[29] They do not change or move, rather they change us. Thus, the young man on a stroll on a warm day who changes his direction once he sees an ice cream vendor evinces the action of an unmoved mover just as surely as a person who makes a resolution and attempts to adhere to it. In a certain sense, we can say that the object of desire or thought—the ice cream or the resolution—is the agent. Yet, it is also equally true to assert that the young man is the mover. He is this because he is the place where the agent can appear as such. By virtue of possessing sensation and mind, he is where the agents can come to presence as objects of desire or thought. As we cited Aristotle, "the functioning of the sensible object" *is* "in the sensing subject."[30] Similarly, the functioning of the intelligible or the desirable object is in the understanding or desiring subject. Each is an example of his doctrine that "the functioning (ἐνέργεια) of the agent and mover occurs in what is acted upon."[31] When such functioning involves moving as an object of desire or thought, the motion occurs within the desiring or thinking person. There is no point in looking beyond or "outside" of this person for the reality of the agency. The reality occurs in the only "place" where objects of desire or thought can actually function, this being the perceiving subject.[32]

Agency and Openness

If the soul really is a "place" or "theater" of forms, it must move us as such. It must move us as the place where objects of thought or desire can appear. Its motion must be their motion. Such objects, as is obvious, move us as goals. If, for example, I desire a cold beer, my desire is to drink it. The act of drinking the beer is not a present reality, but rather a "not-yet." It is a *future* condition whose desirability determines my present actions. It moves me to bring about its *present reality*. Of course, I can "change my mind" and, with this, the goals I have "in mind." Considered in their formal character, however, the goals do not change. They are either entertained, i.e., function as such in me, or they are not. When they do function, they do not do so in terms of their physical reality, which is something not yet realized. They function simply in terms of their "what" character. They operate as forms whose action determines me to accomplish their physical reality. As Aristotle puts this, "there are two principles that cause physical movement." One is obviously physical, as when I am pushed or pulled by something. One, however, is not, "for it has no tendency to change with itself." This is "an unmoved mover." It is also "what anything is or its form," this, insofar as the form functions as "a final cause or goal."[33] Given that goals do move us without themselves being moved, they are a pre-eminent example of one way touch. One way touch is, in other words, inherently teleological. It is the action of forms functioning as final causes. Insofar as the soul is the place of such functioning, its action must also be regarded as teleological. The relation of one way touch the soul has to the body is, then, that of the goals it entertains.

We can put this in terms of the openness to forms (both sensible and intellectual) that characterizes the human soul. This openness to forms is also an openness to the agency or functioning—the *energeia* (ἐνέργεια)—which *is* such forms.[34] Forms, for Aristotle, always act as final causes, and one of the places where they can so act is ourselves. When they do, the actuality of their functioning is our own. We are thus both passive and active at the same time. Undergoing their action, we act on our own. I am the one who reaches for the cold beer. I am the person who is touched by the person in sorrow. Their agency is also my own. The fact that I did something *for some purpose* in no way stands opposed to my *doing it myself*.

Once I do equate my openness and my agency, a rather surprising epistemological implication comes into view. Identified with my openness to my world, my agency or behavior is "disclosive" in a Heideggerian sense. The desired object manifests itself in and through my behavior. Its being, which is its *energeia* (literally, its "at workness") as a form, informs me. It shapes my activity making me disclose it. For Aristotle, as we noted, it is senseless to speak of the actuality of a sensible object qua sensible apart from the sense organ. Given that such actuality is in the organ, there is no original with which we could compare our sensation. The same point holds here. Insofar as our behavior manifests the world, it expresses a relation which *does not involve the notions of original and image*. Our functioning in the world is not to be seen as a copy of it. It is part of an original functioning.[35]

Body and Soul

Thus far, I have been considering soul rather narrowly. To understand the ancient view of the soul's (and hence the mind's) relation to the body, we must note with Aristotle that the soul involves a multiplicity of functions. These include our abilities to feed ourselves, to grow, and to reproduce, as well as our capacities to sense, to desire, and to move to attain the things we desire. In general, "the ensouled is distinguished from the nonsouled by life."[35] Soul includes whatever functions we ascribe to life. Aristotle puts this in terms of a rather striking example. He writes, "if the eye were a living creature, its soul would be its sight."[37] Sight would be the functioning which distinguishes its life. Now, when we say that seeing is the point of being an eye, we are also asserting that seeing is the goal or purpose of its particular material structure. When it sees, it is actually an eye. To use a word Aristotle coined, seeing, the eye is "at-its-goal." Soul itself is defined in terms of this "being at the end or goal" (ἐντελέχεια). In Aristotle's words, soul is "the primary *entelechia*—ἐντελέχεια—of a physical body capable of possessing life."[38] Soul, in a broad sense, can thus be defined in terms of the goals or purposes peculiar to bodies capable of possessing life. Such capabilities, Aristotle notes, imply the possession of distinct organs. Being alive is the actual exercise of such capabilities, i.e., the actual functioning of the different organs. "Being at its end," i.e., actually accomplishing the purposes of its structure, the body is ensouled. The goals of its structure are realized within it.

This definition allows us to specify the soul's relation to the body. According to this ancient view (which Aquinas shares), the relation is essentially teleological. If we ask *what is a soul*, we have to reply that it is a set of goals a thing must embody if it is to be alive. Insofar as the soul is considered an active (causal) principle, such goals are taken as active. They are understood as final or formal causes. Our reply to the question *what is an animate body*, follows from this. A living body is such only as material for the purposes which are its soul. In Aristotle's words, "the soul is the cause [of the body] as that for the sake of which [it is]—ὡς καὶ οὖ ἕνεκεν ἡ ψυχὴ αἰτίας.[39] As "that for the sake of which it is," it is the body's purpose. The living body lives to provide the material means to accomplish this goal. Since, as Aristotle also writes, it is "because of the goal that potentiality is possessed," we can say that without the soul, i.e., without the set of goals definitive of life, there would be no bodies with the potentiality for life.[40] The category of living bodies, the category of what we can call *flesh*, would disappear.[41]

Once we say that the relation of soul to body is that of a *purpose* to the *material required* for its accomplishment, a number of points follow. The first is that their relation does not involve two separate realities. What confronts us are rather two separate ways of considering one and the same process. We can consider the process in terms of its "wherefore," i.e., in terms of the end it seems to be achieving. We can also regard the material conditions for this achievement. The process of such achievement is that of life. Concretely, it is the living being taken as a particular process. To turn this about, we can also say that the living being is the sort of reality we can examine according to the perspectives of body and soul. Those goals discernable in the processes of its life determine our account of its soul. Correspondingly, the material requirements for such processes set the parameters for the account of its body. The second point is that this view allows us to speak of many different types of soul. We can, for example, speak of the souls of plants. We can also, of course, speak of human souls. It all depends on the goals the processes manifest. Thus, a plant's reaching for the light, an animal's reaching for an apple, and a person reaching for the "good" in terms of attempting to make a morally correct decision are all examples of goal-directed activity. Such goals are linked in the sense that some—such as those of nutrition—have to be accomplished for others to be possible. They are also tied together in the sense that not just the higher, but also the lower, are disclosive. The third point, then, is that life itself may be considered an inherently disclosive process. Given that the movement of the mover, which acts as a final cause, is in the moved, the goals of life all involve the world in its functioning through the animal. The goals are part of the world's original functioning, its original disclosure.

On one level such disclosure involves consciousness as we experience it. It involves it as capable of voluntary choice. On another level, that, say, of plants, it obviously need not. It all depends on the goals that can come to presence on a particular level. Thus, voluntary choice, insofar as it involves choosing between competing goals, requires an openness not just to such competing possibilities, but also to ourselves as open to them, i.e., as a place where they can be realized. As such, it requires reflection, a reflection in which we explicitly grasp our own openness. To grasp such openness is to apprehend ourselves as *not being* any of the things we are open to, i.e., our *not being* any of the things in the world. It is, thus, also a grasp of our nothingness. For both Sartre and Hegel, this intuition (which often must be violently forced upon us) confronts us with our freedom.[42] For Aristotle, such nothingness is our immateriality. It is our being as a place of forms rather than any particular form.

Consciousness

Soul, as we have defined it, allows for this grasp of freedom, but does not require it. To speak of matter as ensouled only requires us to take it as manifesting the disclosive, goal-oriented behavior characteristic of life. Speaking from a human perspective, we can say that the "inner" of this goal-oriented behavior is some form of consciousness. Does this mean that we can proceed from types of disclosive behavior to imagine the types of consciousness they involve? As we ascend the animal phyla, adding features such as retention to perception, can we conceive the point where goal-directed behavior implies consciousness in some recognizable form? Leibniz certainly thought so. He was one of the first to speak of different levels of perception.[43] The lower levels, those of perception without retention (perception without any long- or short-term memory) are described as those of monads that are in a "swoon." On their level, there is not yet a distinction between the conscious and the unconscious in any phenomenological sense. This means that the notion of consciousness as we experience it is simply not operative. The implication is that consciousness needs something more than the goal-directed activity which characterizes life in general. It also requires memory. Such memory should not be thought of as an after the fact retention of what we, as conscious subjects, have already perceived. As Husserl's analysis of the retentional process makes clear, it is integral to the perceptual process. Retention is, in fact, what first makes the process a conscious one.

"Consciousness," we may recall, has a specific sense. To be conscious of something is not just to have a bodily, physical relation to it. Consciousness is more than a relation of physical contact. It involves the "intentional" relationship. This means that we are conscious "of" something when we entertain it as an object. The last implies a certain nonidentity. As the German word for "object," *Gegenstand*, indicates, the object is that which can "stand against' one. It stands at a certain remove from the perceiving that grasps it. Consciousness, taken generally, is this remove.

Husserl's remarkable insight, which was traced in the previous chapters, is that this remove is temporal. The perceiver remains now, while his perceptions depart from him into pastness. The necessity for this departure is twofold. On the one hand, if the object is to show more than one side to the perceiver, the appearance it is presently showing must depart into pastness. On the other hand, given that perception occurs in the present, the perceiver must remain now. Thus, were he to remain fixed in the fleeting moment when he perceived a particular appearance, he could not apprehend any others. Equally, were the particular appearance to remain constantly now with him, it could not give way to any others. The original nonidentity between perceiver and his object is, then, occasioned by this giving way, this departure into pastness from the ongoing nowness of the perceiving. It is a nonidentity between the present and the past.

For it to be maintained, i.e., for the intentional relationship founded on this temporal remove to continue, the past must itself be preserved. Without its retention, consciousness, which is the temporal remove of the relationship, would immediately collapse. Like Liebniz's lower level monads, a person would remain in a "swoon" if his impressions were to vanish without record the moment after their reception. What prevents this is the retentional process. With regard to Husserl's account of this process, it is sufficient to note that, in spite of our shift to an Aristotelean context, all its descriptive necessities continue to apply. The intentional relation still requires preservation and temporal tagging of contents. It also requires identification. Thus, the momentary apprehension, with its sensuous contents, becomes "of" the object insofar as its contents are identified with similar ones I have already retained in my past experience of it. For example, turning a die in my hands, the same contents occur again and again. The identification of what I presently experience with what I retain, makes the experience "of" what I grasp *through these retentions*. Thus, the figure of six dots on the surface of the die is not just a content of my present perception. I also find the same figure recurring among my retained experiences. It is because of this sameness that I can say that the experience of the dots gives me the content "of" the die, that, in fact, it is an experience "of" the latter. This "ofness" never collapses into an identity since, in spite of the identity of sensuous content, a temporal difference remains. The presently experienced content is now, while the retained content which allows its predication of the enduring object has, in the process of its retention, been tagged as past.

Even though the descriptive details remain the same, we do require a certain "change of sign" to adapt this descriptive account to the Aristotelian paradigm. We have to reverse the origin of time. For Husserl, temporalization begins with the self in its identity with the Absolute. For Aristotle, the origin is the world. More narrowly, it is the presence of some entity to us. The constancy of its presence is the constancy of our nowness. Time's continuity is its continuity. Insofar as the interdependence of moments expresses this continuity, it is ultimately a *dependence—not, as Husserl thought, on time itself as an unending whole—but rather on the entity in the continuity of its presence*. As we noted in our last chapter, the shift of the entity's presence with regard to its environment is registered by us as the shift of our nowness. The shift, however, does not break time into atomic units. Its result is simply our nowness resituated in a new context. The retention of these past situations (these past presences) gives time its "depth." With this, we have the copresence of retained and actual impressional moments required for the consciousness of some object. As in Husserl's analysis, each further registering of the shift in the body, as it passes over into a retention, increases the pastness of the already retained. This is because the retention of the shift of the entity's presence is also a retention of the shifts in presence which have already been retained. It is a retention of their retentions.

This "change of sign" does not affect the basic point at issue. Wherever we place the origin of time, retention is required to turn the physical receiving of impressions into the conscious process of an actual perception. It is not, however, sufficient for *self*-consciousness. Perceiving, we can remain absorbed in the world. Our attention can remain on its objects indefinitely. Per se, there is nothing in the notion of consciousness, taken as a pure seeing abstracted from any practical necessities, that would demand a shift of attention from the perceived to the perceiver. For the latter, we must consider the process of perception in terms of the flesh of the perceiver. This means considering it, not just as an "openness" to the seen, but as the embodiment of the seen. What we require, to lay the groundwork for self-consciousness, is, in other words, a definition of the openness of consciousness in terms of embodiment through flesh.

Flesh and Openness

To begin on the most general level, we can say that the notion of flesh requires a radical redefinition of the Cartesian notion of "subjectivity." Rather than designating a nonextended self, set apart from and doubting its world, it indicates a kind of disclosive behavior. Engaged in such behavior, the subjectivity that is flesh behaves "in tune" with the world. What tunes it are its goals. It, thus, exhibits the phenomena of one-way touch. Animated by goals, it manifests an openness to their action.

The particular type of openness it displays depends upon its receptivity. This, in turn, depends upon the type of senses it has. Hearing, for example, is an openness to sound as sound—not to the moving pressure ridges in the air but to the actual sounding note. Similarly, the sense of sight is an openness, not to a particular range of electromagnetic fluctuations, but to color. Following Aristotle, we can say that each type of sensory openness involves a particular ratio. It is contingent on a particular material organization of the sensory organ. Corresponding to each is a type of disclosive behavior, the type that is directed toward the particular sort of object it receives. Considered as a phenomenon of one way touch, this behavior can be described as the movement of the mover in the moved.

The same pattern holds for that part of subjectivity we designate as mind. In distinction to the particular senses, it has, of course, an unlimited openness. Thinking, the mind is open to every possible thought. Its disclosive behavior with regard to such thoughts is correspondingly unlimited. This does not mean that the flesh that is mindful—i.e., human flesh—can literally do or be anything, i.e., escape its physical limitations. A sheer openness on the level of thought does not imply a corresponding openness on the level of those senses which first provide the mind with the materials for its thinking. Here, we may note that the immateriality of mind does not mean that we must think of it as somehow apart from flesh. This immateriality simply designates a particular type of openness, one which manifests itself in a particular type of disclosive behavior. In a certain sense, human evil shows our immateriality. Capable, within certain physical limits, of doing anything, we are also capable of "stopping at nothing." The last is a good definition of a scoundrel. Mind, of course, can also be said to be immaterial in the sense of being the "place" where the forms appear. As such, it has the immateriality of a formal or final cause, the cause that can move us without itself being moved. The same thing, however, can be said about the senses of animals not possessing mind. They, too, are immaterial in the sense of being open to their special objects. What moves in each case is the object which appears through them. This is not the object as a physical presence, but rather the object as a "nonphysical . . . unmoved mover," the object that is functioning as a "final cause or goal."[44] What is moved in each case is, however, material. It is flesh.

We can avoid a possible misconception with regard to its openness by noting again that we should not apply the schema of original and replica to such movement. In the paradigm we are exploring, the movement of the mover is *in* the moved. The movement itself is that of embodiment. The desired object embodies itself (manifests its desirability) in the actions of a desiring agent. To be open in this sense is thus to provide an appropriate place for embodiment. It can be defined as the capability to provide a place where the original can come to be—i.e., embody itself.

Perception and Embodiment

This notion of openness as embodiment can be used to analyze perception. An actual perception involves the identification of a presently experienced and a retained content. As we saw, the result of this identification is an intuitive presence. It is the objective givenness of an enduring content. The present momentary experience becomes an experience *of* this content which, as enduring, "stands against" it. Now, although retention and identification are necessary conditions for the perceptual process, they do not exhaust its analysis. In fact, as the chapter on Husserl and Searle shows, they give only half the story. The intuitive presence they generate functions on the side of fulfillment. What is fulfilled or embodied by this presence is what Husserl calls the perception's *interpretative intention*. In Husserl's words, "It belongs to perception that something appears within it, but *interpretation* makes up what we term appearance. . . . The *house* appears to me through no other way but that I interpret in a certain fashion actually experienced contents of sensation."[45] This interpretation, which takes these contents as embodying the sense of the object, "is a character of experience which first constitutes 'the being of the object for me'."[46] What this means, concretely, is that the perceptual contents are grasped as pertaining to a given object when they fulfill an interpretation, one that sees them as fitting together to form the recurring pattern of contents through which the object exhibits its specific sense. Thus, the recurring pattern of the different faces of the die, a pattern that makes each face show itself between its specific neighbors, gives me the sense of the die as a whole. This sense is not just the result of the contents given in the perceptual process. The contents "make sense" only through my interpretation's "making sense" of them. If the interpretation is successful, then its sense is fulfilled or embodied by the perceptual flow. The identification between the presently experienced and the retained contents of experience results, in other words, in the intuitive presence of the intended sense.

Perceptual mistakes provide the best examples of this. Suppose, for example, that I assume I see a cat crouching in the shadows under a bush on a bright sunny day. Moving to get a better look, its features seem to become more clearly defined. One part of what I see appears to be his head, another his body, still another his tail. Based upon what I see, I anticipate that further features will be revealed as I approach it. This shadow will be seen as part of the cat's ear; another as his eye, and so forth. If, however, I am mistaken, at some point the data will fail to fulfill my expectations. My perceptual experience, rather than embodying the interpretative sense, "cat," will dissolve into a collection of shadows. Turning away, I will realize that I was mistaken.

This example illustrates a number of points. The first is that interpretation always involves anticipation. When I interpreted the shadows as a cat, I anticipated that further perceptions would confirm this interpretation. Moving to get a better look, I anticipated that a certain pattern of perceptions would unfold itself over time. The recurrent elements of what I perceived would, so I assumed, become for me the features of a cat. In anticipating this, I simply took my perceptions as determined by an object—in this case, the cat, "out there." Because of this, my perceiving was marked by a special, teleological relationship. In this, the whole that I was attempting to grasp—i.e., the whole which, in anticipation, stood as the *telos* or goal of my perceiving—determined the interpretation I placed upon my individual perceptions. Thus, because I assumed that I was seeing a cat, each of my interpretations was guided by this sense. This is what made me assume that one shadow was part of the cat's ear, another was its eye, and so forth. If my initial interpretative intention had been correct, then the data I experienced would have formed part of an emerging pattern which exhibited these features. That I was mistaken points to the fact that the actual presence of the object involves more than the interpretative intention. It requires the embodiment of this by the objective perceptual presence given by the identification of the presently experienced and the retained contents of the ongoing perception.

A further point, then, is that both intention and fulfillment, both interpretative anticipatory sense and intuitive embodiment, are required. As our example indicates, there is a certain dialectic between the two. Within it, neither side is given the edge. Their relation is such that, even though every sense of the object is a sense intended by consciousness, consciousness cannot, in its interpretative intentions, inform the object with every possible sense.[47] Because of this, there is a constant probing of intentions. Interpretations are advanced or abandoned accordingly as they are supported by perceptual experience. More closely regarded, the interplay between intention and fulfillment shows a certain circularity. The interpretative intention must be drawn from the contents retained from the ongoing perceptual experience. Yet, what we retain contains more than the contents of the specific object. It includes the whole visual field with its multitude of possible objects of attention. To attend to a particular one—say, the cat under the bush—is to select among the retained those contents which make up the pattern of its appearing. But for this selection, we require an interpretative intention, an intention to see just such a pattern. Thus, the circle is such that the interpretative intention to this pattern determines what is to count as the content of the object; yet such content determines the sequence of the pattern. This follows because the sequence, if it is to be fulfilled, must be drawn from the experienced contents themselves. Now, the fact that the interpretation determines the content that determines the interpretation does not mean that we are trapped in a vicious circularity. As we saw in the seventh chapter, the result is rather a codetermination in which interpretations are put forward, determine a selection of contents from our retained experience, are tested against these, are modified, and tested again. Integral to this process is the continual enrichment of our retained experience as we move to get a better look at what we originally intended to see. As a result, the perceptually embodied sense which arises from the fulfillment of our original intention is itself continually enriched. On the one hand, it undergoes a narrowing. We move from seeing "something" under the bush to seeing it as a small animal, as a cat, as a spotted brown and yellow cat, etc. On the other hand, it becomes more detailed. As I move closer, the intention that is fulfilled includes more than just the head, it includes the pattern of perceptions which would give the cat its particular features: its eyes, ears, whiskers, etc.

So regarded, the perceptual sense appears to be teleologically determined in a way that involves both the future and the past. The line of determination is that of the future determining the past in its determination of the present. Thus, the future in the form of what we intend to see determines the selection of the content we have retained from the past. This, however, fulfills or embodies the intention to give us the ongoing, present perceptual sense. The goal of our seeing thus brings itself about by making what we have seen into the material for its present realization. This does not mean that every material can fulfill its purposes. If it did, then the content we experience would be reduced to a kind of undifferentiated "prime matter" capable of sustaining every kind of interpretation. This would eliminate the causality of the past, since only the future in the form of the goal of our seeing would determine the present perceptual sense. With every intention being fulfilled, it would also eliminate the possibility of the *failure* of our interpretative intention. Such failure, we may note, is also impossible if the retained contents by themselves determine the perceptual sense. If a shift in these contents automatically resulted in a shift in this sense, then we would be left with just the causality of the past. The self, in this essentially Pavlovian view, would act only in response to the material changes of its environment and would never have a goal against which success or failure could be measured. Success and failure, thus, require the causality of both the past and the future. The fact that each causality works through the other is, of course, the point of the dialectic of intention and fulfillment. The dialectic, then, brings with it the possibility of success and failure. Its instantiation in the perceptual process is the instantiation of the context for their possibility. This context is that of teleological action. As involving a goal which can act as a standard, it allows the possibility of success or failure in achieving this standard.

Given this, we can also say that the dialectic is, itself, our openness to such tele-ological action. Through our instantiating this dialectic, we are "open" to the final causality of perceptual forms. Through it, we become the place where they can come to be as perceptually embodied senses. The dialectic, in other words, gives us the mechanics in the perceptual sphere of the operation of the "one way touch" relation described above. Its instantiation is the instantiation of the relation. This can be make concrete by noting that the chapter on Husserl and Searle can be read as showing how this can be done in terms of the "flesh" of a computer.

A final point can be drawn from the example of seeing the cat: neither the interpretative sense nor the retained content fulfilling its intention is the "actual" sensible object. This object is their intersection; it exists as the point of their ongoing interpenetration. It is, then, present only so long as my perceptual interpretations are embodied by the appropriate content. Given that the resultant sense is the actual sensible object *qua* sensible, it immediately follows that there is no other original "out there" functioning as a standard for my perceptual act. Neither is there an "inner replica" of this outer object as Descartes thought.[48] When Aristotle says that the sensible object qua sensible is in the per-ceiver, he does not mean that it is "in" it as a replica. Understood phenomeno-logically, the original is just the ongoing perceptual presence which exists by virtue of a successful interpretation.

Granting this, "openness" does not mean being open, "transparent" to some original out there. If the actuality of the sensible object is in the per-ceiver, then the perceiver is the place where the original comes to be as some-thing sensible. It is the place of its embodiment. In other words, my openness to the forms or senses of things is that of providing the place where they can realize themselves as sensible objects. Openness, then, is a kind of transparency, a kind of "letting objects be" in the Heideggerian sense. It is not, however, a "pure" transparency to the other as Sartre maintained.[49] It can, rather, be defined as the capability to provide the ground, the material, in which the original can come to be, i.e., embody itself. In perception, this capacity requires our open-ness to its teleological action. This is the action in which the original, rather than being something already given, first brings itself about by determining, as a goal, the process of its realization. As we said, this capacity requires our instantiation of the dialectic of intention and fulfillment.

The Temporality of Desire

Crucial to the above account is the fact that the perceptual process is not a static gazing at the object. It involves the shifting patterns of contents which arise and are retained as we move to get a better look at what we intend to see. Moving to get a better look is movement animated by a particular passion.

So is attempting to find a solution to a philosophical or mathematical problem. So, for that matter, is reaching for the cold beer on a warm Sunday afternoon. In each case, the unmoved mover moves through desire. Desire, we can say is the felt presence of the goal. It is the experience we have when we are touched by it. More concretely, it is our experience of *its* moving us, its manifesting itself in the motivations of our disclosive behavior. Thus, as long as desire is operative, the person moves closer to get a better look. What he wants to see works on him, i.e., moves him, through desire.

Desire has a special quality. It does not just animate my motion toward some object. It also makes me realize that I am not that object. Confronted by something I want but do not yet possess, I am, when I compare myself to it, its absence. Hungry, I am the absence of food; thirsty, I am the absence of water. The desires that link flesh to the world, thus, also separate it. The behavior they animate discloses flesh as *directed towards* and yet as *other than* the world.[50] This otherness is at the root of the separation of self from the world which is required for self-consciousness.

The best way to express the relation of desire is in terms of the peculiar temporality of flesh. Such temporality is *not* that of the past determining the present, which determines the future. In this Cartesian view of temporal determinism, the state of the world at one moment is seen as being its necessary and sufficient cause for its state at the next. Our account of perception as embodiment suggests that flesh has a different line of temporal determination. In flesh, the future determines the past in its determination of the present. As desired, the future stands as a goal, as a "final cause" of the process. The goal makes the past into a resource, into a "material" as it were, for its own realization. It thus determines the past in the latter's determination of the present by structuring it as a potential for some particular realization.

What we are pointing to can be illustrated by a number of examples. In perception, as we said, what we intend to see—the anticipated object—stands as the goal. The material for its realization is provided by the past in the form of the contents we retain. Together they determine our present, ongoing action of perception. The result is the embodiment of the intended perceptual sense by the changing field of contents occasioned by our moving to get a closer look. The desire to attend to and have a better look at the object is, of course, essential to this process. Manifesting its desirability in the actions of the perceiver, the desired object embodies or realizes itself as a sensible presence. The same point can be taken from the example given earlier of a woman who decides to become a marathon runner. Her being as an actual runner is not a present reality. Neither is it past. It "exists" as a desired *future* whose determining presence is that of a goal. How long she has to train is determined by the resources she brings to the goal—i.e., how long she has trained in the immediate *past*. Once again, the determination by the future is not absolute but occurs through the past. The determining presence of the past is that of the materials or resources it presents us to accomplish the goal. It is, of course, the goal which allows us to see such materials as materials for some purpose. The goal is what turns the past into a potential to be actualized by our ongoing, *present* activity. To take another example, it is the goal of baking which makes flour into a required ingredient. Similarly, the potential of timber to be a boat as opposed to firewood demands the entertaining of a corresponding goal. Other animate beings have their goals. A bird, for example, turns mud and twigs into materials for its nest. What is common to these examples is the notion of the causality of the completed reality which stands at the end of their processes. It is taken as being not just the goal but also the cause of its own realization. As causally determinative, the goal gives us the temporal determination that stretches from the future to the past to the present. As such, it gives us the movement of nature which situates potentiality as a category of reality.

The Necessary Conceptual Shift

As pointed out in the previous chapter, the notion of determination by the goal requires a fundamental conceptual shift. We must change, not just our account of the flow of time; we must also shift from our usual (Cartesian) way of conceptualizing time. Normally we think of time as a sort of receptacle for events. We take it as a kind of independent reality which exists prior to entities as a *condition* for their existing. Given this, the order of the causality of entities is dependent on the order of time. What is temporally prior we take as the cause of what follows. Assuming, then, that time flows from the past to the present to the future, the future, by virtue of its temporal position, can never be a cause. It is always an effect. At a stroke, the whole notion of final causality (of teleological action in general) vanishes. To assert such action, we must, then, shift this conception. We have to assert that the order of time is dependent on the order of the causality of entities, not the reverse. Given this shift, if the goal is causally determinative then it gives us the causal sequence according to which time moves from the future through the past to the present. This movement, as we said, allows us to take potentiality as a category of reality, such potentiality expressing the causality of the past. As our examples indicate, the potential can "be" without being presently actualized, but not without that which directs this actualization. Thus, timber can be a potential building material even though it is not actually used as such. If, however, all notion of building vanishes, i.e., if the goal of building is never entertained, then its potentiality also disappears. This follows since the causality implicit in its notion comes not from itself, but rather from the intended (future) use of it. To assert this, however, is to assert the causal efficacy of this future use or goal.

The priority of causality over time is actually a priority of that which exercises causality. It is, in other words, a priority of being. Thus, our conceptual shift implies that being, in determining causality, determines time. This is the reverse of the Cartesian view which sees space and time as determining the order of causality and sees being as essentially an event resulting from causal processes. Once we do assert that causality is an effect of being, the origin of the causal sequence must occur where the being capable of initiating it first appears. If this being appears at the end of the process, then this is where the source of the causal sequence must lie. In Aristotle's terms, we must treat the end or "telos" of the process as its source. The "coming into being" must be directed by this end. Given this, the causality characteristic of inanimate nature—the causality which takes what occurs in the past as a necessary and sufficient condition for the present which, in turn, is taken as a similar condition for the future—is inadequate to describe the animate processes where the fully formed, functioning reality only appears at the end. The fact that in certain processes the fully formed being only appears at the end, i.e., in the future, means that this is where we must place the origin of the causal sequence. This, of course, does not mean that all sequences are like this. In the sequence of, say, one billiard ball striking the other, each entity is as fully formed as the next and, thus, each in turn can serve as a cause. The assertion that causality is the effect of being makes us assert the causality of the end only in processes (such as perception) where the fully formed reality (e.g., the sensible object qua sensible) appears at the end.

It may be asked here if we are simply asserting or have actually presented an argument for the causal character of the future. To this, we may reply with the general point that the nature of the argument for this character depends upon the context of its assertion. The context of this book is phenomenological. To argue for a claim is, phenomenologically, to point to the appearances and relations of appearances that justify its assertion. In phenomenological reflection, phenomena are first. They determine the validity and extension of our concepts. This means that we cannot take space and time as providing a framework for phenomena, one that would determine, a priori, the possibilities of their order and succession. Space and time, rather, must be considered as determined by the given phenomena. This holds, in particular, for the phenomena manifested by goal-oriented processes. Thus, the causal character of the future obtains for the phenomena of perception where the positing of the goal is integral to the perceptual process, the goal being what first makes possible the interpretation of the content of perception. Where such goal-oriented behavior appears, then, a corresponding causality and, hence, temporal flow should be assumed. This follows because causality, phenomenologically speaking, must draw its sense from the phenomena. As such, it is, in the first instance, simply a formalization of the observed "logic" of experience, the rules of which, rather than being a priori, must be drawn from experience. So regarded, our claims about the causality (and, hence, the temporality of flesh) are simply an attempt to delineate the "logic" of the experience of flesh. If they are justified by this experience, they cannot be ruled out of court by any a priori frameworks (such as the Cartesian) which would make them impossible.

The Temporal Reflexivity of Flesh

This temporality of goal-directed activity is the innermost layer of the phenomenological structure of flesh. Within it, the future appears as the goal, as the desired but not yet attained result. The past shows itself as the material for its accomplishment, while the present is their ongoing point of interpenetration. The past meeting the future is, concretely, material embodying a goal. As such, it is flesh or (as an Aristotelian would say) matter which is ensouled. It is matter which distinguishes itself from the inanimate by having a distinct temporality. With regard to self-consciousness, the crucial point here is that such temporality involves reflexivity. Directed toward the future, flesh grasps itself when it grasps the goal. This is because its own history is not some "dead weight" of the past. As the example of the marathon runner indicates, what flesh brings to the present is the very material for the goal's embodiment. Its grasp of the goal is thus *through itself*, through its history of realizing it.

The temporal reflexivity which makes this possible may be seen by contrasting the teleological with the Cartesian view of temporal determination. In the Cartesian schema, such determination proceeds without self-reference. The future refers to the present as its immediate cause and through it to the past as its more distant cause. No part of it, however, refers to itself. By contrast, the schema of teleological temporality is one where each of the modes of time refers to itself through the others. As earlier noted, its line of temporal determination is that of the future causing itself to be present and actual through its determination of the past and the present. Thus, the past, as we said, is determined as potentiality (as δύναμις) by the future. So determined, it appears a material for the not yet existent goal. Similarly, the future determines the present as the place where the actualization of this potentiality occurs. Thus, the reference of the future is to itself through the past and present. It is through the latter that the future comes to be present and, hence, is now the actual future understood as that which will actually come to be. Similarly, the past refers to itself through the other two modes of time. They are what makes it past, i.e., determine it as material for a goal. The same holds, mutatis mutandis, for the present. It too refers to itself through the other two modes of time. It is not just the intersection point of the past and the future. Through them it determines itself as the point of actualization, i.e., of embodiment.

This can be related to the reflexivity of touch. When I touch an object, I perceive both what I touch and that by which I touch, my flesh. In a certain pre-Cartesian sense, my flesh is both perceiver and perceived, both subject and object, in this act. Flesh is the subject insofar as it is (or contains) the organ of touch. It is the object insofar as it is, as Aristotle pointed out, the "medium" of touch, i.e., that through which the object appears.[51] Professor Rémi Brague nicely describes the mystery of this dual function when he writes: "the medium [of touch] is inside. Inside or outside of what? . . . Flesh is so to speak added to itself. Flesh is its own addition: an inner distance that cannot be measured from some external point. Flesh is something like dimensionality without dimension."[52] This "inner distance" is between touching and touched, the one taken as the subject, the other, as the object of this act. It is that which separates the two, allowing flesh to grasp itself as not yet being (or embodying) its intended object. Its origin, we can say, is the temporal remove which permits the self-reference of each of the modes of time through the "distance," as it were, of the other two. Granting this, what provides this "dimensionality without dimension" is not some hidden spatial remove or relation. It is rather a form of that temporal remove which defines consciousness as consciousness. More precisely, such dimensionality (or remove) arises through the teleological temporality manifested by flesh. This is what allows flesh to be directed towards its object, understood as the goal of its perceptual process, and, in the same process, allows it to grasp itself as other than its object insofar as it does *not yet* embody it. The separation within flesh arises because flesh itself (in the guise of its *presently accumulated* "history") provides the means or "medium" for the goal's *future* realization.

The Existence of Flesh

There is an obvious interrelation in the elements of our account of flesh. For example, goals and desire are related insofar as the felt presence of a goal is desire. Thus, to speak of goals and one way touch is also to speak in terms of the motion prompted by desire. Similarly, we can also say that the presence of desire implies the presence of a distinct, teleological temporality. Insofar as such temporality is not that of the inanimate world, flesh stands out from the latter. This temporal standing out, this temporal "existence" of flesh, is the way in which desire separates it from the world. Animated by desire, flesh discloses itself as other than the world, an otherness that shows itself in a different temporality. The same temporality, as it functions in the perceptual process, allows objects to have what we may call an "epistemological" as opposed to a mere bodily presence. Bodies are present to one another through the causality of inanimate agents. Perceptual objects, by contrast, come to presence as goals. They are the "not yets" our objectifying interpretative acts attempt to make present. By virtue of its intentional relation to such objects, consciousness itself exists, i.e., stands out as something distinct. That the temporality associated with its embodiment involves reflexivity, gives us, as we said, the possibility of self-consciousness. With this, we have the possibility of grasping ourselves in our flesh as other than the world.

This otherness is shown in the distinction between two types of temporality. The temporality of the animate world is teleological, the temporality of the inanimate world that of the simple time line of Cartesian physics. Does the contrast of these two forms of temporality mean that we have reintroduced the kind of dualism we attempted to dispense with? Have we just substituted for the traditional mind-body dualism, a dualism of two different forms of temporal determination? A sign that we have would be our inability to relate the two. Generally speaking, what is wrong with "dualism" is not the distinctions it attempts to make. It is rather its incoherence, i.e., its inability to relate the duality it uncovers. In the present case, however, *one form of temporality includes the other*. Thus, the circle used in the last chapter to symbolize teleological temporality actually contains two different lines of temporal determination (see Figure 6). Beginning with the past, the line of determination reads: past-present-future. Beginning with the future, it reads: future-past-present. What the circle symbolizes is that the two types of temporal determination are not opposed, they are actually part of one process. Thus, the teleological process that begins with the future must include the mechanical one that begins with the past. It must accomplish the realization of the goal, not by bypassing, but by using, material causal means. This, of course, is what life does in all of its projects. It uses the processes of inanimate nature to accomplish its goals. Only when we fail to acknowledge this, do we fall into the incoherence of opposing the animate to the inanimate, or the soul to the body, or the mind to the brain. Each of these pairs represent opposing, yet complimentary aspects of one and the same line of determination. Flesh, as we have described it, actually involves both.

FIGURE 6

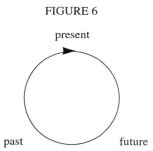

13

NIETZSCHE-DARWIN:
CONFRONTING THE JANUS HEAD

The last chapter left us with a view of the self that made its agency a consequence of its openness. Taking its purposes or goals from its environment, its functioning appears as a set of behaviors disclosive of the world. Such disclosure is not to be thought of under the pattern of image and original. Rather than being a copy, our functioning within the world is part of its original functioning. Granting this, the question still remains as to the nature of the world's functioning. In the nineteenth century, two answers appear which mark a change in the traditional responses to this question. Darwin's response became foundational for modern biology. Nietzsche's became the basis for what came to be called the *postmodern movement*.[1] Since both see our functioning in terms of the world's functioning, both have implications for the "openness" of the self proposed by the previous chapter.

These implications, however, are not straightforward. In Nietzsche's case, the hermeneutical (or interpretative) context generated by his works has a Janus-like character. As the spiritual father of postmodernism, his appeal is to our period's discomfort with foundational, "metaphysical" thinking. He affirms its disquiet with talk of essences. Many find his "deconstruction" of science and morality liberating. Above all his doctrine of "perspectivism" has found a general appeal. The pluralism that is its apparent result is attractive to everyone from feminists to defenders of multiculturalism. There is, however, another, less appealing side to Nietzsche. There is the Nietzsche who speaks of the advance in women's rights as "one of the worst developments in the general *uglification* of Europe."[2] This is the same Nietzsche who teaches that "almost everything we call 'higher culture' is based on the spiritualization and intensification of cruelty,"[3] the Nietzsche, who in answer to his question "whither *must* we direct our hopes," speaks of preparing "for great enterprises and collective experiments in discipline and breeding so as to make an end of that gruesome domination of chance and nonsense which has hitherto been called 'history' . . ."[4] As much as the postmoderns who lay claim to him would like to forget the fact, this Nietzsche became the icon of the Nazis.

How can Nietzsche present such different faces? Is such duality also hidden in the postmodern projects continuing his legacy? Is it implicit in our notion of subjectivity as openness—an openness which can be formed by its environment into different perspectives? Our position will be that Nietzsche's perspectivism finds an essential impulse from Darwin's theory. It can be understood in terms of the Darwinian struggle for existence. The latter has an equally ambiguous character. On the one hand, its notion of preservation through evolutionary adaptation provides the biological underpinnings for a plurality of perspectives. On the other, the very notion of a Darwinian "struggle for existence" gives an adversarial quality to all the processes and perspectives of life. It leads Darwin to deplore society's attempts to lessen the effects of the struggle by looking after the maimed and the weak. "Cruelty," in the organic world, is not immoral but simply part of the processes of life. For Nietzsche this implies that "a genuine and seriously constructed ethical system, based on Darwin's teaching" involves the "*bellum omnium contra omnes* and the privileges of the strong."[5] Nietzsche, however, is no Darwinian. The duality of his own position is that he both maintains and undermines his teaching on perspectivism. Thus, his interpretation of "will to life" as "will to power" transforms the struggle for organic existence into a struggle for power. The latter, whose end is not preservation, but rather endless increase of power, disrupts the Darwinian basis of his perspectivism. Implying a single concept of being and value, its emphasis on the will places Nietzsche within the tradition of subject centered metaphysics. Ultimately, Nietzsche remains within the paradigm that inflates the self to a metaphysical principle.

To escape this tradition, I shall propose a different reading of Darwin. In its radical antifoundationism, it will allow me to place the self's openness in a pluralistic context.

Perspectivism

Heidegger, explaining Nietzsche's doctrine of perspectivism, writes: "a lizard hears the slightest rustling in the grass but it does not hear a pistol shot fired quite close by. Accordingly, the creature develops a kind of interpretation of its surroundings and thereby of all occurrence, not incidentally, but as the fundamental process of life itself."[6] Nietzsche himself put this in terms of the "moral prejudice that truth is worth more than appearance." This, he writes, is "the worst-proved assumption that exists. . . . there would be no life at all except on the basis of perspective evaluations and appearances; and if . . . one wanted to abolish the 'apparent world' altogether, assuming you could do that . . . nothing would remain of your 'truth' either!"[7] What we have here is the abolition of the distinction of the real and the apparent. It is, we claim, motivated by the Darwinian view of organic life. In such a view, each species survives and preserves itself by occupying its evolutionary niche. Each succeeds by taking the world in a certain way, interpreting it according to its survival needs. There is, for example, in the New England Aquarium an exhibition of items found in shark stomachs. Almost everything is there, from diving helmets to old tires. Whatever disturbs the water, the shark takes as food. Is the shark in error? Is its life (or rather diet) one category mistake after another? Not for Nietzsche. For him, "Truth is the kind of error without which a certain species of life could not live. The value for *life* is ultimately decisive."[8] Thus, the "truth" for the shark is precisely the interpretation (the "error") without which it could not survive. That it has survived is the sign of the "truth" of this error.

If we accept this, then what counts as "truth" is utility in the struggle to preserve ourselves. Again and again, Nietzsche draws the epistemological implications of this point. He writes "we have senses for only a selection of perceptions—those with which we have to concern ourselves in order to preserve ourselves."[9] This means that "the measure of that of which we are in any way conscious is totally dependent upon the coarse utility of its becoming conscious."[10] We are conscious of it if it helped preserve us. The same holds for our knowledge. To cite Nietzsche again: "The meaning of 'knowledge' . . . is to be regarded in a strict and narrow anthropocentric and biological sense. . . . The utility of preservation—not some abstract-theoretical need not to be deceived—stands as the motive behind the development of the organs of knowledge—they develop in such a way that their observation suffices for our preservation."[11] Given this, the question is not whether a judgment is true or false. "The question is to what extent it is life-advancing, life-preserving, species-preserving, perhaps even species-breeding." This holds for all forms of judgment—including those with a priori claims. In Nietzsche's words, we must "assert that the falsest judgments (to which synthetic *apriori* judgments belong) are the most indispensable to us, that without granting as true the fictions of logic, without measuring reality against the purely invented world of the unconditional and self-identical, without a continual falsification of the world by means of numbers, mankind could not live . . ."[12] We could not because such notions are *our* survival strategy. As Nietzsche writes in answer to Kant's famous question, "How are synthetic judgments *apriori* necessary," they are necessary "for the purpose of preserving beings such as ourselves . . ."[13] In other words, the use of "the fictions of logic" to interpret the world is simply our way of struggling for existence, of gaining an advantage and preserving ourselves. The same holds for all "the categories of reason." They have prevailed "through their relative utility." Biologically regarded, "they represent nothing more than the expediency of a certain race and species—their utility alone is their 'truth.'"[14] Their truth, in other words, is their value for life; concretely, our success in this struggle is their truth. It is a success written into our very organic structure, a structure that developed through this struggle. Since "our apparatus of acquiring knowledge is not designed for 'knowledge'" but rather success in this struggle,[15] the latter sets both the form and the limits of such knowledge.[16] Thus, different survival requirements would have resulted in a different set of the "fictions of logic." They would have been equally "true," in the sense that each would have been part of an interpretation geared toward survival. In fact, since without life there is no interpretation, since every distinction between the real and the apparent is simply a perspective (a view from some particular survival strategy where what counts for survival is "real," and all else, illusion), Nietzsche's famous doctrine follows: It is all interpretation all the way down.[17] In other words, there is nothing but the apparent. The notion of an identical reality, a substantial "in itself" *of* which the various appearances are appearances, is simply a logical fiction pertaining to *our* perspective.[18]

With this we have Nietzsche's insistence that his truth is his, "that another cannot easily acquire a right to it . . ."[19] The opposition here is to any idea of universal truth, a truth that is truth for everyone. As Kant noted, such truths have objective validity, their universality coming from the fact that all judgments agreeing with the same object must necessarily agree with each other.[20] For Nietzsche, on the contrary, each judgment expresses a perspective, a view whose "truth" is its value for life, the life of the one judging. The basis of truth is, then, not correspondence with some given object, but rather existence. What preserves existence is true. Given this, "the way of knowing and of knowledge is itself already part of the conditions of existence."[21] In terms of the previous chapter, we can say that knowing is an "openness" to the functioning of the world insofar as it itself is a functioning resulting from such conditions. They shape us, determining what we see and what we ignore. This means that the existence of the judger, as resulting from such conditions, *is* the concrete expression of the "truth" of his judgments. Thus, only he can authorize this "truth," and he can do so only through action of his particular existence, his will to life.[22] Because there are no universal truths, to proclaim one's truth as universal, as "true for everyone," is actually to take one's own perspective (ultimately, one's own existence) as universal. To insist upon this is to encroach upon others; it is to override their perspectives, their truths, their existence, forcing them into one's own mold. As such, it appears as expression of a "will to power," this being understood as a will "to grow, expand, draw to itself, gain ascendancy."[23]

One way of reading Nietzsche comes from pursuing this analysis with the depth and patience of a scholarship he himself had increasingly little time for. I am referring to Foucault's painstaking unmasking of one structure of modern science after another as an expression of will to power. For Foucault this is liberating. It exposes alternatives masked by the prestige of science.[24] We thus find the Nietzsche beloved by the postmoderns, the Nietzsche conceived as a pluralist, the Nietzsche who by unmasking the fiction of a "real" world validates multiple perspectives. There is, however, another face of this philosopher, one rooted in his equation of the will to life with the will to power. Here, the will appears not as the expression of a perspective but as an ultimate ground. Rather than being taken as a pluralist, the Nietzsche who proclaims it appears as the last exponent of the tradition of subject-centered metaphysics. He appears, in other words, as the last of the "modern" thinkers.

Nietzsche as a Monist

To draw the contrast with Darwin, we must first note the similarities. Darwin, like Nietzsche, is not shy about drawing the implications of his theory for society. He writes, "with the savages, the weak in body or mind are soon eliminated; and those that survive commonly exhibit a vigorous state of health. We civilized men, on the other had, do our utmost to check the process of elimination; we build asylums for the imbecile, the maimed, and the sick; we institute poor-laws; and our medical men exert their utmost skill to save the life of every one to the last moment. . . . Thus the weak members of civilized societies propagate their kind. No one who has attended to the breeding of domestic animals will doubt that this must be highly injurious to the race of man."[25] At times he is quite gloomy in assessing the prospects for England. If checks are not found for preventing "the reckless, the vicious and otherwise inferior members of society from increasing . . . , the nation," he warns, "will retrograde."[26] At other times he is more cheerful, noting that "civilized races have extended, and are now everywhere extending their range, so as to take the place of the lower races."[27] The problem of the extinction of one of these lower races is, biologically, no different than "that presented by the extinction of one of the higher animals. . . . The New Zealander," he adds, "seems conscious of this parallelism, for he compares his future with that of the native rat now almost exterminated by the European rat."[28] Behind these sentiments lies a view of life as constantly reproducing itself in greater numbers than can possibly survive. The resulting struggle for existence is one in which only the fittest survive to pass on their characteristics to their offspring. Here, survival is the sign of fitness. It is always at the expense of other competing members. When we interfere with this, we interfere with the fundamental mechanism responsible for our success.[29]

Parallel but darker thoughts are expressed by Nietzsche. He writes that "life itself is essentially appropriation, injury, overpowering of the strange and weaker, suppression, severity, imposition of one's own forms, incorporation and, at the least and mildest, exploitation . . ."[30] His celebration of these qualities, in particular, his celebration of cruelty is, in his eyes, a celebration of life. In his view, "to refrain from mutual injury, mutual violence, mutual exploitation, to equate one's will with that of another" is nihilistic. It is a "denial of life." As a "principle of society," it is "a principle of dissolution and decay." Driving this point home, he writes that every social body "must, if it is a living and not a decaying body, itself do all that to other bodies which the individuals within it refrain from doing to one another: it will have to be the will to power incarnate, it will want to grow, expand, draw to itself, gain ascendancy—not out of any morality or immorality, but because it lives, and because life is will to power." "Exploitation," he explains, ". . . pertains to the essence of the living thing as a fundamental organic function, it is a consequence of the intrinsic will to power which is precisely the will to life."[31]

This equation of the will to power with the will to life is crucial, particularly when we interpret the latter as a will to succeed in the struggle for existence, a struggle which necessarily involves the extinction of competing forms. With it, we have a key to a number of Nietzsche's positions. His hatred of women, for example, can be seen as a hatred for the "feminine virtues" of compassion and mildness. His "respect" for her is, contrariwise, a respect for "her genuine, cunning, beast-of-prey suppleness, the tiger's claws beneath the glove, the naïveté of her egoism, her ineducability and inner savagery," all of which does not prevent him from declaring that "her first and last profession . . . is to bear strong children."[32] A similar account of the inequality of women can be found in Darwin.[33] Nietzsche also shares with Darwin the view that the preservation of the "sick and the suffering" is "the corruption of the European race" as well as Darwin's hopes for countering this through the control of breeding.[34]

Nietzsche, however, goes beyond Darwin, in raising the will to life or power to the status of what can only be called a fundamental metaphysical principle. He gives an ontological ground to Darwin's biologism. This involves not just seeing "our entire instinctual life as the development and ramification of one basic form of will—as will to power . . ." It involves the hypothesis of taking the "causality of the will . . . as the only one." Given that "will can operate only on will—and not on matter," this involves assuming that "all mechanical occurrences, insofar as force is active in them, are forces of will, effects of will." All "efficient force" is thus defined "unequivocally as: *will to power.*" If we accept these assumptions, which Nietzsche characterizes as *his* theory, then, as he states the conclusion: "The world seen from within, the world described and defined according to its 'intelligible character'—it would be 'will to power' and nothing else."[35]

Once we speak of the world "as seen from within," the question naturally arises about its external perspectives. What is the status of the view of it from "without"? If the former is its "intelligible character," what is the latter? It seems that, once we adopt the "foundationalist" stance of asserting a single cause, one to which all others can be reduced, we fall back into the schema of appearance and reality. The view from without becomes that of mere appearance. This is an appearance that must be unmasked to show its true "intelligible character." The exhibition of the latter is an exhibition of it as an expression of "will to power." Thus, again and again, Nietzsche devalues the explicit assertions of (among others) the moralist, scientist, philosopher, scholar, Jew, and Christian. He does not accept *their* self-understanding of their work or motivations. Like Marx before him or Freud who was to follow, there is a reduction of other stances to what the author regards as their implicit ground. Marx does not directly counter an opponent's arguments but reduces them to expressions of the interests of his class. Freud sees such arguments as expressions of the opponent's anxiety, his neurotic resistance to psychoanalysis. In the same vein, Nietzsche sees all other positions as masks, as appearances of a single will to power. In each case we have the devaluation of the apparent in favor of the real. Thus, the famous "nay saying" of *Beyond Good and Evil* is just this—the uncovering of the "real" as opposed to the apparent motives for an activity. The philosophers, for example, "pose as having discovered and attained their real opinions through the self-evolution of a cold, pure, divinely unperturbed dialectic . . ."[36] Nietzsche, however, asserts: "I . . . do not believe a 'drive to knowledge' to be the father of philosophy, but that another drive has, here as elsewhere, only employed knowledge (and false knowledge!) as a tool."[37] The latter "drive is tyrannical." It is, in fact, the will to power.[38] Similarly, in answer to the question of why the "mightiest men have . . . bowed . . . before the saint as the enigma of self-constraint and voluntary final renunciation," Nietzsche does not reply by stating their religious motives. He states, rather, that they "learned in the face of him a new fear, they sensed a new power . . . it was the 'will to power' which constrained them to halt before the saint."[39] In the same vein, he does not see the democratic moment as the political expression of the Enlightenment. Rather, the French Revolution is called the beginning of "the last great slave revolt."[40] The first, incidentally, began with the Jews.[41] The Jews were not what they understood themselves to be, the people of the law, those chosen by the single God. They were rather those whose will to power accomplished that "miraculous inversion of values" which first glorified the weak, the inversion which created the "herd" morality.

The pattern in all these examples is readily apparent. They all exhibit the reductionism common to foundational thinking. Thus, in each case there is an unmasking, a refusal to take assertions at face value. Movements, peoples, and doctrines are not what they claim. Their self-understanding, what they take themselves to be, is just the outer appearance. The reality which founds them is far different since actually they are one and all expressions of "will to power." What we confront here is a far cry from the easy pluralism some postmoderns associate with the doctrine of perspectivism. The notion of the will to power involves an ordering and ranking of perspectives. Indeed, it is itself the principle by which Nietzsche constructs his moral hierarchies. "There is," he claims, "a master morality and a slave morality."[42] Whether a group belongs to one or the other depends on its ability to express and affirm will to power. Thus, on the one side, we have "the great majority, who exist for service and general utility and who *may* exist only for that purpose . . ."[43] On the other, we have the "noble caste," who "accepts with a good conscience the sacrifice of innumerable men who *for its sake* have to be suppressed and reduced to imperfect men, to slaves and instruments."[44] For the former, religion provides "some transfiguration of the whole everydayness, the whole lowliness, the whole half-bestial poverty of their souls."[45] The latter, however, require no such comfort.[46] In fact, the "free spirits," the "new philosophers" of the coming age are precisely those who abandon all the comforting illusions provided by religion, morality, and science and freely acknowledge the sole causality of the will. Their ability to express it, particularly to impose it on others, gives them their rank.[47]

This does not mean that the will they express is their will, that it pertains to them as individual beings. Nietzsche asks, "what gives me the right to speak of an 'I', and of an 'I' as cause . . . ?"[48] The dismissal of this right is, in fact, one of the substantiality of the subject. Adopting Hume's stance, he writes, "The 'subject' is the fiction that many similar states in us are the effect of one substratum."[49] Given this, will is not an individual possession. Individuals do not possess will, it possesses them. They feel their being, their sense of reality through it. In Nietzsche's words, "The degree to which we feel life and power . . . gives us our measure of 'being,' 'reality' . . ."[50] With this, we have the dual character of many of his epigrams. The same philosopher who asserts the sole causality of the will, who ranks individuals and groups according to the strength of their will to life, also asserts, "But there is no such thing as will. . . . No subject 'atoms.' No 'substance,' rather something that in itself strives after greater strength, and that wants to 'preserve' itself only indirectly (it wants to surpass itself—)."[51] The individual may want to preserve itself, but its ground, the will to power as such, wants to surpass itself. The ground *is and is not* the individual. It is his acting center. It is what wills through him.

The key to this duality is a phenomenon we have met before. What we confront is that "inflation of the self," where the self takes on a transpersonal, nonlimited character. Nietzsche calls this character *Dionysian*.[51] It first appears in *The Birth of Tragedy* with its assertion that the lyric poet expresses, not just himself, but also, in identity with this, the self of the god, Dionysius. He may say *I* in his poems, but "this self is not the same as that of the waking, empirically real man, but the only truly existent and eternal self resting at the basis of things."[53] Because this self is the primal ground of appearance, we have the contrast between "the worlds of everyday reality and of Dionysian reality."[54] The distinction is actually "between the [Dionysian] eternal core of things, the thing-in-itself, and the whole world of appearances."[55] The principle of individuation reigns in the latter world. It is composed of individual entities. As for the former, it is made up of "the one living being."[56] More precisely, what we confront here is "the will itself."[57] This is the "will in its omnipotence," the will "behind the principium individuationis, the eternal life beyond all phenomena, and despite all annihilation."[58] Such statements place us clearly within a foundationalist paradigm, one with a corresponding schema of appearance and reality. Thus, on the one side, we have the notion of a primal ground which exists prior to all pluralization. On the other, we have the grounded which consists of particular things marked by particular features. The latter are what appear. They constitute the visible realm. The former, the ground which is "the innermost kernel which precedes all forms or the heart of things" does not. Its universality is *before* things.[59] It appears only through them and, then, only as the source of their functioning.

By the time of *Beyond Good and Evil*'s invocation of Dionysius, this early "artist's metaphysics" has shed its Schopenhaurian origins. The "will in its omnipotence" now appears as the "will to power," understood as a "will to life." This will is not just a feature of the organic realm. It has a universal agency. As Nietzsche writes in 1885, "The victorious concept 'force' by means of which our physicists have created God and the world, still needs to be completed: an inner will must be ascribed to it, which I designate as 'will to power,' i.e., as an insatiable desire to manifest power."[60] This completion gives us the doctrine of the sole causality of the will. Will becomes the principle of rank and order. Individuals are taken as *its* expressions, rather than the reverse. It is the inner of which their conscious intentions are the phenomenal outer. If we accept this, then we also accept Nietzsche's 1887 assertion, "There is nothing to life that has value, except the degree of power—assuming that life itself is the will to power."[61] What has not changed from the initial "artist metaphysics" of the *Birth of Tragedy* is the fact that such "will" is not a personal, but rather a metaphysical power. It belongs to the ground of things rather than to any particular individual.

The Dual Grounding

As Heidegger notes, an identification of Being with will is characteristic of German idealism. It is asserted by Leibniz, Kant, Fichte, Hegel, and Schelling. It forms the main theme of Schopenhauer's major work, *The World as Will and Representation*. "Nietzsche," Heidegger adds, "is thinking the selfsame thing [as his predecessors] when he acknowledges the primal Being of beings as will to power."[62] In fact, the movement to which Nietzsche belongs began with Descartes. It was the latter who initiated modern philosophy with his attempt to see the self or subject as an ultimate ground. The figures Heidegger mentions continued this movement by working out the identity of the self and the will. In this subject-centered metaphysics, an apparent subjective function—the will—comes to be seen as an ultimate ground or, in Heidegger's terms, as the "Being of beings."

Nietzsche's contribution to this is twofold. On the one hand, he identifies the will with will to power. On the other, he equates this with the will to life. Life involves "appropriation, injury, overpowering of the strange and weaker, suppression, severity, imposition of one's own forms, incorporation and, at the least and mildest, exploitation." The reference, at least on the surface, seems to be to the Darwinian account of the struggle for existence.[63] The epistemological implications of Darwin's theory, the implication, for example, that "even logic alters with the structure of the brain," allow Nietzsche to advance his perspectivism of appearances. As we saw, the demands of preservation (or survival) in the struggle are taken as shaping both our senses and intellect. Different conditions of existence lead to different demands and hence to the organic shaping of consciousness to particular perspectives. We are, thus, lead to assert the reality of a plurality of ways of bringing reality to appearance, while denying the claim of any to exclusively represent the "real" as it is "in itself." If Nietzsche had remained here, he would have been unambiguously postmodern. Not only would he have denied the possibility of any "grand narrative" (a metadiscourse that would account for the different perspectives), his thinking would also have been postmetaphysical, It would have refused to make the distinction between the real and the apparent (in Heidegger's terms between "what truly is" and what, measured against this, "is not truly in being").[64] Nietzsche, however, attempts to produce a "grand narrative." He seeks a ground for the appearances. He looks for a reason why one perspective rather than another is given. His answer, as we have seen, is "its value for life." More precisely, what decides is the will to life understood as a will to power. We thus enter into a foundational mode of thinking that attempts to reduce everything to the will. A sign of this is Nietzsche's assertion that there is no free, as opposed to unfree, will (the question of such being a question of morality), only "*strong and weak* wills," the question here being that of power.[65] He brushes aside all other grounds by adding "It is *we* alone who have fabricated causes, succession, reciprocity, relativity, compulsion, number, law, freedom, motive, purpose."[66] Engaging in such fabrications, we behave "mythologically." With his metaphysical doctrine of the sole causality of the will, the result, then, is not a perspectivism, but rather a monism. We assert that "all events that result from intention are reducible to the intention to increase power."[67] We, thus, have both a ranking of life according to the strength of the will and a *clearing of the field of behavior* of all other values, all other life practices, so that power alone decides.

To assert the will to power as a sole causality is to leave Darwin far behind. As we said at the beginning, Nietzsche is no Darwinian. He is not because the goal of will to power is not mere preservation, not simple survival. Its goal is simply itself: a constant increase of its power. Thus, Nietzsche complains of "the inconceivably one-sided doctrine of the 'struggle for existence'" with its emphasis on the "so-called preservative instinct."[68] Having made preservation formative of our senses and intellect, he goes on to assert, "the struggle for existence [understood as simply a struggle to preserve oneself] is only an *exception,* a temporary restriction of the will to live; the struggle, be it great or small, turns everywhere on predominance, on increase and expansion, on power, in conformity to will to power, which is just the will to live."[69] The struggle is not just for "self-preservation," but "aims at the *extension of power.*"[70] Its object is the unlimited increase of power. This, of course, is different than the Darwinian struggle. The latter is based on the Malthusian principle that species, unchecked, tend to increase their numbers geometrically, thus increasing the competition between individuals for limited resources. Against this, Nietzsche asserts: "the general condition of life is not one of want or famine, but rather of riches, of lavish luxuriance, and even of absurd prodigality—where there is struggle, it is a struggle for power. We should not confound Malthus with nature."[71] From the Malthusian perspective, the struggle for scarce resources is one for self-preservation, scarcity being the motivating force. As Nietzsche came to realize, the primacy of will to power implies that the struggle continues even when resources are plentiful. It stems not from scarcity. Its source is the unlimited character of the desire for power.[72]

With the above, we have the collapse of the perspectivism Nietzsche bases on preservation. Instead of asserting that life adapts to different conditions of existence, we assert, "A living thing desires above all to *vent* its strength—life as such is will to power: self-preservation is only one of the indirect and most frequent *consequences* of it."[73] This shift can be put in terms of the openness of the subject. If preservation is our principle, then such openness becomes a matter of life adapting to "its" world. It becomes shaped by it into a plurality of forms and perspectives. Insofar as its functioning is the original functioning of the world, this points to the world's pluralization. If, however, preservation is simply a *consequence,* i. e., if the principle is will to power as such, openness has a different cast. Given that life is open to what functions through it, openness now becomes a transparency to will to power. As we said, such "will" is not "mine" in the sense of being the result of my agency. It is rather the cause of such agency. My openness to it is a transparency to the preplural ground of the world—the single force that manifests itself in all the plural, competing forms of life. The paradigm here has the same form as the one we uncovered in our analyses of Augustine and Husserl. Initially, the ultimate functioning is given a subjective cast. Yet, this subjective appearance is deceiving. To bear this functioning, to be adequate to it, the subject must become more than itself. It must suffer a dramatic inflation if it is to be equal to an all encompassing metaphysical principle.

Closely regarded, there is a twofold instability in Nietzsche's position. His thought displays a duality which is responsible for the dramatically different hermeneutical contexts—ranging from postmodernism to Nazism—claiming his thought. The first instability is theoretical. Nietzsche affirms his doctrine of perspectivism as based on utility and preservation *and* undermines this by reducing preservation to a consequence of will to power. To assert the primacy of the latter involves a second, practical instability. Will to power is the power to overcome, exploit, and encroach upon the other. Insofar as will expresses an ultimate ground, its exercise by an individual struggling with its competitors can know no limit. The same holds for collective subjects, groups and races. In each case, the subject in its identity with its ground, in its identity as expressing will to power, takes on a universal, "pre-plural" character. It cannot limit its claims since not only does it not recognize any others like itself, but the self which it does express is (qua will to power) all encompassing. The situation this doctrine leaves us with is, thus, highly unstable. The lack of limits of will to power encompasses the possibility of an ultimate winner in the competitive struggle. Biologically, such a possibility is realized in the disease which kills its host, thus bringing about its own demise. The same sort of unstable victory of the one over all can be seen in the planetary domination of man, a domination Heidegger saw expressed in technology.[74]

Crossing the Line

Does the postmodernism which claims Nietzsche for its ancestor also betray this same Janus face? Is there a subject centered principle lying concealed within its embrace of perspectivism? The jury I think is still out on this question. Certainly the example of Heidegger (another figure claimed by postmoderns) is decidedly ambiguous.[75]

To genuinely cross the line from the modern to the postmodern, we would have to abandon the subject-centered metaphysics at the core of modernity. This implies more than simply abandoning the notion of the subject as an ultimate ground. We would also have to abandon the typical strategy of German idealism, which is to pass through the subject to some ultimate ground. A ground which is uncovered in the depths of the subject may be ultimately pre-plural. Its expression, however, remains subjective. Thus, the will to power which expresses itself through individuals, may be nonpersonal; yet the expression of its unlimited claims still occurs through individuals. To avoid all such claims, the notion of an ultimate ground must itself be abandoned. It must not just be reversed as Nietzsche tried to do with his inversion of all values. It must rather be dissipated in such a way that we cannot distinguish the ground from the grounded. How are we to do this?

One way of proceeding is suggested by a number of Darwin's examples. To read them as clues we must of course first strip from them the rhetoric of will or "struggle" which Darwin shared with most of his contemporaries. Two such examples stand out. The first is his description of the relationship between humble bees and cats. He begins by observing that "humble bees alone visit red clover, as other bees cannot reach the nectar." He then notes that "the number of humble bees . . . depends . . . upon the number of field-mice, which destroy their combs and nests. Now the number of mice is largely dependent, as everyone knows, on the number of cats." The conclusion, then, is that "the presence of a feline animal in large numbers in a district might determine . . . the frequency of certain flowers."[76] One could, in fact, imagine a dairy which, saving the milk cats drank by eliminating them, actually ended up by decreasing the available milk—this, given that its cows fed on red clover. Darwin presents this instance as an example of the "web of complex relations" binding different species together. The second example is that sowing a plot of ground with "several distinct genera of grasses" produces "a greater weight of dry herbage" than sowing it with "one species of grass." This shows that the presence of different species increases the presence of life, in Darwin's words, "that the greatest amount of life can be supported by great diversification of structure."[77] Such examples do not just point out that diversity increases life and that the life of any one species is dependent in often incalculable ways upon others. They also call into question the notion of a "struggle" for existence, at least in its anthropomorphic sense of a subject-centered desire. In the account of the cat and the humble bee, as in any account of a complex web of biological relations, it is extremely difficult to speak of *the* actor in the sense of a particular bearer of the will to life. To think in terms of the "authorship" of a "will to life or power" is not to think of an individual, race or species in competition with others. Such authorship, if it lies anywhere, lies in the whole complex web or system. Its "will" to life is a will to increase it through diversity. In other words, the multiplication of perspectives (biologically, the diversification of the forms of life) is the way life increases. If we grant this, then the ultimate author of a particular "perspective" is neither the individual in his struggle with others nor the will to power working through him to make unlimited claims. It is rather the world which includes the individual.[78]

The best way to put this is in terms of a hermeneutical circle involving both the individual and its surrounding world. On the one hand, we have to say that it is individuals who act: individual cats which hunt individual mice, individual mice which destroy the nests of bees, etc. Yet each action necessarily affects the individual's environment, the very environment which situates and hence motivates the actions (the "willing") of the individual. We thus have a circle of "will" determining the environment, and the environment (through the objects it presents) determining the "will." Given that this environment necessarily includes other actors, the whole is necessarily quite complex. If we wish to continue to speak of the will, its result is a kind of perspectivism of the will; it is the will's pluralization by different motivating contexts. In such a situation, an individual's identification with the ground of action—his openness as a self to what surrounds him—particularizes rather than universalizes his categories. This is because his ground is not some "preplural," preindividual foundation— one which would ultimately lead to a monism with its corresponding reductionism. It is rather the world understood as a self-determining plurality of individual activities and actions, each of which is open to the others which situate it. To accept this is, in fact, to dissipate the notion of a ground. Once we equate agency and openness, we have a situation of individuals determining environments determining individuals. In such a context, there is no first cause, no ultimate determinant. Where each act is both ground and grounded, the notion of a ground is robbed of its foundational character.[79] Embracing the circle of such determination is, then, to abandon any claim to a foundationalist metaphysics. It is to cross the line from the modern to the postmodern.

This crossing the line, as our next chapter will show, requires an acknowledgment of the fragility of the self. The equivalence of agency and openness signifies that the self as an acting center can suffer fragmentation. Open to the world, it can, through its assaults, become multiple.

14

The Splitting of the Self

A striking feature of postmodernism is its distrust of the subject. If the modern period, beginning with Descartes, sought in the subject a source of certainty, an Archimedian point from which all else could be derived, postmodernism has taken the opposite tack. Rather than taking the self as a foundation, it has seen it as founded, as dependent on the accidents which situate consciousness in the world. The same holds for the unity of the subject. Modernity, in its search for a *single* foundation, held the subject to be an indissoluble unity. Postmodernism takes its lead from the Nietzsche who "deconstructs" the subject.[1] This is the Nietzsche who speculates: "The assumption of one single subject is perhaps unnecessary; perhaps it is just as permissible to assume a multiplicity of subjects, whose interaction and struggle is the basis of our thought and our consciousness in general? . . . My hypotheses: The subject as multiplicity."[2]

Given this, there is a natural correspondence between the success of postmodernism and the current interest in multiple personality disorder. In the latter, we actually have the experience of a "multiplicity of subjects" in their interaction and struggle. The subject stands there before us "as multiplicity." It gives us a concrete case, one which raises some of the pressing questions associated with the denial of the subject. Confronting it, we ask, How real are the personalities composing the multiplicity of this disordered self? What, in fact, does this multiplicity tell us about the self? About its genesis and status? What does it reveal about "our thought and consciousness in general"? Using the insights of both Husserl and Aristotle, I am going to sketch some answers to these questions. The result will be an account which will appear postmodern, yet will differ from this in its deriving the self's vulnerability from its openness as "flesh" to the assaults of being.

A Brief Description of MPD

The American Psychiatric Association gives two criteria for multiple personality disorder (MPD). First, and most obviously, there is "the existence within the person of two or more distinct personalities or personality states, each with its own relatively enduring pattern of perceiving, relating to, and thinking about the environment and self." Second, "at least two of these personalities or personality states recurrently take full control of the person's behavior."[3] There is, in other words, a "switching" of control from one distinct personality to another.[4] Additional criteria include a certain "wall of amnesia" existing between the different personalities. Memories in a patient suffering from MPD are not necessarily transparent to one another nor to some overseeing ego. By this, I mean that they do not remember each other, nor are they simply "there," present as objects for an already given ego. Memories are linked to memories "by common affective themes," common contexts and contents.[5] These provide the medium of transparency. As such, they seem to provide the medium where the remembering ego can appear. According to the standard view, the ego exists in and through "the chaining of memories." Different chains give us the different egos or personalities of the patient, each with its own distinguishing memories.[6]

Why are there multiple chains? Why are not all the patient's memories transparent to each other? With these questions, we come to the single most important descriptive fact of MPD: Abuse. An overwhelming percentage (95–98 percent) of patients with MPD "report a history of child abuse."[7] Of course, not every one who is abused experiences a splitting of his or her personality. An abusive family situation, one where the child is repeatedly exposed to the stress of "unpredictable nurturing and abuse" is just one of the factors leading to MPD. Another is the "capacity to dissociate, usually identified with a high responsiveness to hypnosis." Beyond this, there is also a "precipitating event." This is "a specific, overwhelming, traumatic episode to which the victim responds by dissociating." A single episode, however, is normally not sufficient. There must be repeated episodes, each marked by a dissociative response, the result being "separate memories for each dissociative episode."[8] The linking or "chaining" of these by common themes yields the personality, the self that is the rememberer of the chain. To mention one final factor, we may note that the naming of this self, especially under hypnosis, seems to act as a catalyst, causing it to crystallize into something definite. As Pierre Janet, the pioneer in this field, writes: "Once baptized, the sub-conscious personage grows more definitely outlined and displays better [its] psychological character."[9]

How Real are the Selves?

The fact that naming a self under hypnosis seems to stabilize it immediately raises suspicions about its "reality." People suffering from MPD have a high capacity to dissociate; but this, as just noted, is correlated with a high hypnotic ability. Could not naming the self be a factor in its creation? Freud thought so. So have a number of contemporary critics. Kenneth Bowers, in his presidential address to the Society for Clinical and Experimental Hypnosis, makes the charge "that many of the symptoms and reported experiences of MPD are in fact implicitly suggested effects . . ." As such, they are "relatively independent of executive initiative and control." They have the reality, in other words, of trance states induced by the hypnotist. Thus, they are *not* "an outcome of a second executive system or personality"—a second self—that is "responsible for initiating or guiding the suggested outcome."[10] There is no secondary self or personality there. The behavior that seems to point to such a self is actually the result of hypnotic suggestion, made either by the physician or by the patient. In the latter case, we encounter a form of autohypnosis.

Bowers' description of this is revealing of both the strengths and the weaknesses of this claim. It is worth quoting at length. He writes:

> People prone to MPD are very high in hypnotic ability and are, therefore, vulnerable to the suggestive impact of ideas, imaginings, and fantasies; what is more, they are high in hypnotic ability because they have learned to use dissociative defenses as a way of dealing with inescapable threat— such as physical and sexual abuse (Kluft, 1987).[11] The chronic tendency to indulge in solacing fantasy . . . makes it increasingly difficult for a person to deal effectively with reality. Fantasied alternatives to reality (including a fantasied alter ego—stimulated, perhaps, by media accounts of multiple personality disorder) can become increasingly complex and differentiated. Gradually these fantasied alternatives begin to activate subsystems of control more or less directly—that is, with minimal involvement of executive level initiative and control.[12]

Because of this, "one's actions are experienced as increasingly ego-alien." When "the activating fantasies and resulting behaviors become sufficiently threatening, they can also be repressed into an unconscious (i.e., amnesic) status." The result is, thus, "an individual who is subject to profound discontinuities of his or her sense of self" (ibid., p. 169). It is, in fact, an individual exhibiting all the signs of multiple personality disorder. The "subsystems of control"—the systems responsible for purposeful behavior—escape the control of the self taken as an "executive system." Its "fantasied alternatives" more or less "directly" control them. Now, the difficulty with this account is precisely its strength in accounting for the different selves taken as "fantasied alternatives." If these alternatives do control behavior, then they are alternate or secondary "executive systems." As far as their agency is concerned, they seem as real as the primary self or "executive system." Thus, the fact that this disorder can be created by hypnosis does not mean that the alternate selves so created are less "real." It signifies, rather, that hypnosis—in particular, the autohypnosis that allows a patient "to dissociate defensively"—can be taken as creative of the self, i.e., of it as a *particular* agency.

If this conclusion is discomforting to those who attempt to see hypnosis as a way to disprove the "reality" of the selves of the MPD patient, it is equally so to those who argue against Bowers' thesis. Their position is that in genuine MPD the different personalities "have a life history of their own as a result of repeated dissociations."[13] They claim that "in hypnotically induced MPD," by contrast, "the 'personalities' are created by the operator who supplies all the necessary information. Details which are not given are often spontaneously fabricated by the subject" in his adoption of "the role suggested by the hypnotist." The question, here, is, How can one tell whether the personalities one encounters are hypnotically induced or have "developed naturally in response to stress over the course of many years"? The phenomena seem the same. Even the type of causality bears a certain similarity. As Braun (a defender of the "reality" of the different selves) acknowledges, "many consider MPD to be a maladaptive form of dissociation or self-hypnosis in response to environmental stress."[14] If the disorder can result from self-hypnosis, then the assertion that a personality is hypnotically induced is not necessarily a denial of its reality. Here, of course, we must add that what such "reality" is remains to be seen.

The Self as Synthesis

Freud, as we indicated, took an antirealist stance. The whole notion of a consciousness of which the owner is not aware is, he writes, "based on an abuse of the word 'consciousness.'" The fundamental relation is not between selves, but rather between consciousness and unconsciousness. What appear to be separate selves taking control is actually a "shifting of consciousness," an "oscillating between two different psychical complexes which become conscious and unconscious in turn."[15] Only at the end of his life does he begin to speak of the splitting of the ego as a positive phenomenon, something involving separate selves. When he does, he finds himself, as he admits, in the "position of not knowing whether what I have to say should be regarded as something long familiar or something entirely new and puzzling."[16] The "familiar" aspect concerns the type of case that Freud, hitherto, had discussed in terms of repression: that of an instinctual demand which apparently cannot be satisfied. A little boy, who is acquainted with the female genitals, is caught masturbating. Threatened by his nurse with castration by his father, he fears that, like the girl, he too will lose his penis. Instead of discussing the repression of sexual desire, Freud now speaks of "a 'rift' in the ego which never heals but which increases as time goes on."[17] What occurs, concretely, is a splitting of the boy's interpretative stance. One part of it is directed to reality, to acknowledging the danger. A second part, however, directs itself to reinterpreting reality so that the danger no longer exists. The boy comes to believe that women have and do not have a penis. Their bodily image is split according to the stance. Consistent with the first interpretation, he overcomes his fear by creating "a substitute for the penis which he missed in women, that is to say, a fetish."[18] Thus, he is "not obliged to acknowledge that women have lost their penis" and deflects the threat. On the other hand, he cannot "simply contradict his perceptions and hallucinate a penis."[19] The "disavowal of the perceptions," as Freud elsewhere writes, "is always supplemented by an acknowledgment; two contrary and independent attitudes [two interpretations] always arise and result in the situation of there being a splitting of the ego."[20] Freud emphasizes that the phenomenon of such splitting is much wider than this example indicates. Fetishism does not, he writes, present "an exceptional case as regards a splitting of the ego."[21] Such splitting occurs in psychoses, neurosislike states and, indeed, in "neuroses themselves."[22] In the latter, however, repression plays its role, forcing one of the sides to belong to the id.[23]

How does this split in the interpretative attitude or stance "result in . . . there being a splitting of the ego"? Freud's answer points to what he finds "entirely new and puzzling." It is the fragility of the self's synthetic function. In his words, "The whole process seems so strange to us because we take for granted the synthetic nature of the workings of the ego. But we are clearly at fault in this. The synthetic function of the ego, though it is of such extraordinary importance, is subject to particular conditions and is liable to a whole series of disturbances."[24] The disturbance of this function results in the disturbance of the ego. Its disruption is also the ego's disruption. What is pointed to in this last, unfinished work of Freud, is not just the tie of the ego's interpretative stance to the "synthetic nature of the workings of the ego." It is the thought that such workings (and, hence, also the stance) are somehow *prior* to ego. If the ego can be split by a disruption of workings of this synthetic function, then it must in some way be considered as a *result* of it.

Freud, of course, is not the first to see the ego as resulting from synthesis. The view is implicit in the standard dissociative model of MPD. As a psychiatric concept, "dissociation" is derived from the doctrine of "association." This holds that memories are brought to consciousness by way of association of ideas. The memories not available to be associated are, by contrast, termed *dissociated*.[25] It is the association of these dissociated elements, i.e., their *synthesis* or coming together, which results, according to Pierre Janet, in an alternate self with its own set of memories. In his words, "Dissociated states become synthesized among themselves into a large, self-conscious personality to which the term 'self' is given. Subconscious states thus become personified. . . . The subconscious synthesis can be enlarged into something that is self-conscious and which can speak of itself as an 'I'."[26] Such a statement, of course, does not tell us how the association or synthesis works. Current models speak of "state dependent learning" where information acquired in one state is "most expeditiously retrieved" in a similar neuropsychological state.[27] There are also models which emphasize the "chaining" of memories or, in the BASK model, the chaining of behaviors, affects, sensations, and knowledge according to common themes.[28] Unfortunately, such models do not tell us how such chaining comes about. As explanatory vehicles, they hardly get us any further than Hume's original insights regarding resemblance, contiguity, and habit as factors in associative synthesis. As readers of Hume's *Treatise* know, such factors might give us the "fiction" of the self. They seem, however, incapable of yielding the self as an agency, the self that exercises "executive control" over its functions.

To see such agency as a result of synthesis, we cannot presuppose it. This means we have to be able to conceive the "synthetic nature of the workings of the ego" in a pre-egological way. We must also see such pre-egological workings as resulting in egological or "executive" agency, the latter taking them over as its own. Such a demand, as Freud implies, is highly puzzling, not to say paradoxical. How are we to meet it? In Freud's example, it is the split in interpretation—one which took the woman as having and not having a penis—which resulted in the splitting of the person. Since such a split is also a split in the synthetic function, what is pointed to here is the dependence of this function on interpretation. In fact, as we shall now see, interpretation is the key element in synthesis.

Interpretation and Selfhood

Husserl's is still the most convincing description of the role interpretation plays in synthesis. As our chapter on Husserl and Searle shows, he makes interpretation prior to the syntheses that result in the sense of self. His account can be summarized in a couple of pages. Its basic position is contained in the assertion: "perception is interpretation . . . *interpretation* makes up what we term appearance—be it correct or not, anticipatory or overdrawn."[29] This means that I see an object by interpreting the actual contents of my perception as contents *of* some given object. The interpretation is directed to what I *intend* to see. As such, it is, necessarily, an anticipation. Optical illusions make use of this fact. The shift in what we see—such as, the arrow that appears to point towards us and then away—is not a shift in sense contents but in the anticipatory interpretation we place on them. The illusion is constructed to support two opposing intentions. It works only because our perceptions are put together, i.e., synthesized, by placing them within some given interpretative schema. The same holds when I move to get a better look at an object. Thinking that I see a cat crouching under a bush, I interpret the shadows I actually see according to this belief. I take one as part of its ear, another as presenting its eye, and so on. Advancing, I fill in the elements of my perceptual synthesis accordingly. The

synthesis is actually an interpretation of what I see according to some anticipatory guiding schema—here, the thought that I am seeing a cat. In Husserl's
words, "different perceptual contents are given, but they are interpreted, apperceived 'in the same sense'."[30] This sense is what I intend to see, it is the anticipated *goal* of my perceptual synthesis. As goal driven, the process of this synthesis is inherently teleological.

In his later years, Husserl generalized this account to apply to all sorts of
syntheses. They all involve two different elements which give rise to a third. On
the subjective side, we have *contents* there to be interpreted and the *interpretative intention*. When the intention is successful, when it presents an interpretative schema which the contents can embody, the result is the presence of the
intentional object. The latter is what I *intended* to see. The object presents the
sense that is the goal of the act. Present to me, the sense is actually filled out or
embodied by the given contents. What about the syntheses which result in our
self-presence? The account implies that selfhood is interpretation. The "self"
which we are is the self that we take ourselves to be; and this depends upon the
interpretative function. This implies that this function is not just carried on by
the self, i.e., by its executive agency. It also grounds the self in its agency.
How is such self-grounding possible? For Husserl, it does not occur directly.
We are not the *immediate* objects of our self-interpretation. The interpretation
is mediated by the world. The world, which is present by virtue of our interpretative activity, situates the self. It provides the categories that give it shape.

Husserl expresses this point in a number of ways, many of which we
cited in our chapter, "Husserl's Concept of the Self." He writes, for example,
that, abstractly considered, the ego has no "material content" of its own. "It is
quite empty as such." It is, in itself, "an empty form which is only 'individualized' through the stream [of experiences]: this, in the sense of its uniqueness."[31]
The empty form is that of synthesis with its threefold structure of interpretative
intention, material content, and intentional object. The stream of experiences
provides this synthesis with a specific, material content, one that can be synthesized through the interpretative intention into an environment of objects.
As we recall, the presence of this environment is also that of the ego. As an
individual reality, "the ego," Husserl writes, "is only possible as a subject of an
'environment,' only possible as a subject who has facing it things, objects,
especially temporal objects, realities in the widest sense."[32] The dependence
here is, in a certain sense, mutual.[33] On the one hand, such objects are only
present through its perceptual syntheses. Their presence is a measure of the success of the ego's interpretative intentions. On the other, the very presence of the
ego as a subject *in this environment* depends on such success. The self-consis-
tency or identity of the world which confronts the ego is also the ego's own
identity. In Husserl's words, "the subject of the egological performance . . . is
of such a character that it can only preserve its self-identity when it can, in all

the processes of thought, constantly maintain the self identity of the objectivity it thinks."[34] This means that it preserves itself "through correcting itself as it takes positions based on experience." Only as such has it a "personal unity as someone who always possesses a world: the one single world as a fact."[35]

The simplest example of what Husserl is talking about is that of the perceptual syntheses which give us a three-dimensional, spatial-temporal world. The unity of this world is our unity as its center. Our givenness as "here," i.e., as viewing it from a unitary spatial perspective, is correlated to the perspectival unfolding of its objects as we make our way through it. The interpretation of such unfolding which yields a spatially consistent world is *also a self interpretation* insofar as it gives us a "here," i.e., a consistent O-point, as it were, from which we measure distances.[36] The same holds for the interpretations which yield temporal objects. Their correlate is my constant nowness, taken as the point from which both the expired past and the anticipated future are measured. In other words, the "intentional modifications" which yield the continua of the retained past and anticipated future also result in the nowness of my acting self.[37] On the one side, then, we have the interpretative function which yields a surrounding, centering world. Given that this world situates this functioning at its center, we have, on the other side, the specification (particularization) of this functioning as its "subject." In Husserl's words, "subject here is only another word for the *centering* which all life possesses as egological life . . ."[38] Concretely, the subject is both the functioning and the centering of such functioning which results from the success of its interpretations.

Trauma and the Splitting of the Self

What happens when the interpretations fail? For Husserl, as we have seen, "the assertion that I remain who I am . . . is equivalent to the assertion that my world remains a world."[39] Indeed, the interdependence of the two is such that we have to say that a "complete dissolution of the world in a 'tumult' [of experiences]" through the failure of our interpretations brings about a corresponding "dissolution of the ego."[40] The centering which characterizes it as a subject no longer holds. The same point can be made about the splitting of this world. Such splitting is, correspondingly, a splitting of the self. It is its decentering into two or more centers. When we talk about the splitting of the world, we mean, of course, the splitting of its intended sense, the overall meaning which is supposed to give it its unity. Given that this sense is a result of synthesis, its root is the splitting of the interpretative function which guides the action of synthesis. This function, as we said, is teleological or goal driven. Its overarching goal is the unity, the coherent sense, of the world we experience. What we face in MPD is the fragmentation of this highest goal. Each fragment now bears its own sense of the world as an anticipatory unity, a schema into which experiences are fitted as experiences *of* a given world fragment. The splitting of the world's sense into incompatible unities is, in other words, *not* the dissolution or end of the interpretative function. As a teleological, goal-directed function, it continues. It is, however, now particularized by two or more distinct goals.

According to the above, the splitting of the sense of the world results in the splitting of the self. To concretely grasp this split in the self—i.e., to see how it results in selves distinguished in their inner temporality—a couple of intermediate steps linking sense and temporality are required. The first is that the split in the sense of the world is a split in its presence, its being there for us. The second is that this split in presence is, subjectively, a split in the nowness which frames the self's experience. As such, it results in parallel now-streams, each stream defining a self with *its* centering, temporal environment. Let us consider these steps in somewhat greater detail.

That a split in the world's sense is a split in its presence results from presence being a function for us of sense. Things are present because of the sense we make of our experiences. The result of this "making sense" is the object that appears—is present—in the flow of our perceptions. As we cited Husserl on this point: "The object of consciousness, in its self-identity throughout the flowing of experience, does not come from outside into such flowing; it is, rather, present within it, determined as a sense. It is an intentional accomplishment of the syntheses of consciousness."[41] Behind such syntheses lies the interpretative function, the function which takes different experiences as experiences of one and the same object. Guiding the syntheses, it makes the object present. In Husserl's words, "the interpretation according to this [same guiding] 'sense' is an experiential character that first yields 'the existence of the object for me'"[42] The essential point here is that "all real unities"—all actually experienced unitary presences—"are unities of sense."[43] They are guiding senses which have become perceptually embodied, because they are the senses of successful interpretations. Granting this, the split in the interpretative function which results from the splitting of its guiding senses can result in a splitting of presence. To the point that the interpretations guided by the different sense fragments are successful, they will become perceptually embodied. The sense fragments will be experienced as real unities—as actually present. The same holds for the split in the overarching sense of the world. The resulting fragments, to the point that they still can function as guiding senses, split the world's presence. Its being there, its presence or existence for an individual, becomes multiple.

If we stay strictly within the Husserlian paradigm, there is a level of identity not touched by this splitting. The splitting affects the ego, but not the temporalization that Husserl takes as a pre-egological function. For Husserl, as we recall, "subjective time constitutes itself in an absolutely timeless subject who is not an object."[44] Not being an object, such a subject is untouched by the splitting of the interpretative function. As the timeless origin of time, it us ultimately identified with God.[45] If, however, we adopt the reversal suggested by our reflections on Aristotle, the splitting does affect temporalization. This is because this split in the world's *presence* is also a split in the *nowness* which defines the self as a temporal center. Both splits are the same since such nowness *is* the presence of the world. Nowness is its presence to us, i.e., is our registering the world. The best way to elucidate this is in terms of our actual experience of time. Two features characterize this experience: an unchanging now and a changing content. The first is exhibited in the fact that it is always now for me. Whatever I do, think, or experience, the now frames its content. I may, for example, remember something that occurred in the past, but the actual remembering occurs in the now. The now frames the experience of remembering as it frames every other experience I have. That this frame is constant does not, of course, mean that what it frames, the experience itself, is constant. It is, in fact, in constant flux. Experiencing its change, we experience the change of time. Contrariwise, as Aristotle first noted, "when we have no sense of change or are inattentive to any change, we have no sense of the passage of time."[46] Combining the features of nowness and flux, we have to say that our experience of time is that of constant passage within the now. The now that remains continually exhibits the new. In doing so, it seems to shift or stream. In Husserl's phrase, our experience of time is that of the "stationary streaming now." It is an experience of a now that remains even as what is present in the now—the actual perceptual content—streams away.

It seems to be an empirical fact that, when we have no consciousness of time, we have no consciousness of anything at all. Contrariwise, unconsciousness and a loss of any sense of time are synonymous. This indicates that time is the registering of presence. The two features of time point to corresponding aspects of this registering. Thus, the lasting now registers the lasting presence of the world. It remains insofar as the world stays *the world*—i.e., keeps its presence as embodying *a unitary, coherent sense*. As perceptually embodied, this sense is established through a constant flow of contents. Given this, the experience of the world is also an experience of the streaming of the now. The now streams insofar as the world's presence continually manifests a shifting content. Thus, my experience of time's flow is my experience of the shifting presence of the now, and this is an experience of the shifting presence of my experienced world. Summing up, we can say that the constancy of the now which frames this presence registers the constancy of the "sense" world, while its streaming registers the change of contents which make this sense perceptually present.

Nothing prevents us from combining this view with Husserl's insight that being comes to presence through the interpretative function. If we do, then the splitting of this function is not just a fragmentation of the presence of being, it is also a breaking apart of the temporality generated by such presence. Thus, to the point that a split in this function breaks apart the sense of the world into incompatible unities, the split results in the fragmentation of the now which registered the world's unity. This lasting now acted as a frame for the shifting perceptual content which we registered as temporal passage. Accordingly, its fragmentation is the splitting of this frame and, hence, of the identity of the passage itself. The result, then, is separate, yet contemporary inner times—i.e., distinct, yet parallel now streams. With this, we have the split in the self in its inner temporality. It is easy to see how this split touches the self in its identity. The self is present to itself in its experiences, but these experiences are its registering of the world. What marks the self as a self is its registering of the world's presence as time. Formally regarded, i.e., distinguished from the specific material content of its world, the self is just a series of temporal relations. Thus, although we can say that objects in the world are spatially ordered, it makes no sense, as we have often noted, to say that one experience is so many feet or meters from another. It is equally absurd to give an experience a definite size— e.g., to say that my perception of an object is five inches high. Only the relation of before and after orders the experiences which give me my content as a streaming field of consciousness. Granting this, the splitting of the presence of the world is not just a splitting of the temporality which registers this presence. It is also the splitting of the self in its temporal self-presence as a now stream. The resulting distinction in now streams is precisely that which applies to separate yet contemporaneous selves. Each self has a nowness out of which it functions. As a temporal center, it becomes particularized as the point from which its expired past and anticipated future are measured. It, thus, becomes correlated to the givenness of *its* world as a registering of *its* presence.

We are now at the stage where we can propose a more detailed account of what happens in MPD. In MPD, an event occurs which does not just result in a *change of presence*—i.e., in the change which we experience as the advance of time. It results in the *splitting of presence* itself. This is because the event overwhelms the interpretative function responsible for this presence. Accordingly, the traumatic event can be defined as any occurrence whose horrific, exceptional character prevents its sense from being integrated into the experiencing subject's world. The world in which it happens bears a nonintegratable, separate sense—the sense, for example, of a world where abusive sex "normally" occurs between parent and child. The dissociation that occurs through the repetition of trauma is, then, a function of the splitting of the sense, "world." As involving such sense, it is a *cognitive event*. It can be described in terms of a person's conceptual framework. Yet, because the sense is perceptually embodied, its presence is more than that of a series of concepts. Given through the person's actual perceptions, the presence of the sense "world" is the presence of its being.[47] Accordingly, the traumatic event has an ontological aspect. It occasions a split in the presence which times the subject and, hence, a split in the subject itself in its temporal self-presence.

Within this framework, several points stand out. The first concerns the body that is the subject of traumatic abuse. In the constancy and immediacy of its presence, the central object of the self's world is its body. Thus, the presence of the world, which it registers as nowness, is first and foremost the presence of its body. Otherwise put: my physical self-presence is the chief determinant of the nowness that frames my changing perceptions. Given this, the abuse that disrupts the body's sense has a direct effect on my now stream. Splitting the body's sense, it can split the nowness which is the defining place of my executive agency. One way to express this is in terms of the reflexivity or self-presence which, as our last chapter on Aristotle stressed, is inherent in the animate body. Touching an object, I sense myself touching it. My flesh is both subject and object in this act. It is the *subject* insofar as it is (or contains) the organ of touch. It is the *object* insofar as it is the medium of touch, i.e., is that through which the object appears. We can link the two by saying that in a certain sense, flesh grasps an object by embodying it. It does so by providing the material for this embodiment. Thus, grasping the object, I *grasp myself* as embodying it. Suppose, for example, I wish to see a certain object. To do so, I move to get a better look. Here, the material for embodiment is the presence of the appropriate perceptual contents. Reflexivity or self-presence comes in because my grasp of the object is through myself, i.e., through my possessing the appropriate sense contents—the very contents I hope will arise in my moving to get a better look. In this action, I can be aware of the object as the goal of my perceptual process and of myself as *other* than the object insofar I have not yet embodied it, i.e., have not yet provided the contents which would satisfy my intention. Both awarenesses are possible insofar as I myself, in my flesh, provide the means or medium for the object's presence. If this is correct, then the disruption flesh suffers during abuse has a cascading effect. First, there is the disruption of flesh as the place of embodiment or realization. With this is the disruption of the reflexivity or self-presence involved in such embodiment. It is through my self-presence as embodying the object—as possessing the appropriate sensations—that I gauge and correct the interpretative intentions I direct to objects. Thus, the disruption of my bodily self-presence is also a disruption of my interpretative function. The coherency of the sense of my bodily presence and, hence, of the world which appears through it breaks down if the physical abuse is sufficiently severe. With this, there occurs the fragmentation of the unitary character of the nowness which registers the coherency of this sense. The result, then, is a split in the selfhood framed by this nowness. The self is split into distinct now streams.

A further point concerns the correlation between the severity of abuse and fragmentation. The more traumatic the abusive event, the greater is the self's splitting.[48] Each split has its memories, its fragments of the original episode which are organized into a "world" with its distinct sense.[49] Each such world has its personality, its central focus. The account just given differs from the standard one which sees the personality fragment as resulting directly from the chaining (or "association") of multiple memories. A single, sufficiently traumatic event can create a dissociated self. The break-up of the unity sense, "world," creates a personality fragment. Repeated dissociative episodes, to the point that they manifest this same sense, can enlarge this fragment. The dissociated self, however, is there from the first episode. It is not the result of a chaining of memories from a number of episodes. This interpretation, thus, overcomes the difficulty of the standard view, which is that of determining how many such episodes would be enough to provide the chain through which the self could appear. The problem does not arise because personality (or selfhood) is not a function of memory. Memory, rather, is a function of personality, which is *itself a function of interpretation.* The interpretation sets the schema for the personality to which the memories are referred. It does this not just by determining the personal ways an individual understands his world—and, hence, acts in it. It also determines the nowness which is his self-presence. This is the same nowness which situates his memories by being the point from which their presence has elapsed. We can, thus, say that the compartmentalization of memories has its origin in the separation of the temporal frames which organize them. At the basis of such separation is the compartmentalization of the senses of the world guiding the self's interpretation. This, as we said, results from the abuse which disrupts the body's role as the place (or "medium") of presence. The consequence is a splitting of the victim's self-presence and, hence, his temporal frame. With this, comes the dissociation of memories. The memories which do not fit in with a guiding interpretative sense of the world are also not part of the temporal frame correlated to this sense. As a result, they are "dissociated"—referred to another self with its distinct bodily presence, temporal frame, and corresponding world.

Having spoken of nowness as situating memories, i.e., as serving as the point from which their pastness is gauged, we must take note of the breakdown of this function. Severe trauma may result in the apparent nowness of the remembered. The personality which "owns" the memory of a traumatic event may, when activated, live in its immediate presence. It experiences the event as "right now," i.e., as actually occurring at the present moment. We can explain this by noting that in severe trauma the sense of the event is so exceptional that it does not connect with what preceded and followed it. Normally, every movement, every action occurs within a sense giving horizon which involves both the past and the future. They bear as part of their sense, the intention of "after this I am going to do or experience x," x being the follow through of the action or experience. It is, for example, the next step in walking, the next sensation, such as the taste of the coffee as you put the cup to your lips, etc. The exceptionally traumatic event disrupts this process of temporal linking. As traumatic, it does not fit in with the meanings the person gives to a particular situation, circumstance, or individual. It is outside of his conceptual map—i.e., outside of those organizing senses which (as principles) give him his standard interpretations of his unitary world, the standard anticipations of what it offers. Not connected to either what precedes or follows it because of the lack of the fit of its sense with these, its recall does not bring in this locating temporal frame. In other words, the breakdown of the syntheses which would have placed the event in sequential time make it inherently timeless. Not having any inherent temporal tag, it gets its stamp of immediacy from the nowness of the situation of its recall. It picks up its presence from the self-presence of the person reliving it. This presence, however, changes its own sense. Animating the memory of the abuse, it becomes the presence of a self who interprets himself in terms of the abusive event. To the observer it thus seems that the ego actually suffering the abuse takes over the person during the recall.

To speak of one personality "taking over" another implies a certain agency on its part. This has led some authors to see splitting, itself, as an action to protect the "host" or primary personality from the memory of abuse. Some support for this view comes from the testimony of the different personality fragments. Alper, for example, observes "these secondary personalities experienced episodes of abuse and reported maintaining those specific memories, 'protecting' the hosts through amnestic barriers." Such protection, however, is limited since as he also notes, "Host personalities tended to be self-attacking, paralleling the hostile initiator [the abuser's] behavior." In fact, studies by Ross, Norton, and Worney in 1989 reported a 72 percent attempted suicide rate among patients with MPD.[50] Such facts call into question the notion that splitting is a defensive maneuver by the abused ego. The dependence of self on interpretation implies, in fact, the opposite. Rather than anything done by the ego, splitting is something that the ego suffers by virtue of the fragmentation of the interpretative function.[51] As for the "self-attacking" tendencies displayed by the host, these can be traced to the common syndrome in which the victim identifies with the victimizer. In splitting, that part of the interpretative function which identifies with the abuser, i.e., which takes the abuser's agency as the victim's, could very well remain with the host personality. It keeps the identification, even after the conscious memories of abuse have been localized about another personality.

Such localization is their dissociation from the host personality. This leads me to make a final point about the reality of the personalities arising through hypnosis. As noted, a tendency to dissociate is correlated with a high hypnotic ability—the ability to accept suggestions as if they are real. Insofar as such suggestions affect the subject's interpretation of his world, by suggesting a guiding sense for it, the suggestions must, in my account, also affect the subject's sense of self. Situating the subject in the suggested world, they provide it with a distinct centering of experience—a distinct personality—around which particular memories can accumulate. Given that the self is the particularization of the interpretative function, the self thus actualized is as real as the self created through trauma. As long as the suggestion maintains its power, it is as capable of "executive agency" within its world as the trauma-created one. That both can claim to be "real" points to Nietzsche's speculative hypothesis: "the subject as multiplicity." Practically, in terms of the sufferer, it points to the fragility of what we call a *self*.

15

POST-NORMATIVE SUBJECTIVITY

It is time to draw some conclusions from the attempt of these chapters to think about the themes of self, time, and being. Our reflections have been by and large historical. They have been prompted by the fact that, as our century draws to a close, we seem to be at the end of an age. We are no longer moderns, but—as the contempory catchword goes—"postmoderns." A sign of this change is the pluralism which has spread across our culture. In the arts, every style is acceptable from abstract expressionism to photographic realism. Traditional harmonies reappear in music, often alongside the most severe atonalities. "Postmodern" architects, who coined the term *postmodernism* some thirty years ago, feel free to use an often bewildering variety of architectural styles. Even in philosophy, where once a rigid dogmatism reigned, "doing philosophy" is no longer limited to a set of particular problems or methodologies. Here, too, postmodernism is taken as implying pluralism with its corresponding lack of determining norms. The postmodern period is thus post normative. By contrast, the modern period was pre-eminently normative. In philosophy, its birth was announced by Descartes' *Rules for the Direction of the Mind*, prescribing a set of norms for correct thinking. Since then, it has produced rules for practically everything. From the Kantian conditions for the possibility of experience to the Marxian laws of dialectical materialism to our century's various guides on everything from sexuality to accounting, modernity has been intent on declaring *in advance* how things must be. In this final chapter, I am going to examine the roots of modernity in order to sketch how this attitude came about. I will then look at a few of the implications of the shift from the modern notion of subjectivity. Here, my goal is to draw from the previous chapters a proposal for a new way of doing philosophy.

The Origin of Modernity

Philosophical modernity has some unlikely sources. Its immediate impulses came from reports on cannibals and dreams. Montaigne in his essay, "Of Cannibals," declares that "we have no other criterion of truth and reason than the example and pattern of the opinions and customs of the country wherein we live."[1] After praising the virtues of the cannibals and finding them in no wit inferior to those of sixteenth century France, he laughingly concludes: "But hold on! They don't wear breeches."[2] Pants alone make Europe superior. A similar, but much more penetrating relativism is advanced by Cervantes' *Don Quixote*, the international best-seller of the seventeenth century. For the Don, dreams have the force of reality. Any evidence to the contrary is explained by the "enchanters [who] have persecuted, are persecuting, and will continue to persecute me."[3] Evil and all-powerful, they make it impossible to decide on what precisely is real, what is a dream and what not. Indeed, on one level, the whole book can be considered a meditation on the impregnability of the Don's argument. It exposed the bankruptcy of contemporary claims regarding reality and illusion.

Modernity in philosophy begins with Descartes' response to this. The first of Descartes' *Meditations* considers the possibilities that everything we now sense and experience is actually a dream and that "an evil genius, as clever and deceitful as he is powerful" prevents us from realizing this.[4] To banish this enchanter, Descartes searches for something that is absolutely certain, something that he cannot doubt. He finds it in the "I" or subject of the "I think." Even if we doubt every object of this subject's thought, we cannot doubt it. It becomes the *ens certissimum*, the being whose certainty is such that it can stand as a norm, a standard against which to judge all other claims to knowledge. This norm is mediated through the concepts of clarity and distinctness. To the point that our perceptions and thoughts of other objects approach the clarity and distinctness of our grasp of the subject, to that point we can be equally certain of the reality of their objects.

This positioning of the subject or self as normative has worked for hundreds of years. In fact, in a broad sense, modernity is this appeal to subjectivity. Descartes' argument, however, for all its apparent force, has a fateful contradiction. The subject to whom he appeals is not an object like other objects. It is a subject who thinks objects, who doubts or sensuously perceives them as the case may be. Descartes argues that all the objects of its attention can be doubted; what cannot be doubted is simply the attending itself. Qua attending, however, the subject is not an object, but rather that which directs itself to objects. As such, Descartes' attempt to turn it into a "thinking thing"—an entity whose perception can stand as a norm for the perception of other objects—is highly problematical.

This point may be put in terms of our remarks on the mind-body problem. The abstraction which Descartes engages in to make the subject indubitable leads directly to it. For Descartes, as we said, what cannot be doubted is not myself as having a "face, hands, arms and this entire mechanism of bodily members." It is not the self that perceives through its bodily organs. It is rather the self that doubts whether any of this pertains to it. Such a self, then, is "only a thing that thinks." Its "essence," he asserts, "consists in this alone." As such, it is completely nonextended. If I am, then, only what I can be certain of, it follows for Descartes "that I am truly distinct from my body." Indeed, reduced to what I can be certain of, it follows that "I can exist without [this body]."[5] How can this abstract, nonextended subject interact with the body? The body is extended while the mind or soul is a unity of attending. Descartes' attempt to combine the two is instructive. He writes in *The Passions of the Soul*, "we have two eyes, two hands, two ears," etc., yet "we have but one solitary and simple thought of one particular thing at one and the same time."[6] There must, he reasons, be "a place" where the impressions "can unite before arriving at the soul." This is the "little gland" (the pineal) which alone of the brain's structures is not bifurcated.[7] Body and soul communicate by moving this little gland. In Descartes' words, the soul "possesses as many diverse perceptions as there are diverse movements in this gland," such movements being caused by the "impressions" made on the sense organs. "Reciprocally, . . . this gland is diversely moved by the soul" which thereby communicates through it to "the machine of the body."[8] How a nonextended substance is to move something extended, even if it is just a "little" gland suspended in "animal spirits," is not explained. Given that between the extended and nonextended there can be no point of physical contact, the failure of this attempt was to become paradigmatic, echoing down the centuries in the characteristic mind-body dualism of modernity.

When we recall the motive for positing subjectivity as nonextended, which is that of making it normative, there is more than a little irony here. As our first chapter indicated, the perceived failure of ancient philosophy involved its inability to relate its standard of certainty, the ideas or εἴδη, to the physical world. In the premodern period, the failure to solve what was called the *problem of the universals* led to the nominalism and relativism which set the climate for Descartes' reaction. With Descartes, the problem reappears as that of the reduced subject's relation to the world. The otherworldliness of the Platonic norms is matched by a similar otherworldliness of the normative subject. As this brief reading of intellectual history indicates, the key to this dualism is the attempt to make subjectivity normative. This is what requires the abstraction which makes it nonextended.

Synthesis and the Crisis of Modernity

Kant, Descartes' greatest successor, took up the Cartesian project with his typical thoroughness. The subject, he asserts, is a "thoroughgoing identity."[9] When we regard it, "nothing multiple is given."[10] As Kant explains, I am always "conscious of the self as identical with respect to the multitude of the representations which are given to me in an intuition."[11] Whatever I represent myself as experiencing or doing, I am always conscious of myself as the same. This unitary self is also normative. Indeed, for Kant, without it "there would be no nature, i.e., no synthetic unity of the multiplicity of appearances according to rules." Taken as a "unity of apperception," it is, in fact, "the transcendental ground of the necessary lawfulness of appearances composing an experience."[12]

Kant does more than simply reaffirm the normativity and unity of subjectivity. It was his genius to unite these two insights in a radical manner. For Descartes, subjectivity was normative in the sense of providing the most certain object we could perceive. Its perception was supposed to set the standard for clarity and distinctness. Kant asks what we mean by "clarity and distinctness" and, as a prior question, what is meant by the perceptual process itself. His answer is that the process is one of synthesis, of connecting perception with perception so that, through their ordering, we can have an extended intuition of a unitary object. Clarity and distinctness involve following the rules of this ordering. To the point that such rules are violated, the object fails to appear. Such rules, in other words, are viewed as "conditions for the possibility of experience." They determine in advance how the object can appear. Thus, in the Kantian view, subjectivity is normative insofar as it is seen as constitutive, through its synthesis of perceptions, of the appearing of the world. The norms we draw from it, those of the synthetic a priori judgments, are those based on the "universal and necessary connection of the given perceptions," a connection which is required if we are to intuit a unified, self-consistent world.[13] Thus, instead of Plato's forms, we have synthetic a priori judgments, and behind these we have the rules for connecting or synthesizing our perceptions. They are rules which must be followed if objects are to appear. The step from this to the unitary subject is simplicity itself. It occurs once we admit that synthesis requires a synthesizer. As Kant expresses this deduction, there is "an action of the understanding which we may name with the general title of *synthesis* in order, thereby, to draw attention to the fact that we cannot represent to ourselves anything as combined in the *object* without ourselves first having combined it and that combination . . . can only be performed *by the subject itself* since it is an act of its selfhood."[14] The deduction, then, is from the givenness of the *action of synthesis* to the necessity of the subject as an *active synthesizer*. Now, admitting that all combination requires a combiner, this subject must be uncombined. Otherwise it would be the result rather than the ground of combination. In Kant's words, given that it is what "first makes possible the concept of combination," this self must be an absolute unity.[15] If it were not a unity, it would be combined, but then there would have to be another self behind it, acting as *its* combiner.

Ingenious as this analysis is, it sharpens rather than solves the problem of the subject's relation to the world. Given that appearing is a result of the synthesis (or combination) of perceptions, the subject taken as a cause of synthesis (and, hence, of appearing) cannot appear. If it did, it would be a result rather than a cause of synthesis. In Kant's terms, this means that the subject, taken as an uncombined combiner, must be a *noumenal* rather than a *phenomenal* subject. None of the categories we draw from experience can apply to it. Indeed, given that the action of synthesis is that of placing its perceptions in time, even the categories of temporality fall away. Not only is it nonextended, it is out of time. Its relation to the world, in particular, its relation to the "transcendent affection" by which the world provides it with the material of its synthesis, cannot be known.

With Kant the mind-body dualism becomes explicitly that of self and world. Strictly speaking, neither of these poles is knowable "in itself." The noumenal self is matched by the noumenal world. This last is the world that remains once we abstract from its notion all the categories (all the rules of synthesis) the self imposes upon it to make it intuitable. A dualism in which both sides are unknown is, as Fichte realized, inherently unstable. Once we think it through, it requires that we choose between two incompatible alternatives. Either we embrace a thoroughgoing idealism and assert that the ego produces the world, positing itself as finite within it, or else, taking the opposite "dogmatic" stance, we "construe the self merely as a product of things, an accident of the world."[16] Fichte asks, "which of the two [self or world] should we take as primary?" Given that both are inherently unknown, we cannot decide. As Fichte says, "reason provides no principle of choice." It cannot because what is at issue is not "a link in the change of reasoning," but rather "the beginning of the whole chain."[17] In other words, what is at issue is the ground of reason itself.

With this we come to the special crisis of modernity. The Cartesian attempt to ground reason in subjectivity by making the latter normative ultimately results in a kind of philosophic schizophrenia. Either we embrace an idealism which ultimately positions subjectivity as an unknowable ground of the rational or else turn and place this ground in the world. In the former case, as we saw with Husserl, subjectivity undergoes a kind of unlimited inflation. In the latter, the subject becomes an accident of the world in the sense of being contingent on such nonsubjective factors as the particulars of its biology, chemistry, and physics.

The scientific attempt to work out this second alternative displays an instructive circularity. To explain how the physical structure of the subject determines the nature of its perception and thought, science, as it must, uses this perception and thought to investigate this structure. Such perception and thought give us our general knowledge of anatomy, chemistry, and physics. We use this to examine the brain—with the object of ultimately knowing how the brain determines such knowledge. With this, we have the explanatory circle discussed at the beginning of our third chapter: our knowledge is explained by the structure of the brain and the operation of this structure is itself explained by our knowledge—i.e., by the scientific laws we discover through our perception and thought. Given that the structure of the brain is contingent—is something which in the course of evolution could have been different—science finds itself in the unpleasant situation of relativizing itself. Since it can never know whether the brain is so structured that it gets the world as it is in itself, it is, like its idealist alternative, reduced to a level of sheer appearance. Beyond the appearing world lies the "in itself," the unknown, nonrational ground of the rational.[18]

Overcoming Modernity

Given the above, the failure of modernity is the failure of its central project. This is to make subjectivity normative, in broad terms, to make it serve as a substitute for the ideas or forms of ancient philosophy. The forms were to be reinterpreted as rules for synthesis while the synthesizing subject was to be seen as the most certain, the most clear and distinct, of the objects we could grasp. In this way, it would serve as a new foundation of knowledge, one whose openness to inspection would be its bulwark against the skepticism of a Montaigne. Unfortunatley, subjectivity was not up to the task. The history of modernity can be read as the story of its disappearance under the weight of the requirements placed upon it.

The fault here lies not with any of the philosophers who pursued the modern project but rather with subjectivity itself. Whatever it is, it is an openness to the world. Capable of becoming anything in the peculiar identity that mind has with its objects, it is, "in itself," nothing but this openness. As Aristotle put this, "before it thinks," that is, before it grasps an object, "mind has no actual existence."[19] It is "potentially identical with the objects of its thought," indeed, this potentiality is its openness. But, as Aristotle immediately adds, it "is actually nothing until it thinks."[20] This means that it has no inherent content, all such content being derived from the objects which it thinks. If Aristotle is right, then the attempt to grasp the subject as an object is bound to fail. It cannot be an object, for to be such demands a definite, distinguishing content. But a subject has content only in its temporary identity with what is not itself. (This, incidentally, is the curse of psychology. Infinitely adaptable, the subject in its content seems to support every form of analysis from the Freudian to the cognitive.) Given this, the subject is the last place we should look to for normative structures. It is open to such structures. It can take them on in its identity with its objects. This very openness, however, signifies its lack of any *inherent* normative structures or laws. On this point at least, our position is Sartre's: "there is no law of consciousness, but rather a consciousness of law."[21] You cannot, he notes, have both; you cannot make consciousness an openness and require from it a set of normatively prescriptive laws. Such laws make it "opaque" rather than open. As our account of Kant indicates, they ultimately conceal rather than reveal what is not consciousness, consigning it to the "noumenal." This openness does not mean that we shall ever encounter consciousness without its manifesting laws. These laws, however, come not from itself, but rather from its identity with its objects.

The best way to express this point is in terms of temporalization. As Kant observed, all "our representations . . . are subject to time, the formal condition of inner sense. Time is that in which they must be ordered, connected and brought into relation."[22] On the level of "inner sense," the sense by which we grasp subjective processes, we are, formally regarded, simply a series of temporal relations. We say temporal, as opposed to spatial, since, as often noted, it makes no sense to say that one representation is so many feet from another or is a certain size. We can, however, talk about one being before or after another and, indeed, about the processes by which we grasp this. This insight allows us to see why the subject cannot have any inherent content. Time per se is capable of exhibiting every sort of content precisely because it lacks any content of its own. Its moments are, as it were, empty containers—or rather, place holders—of possible contents. Indeed, this very lack of any inherent, distinguishing content undercuts the notion of discrete moments. It is a correlative of the continuity of time. Granting this openness of time, if subjectivity is a field of temporal relations, any content it has must come from its objects. Its being as such a field *is*, in other words, *its openness* to what is not itself.

It is possible to draw a radical conclusion from the above. If we really hold that subjectivity is temporality, then the implication is that it has as many forms as time has. This means we can speak of subjectivity as sheer nowness, subjectivity as temporal flowing, subjectivity as the form of objective synthesis, subjectivity as our being-there in and through other persons, and even of subjectivity as the unidirectional flow of objective causality (the flow that allows us to suppose that our own inner relations are subject to causal laws). Each corresponds to a different sort of object. When I grasp a mathematical relation (when at the moment of insight I am no longer conditioned by the before and after of time) then I exhibit the first form of subjectivity. I exhibit a very different form playing with others as a member of an ensemble. In none of these manifestations are specific contents suggested. Subjectivity so conceived is silent (1) on the nature of nowness, (2) on the contents which might occupy its temporal stream, (3) on the nature of its relations with other subjects, or (4) on the type of causal laws it might assume it is subject to. As a sheer openness, it has a perfect plasticity. It simply provides a place for different types of objects to appear.

Post-Normative Subjectivity and Temporalization

To arrive at this notion of subjectivity a crucial transformation of the modern view of temporalization is required. Since the seventeenth century, subjectivity has been normative by virtue of serving as the ultimate focal point for the constitution of experience. For this, it must, as Kant saw, involve itself in temporalization. Its universal and necessary rules for connecting perceptions are normative in the sense that they are what first make experience possible. They perform this function by being rules for temporalization, rules for inserting experiences in the before and after of time. In other words, subjectivity is normative because time is what we bring to the data of experience to make objective experience possible. If this is right, then the reversal of the normativity of subjectivity is the reversal of this temporalization. The object must time the subject. It must be what inserts it in the before and after of time.

To see how this is possible requires something more than the description of the mechanics of the process. The process, to be comprehensible requires a shift in the metaphysics which underlies modernity. This metaphysics can be summed up in a single sentence: The whole notion of the constitution of reality by the subjective act of temporalization assumes the dependence of reality on temporalization. In other words, "modernity" presupposes the dependence of being on time.[23] A metaphysics that crossed the line from the modern to the postmodern would assert the reverse. It would rethink and renew the pre-Cartesian claim that time was dependent on being.

Its starting point would be the fact that we have no sense of time as a flow of moments without a sense of change. It would interpret this by saying that the presence which characterizes the "now" of time *is* the presence of the entity. The continuity of time is a correlate of this continuity, this lack of any gaps in the entity's presence as one and the same object. The entity is registered as the now in which we always dwell. The fact that we experience this now as flowing, as maintaining its presence by shifting its relation to the before and after, is a consequence of the change of the entity. For example, moving, the entity remains the same while shifting its relation to its environment. Our registering this fact is its timing us, the result being that we experience ourselves as dwelling in what Husserl called the "stationary streaming" of the present. This is the present that appears to remain now by advancing from one momentary present to the next. As our previous chapters have argued, this streaming is simply the result of the advance of the entity, it is our registering *its* shift with regard to its environment.

To flesh out the details of this we would have to take account of the one subjective capacity it presupposes: that of retention. This is our ability to retain (or, as Kant would say, "reproduce" in the present) the impressions an entity makes on us. Husserl's early work on retention, particularly his account of how we are timed through it, is of particular value here. As we have seen, a great part of his *Phenomenology of Internal Time Consciousness* can be read, not as describing how we time the world, but rather how we are *placed in time* by the world.

Postmodern Philosophy

Rather than getting further into the mechanics of this process, I want to conclude with a general description of post-normative subjectivity and the philosophy it implies. Here, several points can be made. The first is that such subjectivity is not epiphenominal. In spite being determined, both in its laws and its content, by the world, it is not an "accident of the world." It is rather an openness that lets the world be. Such "letting be" is not to be conceived in the Heideggerian sense of letting the world reveal itself through *our* projects, goals, or criteria for being.[24] *Letting be* in the post-normative sense means letting the world temporalize itself in and through an apprehending subject. This subject times the world, not by being the origin of time, but by letting itself be timed by it. In the process, it lets the world be by letting the world set the laws of its appearing. In itself, it is simply an openness to these laws. We essentially say the same thing when we assert that its "laws," if such we wish to call them, are basically those by which it maintains and preserves its openness to beings.

Such openness is its "no-thingness" and its receptivity. Both are a result of its being as a temporal form (essentially that of retention) which allows it to be timed by the different forms of motion surrounding it. So timed, this subject is always on the level of ontological identity with its object. It is inherently pluralistic. Attentive to mathematical objects, it has one form of being, attentive to another (e.g., to another musician playing in a quartet), it has another form of being. For Kant, of course, a similar kind of ontological identity held between the subject and its appearing objects, but only because the subject, through its syntheses, set the laws for the latter. When we reverse this determination, the identity continues to hold, but it does lose its normative component. There are, as we said, as many forms of subjective being as there are forms of time, such forms being determined by the way objects come to presence.

An example will help us understand this reversal. As I walk through a forest, the trees that surround me unfold themselves in perspectival patterns. Those that are nearer do so more quickly. Those on a distant hillside hardly seem to move. All this is correlative to my having a finite standpoint, more particularly, to my being an embodied perceiver. Such unfolding requires that I have a finite "here," one which I can, through my bodily motion, continuously shift. In a word, my openness to finite beings seems to rest on my own embodied finitude. A "modern" standpoint would take such finitude as constitutive of the presence of the finite things which surround me.[25] My body (and its motion) would be taken as part of the way I "time" the world so as to apprehend finite beings. The "postmodern" perspective would reverse this. It would assert that it is by virtue of my being timed by finite things that my subjectivity displays the features of embodiment. It is through my registering their motion, including especially the motion of my own limbs, that I become finite, i.e., become a subject capable of being definitely described by a here and a now. The laws which are applicable to me as such as subject—i.e., to me as "flesh"—are those of my openness to finite beings.

Because these laws of openness have a foundational character, there is here a possibility of an ethical standpoint. Briefly put, its moral ideal would be that of "fullness of being," something which would be achieved by maximizing the possibilities of the subject's openness to being. This can be expressed in terms of the concept of radical evil. As that which cuts things off at their roots, such evil consists of actions which permanently foreclose possibilities of openness. The sexual abuse of children is one example of this. It seems to structure the subject so as to close off the possibilities of its being open to others on certain fundamental levels of sexual intimacy. The key point here is the open acknowledgment of the vulnerability of the subject. As constituted in and through its world, it is capable of suffering all sorts of indignities, of having its possibilities prematurely and permanently foreclosed. A moral concern for the subject should begin with this acknowledgment of its vulnerability. From this comes the sense that actions can have permanent consequences, that there are things we can do that cannot be undone, words that, once spoken, cannot be unsaid.

Kant announced his new philosophy as a "Copernican Revolution," one that reverses the view that knowledge must conform itself to objects. Objects, he asserted, must conform themselves to knowledge—that is to the subjective conditions by which we know them. In fact, his revolution, in making the subject the active, determining center of the world, might properly be called Ptolomaic. It was after all Ptolomy who put our earth and ourselves at the center of things. Kant claimed that only through his reversal is a priori knowledge of objects possible.[26] Does our reversal, which involves a genuine Copernican shift of standpoint, imply the abandonment of this possibility? Do we relativize truth when we assert that the subject is constituted by the world? The objection, I think, is based on a misunderstanding. Relativism in the classic sense presupposes a subject to which things are relative. Its assertion is that different subjects imply different truths. What is true for me (or for my clan, race, epoch) is not true for you, for we are differently constituting subjects (or subjective collectivities). Our position, however, makes the subject relative to the world. Where subjects agree, the world is the focus of their agreement. We, thus, can accept Kant's correspondence between universal and objective validity. We can say that there would be no reason for subjects to "universally" agree with one another if there were no object to which their judgments refer and with which they all agree.[27] The object mediates their agreement with one another. Is such "universal agreement" a priori in the Kantian sense? For us, it cannot be since subjectivity is posterior to the world. For Kant, it can be since the appearing object is constituted by the subjects, while the necessary and universal connections of such constitution make possible *in advance* universal validity. This does not mean that we cannot speak of an a priori, but only that, following our own Copernican revolution, we must reverse its sense. All a priori's must be taken from those conditions by which the world constitutes the subject. Thus, it is perfectly possible for us to affirm regional ontologies with their corresponding universal truths. Their root is the constitution *by* the world of a particular openness of the subject. Indeed, there may even be nonregional, formal ontologies which would be rooted in the world's constitution of the subject in its openness as such. None of this implies the traditional notion of relativism, which is based on the notion of subjective constitution. "True for me" does not signify a private, subjective claim but rather one of a certain correspondence to the world.

With this, the "weight" of normativity is placed on the one object that can bear it: the world itself. That the world supports a plurality of overlapping norms is simply a reflection of its containing a plurality of types of being. In its post-normative interpretation, the world simply does not permit any metaphysical monism, any appeal to an exclusive standard of what being must be. Needless to say, the philosophy we are proposing is equally hostile to any form of reductionism. Given that from its perspective the subject is always on a level of identity with its object, it is in the curious position of offering us epistemological certainty without ontological normativity—the normativity of one form of being to the exclusion of others. Here, of course, we have to add with Aristotle that such certainty is never absolute, but only that appropriate to its object.[28] The object rather than the subject sets its limits. Once we disengage philosophy from its task of laying down subjective norms (a task which in subtle and not so subtle ways allowed it to serve as an organ of political control), we can also permit it another ancient truth. For the first time in many centuries, we can affirm with good conscience: "being can be said in many ways."[29]

NOTES

Introduction

1. *Sein und Zeit*, §6 (Tübingen: Niemeyer, 1967), p. 25.

2. Ibid, p. 26.

3. Ibid. Heidegger's later work, of course, no longer limits the interpretation of time to human temporality, but ties it to Being as such, i.e., to its unhiddenness. There is a corresponding change in the critique of being as presence. The contrast of our position with Heidegger's thus holds only for *Being and Time*.

4. This is why Hume, having made the analogy between the mind and a theater, adds: "The comparison of the theater must not mislead us. They are the successive perceptions only that constitute the mind; nor have we the most distant notion of the place, where these scenes are represented, or of the materials, of which it is compose'd" (*A Treatise of Human Nature*, Book 1, Part IV, Sect. iv [Oxford: Clarendon Press, 1973], p. 253).

5. Fichte expresses this point in the following way: "One can ask for a reason only in the case of something judged to be contingent, viz., where it is assumed that it could also have been otherwise. . . . The task of seeking the ground of something contingent means: to exhibit some other thing whose properties reveal why, of all the manifold determinations that the explicandum might have had, it actually has just those that it does. By virtue of its mere notion, the ground falls outside of what it grounds." Ground and grounded are "opposed" and yet "linked" insofar as "the former explains the latter." This opposition means that when philosophy attempts to "discover the ground of all experience," its "object necessarily lies outside of all experience" ("First Introduction," *The Science of Knowledge*, ed. and trans. Peter Heath and John Lachs [Cambridge: Cambridge University Press, 1982], pp. 7–8).

6. Derrida puts this inability to appear in terms of the dichotomy of "center" and "structure." For Derrida, "the center . . . governs the structure, while escaping structurality" ("Structure, Sign, and Play in the Discourse of the Human Sciences," *A Postmodern Reader*, ed. J. Natoli and L. Hutcheon [Albany: SUNY Press, 1993], p. 224). It is responsible for the structure, and yet escapes its characterization. Derrida's notion of the center thus parallels Fichte's concept of the ground. He adds, however, the fact that in the history of metaphysics, one "always attempts to conceive of a structure from the basis of a full presence which is out of play" (ibid., p. 225). This is a presence which is not present. In a passage which recalls the Heideggerian description of the "epochs" of being, Derrida writes: "all the names related to fundamentals, to principles, or to the cen-

ter have always designated the constant of a presence—eidos, arche, telos, energeia, ousia, (essence, existence, substance, subject, aletheia, transcendentality, conscious-ness, or conscience, God, man and so forth)" (ibid.). In each case, there is a recourse to a "full presence" which is absent on the level of the structure it determines. While for Fichte, this absence is simply a result of the logic of the notions of ground and grounded, Derrida sees it as a consequence of the ineradicable presence of metaphysics in dis-course. He writes: "We have no language—no syntax and no lexicon—which is alien to this history [of metaphysics]; we cannot utter a single destructive proposition which has not already slipped into the form, the logic, and the implicit postulations of what it seeks to contest" (ibid., p. 226). It is this fact which makes any attempted refutation of metaphysics self-referentially inconsistent. In my view, the problem is not language, it is that all such refutations share the premises of modernity which are themselves incon-sistent.

7. Habermas links Derrida to this alternative. He writes: "The Young Conser-vatives . . . claim as their own the revelations of a subjectivity, emancipated from the imperatives of work and usefulness, and with this experience they step outside of the modern world. On the basis of modernistic attitudes, they justify an irreconcilable anti-modernism. They remove into the sphere of the far away and the archaic, the sponta-neous powers of imagination, of self experience, of emotionality. . . . To instrumental reason they juxtapose . . . a principle only accessible through evocation, be it the will to power or sovereignty, Being or the dionysiac force of the poetical. In France this line leads from Bataille via Foucault to Derrida" ("Modern versus Postmodernity," *A Post-modern Reader*, p. 103). Habermas sees this as a reaction to the modernist "differentia-tion of science, morality, and art." It is an attempt "to 'negate' the culture of expertise" which results from the specialization that characterizes modernity (ibid., p. 98). I would say that the very possibility of this form of reaction depends on modernity's concealment of subjectivity. It springs from a foundational project which leaves the subject open to every possible interpretation.

8. *Beyond Good and Evil*, §259 (London: Penguin Books, 1990), p. 194.

9. Lyotard calls such an account a *metanarrative*. He uses the example of sci-ence to define it: "But to the extent that science does not restrict itself to stating useful regularities and seeks the truth, it is obliged to legitimate the rules of its own game. It then produces a discourse of legitimation with regard to its own status, a discourse called philosophy. I will use the term *modern* to designate any science that legitimates itself with reference to metadiscourse of this kind making an explicit appeal to some grand narrative such as the dialectics of Spirit, the hermeneutics of meaning, the eman-cipation of the rational or working subject or the creation of wealth. . . . I define *post-modern* as incredulity towards metanarratives. . . . To the obsolescence of the metanar-rative apparatus of legitimation corresponds, most notably, the crisis of metaphysical philosophy . . ." ("The Postmodern Condition: A Report on Knowledge," *A Postmodern Reader*, pp. 71–72).

10. In Derrida's words, "everything became discourse. . . . The absence of the transcendental signified extends the domain and the interplay of signification *ad infini-*

tum" ("Structure, Sign, and Play in the Discourse of the Human Sciences," p. 225). This cutting loose or "free play" happens once one begins to think that the center cannot "be thought in the form of a being-present"—i.e., the being present of the signified understood as a nonlinguistic entity (ibid.).

11. As Lyotard defines them, such games "are composed of sets of statements; the statements are 'moves' made by the players within the framework of generally applicable roles; these rules are specific to each particular kind of knowledge, and the 'moves' judged to be 'good' in one cannot be of the same type as those judged 'good' in another, unless it happens that way by chance" ("The Postmodern Condition," p. 83). The denial of any grand narrative is, in this context, a denial of any legitimating metadiscourse which would arbitrate between their claims. As a result, "each of us lives at the intersection of many of these. . . . There are many different language games—a heterogeneity of elements. They only give rise to institutions in patches—local determinism" (ibid., p. 72). In fact, "the properties of the ones we do establish are not necessarily communicable" (ibid.). This follows because there is no transcendent referent to which we could both refer. If we accept this, then Jürgen Habermas' attempt to overcome the "culture of expertise" which modernity fosters (see note 7) through a "consensus obtained through discussion" is doomed from the start. In Lyotard's words, "Such consensus does violence to the heterogeneity of language games" (p. 73).

12. Kenneth Schmitz thus writes, "in the end post-modernity is a new form of modernity so that its criticisms are not as radical as they first seem to be. Or rather they are radical in terms of certain deeper presuppositions that post-modernity shares with modernity. These presuppositions . . . gather about the human as a contingent yet final horizon. Despite the pronouncement of the death of man and the end of humanism, deconstruction retains the immanence that its denial of transcendence entails" ("Postmodern or Modern-Plus?" *Communio* [Summer 1990]: 166).

13. *Sein und Zeit*, p. 26.

14. *On the Free Choice of the Will*, Book 2, Ch. 3, no. 20; trans. A. S. Benjamin (Indianapolis: Bobbs-Merrill, 1964), p. 40.

15. The same point holds whether we accept the account of him as advocating an essentially idealistic position or attempt to position him as a phenomenological realist. These metainterpretations do not affect the validity of his descriptive account. Thus, although we will argue for the idealistic interpretation, this does not affect the *use* we will make of elements of his descriptive account.

16. See *Will to Power*, §490.

Chapter 1. Between Plato and Descartes—
The Mediaeval Transformation in the Ontological Status of the Ideas

1. Both translations are given in *The Presocratic Philosophers,* trans. and ed. G. S. Kirk and J. E. Raven (Cambridge: Cambridge University Press, 1966), p. 269. The first takes the infinitives νοεῖν and εἶναι as infinitives of purpose.

2. This is the doctrine of the *Book Concerning Unity* by the twelfth century philosopher and translator, Gundissalimus. See *Die dem Boethius faelschlich zugeschriebene Abhandlung des Dominicus Gundissalimus De unitate,* ed. P. Correns (Münster, Westphalia: Aschendorff, 1891), p. 3.

3. See Joseph Owens, "Common Nature: A Point of Comparison Between Thomistic and Scotistic Metaphysics," *Mediaeval Studies* 19 (1957): 4.

4. See ibid., pp. 8–9.

5. As Gilson points out, Scotus influenced Descartes, not directly, but through Suarez's work, the *Metaphysicae Disputationes.* See Etienne Gilson, *Being and Some Philosophers,* 2nd ed. (Toronto: Pontifical Institute of Mediaeval Studies, 1952, pp. 106, 109.

6. By way of contrast, we may observe that for Aquinas grace is emphatically *not* a matter of demonstration. See the *Summa Theologica,* I-ll, q. 112, a. 5.

Chapter 2. Time and Augustine's Metaphysics

1. *Confessions,* Book 11, §8, in *Saint Augustine—Confessions,* trans. R. S. Pine-Coffin (London: Penguin Books, 1964), p. 260. All translations from the *Confessions* are from this edition.

2. See Augustine, "Concerning Eighty-Three Different Questions, Question 46," in *The* Essential Augustine, trans. Vernon J. Bourke (New York: American Library, 1964), p. 62.

3. See, e.g., Heidegger, "Was ist Metaphysik," *Wegmarken* (Frankfurt am Main: Klostermann, 1967). According to Heidegger, "Das menschliche Dasein kann sich nur zu Seiendem verhalten, wenn es sich in das Nichts hineinhaelt" (p. 18). Such thoughts may be also implicit in the critique of the metaphysics of presence.

4. For the original diagram, see E. Husserl, *Zur Phänomenologie des inneren Zeitbewusstseins,* ed. R. Boehm (The Hague: Martinus Nijhoff, 1966), p. 28.

5. The Platonic word for idea is εἶδος (*eidos*). It is derived from εἶδον, the second aorist of εἴδειν, which means "to perceive." Our analysis of perception is, thus, an attempt to get at the root meaning of *eidos.*

Chapter 3. The Temporality of Knowing

1. See E. Husserl, *Die Idee der Phänomenologie,* ed. W. Biemel, 2d ed. (The Hague: Martinus Nijhoff, 1973), p. 21. See also G. Stent, "Limits to the Scientific Understanding of Man," *Science* 187 (1974): 1054.

2. Both time and the line that represents it are, of course, continuous. Thus, there is no discrete "next now point" in time nor is there a definite numerical sum of

such points for some finite stretch of time. When, in our descriptions, we speak of an individual now-point or moment, we are referring to an "ideal limit" of a continuum (see *Zur Phänomenologie des inneren Zeit bewusstseins*, §16, p. 40). Similarly, when we speak of the sum of such moments, we are referring to the notion (from the calculus) of a sum of infinitesimals. This sum gives us a finite length without telling us how many of the infinitesimally small units entered into its composition.

3. As E. Fink points out, when we describe the self-constitution of phenomenological time, we cannot use the schema: subjective act, sensuous contents there to be acted upon. Time constitution is not receptive, it does not require already given material—i.e., "hyle." It is, in fact, an area where talk of the *creative* function of consciousness is fully justified. See Fink, "Die phänomenologische Philosophie Edmund Husserls in der gegenwärtigen Kritik" in *Studien zur Phänomenologie, 1930–39* (The Hague: Martinus Nijhoff, 1966), pp. 141–46.

4. Just as the dependence of the moment requires the independence of time itself, so the intentionality based on this dependence requires time itself as its ultimate and final referent. The latter makes the intentionality of the moment possible in the sense of giving it an object which it is ultimately "of."

Chapter 4. Intersubjectivity and the Constitution of Time

1. This regard to the founding phenomena is something more than a simple reflective glance to the noema—i.e., to the intentional object. Thus, we cannot agree with D. W. Smith and R. McIntyre when they claim: "The epoché is . . . a transition from any given act to a second act of considering the noema of the first act" (David Woodruff Smith and Ronald McIntyre, "Intentionality via Intensions," *Journal of Philosophy* 68, no. 18 [September 16, 1971]: 558). For us, the epoché is a turning to the *evidence* for positing the intentional object or noema. For these authors, "The epoché, in fact, is an heuristic device whose purpose is to acquaint us with noemata" (ibid., p. 543).

Behind their position is a redefinition of the noema, one calculated to erase the difference between Husserlian phenomenology and analytic philosophy. Thus, for these authors, the noema is not the sense of an object, e.g., the perceptual sense of the object of perceptual act, but rather "the sense of an appropriate sentence describing the act" (ibid., p. 547). Were we to accept this, then the phenomenologist, in performing the reduction, and the analytic philosopher, in analyzing language, would be engaged in the same task. In their words, "Thus, phenomenology as conceived by Husserl and analytic philosophy in the Fregean tradition of philosophical semantics become two sides of a common coin" (ibid., p. 549). Both would be analyzing senses understood as propositional meanings.

This view, which was originally put forward by Dagfin Føllesdal in "Husserl's Notion of Noema" (*Journal of Philosophy* 66, no. 20 [October 16, 1969]: 680–87), has been attacked by a number of authors. See, for example, Robert Sokolowski, "Intentional Analysis and the Noema," *Dialectica* 38, nos. 2–3 (1984): 113–29 and "Review Essay: Husserl and Analytic Philosophy and Husserlian Intentionality and Non-Foundational Realism," *Philosophy and Phenomenological Research* 52, no. 3 (September 1992):

725–30. John J. Drummond has devoted a whole book to it: *Husserlian Intentionality and Non-Foundational Realism. Noema and Object* (Dordrecht: Kluwer Academic Publishers, 1990).

In addition to being unfaithful to Husserl's actual texts, it suffers from a number of philosophical difficulties. Chief among these is that, having reinterpreted the noema or intentional object as a propositional sense, it finds itself compelled to distinguish this sense from the actual object. In other words, it finds itself asserting (with Frege) that "meanings direct acts to objects" ("Intentionality via Intentions," p. 547) and that such meanings are *distinct* from the objects they refer to. With this comes a redefinition of *intentionality*. Taking intentionality as a theory of referring and making reference a function of such meanings, intentionality is understood as a theory of semantical meanings (noemata). As Smith and McIntyre put this conclusion, "the theory of intentionality which emerges from Husserl's phenomenology is not a theory of the objects of acts; it is a theory of the noemata of acts" (ibid., p. 558).

Sokolowski writes, this positioning of noemata as intermediate objects misses "what is most distinctive about Husserl's phenomenology." It misses "the nature of intentionality" ("Review Essay," p. 728). More precisely, what is overlooked is the very thing Husserl's theory of intentionality was supposed to solve. It distinguishes itself by attempting to explain our relation to the objects without getting into some sort of representational theory where we relate to the object through some representative (for Smith and McIntyre, the *noemata*). If we do assert an intermediate—in Husserl's words, if we do separate "the actual object (in the case of external perception, the perceived thing of nature) and the intentional object"—then we fall into an infinite regress. This is because, if intentionality required some intermediate entity, one by means of which it could refer, then the relation to this entity (as itself intentional) would require its own intermediate, and so on indefinitely. It is precisely to avoid this, that Husserl asserts: "I perceive the thing, the natural object, the tree there in the garden; this and nothing else is the actual object of the perceiving 'intention.' No second, immanent tree, no inner picture of the actual external tree is in any way given. To suppose such a hypothesis leads to nonsense" (*Ideen I*, §90, ed. R. Schuhmann, p. 208). This means that the intentional object is the actual object—the actual object, for example, of a straightforward perception (*Logische Untersuchungen*, Appendix to §11 and §20, Tübingen, 1968, II/1, 425) or as Husserl also puts this: "The tree *simpliciter*, the thing in nature, is nothing less than this perceived tree as such which inseparably pertains to the perception as the perceptual sense." This holds even though the intentional object or noema—"the perceived tree as such"—is a "perceptual sense" (*Ideen I*, §89, p. 205).

The positioning of the noema as a perceptual sense does not distinguish it from the object as a distinct entity. It rather points to the fact that the object's presence to us in perception is that of a sense. It is the sense of the object as a one in many, i.e., as the one thing which is present in the many different perceptions we have and can have of it. As Husserl explains in the first edition of the *Logical Investigations*, fundamental here is "the fact that all thinking and knowing is directed to states of affairs whose unity relative to a multiplicity of actual or possible acts of thought is a 'unity in multiplicity' and is, therefore, of an ideal character" (*Logische Untersuchungen*, Halle/S., 1900–1901, vol. 2, p. 9). To call the intentional object or noema a "sense" is not to turn it into a propositional meaning. It is rather to recognize that consciousness becomes intentional, i.e., grasps an object, by apprehending this unity in multiplicity. The same doctrine appears some thirty years later in the *Cartesian Meditations*, when Husserl writes of the way an object—a die—is in consciousness: "This in-consciousness is a completely unique being-in. It is not a being-in as a real, inherent component; it is rather a being-in as something intentional, as an appearing, ideal-being-in (*als erscheinendes Ideell-darin-sein*). In other words, it is a being-in as the object's objective sense. The object of consciousness, in its self-identity throughout the flowing of experience, does not come from outside into such flowing; it is rather present within it, determined as a sense" (*Cartesianische Meditationen*, ed. S. Strasser [The Hague: Martinus Nijhoff, 1963], p. 80).

The performance of the reduction does not change this. It is not a transition from actual objects to noemata taken as a distinct set of entities What it does is raise the question of the object's presence as sense, its presence as a "self-identity" occurring in "the flowing of experience." Given that this presence is an "intentional accomplishment of the synthesis of consciousness" (*ibid.*), the question of the *evidence* we have for its positing still must be raised. Bracketing its positing and regarding the founding phenomena, we ask what must be given for this accomplishment to occur, i.e., what are the experiences and connections of experience which allow us to posit this self-identity as the one thing *of which* we are having experiences.

2. See Roman Ingarden, *On the Motives Which Led Husserl to Transcendental Idealism*, trans. A. Hannibalsson [The Hague, 1975]: Martinus Nijhoff, p. 12.

3. Such a perception would be of the other person from the other's point of view. In Sartre's words, "What I must attain is the other, not as I obtain knowledge of him [from some external point of view], but as he obtains knowledge of himself" (*Being and Nothingness*, trans. Hazel Barns [New York: Washington Square Press, 1968], p. 317). Sartre sees the fulfillment of this demand as "impossible. This would, in fact, suppose the internal identification of myself and the other" (ibid.). As we shall see, Husserl actually accedes to this demand. On the ultimately constituting level, there is an internal identification of self and others.

4. Constitution is, thus, a synthetic process. What is founded in each case is a unity in multiplicity—this, through the synthesis of our experiences. Kockelmans writes in this regard: "As Husserl sees it, the question is to be asked now of *how* we can explain and describe the fact that we experience a multiplicity of appearances given in a multiplicity of acts, as the perception of one single thing. Husserl tries to answer this question by suggesting that only in clarifying the concept of synthesis does the discovery of consciousness' intentionality really become fruitful." In each case, "there is a synthesis which gives rise to consciousness of identity of one and the same immanent objective meaning. . . . It is the task of the constitutional analyses of phenomenology to analyze and describe the constitution which takes place in all these syntheses" (Joseph J. Kockelmans, "World-Constitution, Reflections on Husserl's Transcendental Idealism," *Analecta Husserliana* 1 [1970]: 22–23). John Brough objects to this reading because he believes that it leads to idealism. In his words, "if the perceived object is a synthesis of perspectives, then it will be a product . . ." ("Husserl and Erazim Kohak's Idea and Experience," *Man and World* 14 [1981]: 333). "Husserl," he claims, "does not

hold this position." In particular, Husserl does not "claim in *Ideas I* or elsewhere that the object of perception is a synthesis of perspectives" (ibid., p. 334). One such claim, we may note in passing, occurs in a passage earlier cited in part: "The object of consciousness, in its self-identity throughout the flowing of experience, does not come from outside into such flowing; it is rather present within it, determined as a sense. It is an intentional accomplishment of the synthesis of consciousness" (*Cartesianische Meditationen*, Hua I, 80). To be such an accomplishment is to be a "product." As Husserl writes, discussing phenomenology's "systematic explanation of the accomplishment of knowing": "Precisely thereby, every sort of being itself (*Seiendes selbst*), be it real or ideal, becomes understandable as a constituted *product* (*Gebilde*) of transcendental subjectivity, a product that is constituted in just such an accomplishment" (ibid., p. 118).

5. Thus, the time diagram can be read in two different ways. It can be read as a description of how we retain already given moments. In such a reading, the vertical line is the result of the retention of what was successively given along the horizontal line. The data on the horizontal line are first since this reading assumes the objective givenness of successive time. In the second reading, what is primarily given is what is immediately present in the nowness of our ongoing act of apprehension. This is the data on the vertical line. It is through the interpretation of this material that the data on the horizontal line are posited. This interpretation is their temporal constitution. It is their insertion into the before and after of time, being in fact the latter's creation.

6. Insofar as we continue to identify this now with subjectivity, the latter, too, is worldless. With this we have the distinction that Kockelmans draws between Husserl and Heidegger: "the root of all philosophical truth (which for Husserl as well as for Heidegger is to be found in transcendental subjectivity) consists for Husserl in a subjectivity which originally is world-less, whereas for Heidegger the 'ultimate' starting point for philosophy is to be found in man as Being-in-the-world" ("World-Constitution, Reflections on Husserl's Transcendental Idealism," pp. 32–33).

7. What individualizes it is its stream of experiences. In Husserl's words, "The pure ego, it is to be expressly stressed, is a numerical singular with respect to '*its*' stream of consciousness" (*Ideen II*, ed. Biemel, Hua II, 110). As Husserl also puts this: "One can say that the ego of the cogito is completely devoid of a material, specific essence, comparable indeed with another ego, yet in this comparison an empty form which is only 'individualized' through the stream: this in the sense of its uniqueness" (Ms. E III 2, p. 18, 1921).

8. The extended quote here is: "God, the absolute being, who is inherently unchanging, who, himself, does not become, in eternal necessity reveals himself in the form of a pure ego. He externalizes himself in an infinite series of self-reflections in which He depicts (*abildet*) himself in himself as the forms of consciousness. [He does this] first in an obscure form and then with increasing purity and lack of concealment, ultimately coming to the purest self-consciousness. In the process of this development, He splits himself, as it were, into a plurality of finite human subjects. His freedom, the freedom of his absolute self-determination, becomes their personal freedom" (Ms. F I 22, p. 39). This citation is from Husserl's lectures on Fichte's *Menschenheitsideal*. In an

appendix to these lectures, Husserl embraces Fichte's doctrine as containing an insight "which is determined to become a strict theory in the future" (Ms. F I 22, p. 61). Husserl's own expression of this position involves the coincidence of egos on the pre-objective level. He writes in a 1934 manuscript: "All the right paths lead to myself, but to me through my co-egos, my co-egos with whom I am inseparably myself, am inseparably this ego. They lead to God who is nothing other than the pole. The path, beginning with each ego, proceeds as his path (the ego who begins with me is another ego; just as I, who begin with him, am another ego); but all these ways lead to God, the same super-worldly (*überweltlich*), super-human pole; this, not as separate ways, converging at a point [in the future], but rather in an indescribable intermingling" (Ms. K III 2, pp. 105–6, 1934). For an extended account of Husserl's position on God, see Stephen Strasser, "Das Gottesproblem in der Spätphilosophie Edmund Husserls," *Philosophiches Jahrbuch der Gorres-Gesellschaft* 67 (1959); and J. Mensch, *Intersubjectivity and Transcendental Idealism* (Albany: SUNY Press, 1988), pp. 360–74.

Chapter 5. Existence and Essence in Thomas and Husserl

1. Adelgundis Jaegerschmid, "Die letzten Jahre Edmund Husserls (1936–1938)," *Stimmen der Zeit* 199, no. 2 (February 1981): 134. Entry recorded on Sept. 16, 1937. Ibid., p. 131. Entry recorded on April 8, 1937.

2. Ibid., p. 131.

3. *De Ente et Essentia*, ch. 4, ed. Rolland-Gosselin (Kain, Belgium: Le Saulchoir, 1926), p. 34.

4. Ibid.

5. "Ens autem non ponitur in definitione creaturae, quia nec est genus nec differentia; et idea alia quaestio est *an est* et *quid est*. Unde, cum omne quod est praeter essentiam rei, dicatur accidens; esse quod pertinet ad quaestionem *an est*, est accidens," (*Quaestiones Quodlibetales*, II, 3c, ed. P. Mandonnet [Paris: P. Lethielleux, 1926], p. 43). See also the first volume of *Scriptum super libros Sententiarum Magistri Petri Lombardi,* ed. P. Mandonnet and M. F. Moos, 4 vols., (Paris: P. Lethielleux, 1929–47), (hereafter cited as *In I Sen.*), d. 19, q. 5, a. 1, ad 7m.

6. "Non autem potest esse quod ipsum esse sit causatum ab ipsa forma uel quiditate rei, causatum dico sicut a causa efficiente . . ." (*De Ente et Essentia*, p. 35). "Impossibile est autem quod esse sit causatum tantum ex principiis essentialibus rei; quia nulla res sufficit quod sit sibi causa essendi . . ." (*Summa Theologica*, Leonine ed., I, q. 3. a. 4).

7. *Summa Theologica*, I., q. 104, a. 1.

8. *De Ente et Essentia*, ch. 4, p. 35.

9. *Being and Some Philosophers*, 2nd ed., trans. A. Mauer, p. 172.

10. "Per forman enim que est actus materie materia efficitur ens actu et hoc aliquid," (*De Ente et Essentia*, ch. 2, p. 8). "Vnde oportet ut essentia qua res denominatur

ens non tantum sit forma nec tantum materia sed utrumque, quamvis huius esse sua moda *forma sit causa*" (ibid , p. 10, italics added).

11. "Unicuique autem competit habere causam agentem, secundum quod habet esse," *Summa Theol*ogica, I, q. 44, a. 1, ad. 3m.

12. *De Ente et Essentia*, ch. 4, p. 35; see also *In I Sen.*, d. 8, q. 1, a. 1.

13. See *Summa Contra Gentiles*, I. chs. 24–26.

14. See ibid , I, ch. 27.

15. See ibid., I. ch. 43.

16. See ibid., I, ch. 32.

17. "Die letzten Jahre," p. 135. Entry recorded March 16–17, 1938.

18. Ms. C 17 IV, p. 63 als Beilage, 1930; C manuscripts are cited according to their folio page.

19. Ms. E III 9, September 1933; *Zur Phänomenologie der Intersubjektivität, Dritter Teil: 1929–1935*, ed. Iso Kern, Husserliana XV (The Hague: Martinus Nijhoff, 1973), hereafter cited as Hua XV, p. 598. This radically pre-egological factor is "the original present" whose "stationary living streaming" makes it an ultimate origin of constitution. See ibid . As posterior to it, we find as "constituted" entites "all the levels of the existents for the ego, but also correlatively the ego itself" (Ms. C 17 IV, pp. 65a–65b). Thus, "the ego itself is constituted as a temporal unity. It is an already acquired . . . ontical unity" (Ms. C 17, September 20–22, 1931; Hua XV, p. 348).

20. *Cause*, here, signifies origin or ground. Just as *esse* for Thomas is not a thing, so also causality in this context does not signify the action of a thing. As Eugin Fink notes, "The fundamental question of phenomenology . . . allows itself to be formulated as the question of the *origin (Ursprung) of the world*" ("Die phänomenologische Philosophie Edmund Husserls in der gegenwärtigen Kritik," *Studien zur Phänomenologie: 1930–1939* [The Hague, 1966], p. 101). Such an origin is prior to the world and, hence, does not allow itself to be grasped in terms of the worldly causality of things.

21. Ms. C 2 I, p. 8a, September–October 1931.

22. See *Zur Phänomenologie des inneren Zeitbewusstseins*, ed. R. Bohm, Hua X, 74–75, 78, 91–92.

23. Ms. C 3 I, p. 3b, November 1930.

24. Ms. C 17 I, p. 14a, June–July 1932.

25. In Husserl's words, it "is not, in a normal sense (even if we extend this), a present understood as a streaming piece of time which persists for a co-streaming past and future"; i.e., persists as something *fixed between them* as they stream (Ms. C 2 I, p. 10a).

26. Ms. C 10, p. 16b, 1931, see also Ms. C 10, p. 14a. As Husserl elsewhere writes: "I exist, actually and concretely, as a stationary present. This is my concrete being" (Ms. C 7 I, p. 21a, June–July 1932). This means that "the ego in its most original originality is not in time," not something fixed in the order of departing time (Ms. C 10, p. 14a, 1931). This "most original originality" refers not to the ego as a temporal, worldly existent, but rather to the stationary present as "the primal form (*Urgestalt*) of its being" (Ms. C 2 I, p. 10a).

27. Ms. C 17, September 20–22, 1931; Hua XV, 348.

28. Ms. C I, September 21–22, 1934; Hua XV, 668.

29. Ibid., p. 670.

30. Ms. C 10, p. 16b, italics added. In other words, "the ego which is always now and remains now (which, as a stationary and lasting now, is not a now in an objective sense) is the ego of all accomplishing as this living, this 'super-temporal' (*Ueberzeitliches*) now . . ." (ibid., p. 18b).

31. "Ich im 'ständigen' Jetzt, im stehenden Strömen, das ich im ersten Sinn als ein Zeitigen bezeichne. In einem ersten Sinn als Gegenwart, was doch aequivalent gilt für jetzt, also auch erstes 'jetzt'. Dieses Jetzt ist mein ständiges Jetzt und das, *worin oder während dessen ich ständiges (stehende and bleibendes) Ich bin.* In diesem ständigen oder 'stehendem' Strömen aber passiert immerzu neues. . . . Im stehenden Strömen als Zeitigen sind sie das Zeitliche im Sinne des was aufströmt, oder eintritt, verbleibt und wieder verläuft, um anderem Platz zu machen" (Ms. D 13 III, pp. 9–10, July 7, 1933, italics added).

32. "Alles im Strömen Enthaltene strömt, hat die unbeschreibliche Urform des Strömens. . . . Aber das Ich ist in besonderer Weise stehend und bleibend, nämlich es selbst strömt nicht, aber es tut, es setzt seinen Satz, und das Tun ist ein aus sich Entlassen, urquellend—schöpferisch aus sich Hervorgehen-lassen von selbst wieder Strömendem, nämlich den Akten" (Ms. B III 9, pp. 13–14, Oct.ober–December 1931). "Ein Akt, eine Ichtätigkeit ist wesensmässig ein urquellendes 'Ich tue.' Als Urquellendes ist es stehendes und bleibendes Urquellen, aber auch in eins Verströmen in stetige Modifikation des soeben Gewesenen; . . . dieses ganze Urquellende . . . ist Einheit eines stehenden und bleibenden Urphänomens, ein stehender und bleibender Wandel, Urphänomen meines 'Ich tue,' worin ich, das stehende und bleibende Ich bin, und zwar bin ich der Tuende des 'nunc stans.' Jetzt tue ich und nur jetzt, und 'standig' tue ich. Aber das 'Ich tue' verquillt auch ständig, und ständig habe ich zukommendes, das aus mir bestätigt wird" (ibid., p. 25). This temporalization of the ego's acts is the ego's self-temporalization. As Husserl continues: "Also in der Ständigkeit des Urphanomens, in welchem ich das tätige Jetzt bin, entspringt der Aktus als gezeitigter Prozess, in dessen Zeitlichkeit ich selbst als in gewisser Weise mitgezeitigtes Ich meine Zeitstelle und mit dem erstreckten Ichacte meine Erstreckung, meine Zeitdauer habe. So bin Ich als durch die Zeit hindurch Seiendes, strömend als soeben Gewesenes und noch Festseiendes gegeben—mir gegeben" (ibid ., pp. 25–26).

33. Ms. C 7 I, p. 21b, June–July 1932. In other words, "in streaming, a self-transcending is continually accomplished, namely a past is constituted . . ." (ibid ., p. 22a).

34. As transcendent, it is therefore a *constituted*, synthetic unity. The series of temporally distinct perceptions are its constituting phenomena.

35. Ms. C 2 I, p. 3a, September–October 1931; see also Mss. C 2 I, pp. 10a–10b; B I 22, pp. 16–17, May or August 1931.

36. Ms. K III 4, p. 8, 1935; see also Mss. C 3 III, pp. 27a, March 1931, C 2 I, pp. 3a–3b, A VII 11, p. 92, October 26, 1932, B I 14, xi, p. 18, 1934. According to the last cited reference, such functioning is *not* to be understood as a constituted, *namable* given, but rather "as a constitution, a temporalization, a temporal becoming which is a pre-becoming, not a becoming in an ontical, a constituted sense." It is the "creation" of transcendence, of over-againstness which is, itself, *prior* to objective becoming.

37. Thus, the exhibition of the ego's functioning is not direct, but is rather in terms of the results of such functioning. It is an exhibition of what has been temporalized. In Husserl's words, "What is exhibitable is that its functioning is constantly temporalized and that, hence, this functioning exists for the actively functioning ego in the field of its conscious [already temporalized] possessions" (Ms. A V 5, pp. 2–3, January 1933). What is objectively exhibitable are the acts which have been "let loose" in time and, thus, have already slipped into the over-againstness of pastness.

38. See Mss. C 2 I, p. 10a, C 13 II, p. 24a, February 15, 1934.

39. This "transcendental reinterpretation" is used by Husserl to explain how one essence can be present in many individuals. For an account of this, see James Mensch's *The Question of Being in Husserl's Logical Investigations* (The Hague: Martinus Nijhoff, 1981), pp. 182 ff. This account was the basis of my interpretation of Augustine on this point in the second essay.

40. See *Ideen III*, §14.

41. "Jedes konkrete Individuum dauert in der Zeit und ist, was es ist, indem es von Präsenz zu Präzenz, stetig werden, übergeht" (Ms. E III 2, p. 2, 1921).

42. Ms. C 13 III, p. 1, March 1934.

43. Ms. K III 2, p. 9, October 19, 1935.

44. Ms. C I, September 21–22, 1934; Hua XV, p. 670.

45. Ibid.

46. This argument finds a parallel "metaphysical" expression in Aquinas. Commenting on the statement, "Socrates in foro est alter a seipso in domo," Aquinas writes that its assertion follows because Socrates varies "secundum esse, scilicet secundum rationem quam accepit prioris et posterioris" (*In I Sent.*, d. 19, q . 2, a. 2, Solutio; ed. P. Mandonnet, 1929, I, 470). Thus, the otherness of his *esse* is the otherness of the now in

which he finds himself. The fact that this now is constantly departing into pastness and, thus, requires constant replacement distinguishes his *esse* from that of God. God's now is a "nunc aeternitatis." It does not depart, which means that "esse divinum est per se stans . . ." (ibid., d. 11, q. 1, a. 1, Solut., I, 63). In distinction to finite beings, God, Aquinas asserts, has none of his nowness or existence outside of himself. Speaking of the "perfectionem divini esse," he writes: "Illud enim est perfectum cujus nihil est extra ipsum. Esse autem nostrum habet aliquid sui extra se: deest enim aliquid quod jam de ipso praeteriit, et quod futurum est. Sed in divino esse nihil praeteriit nec futurum est; et ideo totum esse suum habet perfectum, et propter hoc sibi proprie respectu aliorum convenit esse" (ibid ., d. 8, q. l, a. 1, Solut., I, 195). The contingency of a finite being follows once we admit that *esse* can be understood "vel *simpliciter* vel *secundum quid*; simpliciter quidem secundum praesens tempus; secundum quid autem secundem alia tempora" (*Expositio in libros Peri Hermenias*, ed. T. Maria. In *Opera Omnia*, vol. 1, Leonine ed. [Rome: Polyglotta, 1882–1948], lect. 5, no. 22). Thus, our being outside of the present—our being "secundum tempus praeteritum aut futurum"—is *esse* only in a relative sense (ibid., lect. 3, no. 13). Our *esse simpliciter* or actual existence is existence in the present. Because our present does depart into pastness, thus making us "outside" of ourselves, this *esse* is *contingent* on our present being renewed. This renewal, we may note, is not something predetermined by our essence. Our essence, as *other* than our existence, is other than our present nowness. Thus, presence or existence in a given time is an accidental, as opposed to an essential, predicate of a finite entity: "Esse autem in hoc tempora vel in illo, est accidentale praedicatum" (*In XII liberos Metaphicorum*, ed. R. Spiazzi [Turin: Marietti, 1950], lect. 3, no. 1982).

47. Ms. D 13 XXI, p. 26, 1907–1909.

48. Ms. F I 14, p. 49, June 1911.

49. *Erste Philosophie, 1923–1924, Erster Teil*, ed. R. Boehm [The Hague: Martinus Nijhoff, 1956], Hua VII, 394.

50. See Aquinas's statement on the essence or nature considered in itself: "Ergo patet quod natura hominis absolute considerata abstrahit a quolibet esse . . ." (*De Ente et Essentia*, ch. 3, p. 26). The corresponding statement by Husserl is "*Setzung* und zunächst anschauende Erfassung *von Wesen impliziert nicht das mindeste von Setzung irgendeines individuellen Daseins; reine Wesenswahrheiten enthalten nicht die mindeste Behauptung über Tatsachen . . .*" (*Ideen I*, §4, ed. W. Biemel, Hua II, 17). This existential neutrality of the essence is behind Husserl's assertions that a "pure" phenomenology "brackets . . . every . . . real positing of existence (*reale Daseinssetzung*) . . ." As he explains, this bracketing follows because its focus is on "the phenomenological intuition of the essences . . ." As such, it brings "die spezifischen Erlebniswesen, die sich in diesen singulären Erlebnissen vereinzelnen, sowie die ihnen zugehörigen (also 'apriorischen', 'idealen') Wesensverhalte zu adäquater Erschauung" (*Logische Untersuchungen*, V, §27; 5th ed., 2 vols., Tübingen: Niemeyer, 1968, II/1, 440; see also ibid , V, §16; II/1, 398–99). Thus, for Husserl, a pure phenomenology is an essential doctrine of the phenomena of consciousness: "Die reine phänomenologie ist dann die Wesenslehre von den 'reinen Phänomenenen,' . . ." (ibid ., VI, Beilage, §5, II/2,

236). It cannot make any existential assertions since essences per se (as in Thomas's philosophy) are considered to abstract from questions of existence. This doctrine, we may note, can lead to a radical *misunderstanding* of Husserl. In it, one equates this "pure" or "eidetic" phenomenology with phenomenology per se and asserts that the latter, too, must be silent on the question of existence. For the later Husserl, such a misunderstanding is almost total. He labels it *ontologism* and remarks with regard to it: "Der Ontologismus ist eine ganz gefährliche Irrlehre. Die Neuscholastik hat mir damals zugestimmt, als ich soweit war. Aber sie konnte später nicht begreifen, dass es nur eine Station auf meinem Weg war. Man abstahiert das Sein schlecthin und schaltet das Bewusstsein aus, in dem doch erst das Sein lebendig wird und lebendig bleibt" ("Die letzten Jahre," p. 131; entry recorded on April 8, 1937). The term *ontologism* most probably refers to *Ideen I*, §§ 4, 9–10 as well as to the sections of the 2d ed. of the *Logische Untersuchungen*, which present the same doctrine, having been composed at the same time.

51. *Erste Philosophie I*, Hua VII, 393.

52. Once again there is a parallel with Thomas, at least if we follow Gilson's interpretation. For Thomas, according to Gilson: "Essences may well represent the balance sheets of so many already fulfilled essential possibilities, but actual existences are their very fulfilling, and this is why essences are actually becoming in time, despite the fact that a time-transcending knowledge eternally sees them as already fulfilled. . . . Thus, becoming through *esse* is the road to fully determined being . . ." (*Being and Some Philosophers*, pp. 183–84).

53. Ms. F I 14, p. 43, June 1911: "in dem Dasein aufgehen und erkannt werden kann."

54. Adelgundis Jaegerschmid, "Gespräche mit Edmund Husserl 1931–1936," *Stimmen der Zeit* 199, no. 1 (January 1981): 49. Entry recorded on April 28, 1931.

55. Ibid., p. 56. Entry recorded in Dec. 1935.

56. Ms. K III 2, p. 106, Autumn 1934: "Alle rechten Wege führen in mir, aber in mir durch meine Mit-ich[e] mit denen ich untrennbar ich, dieses Ich, bin, zu Gott, der nichts ist als der Pol . . ." The same thing can be said by "every ego." Thus, "alle diese Wege führen zu demselben überweltlichen, übermenschlichen Pole Gott . . ." Cf. Husserl's statements: "Das Ich ist Über-zeitlich, es ist der *Pol* von Ich-Verhaltungweisen zu Zeitlichem . . ." (Ms. E III 2, p. 50, 1934). "*Dieses ego ist das im absoluten Sinn einzige, der keine sinnvolle Vervielfältigung zulasst*, noch schärfer ausgedrückt, *als sinnlos ausschliesst*. Die Implikation besagt: Das 'Übersein' des *ego* ist selbst nichts anderes als ein ständiges urtümlich strömend Konstituieren, und Konstituieren von verschiedenen Stufenuniversa von Seienden . . ." (Ms. B IV 5, 1932 or 1933; Hua XV, p. 590). The reference of this last passage is to the "primordial ego" that each subject can uncover through the "reduction."

57. See Mss. M III 3, xi, p. 21, September 1921, C 3 III, p. 26a, March 1931, C 2 I, p. 4b, 1931, E III 2, p. 50.

58. Ms. C 3 I, p. 3b, 1930. Thus, in this present, "my ego and its life and the other ego and its life do not have any extensive [temporal] apartness" (*Abständigkeit*) (Ms. C 16 VII, p. 100a, May 1933). In other words, because nowness per se is preindividual, "I discover that 'in my now, I experience the Other' and his now. I discover my own now and his now as existing in one (*als in eins seiend*) . . ." (Ms. C 17 I, September 1931; Hua 15, p. 332). The level of nowness is, thus, that of "my coincidence with Others, my coincidence, so to speak, before the world . . . is constituted" (Ms. C 17 V, p. 84a, 1931). Insofar as primal constitution can be attributed to it, "the ego is in coincidence with Others" (Ms. B III 4, pp. 65–66, ca. September 1, 1931). This last statement follows analytically from (1) the preindividual character of nowness per se and (2) that such nowness is primally constituting. Husserl's efforts in the 1930s to describe the constitution of a common, intersubjective world (and, thus, to overcome the *Cartesian Meditations*'s problem of transcendental solipsism) are based on these premises.

59. Ms. C 10, p. 16a, 1931. What is temporized here is the *hyle*. As the temporal centering of the *hyle*, the ego, of course, is "immer dabei."

60. See Mss. E III 2, p. 46, C 7 I, p. 9a, June–July 1932.

61. The same doctrine is expressed with regard to my "primal now" understood as a central now—i.e., as a "*Mittelpunkt.*" With the streaming constitution of time, "ist ein *stehendes und bleibendes Ur-Jetzt* als starre Form für einen durchströmenden Gehalt konstituiert und als Urquellpunkt aller konstituierten Modifikationen. Konstituiert aber ist in eins mit der starren Form des urquellenden Urjetzt eine zweiseitige Kontinuität von ebenso starren Formen; also im Ganzen ist konstituiert ein starres Kontinuum der Form, in dem das UrJetz urquellender Mittelpunkt für zwei Kontinua als Zweige der Abwandlungsmodi: das Kontinuum der Soebengewesenheiten und das der Zukünftigkeiten" (Ms. C 2 I, p. 11a, August 1931). Husserl's point here is *not* that the "primally productive," ultimately constituting now is, itself, constituted. What is constituted is its environment and, hence, its being as a middle point of this environment.

62. "So ist auch zu sprechen von der *einen stehenden urtümlichen Lebendigkeit* (der Urgegenwart, die *keine Zeitmodalität ist*) als der des Monadalls. Das Absolute selbst ist diese universale urtümliche Gegenwart, in ihr 'liegt' alle Zeit und Welt in jedem Sinn. . . . Alles ist eins—das Absolute in seiner Einheit: Einheit einer absoluten Selbstzeitigung, das Absolute in seinen Zeitmodalitäten sich zeitigend in dem absoluten Strömen, der 'strömend lebendigen', der urtümlichen Gegenwart, der des Absoluten in seiner Einheit, All-Einheit!, welche alles, was irgend ist, in sich selbst zeitigt und gezeitigt hat" (Ms. C I, September 21–22, 1934; Hua XV, pp. 668–69). See also Ms. C 17 V, p. 80a, 1931, where Husserl writes: "The absolute in 'eternity,' persisting in the streaming changes of its modes. Awakeness, sleep, death as [its] modes. Eternity, nontemporality and temporality. The all-temporal identity of structure; the invariant forms of temporality and the temporalized. What is invariably stationary and remaining fills up (*erfühlt*), stationary and remaining, a transcendental-absolute egological community. It accomplishes (*erfühlt*) a stationary-remaining coexistence of egological subjects of an experiencing (conscious) life, this in the stationary and remaining streaming of a primal present."

63. Ms. E III 9, November 5, 1931; Hua XV, p. 386.

64. Ms. B I 14, xi, p. I9, September 1935.

65. According to Husserl's lectures on Fichte's *Menschenheitsideal*, this means that God's objective self-understanding occurs through the individual subject's consciousness. This follows "weil *wir erkennende Menschen aber doch Iche sind, in welchen dies absolute Ich sich in sich zerspalten hat . . .*" (Ms. F. I 22, p. 22, November 1917). As he also expresses this: "Gott ist . . . *das ewige, unveränderliche, einige* Sein, das sich im Ich offenbart. . . . Es offenbart sich, das sagt wieder: es *reflektiert sich*, es schafft sich *ein Abbild*, nämlich im Form des Bewusstseins, ein Abbild, das anderseits doch nicht von Gott selbst Getrenntes ist" (ibid., p. 38). As not "separate" from the individuals which he has become, the latter become the means of his self-understanding: "*Gott, das in sich selbst ungewordene und wandellos absolute* Sein offenbart sich in ewiger Notwendigkeit in der Form des reinen Ich. Er entäussert sich so *in einer unendlichen Stufe von Selbstreflektionen, in denen als Bewusstseinsgestaltungen er sich im sich selbst zuerst in verdunkelter Form, dann in immer höherer Reinheit und Hüllenlosigkeit abbildet und schliesslich zu reinstem Selbstbewusstsein kommt. In diesem Entwicklungsgang zerspaltet er sich gleichsam in eine Mannifaltigkeit endlicher Menschensubjekte auf die seine Freiheit, die der absoluten Selbstbestimmung, übergeht als ihre personale Freiheit*" (ibid., p. 39). What we have here is an early expression of the docrine that "God, the absolute" is the nowness by which each subject is a subject and, in fact, constitutes the individuality of such subjects by grounding their being as central egos—i.e., as constituted "middle points" of their temporal environments. It is in this sense that he can be said to "split himself" into a plurality of functioning subjects. Thus, the original identity of God and his "reflections" becomes understood as that of nowness per se. It is in terms of this nowness that Husserl can later assert the primordial "coincidence" of egos with one another and with God himself as a "super-worldly, super-human pole." Given that "the absolute has his ground in himself"—i.e., that he possesses an "absolute self-determination"—this coincidence is phenomenologically manifested in our "freedom" as we function in the now.

66. Prof. Dupré writes in criticism of Husserl's position: "No theism, however, could accept a God who is identical with transcendental subjectivity or even one who needs it as an essential part of himself. From this point of view, Husserl's later philosophy is perhaps even further removed from a true transcendence than his earlier. A strange observation in view of the fact that his personal convictions became increasingly theistic!" ("Husserl's Thoughts on God and Faith," *Philosophy and Phenomenological Research* 29 [December 1968]: 212). Against this, it must be noted that God is *not*, strictly speaking, "identical" with subjects. He is their nowness, but this nowness, qua existence, is distinct from the finite, objectively present subjects. Thus, for Husserl, "the transcendental totality of subjects is contingent . . . ," not the absolute ground of such a totality (Ms. K III 12, p. 39, 1935). The contingency of the subjects composing this totality is that of entities which exist by persisting in time—i.e., by departing from the "to be" of their being. It is because of this continual departure from constituting nowness that Husserl can write: "Present (*Gegenwart*), I exist in continual dying as something present . . ." (Ms. D 14, May 7–9, 1934; *Philosophical Essays in Memory of*

Edmund Husserl, ed. M. Farber (New York: Greenwood Press, 1968), pp. 324–25). This dying is a "dying away" into pastness of the moments which make up my objective life. It is their separation from the now which is the source of this life.

67. Ms. C 1, September 21–22, 1934; Hua XV, 669.

68. "Gespräche," p. 55. Entry recorded on September 4, 1935.

69. Ms. E III 10, p. 18, 1934. This is our own opinion. Husserl's position is: "Philosophy, continually becoming more concrete, and theology, continually becoming more philosophical, coincide in the infinite" (ibid., p. 19). His belief in the ultimate identity of the two is expressed, with variations, throughout his career. See, e.g., Mss. F I 14, pp. 43, 45 f, 58 ff, June 1911, F I 22, pp. 54 ff, November 1917, E III 9, p. 31, 1929, E III 10, pp. 19 ff, 1934.

Chapter 6. Radical Evil and the
Ontological Difference Between Being and Beings

1. "Die Bedeutung der phänomenologische Methode für die Neubegrundung der Metaphysik," *Proceedings of the Tenth International Congress of Philosophy*, eds. E. Beth, H. Poss and J. Hollak (Amsterdam: North Holland, 1949), p. 1219.

2. Ibid., p. 1221.

3. Ibid., p. 1220.

4. *Ideen I*, ed. W. Biemel, Hua III, 121.

5. Ibid.

6. *Zur Phänomenologie der Intersubjektivität, Dritter Teil: 1929–1935*, ed. Iso Kern, Hua XV, 669. This assertion is a rather typical expression of Husserl's "transcendental idealism." Perhaps no other subject has occasioned such controversy. Opinions regarding its place in Husserl's phenomenology are sharply divided. European commentators generally see Husserl as continuing (with important modifications) the tradition of German idealism. Karl Schuhmann, for example, gives a number of citations where Husserl's assertions closely parallels "Wilhelm Windelband's famous [1900] definition of idealism as 'the dissolution of the experiential world into the processes of consciousness" (Karl Schuhmann and Barry Smith, "Against Idealism: Johannes Daubert vs. Husserl's *Ideas I*," *Review of Metaphysics* 38 [June 1985]: 774). These formulations attest to the "rather traditional character" of Husserl's idealism (ibid.). Many North American commentators, however, attempt to give a more realistic cast to Husserl's phenomenology. An important exception, here, is Henry Pietersma. See his "A Critique of Two Recent Husserl Interpretations, *Dialogue* 26, no. 4 (Winter 1987): 695–704. Unfortunately, as Pietersma points out, this attempt often results in readings which ignore or distort basic phenomenological concepts.

For the purpose of this note, our discussions will have to be limited to two of these. The first is the concept of constitution or synthesis. Admitting that "if the perceived object is a synthesis of perspectives, then it will be a product . . . ," John Brough declares that "Husserl does hold this position" ("Husserl and Erazim Kohak's Idea and Experience, *Man and World* 15 [1981]: 333). For Brough, the stress on synthesis gives phenomenology an inadmissible Kantian cast. Smith and McIntyre do not mention constitution at all; they do, however, assert that the identification of the actual and the intentional object (the noema) is a "misinterpretation" which "is probably truer to the godfather of Husserl's transcendental idealism, Immanuel Kant" (David Woodruff Smith and Ronald McIntyre, "Intentionality via Intensions," *Journal of Philosophy* 68, no. 18 [September 16, 1971]: 560). Husserl, however, identifies his own project with Kant's. He writes, for example, that his phenomenology is "an attempt to realize the deepest sense of Kantian philosophy" (*Erste Philosophie I*, ed. R. Boehm, Hua VII, 286; see also ibid., pp. 235, 240). This involves Kant's proposing "a transcendental, scientific theory of the essential possibility of the constitution of a true objectivity in transcendental subjectivity . . ." (ibid., p. 227, see also Ms. F I 32, "Natur und Geist," 1927, p. 114a).

Where Husserl does depart from Kant, he reinforces rather than mitigates the idealistic consequences of Kant's doctrine. This occurs, most notably in his explicit denial of Kant's assertion of the existence of things in themselves. This is also a denial of the receptivity of consciousness—i.e., its dependence on data provided by the thing in itself. In Husserl's words, transcendental idealism is unconcerned with "inferences leading from a supposed immanence to a supposed transcendence, the latter being some undetermined thing in itself . . ." It is, thus, "not an idealism which seeks to derive a world full of sense from senseless, sensuous data" (*Cartesianische Meditationen*, ed. S. Strasser, Hua I, 118.).

This denial is for many commentators the key to Husserl's idealism. For Joseph Kockelmans, it signifies that "the world does not have any for-itself, but merely is a being-for-us." This means that "the world itself is considered from the viewpoint of genetic constitution as nothing but a product of the constituting subjectivity" (Joseph J. Kockelmans: "World-Constitution, Reflections on Husserl's Transcendental Idealism," *Analecta Husserliana* 1 [1970]: 27). Eugen Fink makes the same point in his famous *Kant Studien* article. Husserl's denial of the receptivity of consciousness exhibits, according to Fink, "the *productive* character of transcendental intentionality." He writes: "The mental ['innerworldly'] intention is essentially receptive; it is performed with an understanding of itself as an approach to a being in itself that is independent of it. . . . When we no longer interpret transcendental life as receptive, its special character still remains undetermined. It is the constitutive interpretation of it that first exhibits it as creation (*als Kreation*). ("Die phänomenologische Philosophie Edmund Husserls in der gegenwärtigen Kritik," p. 143). When asked by the editors of *Kant Studien* to review this piece, Husserl wrote for its "Preface": "I have thoroughly gone through this article and I am delighted to be able to say that there is not a sentence within it that I do not make my own, that I could not expressly acknowledge as my own conclusion" (*Studien zur Phänomenologie*, p. viii). Given this imprimatur, the assertion of a "creative" function of consciousness is especially significant. Both Ingarten and Schutz also use "creation" to describe Husserl's idealism. Once it is no longer "permissible to speak of what is 'in itself,'" we can, according to Ingarten, "regard this synthetic result [of constitution] as a 'creation' of the set of perceptions. . . . This is what happens to Husserl both in *Ideas I*

and in *Lectures on the Phenomenology of Internal Time Consciousness* and later"
(Roman Ingarten, *On the Motives Which Lead Husserl to Transcendental Idealism*, pp.
20–21). Schutz describes the shift that has occurred from the earlier works in terms of
constitution. For Schutz, "the idea of constitution has changed from a clarification of
sense structures, from an explanation of the sense of being, into the foundation of the
structure of being; it has changed from explication to creation" (Alfred Schutz, "The
Problem of Transcendental Intersubjectivity in Husserl," *Collective Papers III*, ed. I.
Schutz, The Hague: Martinus Nijhoff, 1966, p. 83). Theodor Celms makes essentially
the same point in terms of the two senses of the reduction. There is a shift in its sense
from a "Zurückführung der Betrachtung" to a "Zurückführung des Seins" (*Der
phänomenologische Idealismus Husserls* [New York: Garland Press, 1979], pp. 309–10).

The second key concept that is at issue here is that of the intentional object or
noema. Smith and McIntyre's attempt to position the noema as an intermediate entity—
one that mediates the relation between the intention and the actual object—is intended
to avoid the consequences drawn by the preceding authors. Given that "the point of phenomenology is simply to study noemata, not objects," the reduction (which is conceived by them as a turning to the noema) has no idealistic implications. It leaves the real
world, the world of objects, intact ("Intentionality via Intensions," pp. 560–61). The
same point is made by Harrison Hall in his contribution, "Was Husserl a Realist or an
Idealist?" in *Husserl, Intentionality, and Cognitive Science*, ed. H. L. Dreyfus (Cambridge: MIT Press, 1982), pp. 174 ff. We have already commented on the difficulty with
this solution: When we distinguish between the object and the noema, positioning the
latter as an intermediate, we miss the nature of intentionality. As advanced by Husserl,
it involves a direct reference to the object. If, however, we identify the intentional and
real object, idealism seems inevitable. As Smith and McIntyre admit, the result is "a tidy
ontology of egos and noemata only. This ontology would indeed be an idealism . . ."
("Intentionality via Intensions," p. 560). The authors claim that this would not be a
"transcendental idealism" in a Husserlian sense. But for a number of commentators, De
Boer, Ricoeur, Fink and Ingarten among them, it is precisely this identification of
noema and object—i.e., of perceptual sense and being—which characterizes transcendental idealism. Thus, De Boer writes: "In transcendental phenomenology sense is
being itself. At the end of the *Fundamentalbetrachtung*, when it is said that the world
can only exist as a sense or phenomenon, with this is understood the world's very mode
of being" ("Zusammenfassung," *De Ontwikkelingsgang in het Denken van Husserl*
[Assen, the Netherlands: Van Gorcum, 1966], p. 597). Commenting on Husserl's assertion that sense "presupposes absolute consciousness as the field of sense giving," (*Ideen
I*, ed. Biemel, Hua II, 135), De Boer writes that such sense giving must be taken as a
constitution of being. In his words, "The expressions 'creation' and 'production' do
not appear in *Ideen I*; but when one reads the *Fundamentalbetrachtung* as it wants to be
read, namely, as a discourse about being, then the terms which Husserl does use—
'independence' and 'dependence'—exactly express what he means. At that point there
can be no more talk about realism or even realistic elements in Husserl's thought"
("Zusammenfassung," p. 598). Fink makes the same point when he asserts that "the transcendental noema cannot . . . refer to an object beyond itself that is independent of it; it
is the entity (*Seiendes*) itself" ("Die Phänomenologische Philosophie," pp. 132–33).
Given this, the constitution of this noema is the constitution of the entity. Such consti-

tution, according to Ricoeur, involves the very perceptual fullness which makes the presence of the noema the presence of the perceived entity. As he describes this: "one last gap still remains to be filled in between what we shall henceforth call the 'sense' of the noema and actuality. . . . Transcendental phenomenology aspires to integrate into the noema its own relation to the object, i.e., its 'fullness,' which completes the constitution of the whole noema. . . . To constitute actuality is to refuse to leave its 'presence' outside the 'sense' of the world" ("Introduction to *Ideas I*," *Husserl: An Analysis of His Phenomenology*, trans. E. G. Ballard and L. E. Embree [Evanston, Ill.: Northwestern University Press, 1967], p. 23).

To draw a balance between these competing views is, I think, to recognize the presence of two very different ideals. The European commentators cited are motivated by the ideal of historical scholarship. Their effort is to present Husserl's doctrine according to its original (Husserlian) intent. The North Americans mentioned have a different ideal: that of philosophical truth. Their denial of Husserl's idealism is not primarily motivated by textual considerations—i.e., by attention to the details of what Husserl has actually written. Its primary source is their belief in the untenability of this position. Their faithfulness to what they take to be the truth (including, for some, the truth of the analytic approach to philosophy) often puts them in the position of trying to save Husserl from himself; that is, from what they regard as his unfortunate assertions.

The fact that both sides can find some textual support for their positions indicates a certain level of phenomenological description quite independent of the realism-idealism debate. Having said this, however, we have to admit that Husserl was not content to remain at this level. In advancing his doctrine of transcendental idealism, he is, in fact, a modern, sharing all the presuppositions of modernity. To attempt to turn him into a realist may be to save him philosophically. It is, however, to ignore what constituted a major portion of his later philosophical work, that of accepting and working out the consequences of his idealism—particularly in the area of the intersubjectivity problematic. This is not to say that the descriptive material he left us cannot be fruitfully used to solve philosophical problems. Such employment, however, requires more than a simple adjustment or reinterpretation of his terms, such as *noema*. Given that the path which led him to idealism is inherent in his adherence to the assumptions of modernity, only their overturning will do the trick. Such overturning disqualifies the resultant philosophy from being termed *Husserlian*—this, in spite of its sharing in his descriptive insights. In fact, by virtue of the shift in its assumptions, it will not be "modern," but something quite different.

7. *Cartesianische Meditationen*, ed. S. Strasser, Hua I, 152.

8. See Mss. C III 3, p. 26a, M III 3, xi, p. 21.

9. *Krisis*, 2nd ed., ed. W. Biemel (The Hague: Martinus Nijhoff, 1962), Hua VI, 275.

10. Ibid., p. 276.

11. *Zur Phänomenologie der Intersubjektivität, Dritter Teil*, Hua XV, 595–96.

12. Ibid., p. 380.

13. Ibid., pp. 594–95.

14. *Krisis*, pp. 115–16, 265.

15. *Zur Phänomenologie der Intersubjektivität, Dritter Teil*, Hua XV, 380.

16. Ibid., p. 378.

Chapter 7. Phenomenology and Artificial Intelligence: Husserl Learns Chinese

1. John R. Searle, "Is the Brain's Mind a Computer Program?" *Scientific American* (January 1990): 27.

2. Ibid., p. 29.

3. Ibid., p. 26.

4. John R. Searle, "Reply to Jacquette," *Philosophy and Phenomenological Research* 49 (1989): 702.

5. Searle, "Is the Brain's Mind a Computer Program?" p. 31; "Minds, Brains, and Programs," *The Behavioral and Brain Sciences* (1980): 423 and 453.

6. "Is the Brain's Mind a Computer Program?" p. 26.

7. Ibid., p. 27.

8. "Minds, Brains, and Programs," p. 455.

9. "Reply to Jacquette," p. 704.

10. "Minds, Brains, and Programs," p. 445.

11. "Is the Brain's Mind a Computer Program?" p. 30.

12. Alan Turing, "Computing Machinery and Intelligence" *Mind* 59 (1950): 434.

13. Ibid., p. 435.

14. A. K. Dewdney, "Computer Recreations," *Scientific American* 261 (December 1989): 140C–140D.

15. If, however, we do make this distinction, then the only thing evolution explains is the development of the conditions of the applicability of logic to our mental life. See James R. Mensch, *The Question of Being in Husserl's Logical Investigations*, pp. 18–19.

16. J. C. Maloney, "The Right Stuff," *Synthese* 70 (1987): 367–68.

17. Searle, "Reply to Jacquette," p. 703; "Is the Brain's Mind a Computer Program?" p. 27.

18. See *The Question of Being in Husserl's Logical Investigations*, pp. 53–55.

19. R. McIntyre, "Husserl and the Representational Theory of Mind," *Topoi* 5 (1986): 109.

20. Ibid.

21. Ibid.

22. Ibid., p. 112.

23. Ibid., p. 108.

24. Such a sense is very different from the propositional sense McIntyre imagines it to be. For a critique of McIntyre's position on the noema see Chapter 4, note 1.

25. Husserl also calls it an "appearing ideal being-in (*erscheinendes Ideell-darin-sein*)" (Hua I, 80). Essentially the same position is presented in the first edition of the *Logical Investigations*, when Husserl brings forward the fundamental fact of cognition: "the fact, namely, that all thinking and knowing is directed to states of affairs whose unity relative to a multiplicity of actual or possible acts of thought is a 'unity in multiplicity' and is, therefore, of an ideal character" (Hua XIX/1, 12). Granting this, we have to explain "how the same [perceptual] experience can have a content in a twofold manner, how next to its inherent, actual content, there should and can dwell an ideal, intentional content" (ibid., p. 21), this being the object's content as a sense or a "unity in multiplicity." See also Hua XIX/1, 176, 179 f., Hua XIX/2, 624f.

26. McIntyre takes Husserl's attack on the sense data theories of his time as evidence for his denying "that the meaningfulness, and hence the intentional character, of noematic *Sinne* could be reduced to formal relations among [sensations] based solely on their shapes" (McIntyre, "Husserl and the Representational Theory of Mind," p. 111). According to such theories, at least as Husserl reports them, perception can be reduced to the influxes of the data of sensation, a change in the latter being immediately reflected in the change in perception. Given that we continue to perceive the "same object through the change of experiential contents," there is an obvious error here; and McIntyre correctly reports Husserl's insistence that "senseless sense data" cannot by themselves yield the senses embodied in perception. But this does not mean that such senses have a primitive intentionality, one unrelated to the fact of interpretation (*ibid.*, p. 109). On the contrary, what is wrong with such theories is, in Husserl's words, the refusal to take into account "the phenomenological moment of interpretation (*Auffassung*)" (Hua XIX/1, 528; Findlay's trans. p. 658). This is a refusal to acknowledge that it is in "the animating interpretation (*beseelender Auffassung*) of sensation that what we call the appearing of the object consists" (Hua XIX/1, 361; Findlay's trans., p. 539). Thus, when Husserl writes that the "truly immanent contents, which belong to the real components of the intentional experience, are not intentional," he is referring to them *apart* from the interpretive act (Hua XIX/1, 387; Findlay's trans., p. 559). The act is what makes these nonintentional elements intentional. McIntyre's mention of the "shapes" of these sensations is highly misleading as is his attempt to bolster his position by bringing in Husserl's distinction between phenomenology and mathematics (the latter having to

deal with purely formal elements like "shape"). For Husserl, the interpretative, objectifying act interprets not just the "shape"—the order and arrangement—of the experiences that form its basis. It also interprets their sensuous contents—e.g., such things as color, tone, taste, in short the whole range of what used to be called an object's secondary qualities. Thus, the fact that phenomenology belongs the "material eidetic sciences" in its concern for the object's immediate sensuous content does not mean that it sees itself as incapable of analyzing intentionality into its nonintentional components. It only implies that such elements include the immediate sensuous contents that form the "real components" of the intentional experience.

27. Jacquette vitiates his argument against Searle by not seeing this. For Jacquette, as for McIntyre, intentionality remains something "primitive, ineliminable, and irreducible." This means that "the primacy of the intentional precludes analysis of intentionality, since it implies that nothing is to be found below its conceptual rock bottom" (Dale Jacquette, "Adventures in the Chinese Room," *Philosophy and Phenomenological Research* 49 [1989]: 622). Bynum, in giving a version of the "robot reply" to Searle's position, does grasp the connection between intentionality and interpretation when he insists that the robot's "states *are* subjective in the sense that they involve a specific point of view or interpretation of the world" (Terrell Ward Bynum, "Artificial Intelligence, Biology, and Intentional States," *Metaphilosophy* 16 [1985]: 366). Unfortunately, Bynum never goes beyond the mechanics of contemporary robotics to analyze this further.

28. Husserl writes in this regard, "What is called constitution, this is what Kant obviously had in mind under the rubric, 'connection as an operation of the understanding,' synthesis. This is the genesis in which the ego and, correlatively, the surrounding world of the ego are constituted. It is *passive genesis*—not the [active] categorial action which produces categorial formations" (Ms. B IV 12, pp. 2–3, 1920). See also Mss. A VI 30, p. 9b, November 1921; C 17 IV, pp. 63a–63b, 1930; B I 32 I, p. 16, 1931.

29. Thus, for Husserl, "The assertion that I remain who I am as the same transcendental ego—as the same personal ego—is equivalent to the assertion that my world remains a world" (Ms. B I 13 VI, p. 4, December 15, 1931). Granting this, "One can also say: a complete dissolution of a world in a 'tumult' [of experiences] is equivalent to a dissolution of the ego . . ." (Ms. F IV 3, p. 57a, 1925). An important part of this doctrine is the notion of the ego as the "centering" of its constituted environment. See James R. Mensch, *Intersubjectivity and Transcendental Idealism* (Albany: SUNY Press, 1988), pp. 94–99 for an account of this.

30. Hubert Dreyfus, "Introduction," in H. Dreyfus, ed., *Husserl, Intentionality and Cognitive Science* (Cambridge, Mass.: MIT Press, 1982), p. 10.

31. C. A. Fields, "Double on Searle's Chinese Room," *Nature and System* 6 (1984): 51.

32. Dreyfus, "Introduction," p. 20.

33. Ibid.

34. Ms. C 7 I, p. 19a, July 9, 1932.

35. Ms. C 7 I, p. 21b.

36. *Kritik der reinen Vernunft*, A 99.

37. Ibid., A 102.

38. Ibid., A 103.

39. As we noted in our third chapter, if the sense of pastness is simply that of not-newness, this sense is a relational one. It is a sense of the stretch of retentions of retentions that intervene between the present retention and the original impression. Regarding the impression's content through such retentions, each of which presents itself as a not new or past moment, *is* grasping this content through a stretch of past time. Similarly, if in retaining the impression, we also retain the pastness presented by the retentions of its content, then the appearance of the retained content is also the appearance of the pastness *through which* it is given.

40. In LISP a very simple way of expressing retention would be: (defun retention (impression) (list impression)). The value of the expression, (retention (retention (retention 'i))), would be: (((i))). This points to the fact that retention is inherently recursive or definable in terms of itself. The implication is that all the functions governing the temporality of consciousness, insofar as this is based on retention, are similarly recursive. Granting this, LISP, with its abundant resources for writing recursive functions, is an ideal means for modeling the retentional process. A few examples will make this clear. To model the departure into pastness of an "impression" through x number of retentions, we can write the Common LISP function:

```
(defun retention (x impression)
    (cond ((= x 0) impression)
        (T (retention (- x 1) (list impression))))).
```

Thus (retention 3 'i) yields (((i))). This signifies that "i"—the impression—has sunk back to a retention of a retention of a retention of "i." A similar function, based on the preceding, for modeling the sinking back into pastness of a phrase can written. Its arguments are: "phrase"—e.g., a b c d e—a given "initial element"—e.g., a—and x, which signifies the number of retentions. The function is:

```
(defun phrase-retention (phrase initial-element x)
    (cond ((equal nil (cdr phrase)) (retention (- x 1) initial-element))
        (T ( phrase-retention (cdr phrase) (cons (cadr phrase) (list initial-element)))
            (- x 1))))).
```

Here, (phrase-retention '(a b c d e) '(a) 10) yields ((((((E (D (C (B (A))))))))))). Of the ten retentions, five are used to retain the phrase and result in (E(D(C(B(A))))). Five more occasion the sinking down of the phrase as a whole five further degrees of pastness. This symbolizes that a temporal remove occasioned by five retentions separates the phrase from the present act of perceiving.

As noted in our text, retention also involves interpretation. The grasp of the temporal tags—in our model, the parentheses—marks the past as past. Recursive functions can be used to model this interpreting of what we retain. Thus, the function

```
(defun time-elapsed (retention)
  (cond ((atom retention) 0)
  (T (+ 1 (time-elapsed (car retention)))))))
```

interprets a retention to see how far back into pastness it has slipped. For example, (time-elapsed '((((a)))) yields four. There are four retentions and hence a sinking back into pastness of four units of the impression "a". A similar function for interpreting a phrase to see how far back its initial element has sunk into pastness is

```
(defun phrase-time-elapsed (phrase)
  (cond ((null phrase) 1)
    ((atom phrase) 0)
    (t (max (+ (phrase-time-elapsed (car phrase)) 1)
    (phrase-time-elapsed (cdr phrase))))))).
```

Applied to the retained phrase, ((((((E (D (C (B (A))))))))))), for example, it would yield ten.

The point of this is not to specify all the functions that can be written to simulate the synthetic processes of consciousness. It is only to illustrate the claim that temporal syntheses, as Husserl conceived it, is essentially a recursive process and, thus, can be modeled by recursive functions. These functions can be used not just to represent the action of retention, but also to model the processes by which we scan our retained perceptions again and again to find those patterns (such as that of the successive faces of a die) that allow the distinguishing of objects from their backgrounds.

41. *Kritik der reinen Vernunft*, A 103.

42. Ibid., A 104–5.

43. Mss. C 15, pp. 2a–4a, C 13 1, pp. 7a ff. Richard Lind seems to come close to Husserl's position with his analysis of "focal attention"—in particular, its two opposing tendencies to fasten on what contrasts with the rest of the field and to "discriminate similar elements" (R. Lind, "The Priority of Attention: Intentionality for Automata," *The Monist* 69 [1978]: 610). Unfortunately, he does not see the role that retention plays in the process. He simply confines himself to the mention of a certain "focal inertia."

44. Z. W. Pylyshyn, "Minds, Machines and Phenomenology: Some Reflections on Dreyfus' 'What Computers Can't Do'," *Cognition* 3, no. 1 (1974–75): 72.

45. Ibid., p. 73.

46. Ibid., p. 70.

47. As we shall see in a later chapter, one way to picture this temporality is to take the time line that runs from past to present to the future and bend it in a circle. At this point, the line of determination is from the future to the past to the present. Thus, the pre-

sent is seen not just as determined by the past, but also by the future (i.e., by the goals) we strive to realize. Such determination of the present is *through the past* since the future determines the past by making us take it as the material (the resources) for meeting our goals. Different futures make us interpret our past in different ways. This goal directed temporality is essential to the way *we* fulfill Pylyshyn's demand for systems that "make use of all available knowledge in working towards their goal—including knowledge gained from the analysis of interim failures" (Pylyshyn, "Minds, machines and phenomenology," p. 70). Our grasp of the goal makes us aware not just of our failures in reaching it, but of what counts as "knowledge" (i.e., a resource) for its achievement. For a machine to possess the equivalent ability, it must be programed with the algorithms which would give it the equivalent temporal determination.

48. P. M. Churchland and P. S. Churchland, "Could a Machine Think?" *Scientific American* 262 (January 1990): 35–36.

49. The result would thus be a network of neural networks, each node acting recursively to process a particular feature.

Chapter 8. Husserl and Sartre: A Question of Reason

1. Fowkes, for example, writes: "an ego of some sort is necessary, that is, practically necessary. . . . without some such ego, we wind up with the notion of a consciousness so spontaneous and impersonal—that is, totally free of any connection or commitment to past or future states—as to be paralyzing . . ." (William Fowkes, "The Concept of the Self in Husserl and Beyond," *Philosophy Today* 24 [Spring 1980]: 47). Stamps makes the same point when she asserts: "if there is not an 'I' at the center of consciousness, constituting a human process of consciousness . . . , then both experience and consciousness are rendered irrational and essentially mindless" (Ann Stamps, "Shifting Focus from Sartre to Husserl," *Journal of Thought* 25 [January 1973]: 52). Here Stamps is echoing Natanson's remark: "Giving up the transcendental ego deprives Sartre of a constitutive' ground for the unity and identity of the self" ("Phenomenology and Existentialism: Husserl and Sartre on Intentionality," *Phenomenology, The Philosophy of Edmund Husserl and Its Interpretations*, New York: Garden City, 1967, p. 345). A variation on this defense is to assert that what Sartre takes to be nonegological functions of constituting consciousness are, in fact, egological. See, e.g, John Scanlon, "Consciousness, the Streetcar, and the Ego: Pro Husserl, Contra Sartre," *Philosophical Forum* 2 (Spring 1971): 332–54; and Ralph Ellis, "Directionality and Fragmentation in the Transcendental Ego," *Philosophical Research Archives* 5 (December 1978): 73–88.

2. Imad Shouery, "Reduction in Sartre's Ontology," *Southwest Journal of Philosophy* (Spring–Summer 1971): 50.

3. "In order that there can be the world and the subjectivity constituting it (the world . . . that has . . . the form of the logos . . .), the world must, proceeding from pre-being to being, also constitute rational persons within itself. Reason must already exist and must be able to bring itself to a logical [rational] self-disclosure in rational subjects" (Ms. E III 4, p. 25, 1934; see also ibid., pp. 29, 31, 33).

4. *The Transcendence of the Ego*, trans. F. Williams and R. Kirkpatrick. New York: Noonday, 1957. Cited throughout as *TE*.

5. There is an implicit idealistic thesis here. As Sartre expresses it in *Being and Nothingness*: "The appearance refers to the total series of appearances and not to a hidden reality which would drain to itself all the *being* of the existent. . . . For the being of the existent is exactly what it *appears*" (*Being and Nothingness*, trans. Hazel Barnes [New York: Washington Square Press, 1968], p. 4).

6. Ms. C 2 I, p. 8a, September, October 1931.

7. Ms. B I 32, I, p. 16, May or August 1931. The same passive constitution applies, not just to the experiential "life" of ego, but also to the world it constitutes from this. As Husserl writes in an earlier manuscript: "In the subjectivity to which essentially belong both the ego and the 'stream of experiences,' the lasting world constitutes 'itself' for the ego, but the ego, as much as it participates by its activity in this constitution, does not create it, does not produce it (*schafft sie nicht, erzeugt sie nicht*) in the usual sense, just as little as it produces its past life, its stream of original sensibility . . ." (Ms. A VI 30, p. 9b, November 1921). Such passive genesis, we may note, is contrary to the notion of the individual ego's being somehow "creative" in its constitution. Such creativity, if we do posit it, pertains to the pre-egological level, the level of the "absolute."

8. Ms. C 17 IV, p. 63 als Beilage, 1930.

9. Shouery, "Reduction in Sartre's Ontology," p. 52.

10. Ibid., p. 53.

11. "Consciousness of Self and Knowledge of Self," in *Readings in Existential Phenomenology*, ed. N. Lawrence and Daniel O'Connor (Englewood Cliffs, N.J.: Prentice-Hall, 1967), p. 137.

12. James writes, "we must remember that no dualism of being represented and representing resides in the experience *per se*. In its pure state, or when isolated, there is no self-splitting of it into consciousness and what consciousness is 'of.'" The distinction only arises through its connection with other experiences, i.e., "when the experience is 'taken,' i.e., talked of, twice, considered along with its two differing contexts respectively, by a new retrospective experience" ("Does 'Consciousness Exist?" *The Writings of William James*, New York: Random House, 1968, p. 177).

13. *Being and Nothingness*, cited throughout as *BN*.

14. For an account of controversy surrounding this issue, see note 6 of Chapter 6.

15. Heidegger presents a similar analysis in *The Essence of Reasons*. "Freedom," Heidegger writes, "is the origin of [Liebniz's] principle of sufficient reason," the principle that nothing is without its cause ("*Grund*"). It also, however, is "the *abyss* of Dasein" (*der Ab-grund des Daseins*), i.e., its ground-less character (*The Essence of Reasons*, bilingual ed., trans. T. Malick [Evanston, Ill.: Northwestern University Press, 1969], pp. 123, 129).

16. "Translator's Introduction, *BN*, p. xlv.

17. "Reasoning," *Psychology, Briefer Course* (Cleveland: World Publishing Company, 1948), p. 355.

18. Ibid., p. 356.

19. Ibid., p. 357.

20. Ibid., p. 354.

21. "Translator's Introduction," *BN*, p. xlii.

22. Ibid., p. xlii.

23. "Reasoning," p. 355.

24. Ibid., p. 356.

25. Ms. E III 2, p. 46, 1921.

26. Ms. B I 13, VI, p. 4, December 15, 1931.

27. "The pure ego, it is to be expressly stressed, is a numerical singular with respect to '*its*' stream of consciousness" (*Ideen II*, ed. W. Biemel [The Hague: Martinus Nijhoff, 1952], Hua IV, 110).

28. "I thus see here *an essential lawfulness of the pure ego*. As the one identical, numerically singular ego, it belongs to 'its' stream of experiences, which is constituted as a unity in unending, immanent time. The one pure ego is constituted as a unity with reference to this stream-unity; this means that it can find itself as identical in its course" (ibid., p. 112).

29. *Ideen I*, ed. Schuhmann [The Hague: Martinus Nijhoff, 1976], Hua III/1, pp. 123.

30. "An ego does not possess a proper general character with a material content; it is quite empty of such. It is simply an ego of the cogito which [in the change of experiences] gives up all content and is related to a stream of experiences, in relation to which it is also dependent . . ." (Ms. E III 2, p. 18, 1921).

31. "One can say that the ego of the cogito is completely devoid of a material, specific essence, comparable, indeed, with another ego, yet in this comparison an empty form which is only 'individualized' through the stream: this, in the sense of its uniqueness" (Ms. E III 2, p. 18, 1921).

32. *Cartesianische Meditationen*, 2nd ed. (The Hague: Martinus Nijhoff, 1963), Hua I, 99, 76.

33. "The Question of the Transcendental Ego: Sartre's Critique of Husserl," *Husserl in His Contemporary Radiance: Proceedings of the 24th Annual Meeting of the Husserl Circle* (Waterloo, 1992), pp. 271–72.

34. "We distinguish the ego and its life, we say that I am who I am in my life and this life is experiencing . . . the ego, however, is the 'subject' of consciousness; subject, here, is only another word for the centering which all life possesses as an egological life, i.e., as a living in order to experience something, to be conscious of it" (Ms. C 3 III, p. 26a, March 1931). As he elsewhere expresses this, "I am I, *the center* of the egological (*Ichlichkeiten*)" (Ms. C 7 I, p. 24, June–July 1932, italics added). Sometimes the "center" is called a "pole": "I exist–I live . . . 'I'—that means here, first of all, only *the 'primal pole'* of one's life, one's primal stream" (Ms. C 2 I, p. 4a, September, October 1932, italics added). "The central ego is the necessary ego pole of all experience and of all noematic and ontic givenness which can be legitimated by experience . . ." (Ms. M III 3, XI, p. 21, September 1921). See also *Ideen II*, Hua II, 105, 109–110.

35. Ms. C 7 I, p. 22a, June–July, 1932.

36. Ms. C 7 I, p. 21a.

37. Ms. C 3 II, p. 37, November 1930.

38. Ms. F IV 3, p. 57a, 1925.

39. Ms. B I 13, VI, p. 5, December 15, 1931.

40. *Cartesianische Meditationen*, §38, Hua I, 111. From collecting, for example, the collection is constituted; from counting, the number; from dividing, the part.

41. Ibid., Hua I, 112.

42. Ibid., Hua I, 113.

43. Ms. C 17 IV, pp. 63a–63b, 1930.

44. Ms. B I 32, I, p. 16, May or August 1931. Such constitution occurs on the "pre-egological level" (Ms. B III 9, p. 10, October–December 1931). Because the ego is not yet present, Husserl also calls this the level of the nonego: The "nonego," he writes, "we can designate as the realm of constituting association which is nonactive, i.e., as temporalization . . ." (ibid. , p. 23, October–December 1931). See also Ms. C 16 VI, May 1932; Hua XV, 355.

45. Ms. B IV 12, pp. 2–3, 1920.

46. This position is first advanced in the *Lectures on Internal Time Consciousness*: "In the same impressional consciousness in which the perception is constituted, precisely through this [process], the perceived object is constituted" (*Zur Phänomenologie des innerern Zeitbewusstseins*, ed. R. Boehm [The Hague, 1966], Hua X, 91). In other words, "necessarily the one is constituted with the other" (ibid., p. 92). As Husserl puts this a few years later, "In the constitutive sense of all life in which the origin of all being is found, we discover that subjectivities and objectivities constitute themselves in parallel and that the subjectivities are constituted unities just as much as their objectivities are" ("Gemeingeist II," 1918 or 1921; *Zur Phänomenologie der Intersubjektivität Zweiter Teil*, ed. I. Kern [The Hague: Martinus Nijhoff, 1973], Hua XIV, 203.

47. *Zur Phänomenologie des Inneren Zeitbewusstseins*, Hua X, 92.

48. *Cartesianische Meditationen*, Hua I, 80.

49. Ibid.

50. Ibid.

51. See in particular Chapters 3 and 7.

52. *Ideen I*, ed. Schuhmann, Hua III/1, 316–17.

53. *Ideen I*, Hua III/1, 359.

54. For Husserl, the equivalence between reason and positing signifies the "general insight . . . that not just 'truly existing object' and 'object capable of being rationally posited' are equivalent correlates, but so also 'truly existing object' and the object which is capable of being posited in an original, complete thesis of reason" (ibid., p. 329). The full assertion here is that the thesis of positing, which is the being there (*Dasein*) of an object, is equivalent to the thesis of reason that focuses on the object as something "rationally motivated." As the correlate of both, an "object" is, thus, defined "as a title for the essential connections of consciousness. It first comes forward as the noematic X, as the subject of sense (*Sinnessubjekt*), as the subject of the different essential types of senses and propositions. It further comes forward as the title 'actual object' and is, then, a title for certain eidetically considered rational connections in which the unitary X, present in such connections, receives its rational positing" (ibid., p. 336). For a more extended account of the equivalents of reason and positing, see James Mensch, *Intersubjectivity and Transcendental Idealism* (Albany: SUNY Press, 1988), pp. 67–72.

55. *Ideen I*, §85, ed. Schuhmann, Hua III/1, 193.

56. There is here a remarkable similarity to Aristotle's position on mind. He writes, "Since it thinks all things, it is necessary that the mind be pure." This is because, "the intrusion of anything foreign hinders and obstructs it so that it can have no nature except its capacity to receive" (*De Anima*, III, iv, 429a 18–22).

57. Ms. A VII 11, pp. 90–92, October 26, 1932. As Husserl elsewhere puts this, "the ego which is the counterpart (*gegenüber*) to everything is 'anonymous.' It is not its own 'counterpart' as the house is my counterpart. And yet I can turn my attention to myself. But then this counterpart in which the ego comes forward along with everything which was its counterpart is again split. The ego which comes forward as a counterpart and its counterpart [e.g., the house it was perceiving] are both counterparts to me. Forthwith, I—the subject of this new counterpart—am anonymous" (Ms. C 2 I, p. 3a, September–October 1931).

58. Ms. K III 4, p. 8, 1934–35. There is a temporal aspect to such anonymity: "In reflection, I encounter myself in the temporal field in which my just past (*mein Soeben*) has functioned. . . . But in the now point, I am in contact with myself as functioning" (Ms. A V 5, p. 3, January 1933). It is as now that I am anonymous.

59. See Mensch, *Intersubjectivity and Transcendental Idealism*, pp. 76–80, for an account of this ego. Our next chapter will also have occasion to speak of it.

60. Ms. C I, September 22–23, 1934, *Zur Phänomenologie der Intersubjektivität Dritter Teil*, ed. I. Kern, Hua XV, 670.

61. As Husserl describes this, "The reduction to the living present is the radical reduction to that subjectivity in which everything is originally accomplished which is valid for me—i.e., to that subjectivity in which all ontological sense (*Seinssinn*) for me is sense as experientially apprehended, obtaining sense. It is a reduction to the sphere of primal temporalization in which the first and originary (*urquellenmässige*) sense of time comes forward—time as the living, streaming present. All further temporality—be it 'subjective' or 'objective,' whatever be the sense which these words might take on—receives its ontological sense and validity from this present" (Ms. C 3 I, p. 4a, 1930). As a reduction to that which is constitutive of being, it is also, as we earlier noted, a reduction to "the pre-being which bears all being . . ." (Ms. C 17 IV, p. 63 als Beilage, 1930).

62. Ms. B II 9, p. 10, October–December 1931.

63. Ms. C 5, p. 5a, 1931.

64. Ms. C I, September 22–23, 1934; *Zur Phänomenologie der Intersubjektivität Dritter Teil*, Hua XV, 670.

65. Chapter 3 gives an account of how such interdependence gives rise to the diagonal and vertical intentionalities and, hence, to retention and merging. For a more extended account, see Mensch, *Intersubjectivity and Transcendental Idealism*, pp. 309–30.

66. Ms. C 3 I, p. 3b, 1930. Husserl sometimes speaks of this as a "reduction within the reduction"—i.e., a reduction within that which first reveals transcendental subjectivity: "One requires a reduction within the transcendental reduction to grasp, in a more complete manner, the streaming immanent temporalization and time, to grasp the primal temporalization, the primal time. . . . This is the reduction to the streaming, primal 'immanence,' to the primal unities constituting themselves in this [immanence] . . ." (Ms. C 7 I, p. 14b, January–July 1932).

67. Husserl also speaks here of the "primal functioning" of temporalization as a "constant letting loose (*Aus sich entlassen*) of retentions" (Ms AV5, pp. 4–5, January 1933). Strictly speaking, it is the retentions, with the interpretations which they carry, that result in the departure into pastness of the moments which well up.

68. Ms. B III 9, p. 25, October–December 1931.

69. Ms. B III 9, pp. 13–14, October–December 1931.

70. Ms. C 2 I, p. 11a, September, October 1931.

71. Ms. C I, Hua XV, 667.

72. Ms. B IV 5, 1932 or 1933, Hua XV, 589-90.

73. James Edie, for example, ends his article with the statement: "The imagined dispute between Sartre and Husserl is, therefore, a merely verbal dispute: *Et non est sapientis mere de verbis disputare*." In a footnote to this remark, he adds: "The final fact of the matter is that Husserl's theory of consciousness is just as non-egological as Sartre's; it is only more complete." ("The Question of the Transcendental Ego: Sartre's Critique of Husserl," pp. 274, 279).

74. Husserl describes this origin as "actuality." Here, all the passages we cited in Chapter 5 apply: "We can, therefore, speak . . . of the primal present which is not a modality of time. . . . The absolute itself is this universal, primordial present. Within it 'lie' all time and world in every sense. Itself streaming, [it is] actuality (*Wirklichkeit*) taken in the strict worldly sense of 'present'" (Ms. C I, September 22–23, 1934; Hua XV, 668). This present is also a making present, i.e, a temporalization: "The [primordial] present is 'absolute actuality' (*Wirklichkeit*), is actuality in the authentic sense as primally productive. As primally productive, it is ontifying (*ontifizierend*) itself into a mode of time; primally temporalizing, it has temporal being as an ontic acquisition, primally productive, it has always been such" (Ms. C 16, September 20–22, 1931; Hua XV, 348). Thus, the absolute's actuality is a being-in-act. Since the act is that of temporalization understood as a granting of existence in time, we have the Husserlian correlate to Sartre's "tireless creation of existence" by the absolute. See also Hua XV, 669.

75. The Jamesian "project" is that of self-making. For Sartre, the past is the self that is surpassed: "The past is the In-itself which I am, but I am this In-itself as surpassed" (*BN*, p. 173). The present is the act of surpassing—this, by virtue of the Nothingness, the inner distance, which makes the present self a For-itself: "In contrast to the Past which is In-itself, the Present is For-itself" (*BN*, p. 175). "The For-itself is present to being in the form of flight; the Present is a perpetual flight in the face of being" (BN, p. 179). The future is the self towards which we surpass ourselves, it is the goal of the project of self making: "The Future is the determining being which the For-itself has to be beyond being. There is a Future because the For-itself *has to be* its being instead of simply being it" (BN, p. 182). For Husserl, time is the condition for all projects. The welling-up of its moments is what first makes action possible. For Sartre, by contrast, the very possibility of time is reduced to that of action, in particular, to the possibility of the action of self-making. While the antecedents to Husserl's treatment go back to Kant, in particular to the Schematism of the *Critic of Pure Reason*, Sartre's stretch from James and Heidegger back to Hegel.

Chapter 9. Husserl's Concept of the Self

1. The continuity of the attempts to pursue it is, in part, shown by the intense efforts now devoted to artificial intelligence (AI). It may be, as Heidegger writes, that philosophy has become "cybernetics." As such, however, it still continues to pursue in AI the question, what is a self? See Heidegger, "The End of Philosophy," in *On Time and Being*, trans. Joan Stanbaugh (New York: Harper and Row, 1972), pp. 57–58.

2. *Cartesianische Meditationen*, §41, Hua I, 118.

3. *Husserl, An Analysis of His Phenomenology*, p. 107.

4. This is the point of the *Schlusswort* to the *Krisis*.

5. Lester Embre gives a framework for investigating them in "Reflection on the Ego," in *Explanations in Phenomenology*, eds. D. Carr and E. Casey [The Hague: Martinus Nijhoff, 1973], pp. 243–52).

6. *Husserl: An Analysis*, pp. 53–54.

7. This, even though it is "no real moment" (*reeles Moment*) of immanent time, (*Ideen II*, §22, Hua IV, 103).

8. I*deen II*, §24, Hua IV, 104, 105; *Ideen II*, §28, Hua, IV, 111.

9. Thomas Seebohm,."The Other in the Field of Consciousness," *Essays in Memory of Aron Gurwitsch*, ed. L. Embree (Washington: University Press of America, 1984), pp. 292–93.

10. *Cartesianische Meditationen*, §28, Hua I, 97.

11. "*Sinn und Seinswirklichkeit konstituierenden transzendentalen Subjektiv-ität*," *Cartesianische Meditationen*, §28, Hua I, 97.

12. To call it creative involves, of course, a shift in the notion of constitution. As we cited Schutz, "At the beginning of phenomenology, constitution meant clarification of the sense structures of conscious life, inquiry into sediments in respect of their history, tracing back all *cogitata* to intentional operations of the on-going conscious life. . . . But unobtrusively . . . the idea of constitution has changed from a clarification of sense structures, from an explanation of the sense of being, into the foundation of the structure of being; it has changed from explication to creation" ("The Problem of Transcendental Intersubjectivity in Husserl," *Collective Papers III*, p. 83).

13. Ibid., p. 77.

14. "*In an absolute sense, this ego is the only one. It does not allow of being meaningfully multiplied.* Put more pointedly: *it excludes this as senseless.* The implication is: The 'surpassing being' ('*Uebersein*') of an ego is nothing more than a continuous, primordially streaming constituting. It is a constituting of various levels of existents (or 'worlds') . . ." (Ms. B IV 5, 1932 or 1933 in *Zur Phänomenologie der Intersubjektivität, Dritter Teil*, Hua XV, 589-90).

15. See Klaus Held, *Lebendige Gegenwart* (The Hague, 1966), pp. 127–28. See also ibid., pp. 124–25 for the first two concepts.

16. See Gurwitsch, "A Non-egological Conception of Consciousness," in *Studies in Phenomenology and Psychology* (Evanston, Ill.: Northwestern University Press, 1966), pp. 287–99. Edie writes, in comparing Husserl to Sartre, "The final fact of the matter is that Husserl's theory of consciousness is just as non-egological as Sartre's; it

is only more complete." ("The Question of the Transcendental Ego: Sartre's Critique of Husserl," *Husserl in His Contemporary Radiance*, p. 279).

17. We are referring, of course, to his first major philosophical work, *The Transcendence of the Ego.*

18. See *The Transcendence of the Ego,* trans. F. Williams and R. Kirkpatrick, pp. 98–99, 106.

19. See Eduard Marbach, *Das Problem des Ich in der Phänomenologie Husserls* (The Hague: Martinus Nijhoff, 1974), pp. 338–39.

20. "The Self," *Psychology, Briefer Course*, p. 203. Husserl acknowledges his debt to "James' genius for observation in the field of descriptive psychology" in a note in the appendix to the Second Investigation. See *Logical Investigations*, II, Appendix, trans. J. N. Findlay, I, 420.

21. *Psychology, Briefer Course*, p. 216.

22. As the passage continues, "In the nature of its contents, and the laws they obey, certain forms of connection are grounded. They run in diverse fashions from content to content, from complex of contents to complex of contents till in the end a unified sum total of content is constituted which does not differ from the phenomenologically reduced ego itself" (*Logical Investigations*, V, §4, II, 541).

23. Ibid., V, §8; II, 549.

24. Ibid.

25. "The Other in the Field of Consciousness," p. 283.

26. *Ideen I*, §57, Hua III/1, 123.

27. Ms. E III 2, p. 18, 1921.

28. Ibid.

29. Ms. C 3 III, p. 26a, March, 1931.

30. Once again, we may observe a difference in relative rates of departure. Temporally distant objects seem to recede into pastness at a slower rate than the objects we have recently experienced. The same holds with regard to the approach of objects in the anticipated future. The nearer they are to the now, the faster they seem to draw near.

31. *Analysen zur Passiven Synthesis*, ed. M. Fleischer (The Hague: Martinus Nijhoff, 1966), Hua XI, 205.

32. Ibid., p. 204.

33. Ms. C 7 I, p. 21b.

34. *Logical Investigations*, V, §8; II, 549. Husserl, in the 1930s echoes Natorp's words. See Ms. C 2 I, p. 3a, September–October 1931, cited in footnote 55 of Chapter 8.

35. Ms. C 7 I, p. 21b.

36. Ms. C 2 I, p. 11a, August 1931.

37. Ms. C I, Hua XV, 667.

38. According to Husserl, my "stationary streaming primordiality" is, itself, the result of an absolute temporalization. The latter, in temporalizing my streaming, allows me to be there as something "primally existing" (Ms. C I, September 22–23, 1934, Hua 15, p. 670). Temporalization is thus an aspect of what is prior to me. The same point can be drawn from a pair of earlier manuscripts. Husserl asserts that "temporalization possesses its 'layers' . . . the 'layers' beneath the ego (*unterichliche 'Schichte'*) and the egological 'layers' (Ms. B II 9, p. 10, October–December 1931). In other words, first there is "the primal being, the inherently self-temporalizing absolute . . . then the primal being as [an] ego . . ." (Ms. C 5, p. 14, 1931).

39. Ms. C III 1, p. 3a, 1930. As we noted in our last chapter, Husserl sometimes speaks of this as a "reduction within the reduction" (Ms. C 7 I, p. 14b, January–July 1932). He also writes: "I must not terminate the reduction with the bracketing of the world and, with this, my spatial-temporal, real human being in the world." I must exercise it "on myself as a transcendental ego and as a transcendental accomplishing, in short, as a transcendental life" (Ms. C 2 I, p. 8a, September–October 1931). When I do perform this reduction, I reach the pre-egological—i.e., what Husserl terms "the pre-being (*Vor-Sein*) which bears all being, including even the being of the acts and the being of the ego, indeed, the being of the pre-time and the being of the stream of consciousness [understood] as a being" (Ms. C 17 IV, p. 63 als Beilage, 1930).

40. See Ms AV5, pp. 4–5, January 1933.

41. Ms. B III 9, p. 25, October–December 1931.

42. Ms. B III 9, pp. 13–14, October–December 1931.

43. The "nonego . . . we can designate as the realm of constituting association which is nonactive, i.e., as temporalization . . ." (ibid. , p. 23, October–December 1931). *Nonactive* refers here to passive (pre-egological) constitution. See also Ms. C 16 VI, May 1932; Hua XV, 355.

44. The latter, the individual ego, can never be regarded as creative. The former, however, might be—insofar as we view it as the absolutely prior source of the actuality that nowness brings. This source, however, could never be regarded as egological because, by definition, it is part of what Husserl calls the *nonego* or *pre-egological* layer of functioning.

45. Passive synthesis is what originally provides me with the objects I manipulate in my active synthesis. In Husserl's words, "anything built by activity necessarily presupposes, on the lowest level, a passivity that gives something beforehand. Pursuing this, we encounter constitution through passive genesis. The ready-made object which, so to speak, steps forward complete as an existent, as a mere thing . . . is given, with the

originality of the 'it itself,' in the synthesis of a passive experience" (*Cartesianische Meditationen*, §38, Hua I, 112). The conclusion then is: "Thanks to this passive synthesis, . . . the ego always has an environment of objects" (ibid., p. 113). Similar assertions are made with regard to the elements of the stream of experiences: "'Passive' signifies here without the action of the ego . . . the stream does not exist by virtue of the action (*Tun*) of the ego, as if the ego aimed at actualizing the stream, as if the stream were actualized by an action. The stream is not something done, not a 'deed' in the widest sense. Rather, every action is itself 'contained' in the universal stream of life which is, thus, called the 'life' of the ego . . ." (Ms. C 17 IV, pp. 62a–62b, 1930).

46. From the perspective of our third chapter, the debt seems considerable.

47. *Analysen zur Passiven Synthesis*, Hua XI, 126.

48. *Ideen II*, Hua II, 112.

49. Ibid.

50. Ibid., p. 113.

51. Ibid., p. 119.

52. Ibid.

53. For an account of this, see Mensch, *Intersubjectivity and Transcendental Idealism*, pp. 309–30 as well as Chapter 3 and 4 above.

54. *Ideen II*, Hua II, 113.

55. Ibid, p. 117.

56. Ibid, p. 251.

57. Ms. C 15, p. 4a; 1931.

58. See Ms. C 13 I, pp. 7a ff, January 1934.

59. See *Ideen II*, Hua II, 251-2.

60. As Schutz expresses this conclusion: "It is to be surmised that intersubjectivity is not a problem of constitution which can be solved within the transcendental sphere, but is rather a datum of the life-world. It is the fundamental ontological category of human existence in the world and therefore of all philosophical anthropology. As long as man is born of woman, intersubjectivity and the we-relationship will be the foundation for all other categories of human existence. The possibility of reflection on the self, discovery of the ego, capacity for performing any epoché . . . are founded on the primal experience of the we-relationship" ("The Problem of Transcendental Intersubjectivity," p. 82).

61. This may be the reason why Husserl, after the *Cartesian Meditations*, turned in the C manuscripts of the 1930s to analysis of the ego as a temporal form. See, e.g., Ms. C 16 VII, p. 5, May 1933; Hua XV, 577.

62. It is, thus, an answer which includes the Sartrean view of the self as embodying freedom and transcendence.

Chapter 11. Aristotle and the Overcoming of the Subject-Object Dichotomy

1. Wittgenstein describes a parallel situation of a person "looking for an object in a room. He opens a drawer and doesn't see it there; then he closes it again, waits, and opens it once more to see if perhaps it isn't there now, and keeps on like that" (Ludwig Wittgenstein, *On Certainty*, §315, trans. D. Paul and G. E. M. Anscombe [New York: Harper, 1972], p. 40). This attitude makes sense if each look can only be verified by the next.

2. As Husserl asks in considering the implications of the theory of evolution: "Do not the logical forms and laws express a contingent characteristic of the human species, a characteristic which could be different and, in the course of its future development, will probably be different?" (*Die Idee der Phänomenologie*, ed. Biemal, p. 21). Gunther Stent raises the same issues in "Limits to the Scientific Understanding of Man," *Science* 487 (1974): 1054.

3. All translations from the *Physics* have been taken from *Aristotle's Physics*, trans. Richard Hope (Lincoln, Neb.: University of Nebraska Press, 1961). All other translations from Aristotle are my own.

4. Only if we ignore the issue of motion can we define *place* as the interface between the body and what immediately surrounds it. Once we do consider motion, then, as Aristotle notes, this definition has to be modified. We have to say that "place is receptacle which cannot be transported" (212a 15). Thus, the place of a motionless boat is given by the surrounding water, but once we consider the boat as moving down the river, "it is the whole river which, being motionless as a whole, functions as a place." (212a 19). As the example of the boat suggests, the place of a body need not be continuous with the body itself.

5. Heidegger gives a good sense of the word when he writes: "What does the word *physics* denote? It denotes self-blossoming emergence (e.g., the blossoming of a rose), opening up, unfolding, that which manifests itself in such unfolding and perseveres and endures in it" (*An Introduction to Metaphysics*, trans. Ralph Manheim [New Haven, Conn.: Yale University Press, 1975], p. 14). It is unfortunate that when he comes to describe Aristotle's notion of time, he fails to avail himself of this insight. See *Sein und Zeit*, §81 (Tübingen), pp. 421–22; Donald Lewis gives a sympathetic account of Heidegger's position in "Aristotle's Theory of Time: Destructive Ontology from Heideggerian Principles," *Kinesis* 2 (Spring 1970): 81–92.

6. According to Heidegger, "the ancient interpretation of the being of entities" is such that an "entity is grasped in its being as presence, i.e., it is understood in terms of a definite temporal mode, the present" (*Sein und Zeit*, §6, p. 25). As we saw, this holds for Augustine. It is, for example, implicit in his statement about predicting the future, "it is only possible to see something which exists; and whatever exists is not future but present" (*Confessions*, XI, §18; trans. R. S. Pine-Coffin, p. 268). It also holds for the mod-

ern period, particular for the tradition stretching from Descartes to Husserl. Husserl is, perhaps, the most explicit in his affirmation of this position. As he expresses it in a pair of late manuscripts: "Temporalization, this is the constitution of existents in their temporal modalities. An existent: a present existent with the past of the same existent, with the future coming to be of the same existent. In an original sense, existent = original, concrete presence. It is persisting presence which 'includes', as non-independent components in the stream of presences, both past and future" (Ms. C 13, III, p. 34b, March 1934). In other words, "Every concrete individual persists in time and is what it is because constantly becoming, it passes from presence to presence" (Ms. E III 2, p. 2, 1934). Yet, as we note in our text, to say that being is *capable* of temporal presence is not the same as asserting that being *is* such presence. Aristotle asserts the former, but not the latter. To the point that Heidegger implies that Aristotle does equate being and temporal presence, he is in error.

7. Failure to grasp this point makes Aristotle's derivation of time circular. If the present is part of time then to use it to derive time from motion by noting the different presents (nows) associated with the different positions of the moving body is to derive time from itself. Bostock seems to assume this in his criticism of Aristotle's derivation. See David Bostock, "Aristotle's Account of Time," *Phronesis* 25 (1980): 151. Sarah Waterlow, by contrast, notes that the present, as grounding the unity of a temporal stretch, "cannot itself be represented as a temporal stretch," i.e., as a part of time ("Aristotle's Now," *The Philosophical Quarterly*, Vol. 34, No. 135, [April 1984]: 127). She bases this, however, simply on the present's function as a reference point for the moments of the stretch rather than on the relation of presence and being (see ibid., p. 124). Our own position comes close to that of Paul Conen who asserts that the "substrate" of the ongoing present (of "the dynamically grasped now") is the entity that is moved. This implies that this now, which Conen says is "not in time," but rather "is time" is the entity's attribute. See Paul Conen, *Die Zeittheorie des Aristoteles* (Munich: C. H. Beck, 1964), pp. 78–84, 167. Our own view, which sees the now as the presence of the substrate (i.e., of the entity itself), may be contrasted with Eva Brann's position. She asserts that "the now" which "hovers, as it were, over the moving thing . . . must be the *presentness of the perception* of the moving thing" ("Against Time," *St. John's Review* 34, no. 3 [Summer 1983]: 75). We are saying that it is the presentness, not of the perception of the thing, but of the thing to perception. The now is, in other words, an attribute not primarily of our perception but of the thing perceived.

8. The same point can be made, mutatis mutandis, about the continuity of motion. As Aristotle writes in *On Generation and Corruption*, motion is not continuous "because that in which the motion occurs is continuous," but rather "because that which is moved is continuous. For how can the quality be continuous except in virtue of the continuity of the thing to which it belongs?" (337a 27–29).

9. As Seth Bernadete writes: "Mind is that part of nature which has no one nature. It is nothing but possible. It is neither a being in itself nor any of the beings it thinks before it things them. It is the 'so called mind of soul.' It vanishes everywhere when it is not at work" ("Aristotle De Anima III, 305," *The Review of Metaphysics* 28, no. 4 [June 1975]: 615).

10. If we accept Kant position that "time . . . is the formal condition of inner sense" and that it is in time that our experiences "must all be ordered, connected, and brought into relation," then this grounding of the temporality of the subject is one with the subject's manifesting itself as a subject (see *Kritik d. r. V.*, A99). Kant, with his doctrine of the noumenal subject's being the ultimate origin of time, would, of course, oppose this conclusion. The way, however, is open to it once we make temporality dependent on being. As we mentioned in our "Remark," the order of dependence then becomes that of subjectivity depending on temporality, which depends on being, i.e.,on its registered motion.

11. If motion is understood in the modern sense of momentum (taken as the "quantity of motion," defined as the mass multiplied by the velocity) then given that velocity is distance divided by time, inherent in motion would be the premise of time. Any attempt to derive time from motion understood in this sense would of course be circular. The "earlier" and "later" in motion would be spatial temporal positions. It would then follow, as Corish asserts, that "the only positions that nows can be associated with are already temporal positions. Nows can be associated with positions in movement precisely because these are spatial temporal entities, and therefore temporal" (Denis Corish, "Aristotle's Attempted Derivation of Temporal Order from That of Movement and Space," *Phronesis* 21 [1976]: 251). That Corish is basing his argument on the modern notion of motion is clear from his assertion that, if the positions of movement did not involve time, we could not tell "in what spatial direction the motion proceeds." In other words, "The asymmetry of movement through space is at least partly a function of time, and cannot be determined merely in spatial terms" (ibid., p. 249). For Aristotle, however, the asymmetry is determined not by time but by the end or goal which, insofar as it does not change, is not in time. Thus, to be further along in motion is to be closer to achieving one's full or complete being. By knowing the latter, one knows the direction of motion. For example, looking at a series of snapshots of a growing child, I can easily tell the direction of the motion.

12. Hippocrates Apostle translates the passage in question by rendering energeia as actuality: "neither is it absurd for the *actuality* of one thing to be in another thing (for teaching is the activity of a man who can teach but it is an activity *upon an other man*; it is not cut off but is an activity of A upon B), nor can anything prevent one *actuality* from being the same for two things—not in the sense that the essence is the same for both, but in the sense in which potential being is related to being in *actuality*." He comments: "the two actualities [of A and B] (if we are to call them 'two') are like aspects of one actuality. . . . In a statue, its *actuality* is the shape and its potentiality is the material (e.g., the bronze). Yet the statue is one thing, and the shape and the material cannot exist apart but exist as inseparable principles of the statue. It is likewise with that which acts and that which is acted upon qua such" (*Aristotle's Physics*, trans. H. G. Apostle [Bloomington: Indiana University Press, 1969], pp. 46, 255). In other words, just as the matter and the form are aspects of one actuality, so also are the student and the teacher.

13. As Deborah Modrak notes, the idea of this unity of functioning can be traced back to Plato. In the *Theatetus* (156 d–e), Plato asserts that the eye becomes an actually "seeing eye" in the same process in which the thing seen (the "other parent of the

color") becomes "a white thing." See Modrak, *Aristotle, The Power of Perception* (Chicago: University of Chicago Press, 1987), p. 30.

14. The use of a circle to designate this natural motion draws its advantage from the lack of contrariety in circular motion. Thus, just as in nature, "man generates man," i.e., formally, the end of the process is the same as its beginning, so in motion about the circle, the end of a cycle is not a contrary of, but rather the same as the starting point. See *De Caelo*, I, 4.

15. Insofar as subjective temporality is a manifestation of the movement of nature, such temporality is, itself, naturally teleological. In other words, given that such temporality defines the being of the subject (see note 10 above), this too is teleological.

16. This implies, as Brann notes, "that there is no mechanical causation, which is a causation where each momentary state fully determines the next" ("Against Time," p. 75).

17. As E. Halper notes, it is because of this timelessness that actualities can be known (See "Aristotle on Knowledge of Nature," *The Review of Metaphysics* 37, no. 4 [June 1984]: 818, 820).

18. The distinction is that when some thing is "'in time' (or 'in process') there is *necessarily*, not coincidentally, a time or a process when *it* is" (*Physics*, 221a 27). As opposed to this, a thing can be "while" time lasts in the sense of not having any necessary relation to a particular time. Thus, in term of his form, a person is only incidentally in time. Were the form of humanity temporally determinate, then it would necessarily exist at one specific time rather than another.

19. The same holds for "knowledge or intellectual perception" (ἐπιστήμη ἢ νοῦς) according to Aristotle (*De Anima*, 428a 18).

20. Aristotle's doubts that sensation involves motion are expressed in *De Anima*, 431a 5–7.

21. For a good description of the distinct "sense" of being involved in the actuality of cognition, see Joseph Owens, "Form and Cognition in Aristotle, " *Ancient Philosophy* 1 (Fall 1980): 17–28.

Chapter 12. The Mind Body Problem, Phenomenological Reflections on an Ancient Solution

1. "Meditations, I," in *Discourse on Method ad Meditations on First Philosophy*, trans. D. Cress (Indianapolis: Hacket, 1980), p. 60.

2. Ibid., I, p. 61.

3. Ibid., II, p. 61.

4. Ibid., VI, p. 93

5. See ibid., II, p. 63.

6. Ibid., IV, p. 93.

7. Ibid., VI, pp. 97–98.

8. Ibid., VI, p. 93.

9. "Article XXXIV," *Philosophical Works of Descartes* (New York, 1955), vol. 1, p. 347.

10. *Summa Contra Gentiles*, Book II, Chap. 50, par. 5, trans. James Anderson, p. 150.

11. Ibid., II, 50, pp. 149–51.

12. *De Anima*, III, iv, 429a 22. All translations from Aristotle are my own.

13. Ibid., 429a 25–26.

14. Ibid., II, xii, 424a 28–32.

15. Ibid., 424a 24. According to Aristotle, the ratio also serves as a mean allowing the sense to judge whether the sensation it receives is excessive or deficient. There is, thus, a certain reflexivity in this judgment. The standard applied by the sense refers not just to object but also to itself. See ibid., II, xii, 424b 2.

16. Cited by Husserl in his *Logische Untersuchungen*, 5th ed., I, 147, n. 1.

17. *De Anima* III, iv, 429a 27.

18. Ibid., 429a 24.

19. See *Treatise of Human Nature*, Book I, Part IV, Section VI, p. 253.

20. See *De Anima*, III, ii, 426a 10.

21. *Summa Contra Gentiles*, Book II, Chap. 56, par. 6, p. 165.

22. Ibid., par. 3, p. 16.

23. Ibid., par. 8, p. 165.

24. Ibid., par. 9, p. 166.

25. Ibid., par. 10, p. 167.

26. Ibid., par. 8, p. 167.

27. *On Generation and Corruption*, I, vi, 323a 15.

28. Ibid., 323a 34–35.

29. *Metaphysics*, XII, vii, 1072a 26.

30. *De Anima*, III, ii, 426a 10.

31. Ibid., 426a 5; see also *Physics*, 202a 13–20.

32. For a more extended account of the epistemological implications of this, see the previous chapter, "Aristotle and the Overcoming of the Subject-Object Dichotomy."

33. *Physics*, II, vii, 198b 1–3.

34. *Metaphysics*, VIII, vi, 1045a 24, 1045b 19–20.

35. One of the ways to see our dependence on such functioning is through experiments involving sensory deprivation. Without a surrounding world, the mind's agency itself degrades.

36. *De Anima*, II, ii, 413a 2.

37. Ibid., II, i, 412b 19.

38. Ibid., II, i, 412a 30.

39. Ibid., II, iv, 415b 16.

40. *Metaphysics* IX, viii, 1050a 8–10.

41. The extended quote here is: "everything that comes to be moves towards its source (ἐπ' ἀρχὴν), that is, toward its goal (τέλος); for its wherefore [final cause] is its source. Its coming into being is directed by the end that is the actuality (ἐνέργεια), and it is because of the goal that potentiality (δύναμις) is possessed" (*Metaphysics*, IX, viii, 1050a 8-10).

42. For Hegel's account of the struggle involved, see his "Lordship and Bondage," *Phenomenology of Spirit*, §187.

43. See, for example, his *Monadology*, §§19, 21, 23–26, 30.

44. *Physics*, II, vii, 198b 1–3.

45. *Logische Untersuchungen*, 1st ed. (Halle a. S.: Max Niemeyer, 1900–1901), II, 704-5. For an extended account of Husserl's doctrine on this point, see Mensch, *The Question of Being in Husserl's Logical Investigations*, pp. 79 ff.

46. *Logische Untersuchungen*, 5th ed., II/1, 383.

47. See ibid., II/2, 74, 188.

48. As the Lafleur translation makes evident, the language of original and replica occurs throughout the *Meditations*. To take but two examples, Descartes writes in the "Third Meditation," "And I see nothing which appears more reasonable to me that to judge that this alien entity sends to me and imposes upon me its likeness rather than anything else." (*Meditations on First Philosophy*, trans. L. Lafleur [New York: Macmillan, 1990], p. 37). The likeness sent by the alien or external entity appears in me as an idea.

As Descartes describes them, "ideas in me are like paintings or pictures, which can, truly, easily fall short of the perfection of the original from which they have been drawn, but which can never contain anything greater or more perfect." (ibid., p. 40) It is, in short, an inner, somewhat imperfect replica. See ibid., pp. 32, 34, 36, 38, 42, 71, 78 f for further examples of this type of talk.

49. Sartre's attempt is, in essence, to define the intentionality of consciousness without any recourse to the notion of embodiment. He writes: "All is therefore clear and lucid in consciousness: the object with its characteristic opacity is before [as opposed to in] consciousness . . ." (*The Transcendence of the Ego*, trans. F. Williams and R. Kirkpatrick [New York: Noonday, 1990], p. 40). As James Edie writes, he sees intentionality as "the key to refuting . . . the whole ancient tradition, going back to Plato and Aristotle, which presents 'knowing' on the basis of the metaphor of the assimilation of food by the biological organism" ("The Question of the Transcendental Ego: Sartre's Critique of Husserl," *Husserl in his Contemporary Radiance* [Waterloo, Ont.: 1992], p. 259).

50. Kojève puts this point rather nicely when he writes: "Desire is always revealed as my desire, and to reveal desire, one must use the word 'I.' Man is absorbed by his contemplation of the thing in vain; as soon as desire for that thing is born, he will see that, in addition to the thing, there is his contemplation, there is himself, which is not that thing. And the thing appears to him as an object (Gegen-stand), as an external reality, which is not in him, which is not he but non-I" (*Introduction to the Reading of Hegel*, trans. James Nichols, Jr. [New York: Basic Books, 1969], p. 37).

51. *De Anima*, II, xi, 423b 14–20.

52. "The Mediaeval Model of Subjectivity, Towards a Rediscovery," Paper presented at the 1991 Hannah Arendt Memorial Symposia for Political Philosophy, New School for Social Research, New York, 1991, p. 7.

Chapter 13. Nietzsche-Darwin: Confronting the Janus Head

1. Ernst Behler, noting that Nietzsche's "writing is perceived today as the 'entry into postmodernity,'" writes: "*Beyond Good and Evil* with its subtitle *Prelude to a Philosophy of the Future* and its repeated addresses to the 'coming' philosophers or the philosophers of the 'coming' century, is a characteristic text for this thinking in historical terms" (*Confrontations, Derrida, Heidegger, Nietzsche* [Stanford, Calif.: Stanford University Press, 1991], p. 1). Because of our focus on his postmodern legacy, we will be concentrating primarily on this text. Contemporary citations from *The Will to Power*, because its influence on postmodernism, will be used to supplement this material.

2.. *Beyond Good and Evil*, §232, trans. R. J. Hollingdale, p. 163.

3. *Beyond Good and Evil*, §229, p. 159.

4. Ibid., §203, p. 126.

5. "David Strauss," *Thoughts Out of Season*, in *The Complete Work of Fredrich Nietzsche*, trans. A. M. Ludovici [New York: Russell and Russell, 1964], vol. 4, pp. 51–52.

6. "The Will to Power as Art," §25, in *Nietzsche*, 4 vols., trans. D. F. Krell (San Francisco: Harper, 1987), vol. 1, p. 212.

7. *Beyond Good and Evil*, §34, p. 65.

8. *The Will to Power*, §493, trans. W. Kaufmann and Hollingdale [New York: Random House, 1968], p. 272.

9. Ibid., §505, p. 275.

10. Ibid., §473, p. 263.

11. Ibid., §480, pp. 266–67.

12. *Beyond Good and Evil*, §4, p. 35.

13. Ibid., §11, p. 42.

14. *Will to Power*, §514, p. 278. Thus, they have no independent validity. "The categories are 'truths' only in the sense that they are conditions of life for us . . . reason . . . is a mere idiosyncrasy of a certain species of animal, one among many" (ibid., §515, p. 278).

15. Ibid., §496, p. 273.

16. In Nietzsche's words, "It is improbable that our 'knowledge' should extend further than is strictly necessary for the preservation of life. Morphology shows us how the senses and the nerves, as well as the brain, develop in proportion to the difficulty of finding nourishment" (ibid., § 494, p. 272). Thus, a mollusk's difficulty relative to an octopus's is small, so is its brain and nerves system. Given mollusk's ecological niche, there was no need for its senses to evolve beyond a certain point.

17. Ibid., §481.

18. "'The real and the apparent world.' . . . We have projected the conditions of *our* preservation as predicates of being in general" (ibid., §507, p. 276). This constant emphasis on preservation and survival leads C. U. M. Smith to write: "Nietzsche is consistent in passage after passage throughout his creative life in deriving the fundamental posits of philosophy and natural science from the biological imperatives of surviving in a Darwinian world" ("'Clever Beasts Who Invented Knowing': Nietzsche's Evolutionary Biology of Knowledge," *Biology and Philosophy* [1987]: 85).

19. *Beyond Good and Evil*, §43, p. 71.

20. Kant, "Prolegomena," §18, in *Kants gesammelte Schriften* (Berlin: Georg Reimer, 1911), IV, 298.

21. *Will to Power*, §496, pp. 272–73. Because for different species these conditions differ, Nietzsche immediately adds. "the conclusion that there could be no other kind of intellect than the one that preserves us is precipitate." As he also puts this, "we would not have [our intellect] if we did not *need* to have it, and we would not have it *as it is* if we did not need to have it *as it is*, if we could live *otherwise*." In other words, "even our intellect is a consequence of the conditions of existence" (ibid., §498, p. 273).

22. There is a parallel here with what Kierkegaard calls "religious and ethical theses." Historical and metaphysical theses, according to Kierkegaard, are true no matter who utters them. Religious and ethical theses, by contrast, require the authorization of a life lived in accord with them. Otherwise, they are "mere chatter." Thus, "in the one case, personality does nothing and in the other, everything . . ." (*Johannes Climacus*, para. 2, a [Princeton, N.J.: Princeton University Press, 1987], p. 152).

23. *Beyond Good and Evil*, §259, p. 194.

24. In Foucault's words, such analysis will "not deduce from the form of what we are what it is impossible for us to do and to know; but it will separate out, from the contingency that has made us what we are the possibility of no longer being, doing, or thinking what we are, do or think. . . . it is seeking to give new impetus, as far and wide as possible, to the undefined work of freedom" ("What Is Enlightenment?" in *Foucault Reader*, New York: Pantheon Books, 1984, p. 46).

25. "The Descent of Man," Chap. 5, in *The Origin of the Species and the Descent of Man* (New York: Random House, 1967), p. 501.

26. Ibid., p. 507.

27. Ibid., p. 502. As Darwin predicts, "At some future period, not very distant as measured by centuries, the civilized races of man will almost certainly exterminate, and replace, the savage races through out the world" (Chap. 5, p. 521).

28. Ibid., Chap. 7, p. 550.

29. Thus, Darwin advises, "Man like every other animal, has no doubt advanced to his present high condition through a struggle for existence consequent on his rapid multiplication; and if he is to advance still higher, it is to be feared that he must remain subject to a severe struggle. . . . Hence our natural rate of increase, though leading to many and obvious evils, must not be greatly diminished by any means. There should be open competition for all men; and the most able should not be prevented by laws or customs from succeeding best and rearing the largest number of offspring" (ibid., Chap. 21, p. 919).

30. *Beyond Good and Evil*, §259, p. 194. Much of his criticism of David Strauss's use of Darwin is that the former glosses over this. He thus avoids constructing "a genuine and seriously constructed ethical system, based on Darwin's teaching." If he had, he would "have established a moral code for life out of *bellum omnium contra omnes* and the privileges of the strong." Instead, Strauss attempts to see the "sum and substance of

morality" in our recognition that we are human and "that all others are human also . . . having the same needs and claims . . ." Nietzsche asks, "But where does this imperative hail from? How can it be intuitive in man, seeing that, according to Darwin, man is indeed a creature of nature, and that his ascent to his present stage of development has been conditioned by quite different laws—by the very fact that he was continually forgetting that others were constituted like him and shared the same rights with him; by the very fact that he regarded himself as the stronger, and thus brought about the gradual suppression of weaker types" ("David Strauss," *Thoughts Out of Season,* in *The Complete Works,* vol. 4, pp. 52–54.

31. *Beyond Good and Evil,* §259, p. 194.

32. Ibid., §239, pp. 168–69. In *The Will to Power,* §864, Nietzsche remarks: "Finally: woman! One-half of mankind is weak, typically sick, changeable, inconstant—woman needs a religion of weakness that glorifies being weak, loving, being humble as divine" (p. 460).

33. Darwin in a sense goes further when he writes: "It is, indeed, fortunate that the law of the equal transmission of characters to both sexes prevails with mammals; otherwise it is probable that man would have become as superior in mental endowment to woman, as the peacock is in ornamental plumage to the peahen" ("The Descent of Man," Chap. 19, p. 874).

34. *Beyond Good and Evil,* §62, p. 88. Cf. Darwin, "The Descent of Man," §21, pp. 918–19. Nietzsche looks to the use of religion to assist in "selection and breeding": "The philosopher . . . as the man of the most comprehensive responsibility who has the conscience for the collective evolution of mankind: this philosopher will make use of religions for his work of education and breeding. . . . The influence on selection and breeding, that is to say the destructive as well as the creative and formative influence which can be exercised with the aid of the religions, is manifold and various . . ." (*Beyond Good and Evil,* §61, p. 86). This reference to "religion" does not, of course, include Christianity. Part of Nietzsche's opposition to *this* religion is its unsuitability for this purpose. As he writes in *The Will to Power,* "If one regards individuals as equal, one calls the species into question, one encourages a way of life that leads to the ruin of the species: Christianity is the counterprinciple to the principle of *selection.* . . . The species requires that the ill-constituted, weak, degenerate, perish: but it was precisely to them that Christianity turned as a conserving force. . . . What is 'virtue' and 'charity' in Christianity if not just this mutual preservation, this solidarity of the weak, this hampering of selection?" (*The Will to Power,* §246, p. 142).

35. Ibid., §36, p. 67. As he writes in *The Will to Power,* "There is absolutely no other kind of causality than that of will upon will. Not explained mechanistically" (§658, p. 347). In other words, his position is "that all driving force is will to power, that there is no other physical, dynamic or psychic force except this" (§668, p. 366). Such passages support Schulz's contention "that Nietzsche undertook, despite or perhaps precisely because of his strict opposition to classical metaphysics, to understand for himself the totality of beings as a unity, that is, to interpret it on the basis of one princi-

ple around which the interpreter must organize all his concerns. On this basis he can, in other words, organize himself, his own thought and action" (Walter Schulz, "Funktion und Ort der Kunst in Nietzsches Philosophie," *Nietzsche-Studien*, 12 [1983], 2–3). While for Schulz, this principle is will to power, for Smith it is Darwinism. In Smith's words, "an evolutionary interpretation of his writings provides a vital organizing principle." This is because "his philosophy emerges out of a profound encounter with nineteenth-century evolutionary thought." Recognizing this, we "give the propositions of his thought an organic consistency," we see "his metaphysics . . . as consistent with and complementary to Darwin's biology" ("'Clever Beasts Who Invented Knowing,'" p. 88). Thus, for Smith, "Nietzsche's concept of the will to power was similar to the Darwinian idea of the individual's struggle for existence" (ibid., p. 75). In our view, the notion of will to power involves claims which far exceed any strictly biological interpretation. Ultimately, these claims undermine the perspectivism Nietzsche seeks to base on preservation and utility.

36. *Beyond Good and Evil*, §5, p. 36.

37. Ibid., §6, p. 37.

38. Cf. the assertion of the *Will to Power*: "The so-called drive for knowledge can be traced to the drive to appropriate and conquer: the senses, the memory, the instincts, etc. have developed as a consequence of this drive" (§423, p. 227).

39. *Beyond Good and Evil*, §51, p. 79.

40. Ibid., §46, p. 76.

41. Ibid., §195, p. 118.

42. Ibid., §260, p. 194.

43. Ibid., §61, p. 87.

44. Ibid., §258, p. 193.

45. Ibid., §61, p. 87.

46. They do not because they are on the top. In Nietzsche's words, "It is quite in order that we possess no religion of oppressed Aryan races, for that is a contradiction: a master race is either on top or it is destroyed" (*Will to Power*, §145, p. 93).

47. A fundamental expression of this is the creation of values. For Nietzsche, "it is the intrinsic right of masters to create values" (*Beyond Good and Evil*, §261, pp. 198–99). The master does this by valuing himself, taking his own existence as a standard: "he knows himself to be that which in general first accords honor to things, he creates *values*. Everything he knows to be part of himself, he honors: such morality is self-glorification" (ibid., §260, p. 195). To get another to accept him as a value is to impose his will; it is to get the other to function as a dependent expression of his will to power.

48. *Beyond Good and Evil*, §16, p. 46.

49. *Will to Power*, §485, p. 269.

50. Ibid., §485, p. 268.

51. Ibid., §488, p. 270.

52. This is the same god he praises toward the end of *Beyond Good and Evil*. It was to him, he writes, that "once I brought in all secrecy and reverence my first born . . ." (ibid., §295, p. 219).

53. *The Birth of Tragedy and the Case of Wagner*, trans. W. Kaufmann (New York: Random House, 1967), §5, p. 50.

54. Ibid., §7, p. 59.

55. Ibid., §8, p. 61.

56. Ibid., §17, p. 105

57. Ibid., §16, p. 102.

58. Ibid., §16, p.104.

59. Ibid., §16, pp. 102–3.

60. *Will to Power*, §619, pp. 332–33.

61. Ibid., §55, p. 36.

62. "Who is Nietzsche's Zarathustra?" in Heidegger's *Nietzsche*, II, 223.

63. Initially, that is, in the period of the polemic against Strauss, it was to this account. See, for example, note 27.

64. "Metaphysical thinking rest on the distinction between what truly is and what, measured against this, constitutes all that is not truly in being" ("Who Is Nietzsche's Zarathustra?" *Nietzsche*, II, 230).

65. *Beyond Good and Evil*, §21, p. 51.

66. Ibid.

67. *Will to Power*, §663, p. 349.

68. *The Joyful Wisdom*, V, §349, *The Complete Works*, vol. 10, p. 290.

69. Ibid.

70. Ibid., p. 289.

71. "The Twilight of the Idols," §14, in *The Complete Works*, vol. 16, p. 71.

72. We, thus, cannot agree with Smith who reduces Nietzsche's criticisms of Darwin to misunderstandings of the latter's position. For Smith, it is as a Darwinian that Nietzsche criticizes what he falsely assumes to be Darwin's position. In Smith's words, "Nietzsche puts his finger unerringly on the Darwinian position and then accuses Darwinists of holding the opposite" ("Clever Beasts Who Invented Knowing," p. 72). While this is true of the criticisms he cites, it does not hold for Nietzsche's attack on the Mathusian basis of natural selection.

73. *Beyond Good and Evil*, §13, p. 44.

74. Heidegger, of course, sees the planetary domination of technology as *the* contemporary expression of will to power. See e.g., *The Question of Being*, trans. J. Wilde and W. Kluback (New Haven, Conn.: Yale University Press, 1958), p. 59.

75. Habermas, for one, claims that Heidegger, having attempted to "de-struct the philosophy of the subject, "falls back into the conceptual constraints of the philosophy of the subject," the result being that "the solipsistically posited Dasein once again occupies the place of transcendental subjectivity" (*The Philosophical Discourse of Modernity* [Cambridge: MIT Press, 1987], p. 150). One of the fateful consequences of this move comes when "he substitutes for this 'in each case mine' Dasein the collective Dasein of a fatefully existing and 'in each case our' people" (ibid., p. 157). At this point the rise of National Socialism can prompt him to assert that "The people is winning back the truth of its *Daseinswille* . . ." (ibid., p. 158). Heidegger's "turn," as worked out in the Nietzsche books, may, as Habermas says, be prompted by an attempt to justify this development (ibid., p. 156). Certainly, there is never an explicit renunciation of (or confession of guilt regarding) his involvement with National Socialism.

76. "The Origin of the Species," Chap. 6, p. 59.

77. Ibid., p. 85.

78. Darwin's preferred term here is *nature*. Comparing its action with that effected by domestic breeding, he writes, "Man can act only on external and visible characters: Nature, if I may be allowed to personify the natural preservation or survival of the fittest, cares nothing for appearances, except in so far as they are useful to any being. She can act on every internal organ, on every shade of constitutional difference, on the whole machinery of life. Man selects only for his own good: Nature only for that of the being which she tends" ("The Origin of the Species," Chap. 6, in *The Origin of the Species and the Descent of Man*, p. 65). The notion of "the being which she tends" and its benefit becomes highly ambiguous once we bear "in mind how infinitely complex and close-fitting are the mutual relations of all organic beings to each other and to their physical conditions of life" (ibid., p. 63) If, in fact, every being is ultimately defined by every other, the "being" tended by nature can be only nature itself understood as the whole web of relations and entities.

79. It is also robbed of its predictive power. What we have here is the classic N body problem where a change any one body changes the others and hence changes their determination of the first, which change then affects the others and so on indefi-

nitely. Newton first realized the nonpredictive character of such systems in his discussion of the three-body problem in the *Principia*, Proposition LXVI. The same character prevents us from making long-range predictions about the evolutionary transformations of organisms.

Chapter 14. The Splitting of the Self

1. That there is another Nietzsche, quite different from this, is the subject of the previous chapter.

2. *Will to Power*, §490, trans. Kaufmann, p. 270.

3. Bennet G. Braun, M.D., "Multiple Personality Disorder: An Overview," *American Journal of Occupational Therapy* 44 (November 1990): 971.

4. Frank Putnam, M.D., "The Switch Process in Multiple Personality Disorder and Other State-Change Disorders," *Dissociation* 1 (March 1988): 26.

5. Braun, "Multiple Personality Disorder," p. 972.

6. In Braun's words, "Continued trauma reinforces the chaining of memories and associated response patterns. The different adaptive response patterns become functionally separated by amnestic barries. Thus, the patient's personality is 'split'" (ibid.).

7. Ibid., p. 971.

8. Ibid., p. 972.

9. Pierre Janet, *The Major Symptoms of Hysteria* (New York: Macmillan, 1907), p. 318.

10. Kenneth Bowers, "Dissociation in Hypnosis and Multiple Personality Disorder," *International Journal of Clinical and Experimental Hypnosis* 39 (July 1991): 166.

11. The reference, here, is to R. P. Kluft's "An Update on Multiple Personality Disorder, *Hosp. comm. Psychiat.* 38 (1987): 363–73.

12. Bowers, "Dissociation in Hypnosis and Multiple Personality Disorder," pp. 168–69.

13. Bennett G. Braun, M.D., "The Role of the Family in the Development of Multiple Personality Disorder," *International Journal of Family Psychiatry* 5 (1984): 305.

14. Ibid. In addition to himself, Braun also names Bliss, Lipman and Fischolz as holding this view.

15. Freud, "A Note on the Unconscious in Psychoanalysis" (1912), trans. and ed. J. Stratchey, in *The Standard Edition*, (London: Hogarth Press), vol. 12, p. 26; see also his "The Unconscious," vol. 14, pp. 170–71, where he writes: "The well-known cases of

'double conscience' proves nothing against our view. We may most aptly describe them as cases of splitting of the mental activity into two groups, and the same consciousness turns to one or the other of these groups in turn."

16. Freud, "Splitting of the Ego in the Defensive Process," in *Collected Papers*, trans. and ed. James Strachey (New York: Basic Books, 1959), vol. 5, p. 372.

17. Ibid., p. 373.

18. Ibid., p. 374.

19. Ibid.

20. *An Outline of Psycho-Analysis*, trans. James Strachey (New York: W.W. Norton, 1969), p. 61.

21. Ibid., p. 60.

22. Ibid., p. 59.

23. Ibid., p. 61.

24. Freud, "Splitting of the Ego in the Defensive Process," p. 373.

25. Braun, "The BASK Model of Dissociation," *Dissociation* 1 (March 1988): 4.

26. Janet, *The Major Symptoms of Hysteria*, p. 23.

27. Braun, "The BASK Model of Dissociation," p. 5.

28. Ibid., pp. 5 ff.

29. Edmund Husserl, *Logische Untersuchungen*, ed. U. Panzer (The Hague: Martinus Nijhoff, 1984), Hua XIX/2, 762.

30. Ibid., Hua XIX/1, 397.

31. Ms. E III 2, p. 18, 1921.

32. Ibid., p. 46.

33. We say, "in a certain sense," because ultimately it is not between the ego and the environment, but between the interpretative function (which underlies the ego) and this environment.

34. Husserl, *Erste Philosophie I*, ed. R. Boehm (The Hague: Martinus Nijhoff, 1966), Hua VII, 398.

35. Husserl, Ms. E III 9, 1931, in *Zur Phaenomenologie der Intersubjektivitaet, Dritter Teil: 1929–35*, ed. I. Kern (The Hague: Martinus Nijhoff, 1973), Hua XV, 404.

36. To be "here" is, phenomenologically, to be at the point from which perspectival series unfold, their relative rates of unfolding giving one the sense of objects'

being near or far. Thus, as you walk through a park, trees close by match your progress by receding at the same speed, objects at a middle range glide by at a more stately pace, and objects marking the distant horizon scarcely seem to move. Each in fact, has its rate of showing its different aspects, and each rate is coordinated to the self taken as a spatial center.

37. See Ms. C 2 1, p. 11a, August 1931.

38. Ms. C 3 III, p. 26a, March 1931. See also Mss. C 7 I, p. 9a, June–July 1932, C 2 I, p. 4a, September–October 1931, M III 3, XI, p. 21, September 1921 as well as *Ideen II*, §25, Hua II, 105.

39. The complete sentence is "The assertion that I remain who I am as the same transcendental ego—as the same personal ego—is equivalent to the assertion that my world remains a world." (Ms. B I 13, VI, p. 4, December 15, 1931).

40. Ms. F IV 3, p. 57a, 1925.

41. *Cartesianische Meditationen*, Hua I, 80. See Chapters 7 and 8.

42. *Logische Untersuchungen*, 5th ed., II/1, 383.

43. *Ideen zu einer reinen Phänomenologie und Phänomenologischen Philosophie. Erstes Buch*, § 55, Hua III, 120.

44. *Zur Phänomenologie des inneren Zeitbewusstseins*, ed. R. Boehm, Hua X, 112.

45. For an account of this, see the chapter on Husserl and Aquinas.

46. *Aristotle's Physics*, IV, 11, 218b 23, trans. R. Hope, p. 79.

47. Because of this, DeBoer says, "In transcendental phenomenology, sense is being itself." ("Zusammenfassung," *De Ontwikkelingsgan in het Denken van Husserl*, Assen: Van Gorcum, 1966, p. 597). It is being insofar as being can appear, that is, be phenomenologically present, only in the guise of a coherent, perceptually embodied sense. The same fact is behind Fink's assertion, "The transcendental noema . . . is the entity itself" ("Die phänomenologische Philosophie Edmund Husserls in der Gegenwärtigen Kritik," p. 133).

48. See Victor Alpher, "Introject and Identity: Structural-Interpersonal Analysis and Psychological Assessment of Multiple Personality Disorder," *Journal of Personality Assessment* 58, no. 2 (1992): 361, as well as Braun, "The BASK Model of Dissociation," p. 8.

49. According to Braun, in severe abuse, the result can be personality fragments exhibiting "memory for circumscribed periods of time—often very tiny snippets of time because events were so overwhelming, such as being present at the murder of one parent by another; the event may have been of sufficient impact to cause the creation of several memory trace fragments to deal with parts of the event, i.e., the argument, the shooting, questioning by the police, etc." ("The BASK Model of Dissociation," p. 8.).

50. Victor Alpher, "Introject and Identity," p. 361.

51. My position, in this regard, is the opposite of Fingarette's and Vargo's positions. Fingarette writes: "the defensive process is a splitting of the ego which is not something that 'happens' to the ego, but something the ego *does*, a motivated strategy" (Herbert Fingarette, "Self Deception and the 'Splitting of the Ego'," *Philosophical Essays on Freud*, ed. Wollheim and Hopkins [Cambridge: Cambridge University Press, 1982], p. 224). He explains that it does this "because the incompatibility between the ego nucleus and the current ego is so great, relative to the integrative capacities of the ego, that the latter gives up any attempt to integrate the ego-nucleus into itself . . . the ego says, 'This is not me.' It treats the ego-like system as 'outside' rather than 'inside.'" In other words, the ego solves its inability to integrate its current experience by establishing a "counter-ego nucleus" (ibid.). The difficulty with this view, which Fingarette ascribes to Freud, is that it contradicts the thesis, which Fingarette also accepts, that "the self is a synthesis, . . . something made" (ibid., p. 215). This making includes the self as "a noticeable autonomous governing centre" (ibid., p. 216). If the self is made, then can we also take it as a maker of selves? Our view is that the synthetic process which results in the self also results, under the conditions of trauma, in the splitting of the self. The original self is not the agent, but the victim of such splitting. I have the same objection to the position Stephanie Vargo takes in her otherwise excellent and moving account. She takes splitting to be a result of subjective constitution. In her view, "the already constituted self," when faced with trauma, preserves itself by constituting a distinct self which experiences "the traumatic event from the spatial perspective of 'from a distance' or 'not there'" ("'I Believe I Have Witnessed a Murder': Trauma, Contradiction and the Creation of Alternative Identities," *Proceedings of the 24th Annual Meeting of the Husserl Circle* [Waterloo, Ont., 1992], p. 177). The reason why the self needs to preserve itself is that the event threatens "the coherent system of meanings which constitute the life history of that self." Their disruption is its disruption. In Vargo's words, "any event which had the capacity to annihilate the coherent meaning structure of the life history of a particular self would also result in the annihilation of that particular self" (ibid., p. 173). But, if this is so, then selfhood is not really a creation of the self. It must, rather, be traced back to that which situates it, to that which gives the underlying pre-egological synthetic (or constitutive) function its egological shape or focus.

Chapter 15. Post-Normative Subjectivity

1. *Montaigne: Selected Essays*, trans. W. Hazlitt [New York, 1949], pp. 77–78.

2. Ibid., p. 89

3. *Don Quixote*, trans. S. Putnam [New York, 1949], p. 722.

4. *Meditations on First Philosophy*, I, trans. D. Cress, Indiannapolis: Hacket Press, 1980, p. 60.

5. Ibid., VI, p. 93.

6. "The Passions of the Soul," Article XXXII, *Philosophical Works of Descartes*, trans. E. Haldane and G. Ross, vol. 1, p. 346.

7. Ibid.

8. Ibid., Article XXXIV, vol. 1, p. 347.

9. "Kritik d. r. V.," A 116, in *Kants gesammelte Schriften*, IV, 87.

10. Ibid., B 135, III, 110.

11. Ibid.

12. Ibid., A 127, IV, 93.

13. "Prologomena," §19, IV, 298; see also ibid., §21a; IV, 304.

14. "Kritik d. r. V.," B 130, III, 107.

15. Ibid., B 131, III, 108.

16. "First Introduction . . . ," §5, *The Science of Knowledge*, trans. P. Heath and J. Lachs, p. 13.

17. Ibid., p. 14.

18. That the world remains unknowable under both alternatives allows Nietzsche to be both a "dogmatist" and an idealist. Using nineteenth century science to reduce the subject to its material basis, he nonetheless takes its functioning (its willing) as the ground of things. Given, as Fichte says, "reason provides no principle of choice," this hybrid position is also an alternative. *Will to Power*, §§478–79 and *The Dawn of Day*, §49 are nice examples of the "dogmatic," materialist side of Nietzsche's thought.

19. *De Anima*, II, iv, 429a 24.

20. Ibid., 429b 31.

21. "Consciousness of Self and Knowledge of Self," *Readings in Existential Phenomenology*, p. 136. For the points of our disagreement, see the chapter on Husserl and Sartre.

22. "Kritik d. r. V.," A99, IV, 77.

23. Given that this definition is prescriptive, not every post-Cartesian philosopher is necessarily "modern" in the sense that we use. Only those who share in the modern project and its accompanying metaphysical commitment are.

24. Such projects would still be our norms, our modes of constituting the world's appearance. Heidegger's notion of this "pragmatic" disclosure is derived largely from William James. James writes that in disclosing an entity, "I am always unjust, always partial, always exclusive. My excuse is necessity—the necessity which my finite and practical nature lays upon me. My thinking is first and last and always for the sake of my

doing, and I can only do one thing at a time." From this, it follows that "the essence of a thing is that one of its properties which is so important for my interest that in comparison with it I may neglect the rest" ("Reasoning," *Psychology, Briefer Course*, pp. 355, 357). The interest, then, is the subjective norm for disclosure.

25. Heidegger's acceptance of this standpoint at the time of *Sein und Zeit* is documented in an October 22, 1927 letter he wrote to Husserl. Remarking that they are "agreed that being (*Seiende*) in the sense that you term the 'world' cannot be explained in its transcendental constitution by resorting to a being of the same type," he continues, "What kind of being is the being in which the world constitutes itself? This is the central problem of 'Being and Time'—i.e., a fundamental ontology of Dasein. One has to show that the type of being of human Dasein is totally distinct from all other beings and that, precisely as such, it conceals in itself the possibility of transcendental constitution. Transcendental constitution is a central possibility of the existence of the factual self" (quoted by Biemel in *Phänomologische Psychologie*, ed. W. Biemel, [The Hague: Martinus Nijhoff, 1962], Hua IX, 601–2).

26. "Kritik d. r. V.," B xvii, III, 12.

27. "Prologomena," §18, IV, 298.

28. *Nicomachean Ethics*, I, ii, 1094b 25.

29. *Metaphysics*, IV, i, 1003a 33.

BIBLIOGRAPHY

Alpher, Victor. "Introject and Identity: Structural-Interpersonal Analysis and Psychological Assessment of Multiple Personality Disorder." *Journal of Personality Assessment* 58, no. 2 (1992).

Apostle, Hippocrates G. "Commentary." In *Aristotle's Physics*, trans. H. G. Apostle. Bloomington: Indiana University Press, 1969.

Aquinas, Thomas. *De Ente et Essentia*, ed. M. D. Rolland-Gosselin, ch. 4. Kain, Belgium: Le Saulchoir, 1926.

———. *Expositio in libros Peri Hermenias*, ed. T. Maria. In *Opera Omnia*, vol. 1. Leonine ed. Rome: Polyglotta, 1882–1948.

———. *In XII liberos Metaphicorum*, ed. R. Spiazzi. Turin: Marietti, 1950.

———. *Quaestiones disputatae de Anima*, ed. R. Spiazzi, 2 vols. Turin: Marietti, 1949.

———. *Quaestiones Quodlibetales*, ed. P. Mandonnet. Paris: P. Lethielleux, 1926.

———. *Scriptum super libros Sententiarum Magistri Petri Lombardi*, ed. P. Mandonnet and M. F. Moos, 4 vols. Paris, 1929–47.

———. *Summa Contra Gentiles*, trans. James Anderson. Notre Dame, Ind.: Notre Dame University Press, 1975.

———. *Summa Theologica*, Leonine ed., 5 vols. Madrid: Biblioteca de Autores Cristianos, 1961.

Aristotle. *Aristotle's Physics*, trans. Richard Hope. Lincoln, Neb.: University of Nebraska Press, 1961

———. *On The Soul, De Anima*, trans. W. S. Hett. London: Loeb Classical Library, 1964.

———. *The Basic Works of Aristotle*, ed. R. McKeon. New York: Random House, 1941.

Augustine. "Concerning Eighty-Three Different Questions, Question 46." In *The Essential Augustine*, trans. Vernon J. Bourke. New York: American Library, 1964.

———. *Saint Augustine—Confessions*, trans. R. S. Pine-Coffin. London: Penguin Books, 1964.

————. *On the Free Choice of Will*, trans. A. S. Benjamin. Indianapolis: Bobbs-Merrill, 1964.

Avicenna. *Logica*. Venice, 1508.

————. *Metaphysica*. Venice, 1508.

Behler, Ernst. *Confrontations, Derrida, Heidegger, Nietzsche*. Stanford, Calif.: Stanford University Press, 1991.

Bernadete, Seth. "Aristotle De Anima III, 305." *The Review of Metaphysics* 28, no. 4 (June 1975).

Bostock, David. "Aristotle's Account of Time." *Phronesis* 25 (1980).

Bowers, Kenneth. "Dissociation in Hypnosis and Multiple Personality Disorder," *International Journal of Clinical and Experimental Hypnosis* 39 (July 1991).

Brague, R. "The Mediaeval Model of Subjectivity, Towards a Rediscovery." Paper presented at the 1991 Hannah Arendt Memorial Symposia for Political Philosophy, New School for Social Research, New York, 1991.

Brann, Eva. "Against Time." *St. John's Review* 34, no. 3 (Summer 1983).

Braun, Bennet G. "Multiple Personality Disorder: An Overview." *American Journal of Occupational Therapy* 44 (November 1990).

————. "The BASK Model of Dissociation." *Dissociation* (March 1988).

————. "The Role of the Family in the Development of Multiple Personality Disorder." *International Journal of Family Psychiatry* 5 (1984).

Brough, John. "Husserl and Erazim Kohak's Idea and Experience." *Man and World* 14 (1981).

Bynum, Terrell Ward. "Artificial Intelligence, Biology, and Intentional States." *Metaphilosophy* 16 (1985).

Celms, Theodor. *Der phänomenologische Idealismus Husserls*. New York: Garland Press, 1979.

Cervantes, M. *Don Quixote*, trans. S. Putnam. New York: Random House, 1949.

Churchland, P. M., and Churchland, P. S. "Could a Machine Think?" *Scientific American* 262 (January 1990).

Conen, Paul. *Die Zeittheorie des Aristoteles*. Munich: C. H. Beck, 1964.

Corish, Denis. "Aristotle's Attempted Derivation of Temporal Order from That of Movement and Space." *Phronesis* 21 (1976).

Darwin, Charles. "The Descent of Man," in *The Origin of Species and the Descent of Man*, New York: Random House, 1967.

De Boer, Theodore. *De Ontwikkelingsgang in het Denken van Husserl*. Assen: Van Gorcum, 1966.

————. *The Development of Husserl's Thought*, trans. Theodore Plantinga. The Hague: Martinus Nijhoff, 1978.

Derrida, Jacques. "Structure, Sign, and Play in the Discourse of the Human Sciences." *A Postmodern Reader*, ed. J. Natoli and L. Hutcheon. Albany: SUNY Press, 1993.

Descartes, Rene. *Descartes Meditations*, trans. L. Lafleur. New York: Macmillan, 1990.

————. *Discourse on Method and Meditations on First Philosophy*, trans. D. Cress. Indianapolis: Hacket, 1980.

————. *Philosophical Works of Descartes*, 2 vols., trans. E. Haldane and G. Ross. New York: Dover, 1955.

Dewdney, A. K. "Computer Recreations." *Scientific American* 261 (December 1989).

Dreyfus, H., ed. *Husserl, Intentionality and Cognitive Science*. Cambridge, Mass.: MIT Press, 1982.

Drummond, John J. *Husserlian Intentionality and Non-Foundational Realism. Noema and Object*. Dordrecht: Kluwer, 1990.

Dupré, L. "Husserl's Thoughts on God and Faith." *Philosophy and Phenomenological Research* 29 (December 1968).

Edie, James. "The Question of the Transcendental Ego: Sartre's Critique of Husserl." *Husserl in His Contemporary Radiance: Proceedings of the 24th Annual Meeting of the Husserl Circle*. Waterloo, Ont.: 1992.

Ellis, Ralph. "Directionality and Fragmentation in the Transcendental Ego." *Philosophical Research Archives* 5 (December 1978).

Embre, Lester. "Reflection on the Ego." In *Explanations in Phenomenology*, eds. D. Carr and E. Casey. The Hague: Martinus Nijhoff, 1973.

Farber, M. (ed.). *Philosophical Essays in Memory of Edmund Husserl*. New York: Greenwood Press, 1968.

Fichte, J. G. *The Science of Knowledge*, ed. and trans. Peter Heath and John Lachs. Cambridge: Cambridge University Press, 1982.

Fields, C. A. "Double on Searle's Chinese Room." *Nature and System* 6 (1984).

Fingarette, Herbert. "Self Deception and the 'splitting of the ego'," *Philosophical Essays on Freud*, ed. R. Wollheim and Hopkins. Cambridge: Cambridge University Press, 1982.

Fink, Eugen. "Die phänomenologische Philosophie Edmund Husserls in der gegenwärtigen Kritik." In *Studien zur Phänomenologie, 1930–39*, Phänomenologica vol. 21. The Hague: Martinus Nijhoff, 1966.

Føllesdal, Dagfin. "Husserl's Notion of Noema." *Journal of Philosophy* 66, no. 20 (October 16, 1969).

Foucault, Michel. "What Is Enlightenment?" in *The Foucault Reader*, ed. Paul Rabinow. New York: Pantheon Books, 1984.

Fowkes, William. "The Concept of the Self in Husserl and Beyond." *Philosophy Today* 24 (Spring 1980).

Freud, Sigmund. *An Outline of Psycho-Analysis*, trans. James Strachey. New York: W.W. Norton, 1969

———. "A Note on the Unconscious in Psychoanalysis" (1912), trans. and ed J. Stratchey. In *The Standard Edition*, vol. 12. London: Hogarth Press, 1978.

———. "Splitting of the Ego in the Defensive Process." In *Collected Papers*, trans. and ed. James Strachey, vol. 5. New York: Basic Books, 1959.

———. *The Future of an Illusion*, trans. W. D. Scott. Garden City, N.Y.: Doubleday Books, 1964.

———. "The Unconscious," trans. and ed J. Stratchey. In *The Standard Edition*, vol. 14. London: Hogarth Press, 1978.

Gilson, Etienne. *Being and Some Philosophers,* 2nd ed. Toronto: Pontifical Institute of Mediaeval Studies, 1952.

Gödel, Kurt. "On Formally Undecidable Propositions," in *Frege and Gödel, Two fundamental Texts in Mathematical Logic*, ed. J van Heijenoor. Cambridge: Harvard University Press, 1970.

Gundissalinus. "De Unitate." In *Die dem Boethius fälschlich zugeschriebene Abhandlung des Dominicus Gundissalimus De unitate*, ed. P. Correns. Munster, Westphalia: Aschendorff, 1891.

Gurwitsch, Aron. "A Non-egological Conception of Consciousness." In *Studies in Phenomenology and Psychology*. Evanston, Ill.: Northwestern University Press, 1966.

Habermas, Jürgen. "Modern versus Postmodernity," *A Postmodern Reader*, ed. J. Natoli and L. Hutcheon. Albany: SUNY Press, 1993.

———. *The Philosophical Discourse of Modernity*, trans. F. G. Lawrence. Cambridge: MIT Press, 1987.

Hall, Harrison. "Was Husserl a Realist or an Idealist?" In *Husserl, Intentionality, and Cognitive Science*, ed. H. L. Dreyfus. Cambridge: MIT Press, 1982.

Halper, E. "Aristotle on Knowledge of Nature." *The Review of Metaphysics* 37, no. 4 (June 1984).

Hegel, G. W. F. *Phenomenology of Mind*, trans. James Baillie. London: Allen and Unwin, 1966.

Heidegger, Martin. *An Introduction to Metaphysics*, trans. Ralph Manheim. New Haven, Conn.: Yale University Press, 1975.

———. *Nietzsche*, trans. D. F. Krell, 4 vols. San Francisco: Harper and Row, 1991.

———. *Sein und Zeit*. Tübingen: Niemeyer, 1967.

———. "The End of Philosophy." In *On Time and Being*, trans. Joan Stanbaugh. New York: Harper and Row, 1972.

———. *The Essence of Reasons*, bilingual ed., trans. T. Malick. Evanston, Ill.: Northwestern University Press, 1969.

———. *The Question of Being*, trans. J. Wilde and W. Kluback. New Haven, Conn.: Yale University Press, 1958.

———. "Was ist Metaphysik." *Wegmarken*. Frankfurt am Main: Klostermann, 1967.

———. "Who is Nietzsche's Zarathustra?" In *Nietzsche, Volumes One and Two*, trans. David Krell. San Francisco: Harper and Row, 1991.

Held, Klaus. *Lebendige Gegenwart*. The Hague: Martinus Nijhoff, 1966.

Hume, David. *A Treatise of Human Nature*, ed. L. A. Selby-Bigge. Oxford: Clarendon Press, 1973.

Husserl, Edmund. *Analysen zur Passiven Synthesis*, ed. M. Fleischer. Husserliana XI, The Hague, 1966.

———. *Cartesanische Meditationen*, ed. S. Strasser. Husserliana I, The Hague: Martinus Nijhoff, 1963.

———. *Die Idee der Phänomenologie*, ed. W. Biemel, 2d ed. Husserliana II, The Hague: Martinus Nijhoff, 1973.

———. *Die Krisis der Europäischen Wissenschaften und die transcendentale Phänomenologie*, 2nd ed., ed. W. Biemel. Husserliana VI. The Hague: Martinus Nijhoff, 1962.

———. *Erste Philosophie (1923–24), Erster Teil, Kritische Ideengeschichte, (Erste Philosophy I)*, ed. R. Boehm. Husserliana VII. The Hague: Martinus Nijhoff, 1956.

———. *Ideen zu einer reinen Phänomenologie und phänomenologischen Philosophie. Erstes Buch (Ideen I)*, ed. R. Schuhmann. Husserliana III, 1. The Hague: Martinus Nijhoff, 1976.

———. *Ideen zu einer reinen Phänomenologie und phänomenologischen Philosophie. Erstes Buch (Ideen I)*, ed. W. Biemel. Husserliana II. The Hague: Martinus Nijhoff, 1950.

———. *Ideen zu einer reinen Phänomenologie und phänomenologischen Philosophie. Zweites Buch (Ideen II)*, ed. W. Biemel. Husserliana IV. The Hague: Martinus Nijhoff, 1952.

——— . *Ideen zu einer reinen Phänomenologie und phänomenologischen Philosophie. Drittes Buch (Ideen III)*, ed. W. Biemel. Husserliana V. The Hague: Martinus Nijhoff, 1971.

——— . *Logical Investigations*, trans. J. N. Findlay, 2 vols. New York: Humanities Press, 1970.

——— . *Logische Untersuchungen*, 1st ed., 2 vols. Halle a.s.: Max Niemeyer, 1900–1901.

——— . *Logische Untersuchungen*, 5th ed., 2 vols. Tübingen: Max Niemeyer, 1968.

——— . *Logische Untersuchungen, Erster Band, Prologomena zur Reinen Logik*, ed. Elmar Holenstein. Husserliana XVIII. The Hague: Martinus Nijhoff, 1975.

——— . *Logische Untersuchungen*, ed. Ursula Panzer, 2 vols. Husserliana XIX. The Hague: Martinus Nijhoff, 1984.

——— . *Phänomologishce Psychologie*, ed. W. Biemel. Husserliana IX. The Hague: Martinus Nijhoff, 1962.

——— . *Zur Phänomenologie der Intersubjektivität Zweiter Teil: 1921–1928*, ed. I. Kern, Husserliana XIV. The Hague: Martinus Nijhoff, 1973.

——— . *Zur Phänomenologie der Intersubjektivität, Dritter Teil: 1929–1935*, ed. Iso Kern. Husserliana XV, The Hague: Martinus Nijhoff, 1973.

——— . *Zur Phänomenologie des inneren Zeitbewusstseins*, ed. R. Boehm, Husserliana X, The Hague: Martinus Nijhoff, 1966.

Ingarten, Roman. *On the Motives which lead Husserl to Transcendental Idealism*, The Hague: Martinus Nijhoff, 1975.

Jacquette, Dale. "Adventures in the Chinese Room," *Philosophy and Phenomenological Research* 49 (1989).

Jaegerschmid, Adelgundis. "Die letzten Jahre Edmund Husserls, 1936–1938." *Stimmen der Zeit*, 199, no. 2 (February 1981).

——— . "Gespräche mit Edmund Husserl 1931–1936." *Stimmen der Zeit*, 199, no. 1 (January 1981).

James, William. "Does Consciousness Exist?" In *The Writings of William James*, ed. J. McDermott. New York: Random House, 1967.

——— . *Psychology, Briefer Course*. Cleveland: World Publishing Company, 1948.

Janet, Pierre, *The Major Symptoms of Hysteria*. New York: Macmillan, 1907.

Kant, Immanuel. "Kritik der reinen Vernunft" (1st ed.). In *Kants gesammelte Schriften*, ed. Königliche Preussische Akademie der Wissenschaften, 23 vols., Berlin: Georg Reiner, 1911, vol. 4, pp. 1–252.

————. "Kritik der reinen Vernunft" (2nd ed.). In *Kants gesammelte Schriften*, ed. Königliche Preussische Akademie der Wissenschaften, 23 vols. Berlin: Georg Reiner, 1911, vol. 3, pp. 1–594.

————. "Kritik der Urteilskraft." In *Kants Werke*. Berlin: Cassier, 1968, vol. 5.

————. "Prolegomena." In *Kants gesammelte Schriften*, ed. Königliche Preussische Akademie der Wissenschaften, 23 vols., Berlin: Georg Reiner, 1911, vol. 4, pp. 253–383.

Kierkegaard. *Philosophical Fragments—Johannes Climacus*, trans. H. Hong. Princeton, N.J. 1987.

Kirk, G. S., and J. E. Raven (eds. and trans.). *The Presocratic Philosophers*. Cambridge, England: Cambridge University Press, 1966.

Kojève, Alexandre. *Introduction to the Reading of Hegel*, trans. J. Nichols Jr. New York: Basic Books, 1969.

Kockelmans, Joseph J. "World-Constitution, Reflections on Husserl's Transcendental Idealism." *Analecta Husserliana*, 1 (1970).

Landgrabe, Ludwig. "Die Bedeutung der phänomenologischen Methode für die Neubegrundung der Metaphysik." In *Proceedings of the Tenth International Congress of Philosophy*, ed. E. Beth, H. Poss, J. Hollak. Amsterdam: North Holland Press, 1949.

Leibniz, Gottfried. *Basic Writings*, trans. Montgomery. La Salle, Ill.: Open Court Press, 1962.

Lewis, Donald. "Aristotle's Theory of Time: Destructive Ontology from Heideggerian Principles." *Kinesis* 2 (Spring 1970).

Lind, R. "The Priority of Attention: Intentionality for Automata." *The Monist* 69 (1978).

Lyotard, Jean-François. "The Postmodern Condition: A Report on Knowledge." *A Postmodern Reader*, ed. J. Natoli and L. Hutcheon. Albany: SUNY Press, 1993.

Maloney, J. C. "The Right Stuff." *Synthese* 70 (1987).

Marbach, Eduard. *Das Problem des Ich in der Phänomenologie Husserls*. The Hague: Martinus Nijhoff, 1974.

McIntyre, R. "Husserl and the Representational Theory of Mind." *Topoi* 5 (1986).

Mensch, James R. *Intersubjectivity and Transcendental Idealism*. Albany: SUNY Press, 1988.

————. "Phenomenology and Artificial Intelligence, Husserl Learns Chinese." *Husserl Studies* 8 (1991).

————. *The Question of Being in Husserl's Logical Investigations*. The Hague: Martinus Nijhoff, 1981.

————. "Husserl and Sartre: A Question of Reason." *Journal of Philosophical Research* 19 (1994).

————. "The Mind Body Problem, Phenomenological Reflections on an Ancient Solution." *American Catholic Philosophical Quarterly* 68, no. 1 (Winter 1994).

————. "Aristotle and the Overcoming of the Subject Object Dichotomy." *American Catholic Philosophical Quarterly* (Autumn 1991): 465–82.

————. "Phenomenology and Artificial Intelligence: Husserl Learns Chinese." *Husserl Studies* 8 (1991): 107–27.

————. "Existence and Essence in Thomas and Husserl." In *Horizons of Continental Philosophy: Essays on Husserl, Heidegger, and Merleau-Ponty*. Dordrecht: Kluwer Press, 1988.

————. "Radical Evil and the Ontological Difference Between Being and Beings." *Philosophy and Culture, vol. 4*, ed. V. Cauchy. Montreal: Montmorency, 1988.

Modrak, Deborah. *Aristotle, The Power of Perception*. Chicago: University of Chicago Press, 1987.

Montaigne, Michel. *Selected Essays*, trans. W. Hazlitt. New York: Random House, 1949.

Natanson, M. "Phenomenology and Existentialism: Husserl and Sartre on Intentionality." In *Phenomenology, The Philosophy of Edmund Husserl and Its Interpretations*. Garden City, New York: Doubleday, 1967.

Newton, Isaac. *Newton's Principia*, trans. A. Motte and F. Cajori. Berkeley: University of California Press, 1960.

Nietzsche. F. *Beyond Good and Evil*, trans. R. J. Hollingdale. London: Penguin Books, 1990.

————. *The Birth of Tragedy and the Case of Wagner*, trans. W. Kaufmann. New York: Random House, 1967.

————. *The Complete Work of Fredrich Nietzsche,* trans. A. M. Ludovici, 18 vols. New York: Russell and Russell, 1964.

————. *The Will to Power*, trans. W. Kaufmann and R. Hollingdale. New York: Random House, 1968.

Owens, Joseph. "Common Nature: A Point of Comparison Between Thomistic and Scotistic Metaphysics." *Mediaeval Studies* 19 (1957).

Pietersma, Henry. "A Critique of Two Recent Husserl Interpretations." *Dialogue* 26, no. 4 (Winter 1987).

————. "Form and Cognition in Aristotle." *Ancient Philosophy* 1 (Fall 1980).

Plato, *Platonis Opera*, ed. John Burnet, 5 vols., Oxford: Clarendon Press, 1957.

———. *The Dialogues of Plato*, trans. B. Jowett, 2 vols. New York: Random House, 1937.

Proceedings of the Tenth International Congress of Philosophy, eds. E. W. Beth, H. J. Pos, J. H. Hollak. Amsterdam: North Holland, 1949.

Putnam, Frank. "The Switch Process in Multiple Personality Disorder and Other State-Change Disorders." *Dissociation* 1 (March 1988).

Pylyshyn, Z. W. "Minds, Machines and Phenomenology: Some Reflections on Dreyfus' 'What Computers Can't Do'." *Cognition* 3, no. 1 (1974–75).

Ricoeur, Paul. *Husserl: An Analysis of His Phenomenology*. Northwestern Studies in Phenomenology and Existential Phenomenology. Evanston, Ill.: Northwestern University Press, 1967.

Sartre, J. P. *Being and Nothingness*, trans. Hazel Barnes. New York: Washington Square Press, 1968.

———. "Consciousness of Self and Knowledge of Self." In *Readings in Existential Phenomenology*, ed. N. Lawrence and D. O'Connor. Englewood Cliffs, N.J.: Prentice-Hall, 1967.

———. *The Transcendence of the Ego*, trans. F. Williams and R. Kirkpatrick. New York: Noonday, 1957.

Scanlon, John. "Consciousness, the Streetcar, and the Ego: Pro Husserl, Contra Sartre." *Philosophical Forum* 2 (Spring 1971).

Schmitz, Kenneth. "Postmodern or Modern-Plus?" *Communio* 17 (Summer 1990).

Schuhmann, Karl, and Smith, Barry. "Against Idealism: Johannes Daubert vs. Husserl's *Ideas I*." *Review of Metaphysics* 38 (June 1985).

Schulz, Walter. "Funktion und Ort der Kunst in Nietzsches Philosophie." *Nietzsche-Studien* 12 (1983).

Schutz, Alfred. "The Problem of Transcendental Intersubjectivity in Husserl." *Collective Papers III*, ed. I. Schutz. The Hague: Martinus Nijhoff, 1966.

Scotus, Duns. *Duns Scotus, Philosophical Writings,* ed. A. Wolter. London: Nelson, 1962.

———. *Opus Oxoniense*, ed. Wadding, Paris: Vives, 1891–95.

Searle, John. "Is the Brain's Mind a Computer Program?" *Scientific American* 262, no. 1 (January 1990).

————. "Minds, Brains, and Programs." *The Behavioral and Brain Sciences* (1980).

————. "Reply to Jacquette." *Philosophy and Phenomenological Research* 49 (1989).

Seebohm, Thomas. "The Other in the Field of Consciousness." In *Essays in Memory of Aron Gurwitsch*, ed. L. Embree. Washington: University Press of America, 1984.

Shouery, Imad. "Reduction in Sartre's Ontology." *Southwest Journal of Philosophy* 2 (Spring–Summer 1971).

Smith, C. U. M. "'Clever Beasts Who Invented Knowing': Nietzsche's Evolutionary Biology of Knowledge." *Biology and Philosophy* 2 (1987).

Smith, David Woodruff, and McIntyre, Ronald. "Intentionality via Intensions." *Journal of Philosophy* 68, no. 18 (September 16, 1971).

Sokolowski, Robert. "Intentional Analysis and the Noema." *Dialectica* 38, nos. 2–3 (1984).

————. "Review Essay: Husserl and Analytic Philosophy and Husserlian Intentionality and Non-Foundational Realism." *Philosophy and Phenomenological Research* 52, no. 3 (September 1992).

Stamps, Ann. "Shifting Focus from Sartre to Husserl." *Journal of Thought* 25 (January 1973).

Stent, Gunter. "Limits to the Scientific Understanding of Man." *Science* 187 (1974).

Strasser, Stephen. "Das Gottesprobleme in der Spätphilosophie Edmund Husserls." *Philosophiches Jahrbuch der Gorres-Gesellschaft* 67 (1959).

Turing, Alan. "Computing Machinery and Intelligence." *Mind* 59 (1950).

Vargo, Stephanie. "'I Believe I Have Witnessed a Murder': Trauma, Contradiction and the Creation of Alternative Identities." In *Proceedings of the 24th Annual Meeting of the Husserl Circle*. Waterloo, Ont., 1992.

Waterlow, Sarah. "Aristotle's Now." *The Philosophical Quarterly* 34, no. 135 (April 1984).

Whitehead, Alfred N. *Science and the Modern World*. New York: New American Library, 1974.

Wittgenstein, Ludwig. *On Certainty,* trans. D. Paul and G. E. M. Anscombe. New York: Harper, 1972.

NAME INDEX

Subject Index